PARIS

D0311020

NATIONAL GEOGRAPHIC
TRAVELER

PARIS

by Lisa Davidson & Elizabeth Ayre
photography by Gilles Mingasson

National Geographic
Washington, D.C.

CONTENTS

Pages 2–3: Night falls on the City of Light.
Opposite: A young visitor sails a rented boat in the Grand Bassin, Jardin du Luxembourg.

TRAVELING WITH EYES OPEN

Alert travelers go with a purpose and leave with a benefit. If you travel responsibly, you can help support wildlife conservation, historic preservation, and cultural enrichment in the places you visit. You can enrich your own travel experience as well.

To be a geo-savvy traveler:

- Recognize that your presence has an impact on the places you visit.

- Spend your time and money in ways that sustain local character. (Besides, it's more interesting that way.)

- Value the destination's natural and cultural heritage.

- Respect the local customs and traditions.

- Express appreciation to local people about things you find interesting and unique to the place: its nature and scenery, music and food, historic villages and buildings.

- Vote with your wallet: Support the people who support the place, patronizing businesses that make an effort to celebrate and protect what's special there. Seek out local shops, restaurants, and inns. Use tour operators who love their home—who love taking care of it and showing it off. Avoid businesses that detract from the character of the place.

- Enrich yourself, taking home memories and stories to tell, knowing that you have contributed to the preservation and enhancement of the destination.

That is the type of travel now called geotourism, defined as "tourism that sustains or enhances the geographical character of a place—its environment, culture, aesthetics, heritage, and the well-being of its residents." To learn more, visit National Geographic's Center for Sustainable Destinations at *nationalgeographic.com/maps/geotourism/*.

NATIONAL GEOGRAPHIC
TRAVELER
PARIS

ABOUT THE AUTHORS

Lisa Davidson is a writer and editor living in Paris. She has written for *Village France, France par Excellence,* and *World Media Network* and has published *Baboushka and Dedoushka,* a memoir of the Russian Revolution. She is currently working with *Beaux-Arts Magazine* and for the Paris-based publisher Gallimard.

Elizabeth Ayre is also a writer and editor living in Paris. She has written for the *International Herald Tribune, The Independent,* and *Village France* and *France par Excellence* guidebooks. She is the author of *They Don't Take No for an Answer* and editor of the journal *Variations.* She is currently working with Paris-based publisher Gallimard and runs a European network for children separated from an imprisoned parent.

Responsible for updating and writing new features for the 2011 and 2016 editions, **Heidi Ellison** is an American journalist who has lived in Paris for more than 25 years. She is the founder and editor of ParisUpdate.com. Over the years, her articles on travel, art, design, architecture, and fashion have appeared in dozens of magazines and newspapers. She has also contributed to a number of guidebooks.

The authors would like to thank the following people for their collaboration in this book: David Applefield (Bridges), John Calder (Literature), Tina Isaac (Fashion), Lisa Nesselson (Cinema), Julian Nundy (Paris Today), A. J. Paterson (Paris Today and research on the History section), Nicolas Petty (Travelwise), and Karen Wells Verlander (Fashion).

CHARTING YOUR TRIP

Paris has changed enormously in the past 30 years, leaving behind many of its provincial ways and becoming an increasingly modern, multicultural, and international metropolis. The new Paris is more user-friendly, staying open all day as the life of a bustling 21st-century city swirls around its historical core.

The pride Paris takes in its history is evident in the ongoing restoration of its monuments, which now sparkle and glow in the sunlight almost as brilliantly as the glittering lights that transform the Eiffel Tower into a giant sparkler every evening on the hour.

The new Paris, however, has not lost its legendary romantic atmosphere. Couples still canoodle on the quays of the Seine, and the ever changing light still inspires painters and poets. Young people still come here dreaming of writing novels in garret rooms and making Hemingway's moveable feast their own. French students still argue vehemently about philosophy in cafés and then go out dancing all night.

Which brings us to one major change that most visitors will find to be a huge improvement. The (once highly accurate) clichéd image of smoky Parisian cafés, restaurants, and jazz clubs is dead forever, killed by a law forbidding smoking in public places. Breathe deeply and enjoy your stay!

How to Get Around

Paris has an excellent transportation system. The 14 lines of the easy-to-use Métro subway system (*ratp.fr*) cover almost every corner of the city and are supplemented by the RER suburban train lines, which can also be used to travel within the city for the price of a Métro ticket. An extensive grid of municipal bus lines, further upgraded in 2019, fills in any gaps not served by the Métro or RER. Almost any location in the city is within a few minutes' walk from one of these transportation options.

While the bus lines are slightly more complicated to use, they offer visitors with time to spare a wonderful way to see the city without tiring themselves out, provided that they travel in off hours (after 10 a.m. and before 5 p.m.). Every bus shelter has a map of the entire system on the outside and details of the line(s) served on the inside. Once the Métro has stopped running, at about 1:15 a.m. (2:15 a.m. on Friday and Saturday night), there are two options: Take a taxi or a Noctilien

■ Rodin's "The Thinker" in the garden of the Musée Rodin

all-night bus (shelters are marked with a big "N"). Zip-car and Mobilib' rentals are available by the hour but require preregistration. Avoid driving in Paris; traffic jams are a given and parking scarce and expensive.

For trips out of town, you can either rent a car at a train station or airport, or take a train to your destination and rent a car on-site if you need one (to tour the Loire châteaus, for example, or Champagne country). In most urban destinations, a car is not nec-essary. It is always wise to reserve a car in advance.

The other suburban railway system serving the Île de France is called the Transilien (transilien.com). Destinations beyond the Île de France are well served by the SNCF (sncf.com), the excellent national railway, which offers high-speed TGV service to major cities (two to three hours to Bordeaux or three and a half to Marseille, for example) and slower Intercités trains to other destinations. The Eurostar (eurostar.com) zips passengers to London in two and a quarter hours, while the high-speed Thalys (thalys.com) serves northern destinations, including Brussels, Cologne, and Amsterdam.

Back in Paris, the more adventurous might want to try the Vélib' short-term bicycle rental system (velib-metropole.fr). Although the city has become much more bike-friendly with over 150 miles (240 km) of new bike lanes (and more planned) and 10,000 bike parking spaces, biking around is still recommended only for those who are confident cyclists. A safer way to visit Paris by bicycle is by taking a tour with a Company like Paris à Vélo (parisavelo.fr).

If You Have One Week

Few first-time visitors to Paris will have a hard time deciding what to do in Paris, since the major sites are so deservedly well known: the **Eiffel Tower,** the **Louvre,** the **Musée d'Orsay,** the **Orangerie,** the **Arc de Triomphe, Sacré-Coeur,** the **Latin Quarter,** the **Champs-Élysées,** and the **quays of the Seine.**

Visitor Information

The official **Paris Tourist Office** website (tel 01 49 52 42 63, en.parisinfo.com) covers just about everything a visitor to Paris would want to know, in English and in great detail. Users can book hotels, exhibitions, and sightseeing excursions through the site. The Tourist Office has branches at the Hôtel de Ville (main office, 29 rue de Rivoli), the Carrousel du Louvre (99 rue de Rivoli), and the Gare du Nord (18 rue de Dunkerque).

More info on what's new in Paris can be found on the city's quefaire.paris.fr and on **Paris Update** (parisupdate.com), a weekly review of cultural events. For excursions nearby, visit the website of the **Paris-Île de France Regional Tourist Office** (visitparisregion.com), which takes in both Paris and its environs. For infor-mation on using public transport, includ-ing maps and suggested itineraries for the Métro, bus, and RER, go to ratp.fr.

When to Go

When you go to Paris depends on what you are looking for. Some people find the Christmas lights on the Champs-Élysées thrillingly romantic, or come in winter to avoid other tourists. "April in Paris" is beautiful, but may be cold and rainy. May and June usually have fine weather. During July and August, the city is fairly laid-back and Paris Plages turns some of the quays of the Seine into beaches and a stroller's paradise; many shops and restaurants are closed in August. September brings *la rentrée*—the return of vacationing Parisians—and an upswing in activity. Paris is lovely in the fall, when the chestnut trees turn rust-colored and children return to school.

It would take a lifetime to discover all of Paris's treasures, but if you have only one week and have never been here before, the sites mentioned above should be part of the master plan. Most of the major monuments are clustered fairly close together on either side of the Seine on the Right and Left Banks, and many are within walking distance. All can be reached in 30 to 40 minutes by Métro from the center of Paris. A Bateau-Mouche *(bateaux-mouches.fr)* ride along the Seine at the beginning of your trip or an Open Tour bus *(open tourparis.com)* will help you get the lay of the land.

Rest & Relaxation

Visiting more than one museum a day is not recommended, except for those high in energy and artistic curiosity, especially since long lines often mean waits to get in. Plan to stop frequently in cafés or restaurants to rest and recuperate and prevent oversaturation blues. In fine weather, a good way to relax and rest your feet is a stop in the **Luxembourg** or **Tuileries Gardens.** When it rains, a film in one of Paris's dozens of cinemas might be in order (check that your English-language films are marked "VO"—for *version originale*—which means they are shown in the original language with French subtitles). A nap at the hotel before dinner is also recommended to keep your strength up and whet your appetite (most restaurants do not begin to serve dinner until 8 p.m.).

For blockbuster temporary art exhibitions, such as those usually held at the **Grand Palais,** it is a good idea to book online far ahead, even before you leave home. The 2010 Monet exhibition, for example, was sold out far in advance—despite offering entrance 24 hours a day.

Top Ten Local Phrases

Where is the bathroom?	*Où sont les toilettes?*
How much does it cost?	*Combien ça coute? Or just Combien?*
Where is the nearest Métro station?	*Où est le Métro le plus proche?*
I don't understand.	*Je ne comprends pas.*
Pleased to meet you.	*Enchanté(e).*
See you later.	*À plus tard.*
Thank you. You are very kind.	*Merci. Vous êtes très gentil(le).*
Do you know a good, inexpensive restaurant in this area?	*Connaissez-vous un bon restaurant, pas trop cher, dans ce quartier?*
I would like to reserve a table for two.	*Je voudrais réserver une table pour deux.*

■ Paris Plages transforms the Quai des Tuileries, facing the Seine, into a beach in July and August.

If You Have More Time

Once you have taken the elevator to the top of the Eiffel Tower, seen the "Mona Lisa," admired the view of the Champs-Élysées from the Arc de Triomphe, and visited the other attractions mentioned above, that does not mean you have done Paris. If you have more than a week or are visiting for the second (or third, or fourth) time, hundreds of other things remain to do, beginning with visits to smaller museums like the **Marmottan-Monet,** near the Bois de Boulogne, or the **Musée Gustave-Moreau,** in the 9th arrondissement.

Cooking classes, many of which include market visits, are a wonderful way to immerse yourself in French culture—or join the crowds in Sunday-morning food markets like the **Marché d'Aligre** near the Bastille. Flea markets are another option. The permanent ones on the outskirts of Paris are open every weekend, but temporary flea markets are often held in different neighborhoods (check the "Brocantes" section of weekly events guide *Pariscope*). During the week, the **Village St.-Paul** in the Marais is a peaceful haven for antique hunters. Other options are to explore Paris's many beautiful parks or join a walking or biking tour.

The possibilities for out-of-town excursions are almost limitless as well. **Versailles** is the most obvious, but there are many other châteaus that can be visited on a day trip from Paris: **Fontainebleau, Chantilly,** and **Malmaison** among them. A number of fascinating sites are only an hour or so away by train and can be visited in one day, among them **Provins, Giverny,** and the stunning **Chartres Cathedral.**

HISTORY &
CULTURE

▪ Above: A clock approaches the
eleventh hour at the Musée d'Orsay.
Opposite: Stained-glass windows at
Notre-Dame

PARIS TODAY

"Paris vaut bien une messe" (Paris is well worth a mass), said King Henri IV on converting to Catholicism in 1593. Then as now it would have been hard to disagree. Paris was the political heart of France, and since then has more often than not been the political as well as the geographical heart of Europe.

Known as the City of Light, Paris is considered by many people to be the world's most beautiful city. Its monuments and treasures are better preserved than those of any rival city. But Paris is much more than that. It is an international city that controls the larger part of France's economy, the second most successful in the European Union in terms of GDP, after Germany.

The French capital for over a thousand years, Paris was central to the establishment of the modern French state, which developed out of the initial domain of the Capetian kings (roughly Paris to Orléans) over some six centuries. The city is the governmental, economic, and cultural axis around which French society has revolved, a trend that has grown since the French Revolution. This historic trend has been diluted by a series of decentralization measures, and Marseille, Lyon, Bordeaux, and other major cities have developed their own identities and clout as a result. Yet France remains the creation of a capital of which it has often been a mere extension—in other words, as the saying goes, when Paris sneezes, France catches cold.

The Importance of "Bonjour"

Walk up to a French person in the Parisian street and say, "Excuse me, where is the Louvre?" and the response is likely to be an intense stare, followed by a pause for effect, and *"Bonjour."* Not saying *"bonjour"* as you enter a shop, or before you launch into whatever you want to say, is considered extremely rude. So be a good visitor and say instead, *"Bonjour, Madame/ Monsieur* [far more polite and respectful]. *Parlez-vous anglais?"* If the answer is affirmative, then ask your question. You may make a friend for life.

The Paris Region & Its Economy

Paris is blessed with great natural assets: Straddling the middle reaches of the Seine, the city lies at the center of Europe's greatest sedimentary basin (the Bassin Parisien). The basin's agricultural resources, which exploit the rich alluvial soils of its plains and low plateaus, have traditionally been the backbone of the French economy. The Paris region dominates a wide area extending from Normandy in the west, around Picardy and Champagne to the north and east, and through the Beauce country of Chartres between the Seine and the Loire to the south. Within this broad geographic area, today's Région d'Île-de-France (one of 13 French metropolitan regions) covers a little over 4,500 square miles (12,000 sq km), forming a threefold concentric ring of eight *départements* (out of a total of 95 départements in mainland France) around the capital, which, since 1976, has resumed its status of commune with its own mayor.

The café scene near the Église St.-Germain-des-Prés

EXPERIENCE: The Personal Touch at B&Bs

How to meet the French? Those who are not naturally chatty could try staying in a bed and breakfast. Parisians who operate B&Bs are generally those who are most interested in meeting foreigners. Some owners sit down with arriving guests for a drink and a snack in their living room or enjoy getting to know visitors over breakfast, and are generally happy to share their knowledge of the city. Try booking through these agencies, whose members have signed the city of Paris's "Quality Charter" specifying standards: **Alcôve & Agapes: Paris Bed & Breakfast** (tel 06 99 44 75 75, bed-and-breakfast-in-paris.com), **Association Française BAB France** (bedbreak.com), **Fleurs de Soleil** (tel 09 51 67 79 80, fleursdesoleil.fr), **Une Chambre en Ville** (tel 09 67 05 22 82, chambre-ville.com). A list of Parisian B&Bs is available and bookable through the tourism office website in the section "Where to stay" (en.parisinfo.com).

One of the great victories of Paris has been to contain the city proper within the Périphérique ring road, keeping it a manageable size. With a clean, extensive, efficient, and constantly modernized transport system, this means that few journeys across town take more than 40 minutes.

The Parisian Population

The city's population began to stabilize during the 1920s and now counts more than 2.2 million inhabitants, while the suburbs began their rapid expansion. Some 3 million people a day travel from the suburbs into Paris to work. The city is constantly evolving; only about one in three Parisians was born in the capital. Immigration also has influenced the city's demographics. From the mid-1950s to the 1970s, labor shortages led to massive recruitment campaigns in North Africa and poorer European regions like southern Italy, Spain, and Greece. Today 15 percent of Parisians are of foreign birth, the predominant groups being Algerians, Portuguese, and Moroccans.

Paris is divided into 20 districts called *arrondissements,* which spiral out in a circle from the center (Châtelet) like a snail shell. Parisians tend to identify strongly with their own *quartier* (neighborhood), whether it be the stodgier 16th arrondissement or one of the lively multiethnic areas of Belleville, Chinatown, or Ménilmontant to the east.

Many American, Japanese, and European nationals opt for the inner-city arrondissements of the center or west. Those from Southeast Asia (primarily Cambodia, Laos, and Vietnam) have gravitated to the 13th; many Chinese and Turks live in the 10th; many people from sub-Saharan Africa or Algeria are in the 18th; and many from sub-Saharan Africa or China in the 19th. The Belleville district straddling four arrondissements (10th, 11th, 19th, 20th) is a melting pot of the various ethnic and religious groups.

The Paris population is young, with over half of the city's apartments occupied by single people. Most Paris apartments are extremely small (over half have only two rooms or less); the housing shortage (construction has shifted from residential to office building in many areas) and exorbitant prices have exacerbated the problem, driving many Parisians, both well-off and less well-off, into the suburbs.

Parisian Life

One of the municipal priorities is to maintain the city's diversity. In practical terms, this means a commitment made in 2001 to create 3,500 new public housing units, seen as a source of vitality, per year. Meanwhile, certain districts of working-class arrondissements to the east are attracting fairly well-off young people, encouraged by lower real-estate prices and the villagelike feel of these neighborhoods. This demographic shift has both negative and positive impacts: Locals welcome the trendy new shops, bars, and restaurants the *bobos* (bourgeois bohemians) bring, yet often bemoan the watering down of the neighborhood's original character.

The bobos have also been active in creating residents' associations and campaigning for more green spaces and bicycle lanes, much to the chagrin of architects and shop owners who maintain that they are an obstacle to the capital's economic development and risk turning Paris into a "pedestrianized museum." But they did have Bertrand Delanoë—Paris's Socialist mayor from 2001 to 2014—on their side. One of his most memorable contributions has been the creation of Paris Plages, a summer operation that transforms stretches of the Right and Left Bank and the Bassin de la Villette with small strips of sand, palm trees, deck chairs, food stands, beach volleyball courts, and swimming pools. The mayor who succeeded him, Anne Hidalgo, moved along a similar line with her Plan Vélo (50 percent increase in the cycle network and creation of 10,000 bike spaces) and the increase in pedestrian areas and green areas. This and a host of restored museums, new restaurants and bars, and improved transportation have injected new life into this ever changing but eternal city. ∎

■ **Lovers on the Pont Neuf near the Île de la Cité, a natural island on the Seine**

HISTORY OF PARIS

The history of Paris is very much present throughout the city today. Various quarters—the Napoleonic Opéra area or the 17th-century Marais, for example—bear the mark of Parisian rulers.

The Celts

The site where Paris is today was occupied from as early as the fifth or fourth millennium B.C. until the early Iron Age (circa 800–700 B.C.). Neolithic humans inhabited the island that would become Île de la Cité, as well as a rocky spur on the left bank that served as an observation point. The island subsequently was abandoned, probably due to climatic changes, until around 250–225 B.C., when a Celtic tribe

Gallic leader Vercingétorix surrenders to Caesar, in a painting by Lionel Royer (1899).

called the Parisii settled there. The Parisii lived mainly from river trade until approximately 90 B.C., when they began to mint high-quality gold coins. This continued until the Romans arrived in the middle of the first century B.C.

In 53 B.C., seizing upon its strategic geographical position, Julius Caesar used the island as his base during his campaign to quell the insurrection of the neighboring Senones. According to Caesar's *Gallic War,* by 52 B.C., the Celt Vercingétorix had convinced the Parisii to revolt against the Romans. When Caesar's lieutenant Labienus and four legions arrived to crush them, the Gauls (Gaul was the Roman name for France) set fire to the Cité and destroyed its bridges. Labienus then surrounded the Gallic positions, killing the Celtic general Camulogenus and routing the other Gauls. (Historians are divided over where the battle took place; it may have occurred on the plain of Grenelle.)

Lutetia, as it was known, flourished under the Romans. The settlement was reconstructed and a wall built around it in the early second century A.D. Rustic Gallic dwellings were

❝ Toward the mid-third century, Lutetia became a Christian center through the efforts of Saint Denis, the city's first bishop. ❞

replaced with homes built along actual streets. A new city sprang up across the Petit Pont on the left bank, around the *cardo,* the main north–south street of the Roman city (the present-day Rue St.-Jacques–Rue St.-Martin). The Romans built baths along today's Boulevards St.-Michel and St.-Germain; a theater beneath what is now the Lycée St.-Louis; a temple to Jupiter and Tiberius (on the site of Notre-Dame); a forum on Rue Soufflot; arenas on Rue Monge; an aqueduct; and taverns serving barley beer and spiced wine.

Toward the mid-third century, Lutetia became a Christian center through the efforts of Saint Denis, the city's first bishop. For years, the Romans tolerated Denis as he converted followers and founded churches. But eventually they clamped down on Christianity and ordered his arrest. According to legend, Denis was beaten, thrown to the lions, and crucified. Refusing to abjure his faith, he was dragged to the Mont des Martyrs (later Montmartre) and beheaded. He then rose, picked up his head, and carried it to a village north of Paris. The Basilica of St.-Denis was later built on the site of the martyr's tomb, and Denis became the patron saint of France.

Christianity & Barbarism

Constantine I made Christianity the official religion of the Empire in 313. His nephew Julian the

Apostate, who rose to the imperial throne in 361, would play a large role in promoting Paris as an imperial city (although a third-century decree renamed Lutetia "Paris," Julian continued to call it Lutetia). He also did a great deal to defend Gaul from barbarian invasions until he was killed in battle in 363. Over the next century, Roman power weakened, and by the early fifth century it had virtually collapsed.

Middle Ages

The Merovingians: The Frankish king Merovech (R.447–457) and his son Childeric I (R.457–481) proved loyal allies of Rome against Attila the Hun and other invaders. As the Empire disintegrated, Childeric's son Clovis (R.481–511) formally added the Roman provinces of western Gaul to his realm in Flanders, thus establishing the Frankish Kingdom, the forerunner of the modern French state. The educated Gallo-Romans found themselves subject to the crude culture of the bloodthirsty Merovingians—called the "long-haired kings" because cutting their hair was seen as a disgrace that barred them from the throne.

In 486, Clovis triumphed over the Romans at Soissons. Although Clovis was a pagan, he married a Catholic, Clothilda of Burgundy, in 491 and was baptized at Reims. Clovis made Paris his capital in 508. Three years later he died, and the Merovingian kingdom was divided into four parts. One of Clovis's descendants, Dagobert (R.628–639), established the annual Fair of St.-Denis outside Paris in 635, and the city once again became a leading commercial and cultural center.

> By Philippe the Fair's reign (R.1285–1314), Paris was the site of political decision-making and the main seat of royalty.

The Carolingians: Dagobert's descendants, nicknamed "*les rois fainéants*" or "do-nothing kings," allowed power to slip into the hands of the palace mayors, and Pepin the Short had himself elected king in 751. His bastard son Charlemagne became king of the Franks in 768 and in 30 years, reconquered a large part of the old western Roman Empire. In December 800, he was crowned emperor by the Pope, choosing Aachen (Aix-la-Chapelle) as the capital of his Holy Roman Empire.

In the ninth century, Paris became a target for Viking raiders in quest of plunder, and the city was repeatedly attacked from 845 to 885. Charlemagne's great empire had now split into three kingdoms and was too disrupted to organize effective resistance. Disgruntled nobles and clergy, therefore, turned to the warrior Robert the Strong, Count of Anjou and Blois. He was killed by Vikings, and his son Eudes (Odo) became Count of Paris (under the Carolingians, palace mayors were replaced by hereditary counts). Parisians placed their trust in Eudes, then restored the Roman walls around the Île de la Cité and built two *châtelets*, or castles.

The Capetians: After Charles III (the Fat) was deposed in 887, the nobles set a precedent by electing Count Eudes king instead of the legitimate Carolingian heir. When the last Carolingian king—Louis V—died, Hugues Capet (Count of Paris) was elected king in 987 and crowned at Noyon. The Capetian dynasty ruled from Paris, imbuing the city with a prestige unknown since Clovis. Trade and commerce expanded on the right bank. The powerful abbeys and fairs at St.-Denis and St.-Germain played a key role in the development, as did Abbot Suger, a shrewd administrator who commissioned the new Basilica of St.-Denis—France's first Gothic building—in 1136.

The royal domains doubled during the reign of Philippe-Auguste (1180–1223), who took a great interest in Paris. He backed a University of Paris charter, paved the main streets, built a market at Les Halles, and laid the Louvre's foundations. Before embarking on the Crusades, Philippe-Auguste ordered the expansion of the city's protective wall, which was to encompass areas on both banks of the Seine. Vestiges of the wall can be seen in the Latin Quarter and the Marais.

Saint Geneviève

When word spread that Attila and his Huns were headed toward Paris in 451, the people panicked and made ready to flee. A young Gallo-Roman woman from Nanterre, named Geneviève, urged the inhabitants to remain, pray to God, and do works of penance to avert the invasion. Luckily for Geneviève, Attila's plan was not to ransack Paris, but to reach the Loire at Orléans and attack the Visigoths. Geneviève was credited with a miracle and proclaimed the savior of Paris. As Saint Geneviève, she was said to continue to protect the city through her relics.

Philippe-Auguste's grandson, Louis IX (R.1226–1270), was known as Saint Louis for his piety. He commissioned Ste.-Chapelle to house part of the True Cross and the Crown of Thorns. By Philippe the Fair's reign (R. 1285–1314), Paris was the site of political decision-making and the main seat of royalty. Philippe made the Parlement of Paris a legitimate court of law (not a governing body) and convoked the first French Estates-General. He also built the magnificent Salle des Gens d'Armes in the Conciergerie. His three sons ascended the throne in succession, following his death in 1314; the last, Charles IV, died in 1328 without leaving a male heir.

House of Valois

Edward III of England (Philippe IV's grandson) believed he had a better right to the French throne than the late king's cousin, Philippe de Valois. This claim was denied on the grounds of a new addition to the Salic Law forbidding matrilineal inheritance. (Edward was the son of Philippe IV's daughter.) Philippe de Valois (Philippe VI, R.1328–1350) claimed the throne, launching the Valois dynasty and precipitating the onset of the Hundred Years' War between England and France.

During this war, Parisians became instrumental in politics, as the king appealed regularly for financial support in raising war revenues. The period was marked by strife, with the Black Death claiming nearly a third of the French population in 1348. Étienne Marcel, who was Merchant Provost, had become a spokesman for Parisians, who were angry over government corruption and the court's lavish lifestyle. He assembled 3,000 armed men and invaded the Île de la Cité palace in 1358, slitting the throats of two advisers of the future Charles V as the boy looked on. The event was said to have traumatized Charles V (the Wise, R.1364–1380), who later moved the royal residence to the more secure Louvre. Charles V beautified Paris, with garden layouts, palaces, and private mansions. He also extended the city walls and built the Bastille in eastern Paris.

Late Middle Ages & Renaissance: France had long been at war with England. Following the Battle of Agincourt in 1415, the English, in alliance with the dukes of

Burgundy, appeared victorious. From 1420 to 1436, Paris was under English rule, and Henry VI of England was anointed King of France in Paris in 1431. Famine and rebellions afflicted the besieged city and wolves roamed the streets. Charles VII (R.1422–1461) finally liberated Paris and retook his capital.

France made an impressive recovery during the late 15th and early 16th centuries. The restored House of Valois regained its royal authority, and the economy began to expand. Printing was introduced, and perfumes, ladies' underwear, and forks were imported. The kings, influenced by Italian urban concepts integrating beauty with functional design, took a growing interest in their city. Gothic designs, such as the Église St.-Séverin, the Hôtel de Sens, and the Hôtel de Cluny, were added to the cityscape.

François I (R.1515–1547), an ostentatious patron of the arts who expanded royal absolutism and fostered intellectual freedom, declared Paris his residence in 1528. The city became more cosmopolitan, and artists such as Leonardo da Vinci and Benvenuto Cellini worked at his court. François renovated the Louvre; built or renovated superb castles at Chambord, Blois, and Fontainebleau; commissioned the lavish Hôtel de Ville; and drew up many of the main streets. Renaissance art found new expression in the Fontaine des Innocents, the Église St.-Eustache, and the Tuileries Palace.

St. Bartholomew's Day Massacre: The Protestant Reformation began in Wittenberg in 1517, with Martin Luther's protest of the Church's sale of indulgences. In Paris, many intellectuals, princes, and wealthy merchants embraced the ideas behind the Reformation, in contrast to the capital's heavily Catholic lower classes. Catherine de Médicis, the wife of François I's successor, Henri II (R.1547–1559), wielded immense power. She played the two ideological groups off each other, permitting an armed conflict to develop that led to the first of the Religious Wars.

> **Absolute monarchy—by divine right—reached its apogee under Louis XIV, 'the Sun King,' who inherited the throne at the age of five.**

Religious strife and paranoia were further exacerbated by factional fighting between the Huguenot Prince de Condé and the Catholic Duc de Guise. Accused heretics were burned at the Place Maubert. The planting of a rumor that Huguenots (French Calvinist Protestants) were planning to "cut the king's throat, kill his brothers, and pillage the city of Paris" led to the St. Bartholomew's Day Massacre of August 24, 1572, during which Catholic mobs turned on Protestants. Approximately 5,000 were killed in the capital alone.

Henri III's (R.1574–1589) proposal of compromise made him hugely unpopular. His immediate heir was the Protestant Henri de Navarre, but the population backed Henri Duc de Guise, who became leader of the Catholic League. A revolt broke out following the latter's assassination in 1588, and Henri III and Henri de Navarre besieged Paris. When a League monk assassinated Henri III in 1589, Henri (IV) de Navarre became king, founding the Bourbon dynasty.

Henri IV: Henri IV's (R.1589–1610) Protestantism remained an obstacle to his recognition by royalist Catholics who held Paris against him. In 1593 he converted to Catholicism, a step that all but completed his great task of unifying a fractious

country. A year later, he was anointed at Chartres and entered the capital on March 22, 1594. He then sought to consolidate royal power. Henri IV completed the Pont Neuf (the first Paris bridge that was not lined with houses or shops, but with sidewalks and benches); commissioned the Place Dauphine; and laid out royal squares.

But the Catholic League had not forgiven its old opponent, and—after more than 20 assassination attempts—Henri IV was stabbed to death by the fanatic François Ravaillac, in May 1610, while caught in a traffic jam on the Rue de la Ferronnerie.

Ancien Régime

Louis XIII: Henri IV's son Louis XIII (R.1610–1643) was only eight at the time of his father's death. His domineering mother, Marie de Médicis, served as regent until Louis XIII assumed power in 1617. The real head of his government was Cardinal Richelieu (who became Chief Minister in 1624), a shrewd administrator whose centralizing policies—along with those of his successor, Cardinal Mazarin—paved the way for royal absolutism. He commissioned the Palais Cardinal (later the Palais-Royal), rebuilt the Sorbonne, and founded the Académie Française. The Counter-Reformation fostered the construction of convents, chapels, and churches such as Val-de-Grâce, built in 1638 to commemorate the "miraculous" birth of Louis XIII's son, the future Louis XIV (Anne of Austria's first child at the age of 37).

Rebellious Stirrings: Absolute monarchy—by divine right—reached its apogee under Louis XIV (R.1643–1715), "the Sun King," who inherited the throne at the age of five. The Parlement sought to check the young king's power by drawing up a constitution; the aristocratic opposition wanted shared power, but was fraught with dissension. Rumors that taxes were to be paid in proportion to income resulted in panic and protest. In July 1648, Chief Minister Cardinal Mazarin, co-regent for Louis with Anne of Austria, declared that the young king would not repay his debts.

The Fronde, a series of rebellions by nobles and their supporters against absolutism and tax policy, spread violence in Paris from 1648 to 1653, with troops led by the Prince de Condé besieging the city and blocking its food supply. Louis assumed full power in 1661 following Mazarin's death, and a desire for order ultimately permitted the king's absolutism to flourish.

The Sun King: The 23-year-old Louis embarked on a series of wars to establish France's supremacy in Europe. At first he delegated important affairs of state to

Anne of Austria and the infant Louis XIV in an anonymous 17th-century painting

Mazarin's successor, Jean-Baptiste Colbert, who sought to replenish the royal treasury and make Paris more secure. He introduced an anticorruption campaign, created the Lieutenant General of Police, and organized firefighting. He also ordered the city's reconstruction according to a classical ideal, resulting in Place Vendôme, Place des Victoires, Les Invalides, and the Observatory.

But Louis's attention was focused less on Paris than on Versailles. The Sun King poured vast amounts of money into the palace and moved his court there in 1682, where political power was out of the reach of street movements. Almost 10,000 people worked in the vast palace and its expanse of formal gardens, a virtual city of servants and courtiers. By keeping the aristocracy under his supervision, Louis also severed the independence of high nobles, who were reduced to squabbling over who would—literally—wipe the royal behind.

But financing wars and the king's extravagance put a strain on the economy, as did the exodus of skilled artisans and merchants after the king revoked the Edict of Nantes (which granted Huguenots religious and civil liberties) in 1685. To meet rising expenses, Colbert had been forced to revert to short-term expedients to increase taxation revenue. The root of financial problems, however, was the tax collection system itself more than expenditures. Louis XIV's legacy was a modern system of government financed by a semi-medieval taxation system.

Cour des Miracles

During the 15th, 16th, and 17th centuries, war and the plague spawned masses of homeless people in France. Many came to Paris, gravitating toward the side streets just inside Charles V's wall. By day, they made a living as beggars, pretending to be crippled, maimed, blind, or orphaned, or worked the crowds alongside the swindlers and thieves. At night, they disappeared into the alleyways, miraculously cured—hence the area's name, Cour des Miracles.

The Cour des Miracles was shut down by police in 1667, with the so-called cripples leading the flight from the security forces.

Louis XV: After Louis XIV's death in 1715, the court and young Louis XV (R.1715–1774) moved back to Paris under the regent Philippe d'Orléans, a dissipated rake who allowed the great noble families to regain their former independence. Parisians sought to forget the austerity of Louis XIV's final years, opting for bright colors and a dash of frivolity. This was the age of Watteau's lighthearted paintings and Charles Perrault's fairy tales.

A period of political stability followed under the king's chief adviser, André de Fleury, with overseas trade and improved transportation boosting commercial development. Paris grew on both banks, with the stylish new *faubourgs* (quarters outside the old walls) of St.-Germain and St.-Honoré. After de Fleury's death in 1743, Louis XV took over as head of government. He commissioned the Place Louis XV (now the Place de la Concorde), the Ste.-Geneviève Church (Panthéon), the Odéon Theater, the École Militaire, and the Champ de Mars.

Where the Ghosts Are

With more than 2,000 years of history, the city of Paris cannot help but be haunted by a few ghosts. The prime real estate that is the Tuileries Garden, for example, is said to be haunted by a butcher known as Jean l'Ecorcheur (John the Skinner). His assassination was supposedly ordered by Queen Catherine de Médicis, who built the Tuileries Palace, because he knew too much about her occult activities. "I shall return," he told his assassin. He is said to have appeared to Marie-Antoinette when she was imprisoned in the palace, to Napoleon just before the Battle of Waterloo, and to the Communards who burned the palace down in 1870.

On the Left Bank, the Luxembourg Gardens are visited by a man in a frock coat who may invite visitors to a concert. Beware: The concert took place a century ago. Another park with a ghostly presence is the Parc Montsouris, haunted by the wailing of the headless corpse of Isauré de Montsouris, who was decapitated by a band of thieves in 831. And, of course, many legends surround the Père-Lachaise Cemetery, where black masses and human sacrifices are said to have taken place. And watch out if you spy a huge red cat there with an unusual gait—it may not be what it appears.

The Enlightenment: Louis XV's lack of character resulted in nearly 50 years of weak government. He sought distraction in hunting and in women, one of whom was his famous mistress, the Marquise de Pompadour. She was a friend of Denis Diderot, who recruited the major French thinkers of the Enlightenment to write the *Encyclopédie*, a remarkable compendium of ideas championing skepticism and rationalism. The first volume was published in 1751.

The 18th century brought great interest in reform, as political and financial structures were not keeping pace with social changes. Montaigne, Descartes, Newton, and others had laid the groundwork for unorthodox ideas—stifled under Louis XIV but now flourishing. By the mid-18th century, revolutionary ideas on science and philosophy circulated through the fashionable salons held by influential women such as Madame Geoffrin.

French Revolution

Louis XVI's Government: The Parlements became the center of opposition to Louis XIV's weaker successors. The Parlement of Paris saw itself as the defender of constitutional liberties, and although Louis XVI (R.1774–1792) tried to enact reforms, the Parlement continued to spread opposition and revolutionary ideas.

To gain favor with the people, the king appointed Jacques Necker as Director General of Finances in 1777. Necker was a popular figure, an ally of the commoners. The French government was on the verge of bankruptcy, due in part to expenses incurred by France during the American Revolution. In 1785, work began on the Fermiers Généraux (Tax Collectors) wall around Paris. Heavy taxes were levied on goods entering and leaving the city, fueling popular discontent. The *vingtième*, a tax on one-twentieth of all incomes, had been introduced in 1749, but the nobility refused to pay, and the clergy led the opposition to the tax.

Third Estate: After attempts to avert bankruptcy failed, Louis XVI was forced to convene the Estates-General to try to raise new taxes. The Estates-General was composed of the clergy (First Estate); the nobility (Second Estate); and the commoners (Third Estate), each voting as a block. Its meeting in May 1789—for the first time since 1614—marked the abdication of absolute monarchy and the empowerment of the Third Estate. A new kind of revolution was to emerge, one no longer led by the Parlements, nobility, and clergy. The hidden impetus was the supply and price of food—primarily bread—following the disastrous harvest of 1788.

Representing 96 percent of the population, the Third Estate proclaimed itself the National Assembly on June 17. When their meeting hall was closed, the deputies adjourned to a nearby *jeu de paume*, or indoor tennis court, and took an oath (June 20) to meet until a constitution was drafted. Troops, largely foreign, continued to pour into Paris and Versailles, and on July 11 Necker was dismissed and replaced by Queen Marie-Antoinette's favorite, the Baron de Breteuil.

Revolt Against the Monarchy: On July 14, orators at the Palais-Royal incited the people to take up arms. They attacked Les Invalides to procure munitions, then stormed the Bastille's armory. Refusing to surrender, the Bastille's governor was killed and his head was paraded around Paris on a pike to mark the victory. Louis XVI proceeded to the Hôtel de Ville, where he accepted the tricolor cockade from the new municipal government, or commune.

In October, angry Parisians marched to Versailles to protest high bread prices—when Marie-Antoinette allegedly told them to try brioche instead. In Paris, political clubs guided the National Assembly in drafting a constitution. The king and queen fled the city on June 20, 1791, but were recognized at Varennes and brought to the Tuileries Palace in humiliation. The king accepted the constitution, thus creating a limited monarchy.

> 66 **By the mid-18th century, revolutionary ideas on science and philosophy circulated through the fashionable salons.** 99

Exasperation of Parisians with the government led to the radicalization of the *sans-culottes* ("without breeches"; the lower classes wore trousers instead of aristocratic breeches) in 1792. On August 10, 1792, when a demand that Louis XVI be deposed was refused, they attacked the Tuileries, and an insurrectionary commune replaced the legally elected one.

Reign of Terror: Mobs stormed the prisons during the September massacres, killing nearly 2,000 suspected traitors. The monarchy was abolished on September 22, 1792—the first day of Year 1 of the French Republic, according to the new revolutionary calendar. The king was tried for treason and guillotined on January 21, 1793; Marie-Antoinette followed him nine months later. The Reign of Terror, ostensibly a campaign against foreign spies directed by the Committee of Public Safety—which included the revolutionary leaders Maximilien Robespierre and Louis Saint-Just—was in reality an attempt to purge "enemies from within." Thousands were guillotined, including Robespierre himself, in July 1794.

The National Convention, which had been elected to draw up a new constitution, set up a five-man Directory, fraught with internal dissension and dependent on the army to maintain control. The Directory was overthrown by a coup d'état in November 1799, and army hero Napoleon Bonaparte (R.1804–1814) was declared First Consul.

19th-Century Paris

First Empire: Napoleon's popularity rose as peace returned, and he quickly shaped France into a powerful, centralized state. Although Napoleon distrusted Paris and considered shifting the imperial seat to Lyon, he understood the capital's key position. He set about marking it with his imperial stamp following his coronation on December 2, 1804—building new boulevards, palaces, and imposing Roman-style monuments, such as the Arc de Triomphe, the Madeleine, and the Bourse. He also expanded the Louvre's collections with booty from abroad.

While pursuing military campaigns, Napoleon boosted the economy and trade, established the Code Napoléon for civil law, set up the Grandes Écoles, and revamped the administrative system. But the success of his initial campaigns waned, particularly after the catastrophic invasion of Russia in 1812. In early 1814, Paris was occupied by the allied troops of Russia, Austria, Prussia, and Great Britain, and Napoleon was exiled to Elba. King Louis XVIII (Louis XVI's gout-afflicted brother; R.1814–1824) was restored to the throne with Talleyrand's help, but fled when Napoleon escaped from Elba a year later for his Hundred Days' Rule. Napoleon was crushed in the Waterloo Campaign (June 12–18, 1815) and the British government banished him to the island of St. Helena, where he died in 1821.

> **Although Napoleon distrusted Paris and considered shifting the imperial seat to Lyon, he understood the capital's key position.**

The Revolution of 1830: Louis XVIII returned to Paris on July 8. His chief ministers initially were moderates, but the ultraroyalists eventually got the upper hand. Electoral laws were revised to favor the wealthy, and civil liberties were curbed. Louis's successor, the reactionary Charles X (R.1824–1830), went further, dissolving the liberal Chamber of Deputies in May 1830, banning the press, and modifying electoral laws to favor property owners. On July 27, newspapers published defiantly; barricades soon went up and insurrection committees formed. A new provisional government ordered the tricolor raised, and three days of fighting ensued—the famous Trois Glorieuses (July 27–29)—forcing Charles into exile.

July Monarchy & Revolution: During the reign of Louis-Philippe (R.1830–1848), dubbed "the citizen king," class divisions became even more entrenched. Wealthy families could afford to live in spacious new districts like the 8th arrondissement, while the poor were packed into central districts like St.-Merri.

■ A painting by Lejeune depicts the 1800 Battle of Marengo, an early Napoleonic victory.

On February 23, 1848, troops opened fire on a crowd on the Boulevard des Capucines, killing more than 40. Parisians erected barricades and tore up paving stones on Place Vendôme and the Rue Royale. Louis-Philippe abdicated the next day.

The provisional government, presided over by Alphonse Lamartine, included "Albert the mechanic"—the people's representative. It abolished slavery in the colonies and the death penalty for political crimes, decreed freedom of expression, granted universal suffrage to men, and set up national workshops on construction sites throughout France to ease unemployment.

In April 1848, a conservative commission was voted in, and Parisian revolutionaries and socialists took to the streets. On May 21, the national workshops were suppressed. The next day, rioting broke out to shouts of *"Du pain ou du plomb!"*–"Bread or lead!"– ending in a bloodbath that killed 3,000.

Second Empire: In late 1848, elections overwhelmingly brought Louis-Napoleon Bonaparte (the emperor's nephew) to power as France's first president. He carried out a coup d'état three years later (the constitution forbade running for a second term of office), and the following year he was installed as Napoleon III (*R.*1852– 1870). Paris saw it as the triumph of order.

Louis-Napoleon's plans to modernize the city reflected this sense of order. He called upon Baron Haussmann, Prefect of Paris, to oversee the major projects (see pp. 166–167).

New market halls at Les Halles were built, the Palais Garnier commissioned, and the sewer system expanded. By the end of the Second Empire, Paris was a showcase for industrial exhibitions and the economy was thriving. But this sense of euphoria was shattered when Napoleon III, recognizing that Prussia's rise posed a threat to France, declared war, precipitating the disastrous Franco-Prussian War of 1870.

Paris Commune: Following Napoleon III's military defeat at Sedan, September 2, 1870, and the fall of the imperial regime, a new Republic—proclaimed on September 4, 1870—prepared to face the advancing Prussians. By late September, the capital's troops numbered 500,000 (two-thirds of whom were grossly inexperienced). Although 30,000 cattle and 180,000 sheep were kept in the Bois de Boulogne as a backup food supply, the besieged Parisians went hungry that winter. Horses, dogs, cats, rats—even a few beasts from the zoo at the Jardin des Plantes—were eaten in the effort to survive.

Adolphe Thiers's government negotiated a temporary armistice with Bismarck on January 28, 1871. Terms included the surrender of Alsace and much of Lorraine, and many Parisians saw the armistice as a betrayal. On March 18, Thiers sent troops to confiscate 227 guns from the National Guard in Montmartre. The people refused to give up the guns, and when the troops sent to remove them started fraternizing with the crowd, two of their generals were executed. On March 28, the Commune of Paris was proclaimed, its principal demand being that Paris have a municipal government within a French democratic republic. The Commune laid out plans for compulsory primary education and workers' cooperatives.

Charles de Gaulle leads a march down the Champs-Élysées, 1944.

Bloody Week & Its Aftermath: Thiers and the Versailles troops then began a ferocious, five-week siege of Paris to suppress the Commune, culminating in Bloody Week (May 22–28). The greatly outnumbered Communards barricaded the streets and shot many suspected of not resisting the troops. The government retook the city in a brutal assault, and on May 28, the Commune was defeated. Thousands of Communards were shot in reprisal (147 were executed against the Federalists' Wall of Père-Lachaise Cemetery), with the death toll estimated at anywhere from 17,000 to 35,000.

Despite a mutual wariness between Parisians and the French government, one long-term impact of the siege was a surge in patriotism, which found expression in such spectacular new monuments as the Grand Palais and the Eiffel Tower—the centerpiece of the 1889 Universal Exposition marking the centenary of the French Revolution.

> **In 1936, Léon Blum brought Radical Socialists, Socialists, and Communists together in a Popular Front government.**

20th-Century Paris

Belle Époque & World War I: During the *belle époque*, Paris became as dynamic as it had been under Haussmann. The 1889 exposition featuring the Eiffel Tower was outdone only by the 1900 exposition, when the opening of the first Métro line launched the new century. Paris was the world's cultural capital, and artists, writers, and musicians were laying the foundations of the modern era.

The expansion was halted by the onset of war. By September 2, 1914, the Germans were 15 miles (24 km) outside Paris. Five days later, 4,000 men were shuttled to the front in taxis. Following the Battle of the Marne, a German retreat was ordered and trench warfare began. In four years, Paris was hit by 746 bombs. Big Bertha, the huge cannon in the St.-Gobain forest 88 miles (140 km) away, lobbed more than 300 shells, each weighing 400 pounds (181 kg), on the city. Morale in Paris had been badly damaged by the 1916 Battle of Verdun, when France suffered 163,000 dead and 320,000 wounded. Propaganda campaigns sought to boost morale, but the tide only really turned when the formidable Georges Clemenceau became prime minister in 1917 and led his country to victory.

Postwar Paris: The victory parade on Bastille Day in 1919 marked the end of a nightmare, yet the postwar years were harsh. The Depression exacerbated political crises, and on February 6, 1934, right-wing forces rallied protesters ranging from war veterans to Fascists on the Place de la Concorde, ostensibly against government corruption. Riots broke out, and police killed 15 and injured 1,500, including several "war heroes." Five days later, unions organized a massive strike in support of democracy. In 1936, Léon Blum brought Radical Socialists, Socialists, and Communists together in a Popular Front government. Its achievements included inaugurating collective bargaining and a 40-hour work week.

France and Britain declared war on Germany in September 1939. During the subsequent "Phoney War"—with the side having declared war awaiting attack—truckloads of art left the Louvre for Chambord, the stained-glass windows of Ste.-Chapelle were removed, and gas masks were distributed. Germany attacked France on May 10, 1940, forcing many Parisians into exodus. Paris was declared an open city and the government left for Bordeaux.

On June 14, Paris fell. Marshal Pétain, who became prime minister, demanded an armistice, triggering Charles de Gaulle's June 18 call from London to shore up "Free French" resistance. (De Gaulle, then Undersecretary of State for War, was sentenced to death in absentia by a Vichy court.) The armistice was signed, the Third Republic was dissolved, and Pétain became Head of State of the government of unoccupied France (now at Vichy), with more legal authority than any leader since Bonaparte.

The Occupation: The Germans occupied 60 percent of France, which became an ally in the Holocaust. There is no proof that Vichy acted under Nazi pressure to enact racial laws in 1940, yet it imposed a broader definition of a Jew than the Germans had. The laws also lowered the age of children subject to deportation.

During the Occupation, average Parisians were deprived of cars; bread, sugar, and other staples were rationed. Vegetable patches sprang up on rooftops. Street signs were in German, and the swastika flew over the Hôtel de Ville and the Eiffel Tower.

The Germans required the registration of all Jewish persons and launched anti-Jewish propaganda campaigns. An exhibit called "The Jew and France," designed to instruct the public on how to recognize Jews, featured a huge poster depicting a Shylock-like caricature of a Jewish man. All Jewish people over the age of six were forced to wear a yellow star in the occupied zone. They were barred from public places, many important jobs, and morning shopping hours, and had to ride in the last Métro car, dubbed "the Synagogue." Police sweeps in the Paris region began in May 1941, when Jewish men, at first mostly foreign, were rounded up. The first deportation train left for Germany in March 1942, half of the men being French Jews. During La Grande Rafle in July 1942, more than 8,000 people, including 4,115 children, were rounded up at the Vélodrome d'Hiver bicycle stadium in the 15th arrondissement. During the same period, the first French victims died in the gas chambers at Auschwitz.

The organized Resistance hid many Jewish people and helped them escape. Although one-third of French Jews were deported and killed, two-thirds were saved, largely through the efforts of French citizens and the Resistance.

The Liberation: The Allies landed in Normandy on June 6, 1944, and by August they were fast approaching Paris. An insurrection was launched on August 19, resulting in heavy casualties on both sides. Hitler had instructed German Commander General von Choltitz to reduce the city to ashes in case of defeat, but he did not carry out the order.

On the evening of August 24, an advance detachment from General Leclerc's Second Armored Division burst through the city to the Hôtel de Ville, and hundreds of

Please Sit on the Grass

Paris has become a kinder, more user-friendly city under its past mayor, Bertrand Delanoë, and his successor, Anne Hidalgo, both Socialists and, respectively, the first gay man and the first woman to hold the office. "Keep off the grass" signs are gone from Paris parks; Vélib' and Mobilib' (short-term bike and car rentals) have been introduced; bike lanes have multiplied; Paris Plages, Berges de Seine, and the Parc Rives de Seine have given the quays back to pedestrians and cyclists; and new laws should help clean up the city's polluted air.

President Emmanuel Macron, the youngest in the history of France

church bells pealed above the roofs of Paris. On August 25, the main body of Leclerc's division, in conjunction with the American 4th Infantry Division, liberated the city. The French flag was hoisted over the Eiffel Tower.

Modern France: De Gaulle emerged as the postwar leader of France, but in 1946 he brusquely withdrew during political maneuvering in forming the Fourth Republic. He was called back in 1958 during an uprising led by right-wing elements determined to keep Algeria as a French colony. De Gaulle prevailed, forming the Fifth Republic and becoming its first president. Algeria was proclaimed independent, and Paris at last began to enjoy prosperity.

This lasted until May 1968, when students demonstrated massively against France's obsolete educational system. Workers joined the movement and called a general strike that nearly paralyzed the country. Ten months after this upheaval, De Gaulle resigned, and Georges Pompidou was elected president, succeeded by Valéry Giscard d'Estaing. The latter's projects for Paris included the Musée d'Orsay. In 1981 Socialist François Mitterrand came to power, instituting a series of *grands travaux*. His Bibliothèque Nationale de France was completed after his death in 1996.

Former Paris mayor Jacques Chirac became president in 1995, and was followed by right-of-center president Nicolas Sarkozy, who was voted out of office in 2012 after only one five-year term (two are allowed). He was replaced by Socialist François Hollande, whose ineffectual governance set new unpopularity records for a French president. Although his ratings rose thanks to his response to the shocking terrorist attacks in January 2015, he didn't run for a second mandate in the 2017 elections, won by Emmanuel Macron. Former member of the Socialist Party and Minister of the Economy and Industry, then founder of the centrist movement La République en Marche!, Macron defeated the right-wing nationalist Marine Le Pen and became the youngest president in the history of France at 39. ■

THE ARTS

Paris, the most visited city in the world, certainly owes its fame to its monuments and its history. But above all, this vibrant city basks in a rich cultural heritage and continues to attract leading exponents of literature, art, dance, theater, and opera.

Literature

Paris has always drawn writers looking for recognition and inspiration at the center of European intellectual society.

From the 15th to the 17th centuries, the long-established University of Paris was the home of scholastic philosophy, which tried to reconcile the thinking of Greek

■ **Visitors climb the Louvre's floating staircase.**

philosophers—particularly Aristotle and Plato—with Christian orthodoxy. It also played a part in the French Inquisition, forcing independent thinkers like the 17th-century philosopher René Descartes to choose their words carefully to avoid prosecution. But theater flourished under Louis XIV. The plays of Jean Racine and Pierre Corneille elegantly retold the ancient Greek stories using classical French verse, while the satirist Molière amused his aristocratic audiences with plays depicting the pretensions and ambitions of the growing middle classes.

18th Century: Eighteenth-century literature was greatly influenced by a young aristocrat, François-Marie Arouet, who eventually went too far in his satires and was sent to the Bastille. There he changed his name to Voltaire. Upon his release, Voltaire became enormously popular, but was nonetheless forced to spend most of his life in exile. His contemporaries, Denis Diderot, Jean le Rond d'Alembert, and their circle, stayed on in Paris, producing the first French *Encyclopédie*. They became the center of the Enlightenment, which gradually brought intellectual tolerance to France.

> **In 19th-century Paris, strong personal friendships flourished between creative artists of all kinds.**

Many of the next generation's circle of aristocratic and liberal French writers, whose works circulated through the famous literary salons, died while serving in Napoleon's armies. The most famous was Stendhal (Henri-Marie Beyle), whose historical romances were the first important 19th-century French novels.

19th Century: After 1830, the French novel progressed from Honoré de Balzac through Gustave Flaubert, Victor Hugo, Émile Zola, and Marcel Proust to achieve a new form that described everyday life, investigated character, and propagated social and political ideas, thus enabling a massive, newly literate readership to understand more about the world around it.

Artists and poets were regarded in a new light, suddenly becoming important and influential social leaders. Some 19th-century poets, such as Charles Pierre Baudelaire and Théophile Gautier, shocked society by probing the darker sides of human nature, and were even prosecuted for their work. However, as the notoriety only increased sales, they received more benefit than harm. In 19th-century Paris, strong personal friendships flourished between creative artists of all kinds. Thus, ideas spread rapidly, encouraging the emergence of new styles in painting, literature, and music. With the rise of the comfortable middle classes, survival was no longer the only aim in life, and artists led the way in prescribing the pursuit of pleasure as a new goal.

Throughout the middle years of the 19th century, Paris became a haven for intellectual and artistic refugees from all over Europe, such as Karl Marx, Richard Wagner, and Heinrich Heine, although some—among them Victor Hugo—who angered the monarchy were forced to flee the country. Talk of new systems in art, literature, philosophy, politics, and everyday institutions dominated the conversations at café tables from Montmartre to Montparnasse, bolstering the city's reputation as an artistic and intellectual center.

20th Century: Impressionism, which started in painting, also affected literary and musical techniques. The burgeoning modernism of the first decade of the 20th century took many forms—symbolism, imagism, cubism, and others—which André Breton employed in his surrealist school, perhaps the most successful of the modernist art movements.

When American Sylvia Beach established her Shakespeare and Company bookshop on the Left Bank in 1919, Paris also became a haven for British and American writers, and she was the first to publish James Joyce's *Ulysses*. Dubbed "the lost generation" by Gertrude Stein, the Americans included popular novelists like journalist Ernest Hemingway and F. Scott Fitzgerald; literary magazine editors like the Crosbys and the Jolases, who published in Paris and in England; and others like James Joyce and Henry Miller, whose works were too outspoken and sexually frank to be published in their own, English-speaking countries. The poet T. S. Eliot collected material in Paris for his magazine *The Criterion,* and author and journalist Cyril Connolly came for the wine, food, and culture, and to get published by Jack Kahane's Obelisk Press (which was the first to publish Miller's controversial *Tropic of Cancer*).

Women writers such as Colette and Anaïs Nin also made their mark with their explicit descriptions of love and sex, setting the groundwork for later women who would challenge the predominantly male domain of erotic literature.

Post World War I: In the 1930s, antifascists and Jews fleeing Italy and Germany joined the expatriate Americans still in Paris. The new arrivals included André Gide, André Malraux, Roger Martin du Gard, Jean Cocteau, Franz Werfel, Erich Maria Remarque, and Odön von Horváth. During the war, a great many writers were killed serving in the French army or in the Resistance, in concentration camps, or were shot at borders. But throughout the war, a considerable underground press continued publishing works such as Vercors's novel *The Silence of the Sea*, about passive resistance to the Germans, and Paul Éluard's passionate poem *Liberté,* which was dropped on Paris by the Royal Air Force.

Engineering Marvels

England astonished the world in 1851 with the Crystal Palace, built for the first Great Exhibition to showcase British goods and technical know-how. The French immediately began planning their own world's fair. The first of five *expositions*, most of which were based around the Champ de Mars, was held in 1867.

The greatest French fair was the one held in 1889, when 28 million visitors came to marvel at the glittering cast-iron and glass structures covering the site and to look up amazed at the Tour Eiffel.

Literary Café Life From Postwar Paris to the Present: After the war, a new generation of writers, philosophers, and intellectuals that included Jean-Paul Sartre, Albert Camus, Boris Vian, and Simone de Beauvoir came to prominence. They, in turn, were followed by what became known as the *"nouveau roman,"* a legacy of surrealism. New theater also flourished in the plays written by such major figures as Samuel Beckett, Arthur Adamov, and Eugène Ionesco, who continued in the vein initiated by Antonin Artaud.

■ Today's Shakespeare and Company bookstore is a fixture of the Latin Quarter.

These writers, some not French-born, were soon joined by other expatriates from America and Britain, who produced small magazines in English for another new literary current, the "Beat" movement (whose starting place was thus as much in Paris as in San Francisco).

Although there has been a decline in literary café life in the last few decades, cafés like La Coupole, Flore, and Brasserie Lipp in St.-Germain, where Sartre held court, still recall the heyday of this vibrant past. Paris seems alive with a creativity that still lures artists today, and the city still has a reputation for recognizing talent. One of the more recent literary discoveries—and source of scandal—is novelist and poet Michel Houellebecq, who wrote *Atomized* and *The Possibility of an Island.* In 2014, Parisian novelist Patrick Modiano received the Nobel Prize in Literature "for the art of memory with which he has evoked the most ungraspable human destinies and uncovered the life-world of the occupation."

Art

The art scene in Paris is as diverse and international as its literature, with galleries and exhibitions showing work by artists from Africa, Asia, America, and Europe.

Parisian Galleries: Art is alive and well in Paris, if the several hundred galleries in the city are any indication. Most are concentrated in three main areas:

■ **The Panthéon Bouddhique in the Musée Guimet contains stone carvings and bodhisattvas.**

St.-Germain-des-Prés, the Marais, and the 8th arrondissement, just behind the Champs-Élysées, which is now filled with galleries showing more recognized artists.

New artists are most likely to be found in the Marais area near Rue Vieille-du-Temple and in the 13th arrondissement. Generally speaking, more established artists exhibit in the dozens of galleries clustered around the Rue de Seine and the Rue Guénégaud in the St.-Germain neighborhood. New galleries are scattered around the Belleville area, with a concentration between the Métros Belleville and Pyrénées, and in the third arrondissement on Rue Chapon and nearby streets.

It is possible to see artwork outside the galleries. A number of artists display their work in the square at Montmartre, though you'll have to sift through the purely commercial tourist work. There are also several artists' associations that organize *portes ouvertes,* or open houses, welcoming the public into their studios (usually in May and October). The Génie de la Bastille was the first of these, but others have sprung up in the 13th, 18th, and 20th arrondissements, and in the suburbs of Ivry, Montreuil, and Montrouge, where many artists have moved to escape Paris's high rents.

Several publications (mostly in French) provide information about current shows, including the weekly *Pariscope,* the monthly *Beaux Arts Magazine, Artpress,* and a gallery guide that is available free of charge at galleries. This guide provides a map of the St.-Germain and Marais neighborhoods, with locations and dates of the *vernissages* (openings). The Drouot auction house puts out *La Gazette Drouot,* which features information about upcoming auctions and news on exhibitions and galleries.

Architecture

The architectural history of Paris is densely layered. Time and time again old buildings and monuments have been knocked down or transformed or reused to make way for new ones. For example, vestiges of the Bastille prison were used to build the Concorde Bridge and the Théâtre du Marais (no longer standing), and stones from the Roman baths and Left Bank dwellings were used in medieval times to build a medieval defensive wall on the Île de la Cité.

Paris's earliest architectural elements are over 2,000 years old, dating from the time when the original settlement of Lutetia was only a backwater at the outer reaches of the Roman Empire. The ruins of two characteristic structures remain from this period: the heavily restored 16,000-seat Arena (the Arènes de Lutèce rediscovered in the 19th century) and the baths of Cluny, now part of the Musée de Cluny.

Gothic & Medieval Architecture: The Île de France is the cradle of Gothic architecture, with its luminous churches heightened by their Gothic arches. In 1136, the Basilica of St.-Denis was begun, which was the first Gothic building to combine flying buttresses and ribbed vaulting; it was followed by the Cathedral of Notre-Dame in 1163, and the Flamboyant Gothic-style masterpiece, Ste.-Chapelle, built by Pierre de Montreuil in the following century. The Hôtel de Sens and the Hôtel de Cluny are among the few examples of secular Gothic architecture left in Paris.

Medieval architecture persisted in Paris long after the Renaissance had replaced it elsewhere. Although King François I brought back Renaissance ideas in architecture from his military campaigns in Italy, he only utilized them in the Loire Valley châteaus. Meanwhile, Paris continued to build Flamboyant Gothic buildings for nearly five centuries; they include the Tour St.-Jacques (1509–1523), the St.-Merri Church (1520–1552), and the St.-Gervais Church (1494–1657). Henri IV initiated the great royal squares, the first being today's Place des Vosges.

EXPERIENCE: Gallery-Hopping

To really immerse yourself in Paris's impressive art scene, try a day or two of gallery-hopping. Most high-end art galleries are clustered around Avenue Matignon and Rue du Faubourg St.-Honoré in the 8th arrondissement. This is where Flemish Old Masters, 18th-century French furniture, and Picasso and other 20th-century masters can be found. A must for contemporary art lovers is the **Gagosian Gallery** (4 rue de Ponthieu, tel 01 75 00 05 92), specialist in big-name artists. On the Left Bank, the area around Rue de Seine and Rue Mazarine is home to many 20th-century art and design galleries, as well as contemporary galleries, one of the hottest being **Kamel Mennour** (47 rue Saint André des Arts and 6 rue du Pont de Lodi, tel 01 56 24 03 63). The area around upper Rue Vieille-du-Temple, between Rue des Francs-Bourgeois and Rue de Bretagne, is a hotbed for trendy galleries, among them the **Galerie Rabouan Moussion** (11 rue Pastourelle, tel 01 48 87 75 91), which shows cutting-edge work mainly by French and Russian artists. A number of new galleries have popped up in the last decade on the Rues Chapon, Vertbois, and Notre Dame de Nazareth in the northwestern corner of the Marais.

17th, 18th, & 19th Centuries: The fashionable quarter in the 17th century remained the Marais, where a number of lavish mansions—the Hôtel de Sully and the Hôtel Salé (now the Musée Picasso)—still stand. During the Ancien Régime (France's system of government before the Revolution), some of the greatest architects worked under royal patronage. Salomon de Brosse constructed the Palais de Luxembourg, François Mansart created his eponymous roofline and windows, and Louis Le Vau built Vaux-le-Vicomte. This era also saw the development of formal landscaping, its leading proponent being André Le Nôtre.

> 66 **Paris was radically transformed when Baron Haussmann set about modernizing the city during the Second Empire.** 99

During the 18th century, the aristocracy migrated to the Faubourg St.-Germain, where many *hôtels particuliers,* or private mansions, were built in the rococo style; most of these are now embassies and government institutions.

There was little new building during the Revolution. Churches were either torn down or converted. Many were deconsecrated and used as warehouses or Temples of Reason. Paris was radically transformed when Baron Haussmann set about modernizing the city during the Second Empire (see pp. 166–167). The Prefect of Paris under Napoleon III, Haussmann tore down dilapidated houses, replacing them with entire blocks of apartment buildings, and sliced wide boulevards through old neighborhoods. Another legacy of 19th-century architecture were exuberant iron structures dramatically exemplified by the Eiffel Tower.

Modern Architecture: Technical innovations and a new design aesthetic, devised by Le Corbusier, contributed to the more geometric and functional style of the modern movement after World War I. There are few of Le Corbusier's designs in Paris, although his influence was widespread.

Postwar Paris was marked by experiments in high-rise developments, where entire neighborhoods, particularly in the 19th arrondissement, were replaced by impersonal slabs of apartment buildings. President Mitterrand's *grands travaux* had a great impact on the face of the city, with some of the more admirable monuments including the Louvre Pyramid, the Grande Arche de La Défense, and the Institut du Monde Arabe; others—such as the Opéra Bastille or the stark towers of the new Bibliothèque de France—are more controversial. Among the most recent purchases of the Parisian architectural landscape are the buildings of the Fondation Louis Vuitton and the Philharmonie de Paris, designed by Frank Gehry and Jean Nouvel, respectively.

Cinema

In France, and Paris in particular, an appreciation of the cinema is regarded as a key component of the good life. France has a long tradition of serious writing about cinema. The monthly journals *Positif* and *Cahiers du Cinéma* have been in business for over half a century, each voicing occasionally sharp divisions in taste. Every major general-interest magazine includes extensive movie criticism and director profiles.

The French government encourages its citizens to go to the movies by offering discounts to students, the elderly, members of the military, members of families with three or more children, and the unemployed, while several movie houses offer unlimited access passes at very reasonable rates per month. Whereas box office statistics in the United States are less than scientific, in France the National Center for Cinema (CNC) accounts for every last ticket sold, a percent of which is funneled into future productions of French movies (the *avance sur recettes* system).

The sheer choice of films in Paris is spectacular—more than 400 screens in around 100 theaters—from the latest Hollywood megaproduction to first-person documentaries shot in Super 8 or video formats and blown up for commercial release. Although the art-house and

I. M. Pei's glass pyramid entrance to the Louvre contrasts with the facade of the older buildings.

repertory cinemas remain far more vital in Paris than in any other city on Earth—in Paris, one cinema in five is classed as "art and experimental"—there are also megacinema chains, such as the giants Gaumont and MK2, which threaten independent theater owners.

In addition to the small art-house cinemas and state-of-the-art multiplexes, there is Studio 28 in Montmartre, where Luis Buñuel and Salvador Dalí's notorious surrealist masterpiece *An Andalusian Dog* premiered in 1928, and the huge, lavishly decorated Grand Rex cinema with its star-spangled ceiling, which offers a backstage tour that includes an elevator ride behind the giant screen while a movie is showing. The reopened Cinémathèque Française in a Frank Gehry building on Rue de Bercy offers a series of retrospectives and cinema-related exhibitions. The city also holds annual festivals like Cinéma au Clair de la Lune, and has renovated and reopened the art deco Louxor Cinema.

Purely French Cinema: Although the vast majority of viewers under the age of 25 think "American" when they think "Let's go to the movies," French cinema is back in vogue. In the 1990s, the share of the box office in France for French-made films dropped to 34.5 percent, with 53.8 percent of the moviegoing public opting for American releases, and dipped to below 30 percent in 2000. But in 2001, French moviegoers led a mass revolt against the bulwark of Hollywood productions when record numbers hit movie houses to see a variety of films produced by a domestic film industry that has reinvented itself. The strength of French cinema, regarded as being the champion of European film creativity today, is its diversity. The French have always excelled at more intimate movies, such as those by François Ozon *(Under the Sand, Eight Women)*, but they're now also recording commercial and artistic successes, with everything from lighthearted comedies (Jean-Pierre Jeunet's *Amélie*, Agnès Bacri's *Le Goût des Autres*) to New Wave–inspired pieces by directors like Jacques Rivette *(Va Savoir)*; thrillers (Hitchcock-influenced numbers like *With a Friend Like Harry* by Dominik Moll); hard-line detective films; and action movies, spearheaded by Luc Besson, director of Hollywood-influenced movies like *Nikita* and *Lucy*.

Theater, Dance, & Opera

Ever since Les Confrères de la Passion established the city's first permanent theater in 1547 at the Hôtel du Duc de Bourgogne (see the commemorative plaque at 29 rue Étienne Marcel), the dramatic arts have diversified. They now range from street theater in summer to grandly produced plays, performed everywhere from tiny cellars to sumptuous surroundings. The 1960s counterculture and Culture Minister André Malraux's decentralization plan succeeded in broadening the

---

EXPERIENCE:
Enjoy the Wide World of Dance

The diverse annual multi-arts Autumn Festival *(festival-automne.com)* is a good opportunity to watch dance from around the globe, but dance lovers can also see international dance troupes in the auditorium of the **Musée du Quai Branly** (see p. 175). The **Maison de la Culture du Japon** *(mcjp.fr)* includes dance such as the Jiutamai song and dance of the geishas as part of its varied program of cinema, theater, and exhibitions. The Parc de La Villette (see pp. 208–209) hosts a few free or low-priced performances at different venues.

The Théâtre Rive Gauche hosts plays in Montparnasse.

appeal of theater, and plays everywhere are enjoying increased popularity.

This recent revolution, however, has not dented the deference accorded to the traditional Comédie Française (referred to as the House of Molière), created by Louis XIV in 1680, seven years after Molière's death. This prestigious symbol of French culture purveys classics by Molière, Pierre Corneille, and Jean Racine (see p. 35), as well as plays by such modern authors and playwrights as Jean Genet, Stefan Zweig, Marguerite Duras, and Tom Stoppard.

Contemporary Theater: Contemporary directors such as Ariane Mnouchkine and Peter Brook have opted out of commercial crowd-pleasers to pursue exciting, independent theater. Mnouchkine at the Théâtre du Soleil uses this spacious venue— a transformed armaments factory—to intrigue audiences with evocative plays.

Such unconventional use of space characterizes many Parisian theaters, drawing directors from abroad, such as self-exiled Englishman Peter Brook, whose Théâtre des Bouffes du Nord is exceptional. Together with Micheline Rozan, he founded the Centre International de Recherche Théâtral (CIRT) in 1970 and Le Centre International de Créations Théâtrales in 1974. Although Brooks has now stepped down as the theater's artistic director, the Bouffes du Nord continues to stage productions that exemplify his belief that "opera, popular music, theater and dance can be married in a single spectacle in order to invent new forms."

France's commitment to continuing cross-cultural exchange was exemplified by Harold Pinter's first-time direction of *Ashes to Ashes;* Oscar-winning French actress Juliette Binoche's off–West End appearance in London; and Paris-based playwright Yasmina Reza's *Art,* which has been translated into 35 languages. Resident English-language theater companies, including Dear Conjunction and The International Players, present bilingual productions of well-known plays, as well as their own creations. Another key theater in the artistic exchange between France and the rest of the world is the MC93 in Bobigny, whose eclectic international program has featured American choreographer Lucinda Childs, English producer Deborah Warner, and Irish actress Fiona Shaw.

Dance: As Europe's undisputed dance capital, Paris has a rich selection of festivals, events, spectacles, and dance forms ranging from tango and ballet to hip-hop and contemporary dance.

Productions of the Ballet de l'Opéra National de Paris are held at both the Palais Garnier and the Opéra Bastille. Generous sponsorship by the Ministry of Culture permits extravagant tributes to George Balanchine and Jerome Robbins, alongside standards like *Giselle* and *Swan Lake,* and performances by the Bolshoi Ballet. Since 1973, Carolyn Carlson, Angelin Preljocaj, Jean-Claude Gallotta, and the late Merce Cunningham have revitalized the modern dance repertoire.

The Théâtre de la Ville, backed by the city of Paris, is a dedicated promoter of contemporary dance. It hosts the late Pina Bausch's Wuppertaler Tanztheater almost every year, as well as other regulars, including Belgian choreographer Anne Teresa De Keersmaeker and her company Rosas. Poetry, texts, and slide projections are often interwoven with her dances.

> **Today, major world-class opera productions are held at both the Palais Garnier and the Opéra Bastille (opened in 1990).**

Opera: Today, major world-class opera productions are held at both the Palais Garnier and the Opéra Bastille (opened in 1990). The Royal Academy of Music and Dance (known as l'Opéra), founded in 1669, had monopolized the theatrical and lyrical arts for decades, along with La Comédie Française.

The ingenious use of music and mime in Parisian fairground theaters laid the foundation for today's Opéra Comique, created over 200 years ago. The present building, the Salle Favart, opened on December 7, 1898. A number of operas, including Georges Bizet's *Carmen,* Claude Debussy's *Pelléas et Mélisande,* and François Boïeldieu's *La Dame Blanche,* have premiered at the Salle Favart, which was recently renovated and is a charming venue for lyrical theater. In contrast, the vast Opéra Bastille has also staged *Carmen* as well as weightier productions.

Another leading musical theater is the Châtelet-Théâtre Musical de Paris, which has built its reputation with major conductors and directors, staging operatic productions rivaling those of other, more famous opera houses. Today it presents mostly musicals like *An American in Paris* and orchestrated concerts.

The Théâtre des Champs-Élysées provides a distinguished art deco backdrop—worth seeing for its sculpted facade and beautiful interiors alone—for operas, operas in concert, dance recitals, chamber music, and orchestral concerts. ■

The essence of Paris: the boat-shaped Île de la Cité—long a seat of power—and the Île St.-Louis, a preserve of 17th-century elegance

THE ISLANDS

Statuary saints adorn Notre-Dame's facade.

THE ISLANDS

Paris, in essence, was created by the Seine, which was once twice as large. At one time, a string of islands stretched along the river; now, as a result of natural changes in the river's course and human intervention, there are only two—the Île de la Cité and the Île St.-Louis.

Île de la Cité

"The Île de la Cité is the head, heart, and very marrow of Paris," wrote Victor Hugo in *Notre-Dame de Paris*. Indeed, the Île de la Cité—the geographical center of Paris, itself the cultural center of France—was the birthplace of the city and the site of the French capital's original settlement.

Strategic positioning played a key role in the Île de la Cité's development. Not only was it situated along a major Bronze Age trade route for English tin bound for Central Europe and the Mediterranean, but it also served as a refuge in times of war. During the prosperous time of the ancient Romans, who arrived in 53 B.C. and named the settlement Lutetia Parisiorum, the town

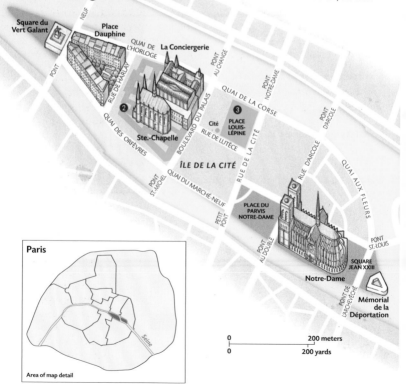

Seine

❶

Square du Vert Galant

PONT NEUF

Place Dauphine

QUAI DE L'HORLOGE

La Conciergerie

RUE DE HARLAY

QUAI DES ORFÈVRES

❷

Ste.-Chapelle

BOULEVARD DU PALAIS

PONT AU CHANGE

PONT NOTRE-DAME

QUAI DE LA CORSE

Cité

❸

PLACE LOUIS-LÉPINE

RUE DE LUTÈCE

ÎLE DE LA CITÉ

RUE DE LA CITÉ

RUE D'ARCOLE

PONT D'ARCOLE

QUAI AUX FLEURS

PONT ST-MICHEL

QUAI DU MARCHÉ-NEUF

PETIT PONT

PLACE DU PARVIS NOTRE-DAME

PONT AU DOUBLE

Notre-Dame

SQUARE JEAN XXIII

PONT ST-LOUIS

PONT DE L'ARCHEVÊCHÉ

Mémorial de la Déportation

Paris

Seine

Area of map detail

0 — 200 meters
0 — 200 yards

spread onto what is now the Left Bank. This golden age lasted about 300 years, until tribes from the outer Rhine invaded in the late third century, and the inhabitants fled back to the Cité. The Romans, Franks, and Capetian kings all expanded the original settlement.

The Île de la Cité has always been an important administrative and religious center. The original seat of the Roman governor is today's Palais de Justice, where judges still dispense justice some 2,000 years later, and both the Conciergerie (the notorious revolutionary prison; see p. 60) and the glorious Ste.-Chapelle (see pp. 56–58) are found within its walls.

Despite the hordes of tourists and unsightly tour buses everywhere, especially around the parvis of Notre-Dame, the Île de la Cité has many charming and secluded getaways. Examples include the Marché aux Fleurs (Flower Market) on the Place Louis-Lépine, the Square du Vert Galant on the far western edge of the island, and the narrow streets off the Quai aux

Fleurs, such as the lovely Rue des Ursins, with its Gothic building that was once the home of the Aga Khan. Although the building is not open to the public, it is a fascinating pastiche of architectural elements. Just beyond, there is a splendid view down the Rue des Chantres of the upper section of Notre-Dame (see pp. 48–53).

Walk around the back of the cathedral for a spectacular view of the flying buttresses; whether illuminated at night or rising over the pale blossoms of spring, this is still one of the city's most memorable sights.

Île St.-Louis

The different histories of the two islands have contributed to their diverse characters. The Île St.-Louis was a quiet, unoccupied island until 17th-century entrepreneurs came up with one of the first planned development projects, achieving a coherent architectural whole that is strikingly well preserved today. This island remains delightfully free of traffic, major shops, Métro stations, and cinemas, and a leisurely stroll around its streets will reveal many discreet vestiges of 17th-century elegance. ■

❶ **Pont Neuf** ❷ **Palais de Justice**
❸ **Marché aux Fleurs**

NOTRE-DAME

Notre-Dame stands out as a symbol of Paris itself. Like the city, it sprang up along the banks of the Seine, its magnificent west facade rising like "a vast symphony of stone," as Victor Hugo described it. The cathedral's site is rich in history. It stands over the ruins of a Gallo-Roman temple to Jupiter, a fourth-century church, and a sixth-century basilica, in whose foundations were found 12 stones originally used in the construction of the Roman temple.

■ The eastern facade of Notre-Dame before the 2019 fire

Notre-Dame
🗺 Map p. 46
✉ Place du Parvis Notre-Dame, Île de la Cité
☎ 01 42 34 56 10
🚇 Métro: Cité
notredamedeparis.fr

By the 12th century, the basilica was in ruins, and Maurice de Sully (who was elected bishop of Paris in 1160) decided to replace it with a superb cathedral to rival the basilica at St.-Denis. Pope Alexander III laid the first stone in 1163, beginning what would become one of the masterpieces of French Gothic design. Work proceeded swiftly, funded by the vast sums Sully collected from the king, the clergy, the nobles, and the poor. When completed, the cathedral dominated all of religious architecture in the Île de France, as the Paris region is called, and had a sweeping impact throughout Europe.

The 19th-century Restoration

In the 17th and 18th centuries,

the Gothic style was no longer in vogue, and the cathedral suffered greatly as a result. Under Louis XIV (R.1643–1715), the chancel screen was partly destroyed, the 13th-century stained-glass windows were replaced with clear glass trimmed in blue and gold, and the rood screen and tombs disappeared. (A fragment of the rood screen, "La Descente aux Limbes," is in the Louvre.)

During the Revolutionary period, the church was pillaged and transformed into a Temple of Reason. Revolutionaries melted down the Treasury, burned the liberty flame on the altar, and smashed the 28 statues of the kings of Judea in the King's Gallery—mistakenly believed to represent the kings of France. Miraculously, 21 of the heads were subsequently found and are now preserved in the Musée de Cluny (see pp. 66–67), except for the head of King David, which is in the Metropolitan Museum of Art in New York.

By 1804, the cathedral was so dilapidated that when Napoleon I crowned himself emperor here, huge tapestries and drapings were hung to mask the damage, and plans were made to demolish it. As Victor Hugo wrote in 1831 in *Notre-Dame de Paris,* "On the face of this queen of our cathedrals, next to a wrinkle you will always find a scar. *Tempus edax, homo edacior*. Which I would freely translate: Time is blind, man is stupid." The publication of Hugo's book inspired efforts to save the cathedral and launched a movement to raise money for its restoration.

The 19th-century architect Eugène Viollet-le-Duc spent nearly 20 years restoring the statuary and glass, although his zealous efforts have been criticized. He added the 295-foot (90 m) steeple embroidered with graceful floral motifs (the main feature destroyed by the 2019 fire), and replaced the sculptures on the western facade and the southern transept, reserving the most delicate work for the bays, which ultimately only succeed in approximating those of the 12th century.

The Fire of 2019

On the evening of April 15, 2019, the flames broke out inside the cathedral, probably caused by a short circuit in the construction site that had been set for some restoration work. The fire destroyed much of the roof and the spire, and weakened the structure of the building. The stained-glass windows, the artwork, and the relics it housed are all safe, in part because they had been removed in view of the works.

After the fire, in a few months hundreds of millions of donations were collected to be used for reconstruction. Consolidation and decontamination works of the structure began immediately, together with the planning of the restoration and reconstruction interventions, which will start only in 2021 and will not be completed before 2024, under the direction of architect Philippe Villeneuve.

Portals

Three portals grace the west facade of Notre-Dame; from left to right, they represent the Virgin Mary, the Last Judgment, and Saint Anne. The statues decorating the portals once were brilliantly painted and stood out against a gilt background. The Saint Anne portal contains the oldest, carved about 1170.

Framing the portals are two elegant towers (the left is slightly higher than the right), each pierced by lancets more than 50 feet (15 m) high, and decorated with gargoyles that lurk behind the large upper gallery between them.

Rose Windows

The size and brilliance of Notre-Dame's glorious rose windows testify to the splendor of Gothic architecture. The **North Rose,** 69 feet (21 m) in diameter, with its nearly intact 13th-century glass,

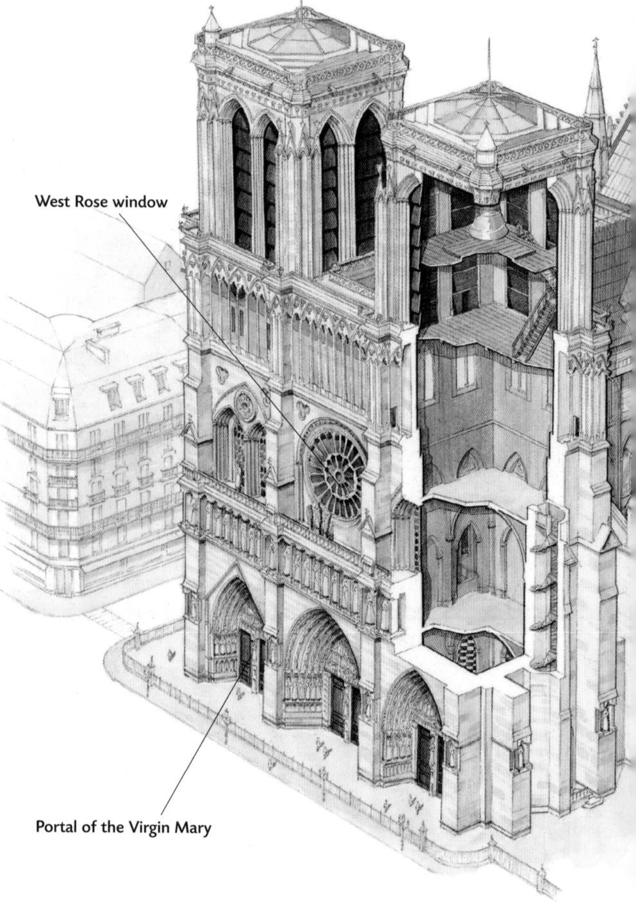

West Rose window

Portal of the Virgin Mary

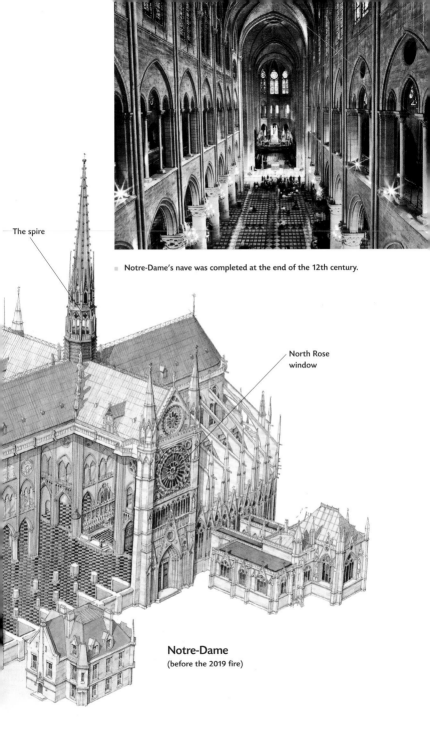

The spire

Notre-Dame's nave was completed at the end of the 12th century.

North Rose window

Notre-Dame
(before the 2019 fire)

Treasury

🕐 Closed until
   further notice

Towers

✉ Rue du Cloître
   Notre-Dame

☎ 01 53 10 07 00

🕐 Closed until
   further notice

features Old Testament figures surrounding the Virgin.

Facing the Seine is the 43-foot-high (13 m) **South Rose,** which was greatly restored in 1737; it depicts Christ surrounded by saints, apostles, and angels. The bays of the nave and the gallery rosettes were redone in 1965 by Jacques Le Chevallier, who imbued the dismal, 19th-century *grisaille* glass with the original medieval colors—rich reds and blues—and materials.

Gargoyles & Flying Buttresses

Although they seem the very essence of medieval art, the cathedral's gargoyles date only to the 19th century and the restoration efforts of Viollet-le-Duc. The term "gargoyle" comes from the word for gullet, and in fact some of the creatures, those at the higher levels, do serve as

waterspouts. Others are more purely sculptural. All were created by the obscure artist Victor Pyanet. Viollet-le-Duc called them "chimeras," and over the years the individual monsters acquired nicknames—such as "The Vampire" and "The Devourer."

Notre-Dame's famous single-arch flying buttresses, so typical of a high Gothic cathedral, were originally built between 1220 and 1230. Each incorporates a channel to allow rainwater to run off. Those at the east end have a span of 49 feet (15 m). The chapels between the buttresses date from 1250 through 1325.

Treasures

The cathedral's sculpted works include 13th-century architect Jean Ravy's ancient choir-screen carvings; Nicolas Coustou's "Descente de croix"; and Antoine

▪ Notre-Dame's famous gargoyles were sculpted in the 19th century.

Coysevox's statue of Louis XIV. Against the southeast pillar of the transept stands a 14th-century statue of the Virgin and Child, known as "Notre-Dame de Paris." Religious paintings by Charles Le Brun are in the side chapels. The cathedral's treasures include the **Crown of Thorns,** a **Holy Nail,** and a fragment of the **True Cross** from Ste.-Chapelle

was in the Middle Ages. The plaques on the ground indicate the old layout of the streets and city landmarks. Where the statue of Charlemagne now stands was the site of the seventh-century Hôtel Dieu, the oldest hospital in France. Patients in the hospital weren't grouped according to gender or disease until the

Archaeological Crypt

✉ Place du Parvis Notre-Dame

☎ 01 55 42 50 10

🕐 Closed until further notice

Quays of the Seine: Walkers In, Cars Out

Appreciating Notre-Dame from the walkways of the Seine is one of the pleasures of Paris. The banks of the Seine are one of UNESCO's 100 World Heritage Sites, but the highways running along them have long blighted this beautiful spot for strollers. The city of Paris has undertaken a project to "civilize" the banks of the Seine without closing the roads entirely (they were already closed to automobiles on Sundays during the day). On the Right Bank, more traffic lights have been installed and the sidewalks widened here and there to slow down cars.

On the Left Bank, automobile traffic has been banned on the "Berges de Seine" between the Pont de l'Alma and the Musée d'Orsay and replaced by walking and biking lanes, gardens, greenhouses, and sports facilities. Artificial island parks float on the Seine near the Port des Invalides.

(see pp. 56–58). These are only on public display once a year, when they are brought out and paraded before the congregation on Good Friday. Other treasures include Saint Louis's rib. The early 18th-century organ on the western wall was restored in 1992 and features 6,000 pipes, 110 stops, and 5 keyboards—the largest in France. Following the 2019 fire, most of the treasures were moved to the Louvre for safekeeping.

Parvis of Notre-Dame

The present parvis (the court in front of the church, derived from the word for paradise) is presently six times larger than it

18th century, and up to six people might have shared each bed. A new **Hôtel Dieu**—the one now on the northern side of the cathedral's parvis—was built between 1868 and 1877, after Baron Georges-Eugène Haussmann (see pp. 166–167) razed the area.

Archaeological Crypt:

Stretching for 394 feet (120 m) beneath the parvis, and also currently not accessible, the crypt hosts the ruins of Gallo-Roman fortifications (including those rooms that used a heating system called a hypocaust) and the remains of the medieval rue Neuve Notre Dame. ∎

A WALK AROUND THE ISLANDS

The islands are the heart of medieval Paris. The lively, bustling Île de la Cité is crammed with architectural gems, such as the magnificent Notre-Dame cathedral. In striking contrast, the smaller, quieter Île St.-Louis offers a peaceful village atmosphere, its shaded embankment lined with elegant private mansions as silent witnesses to a bygone era.

Place Dauphine on Île de la Cité

NOT TO BE MISSED:

Notre-Dame • Ste.-Chapelle • Square du Vert Galant • La Conciergerie • Mémorial de la Déportation • Hôtel de Lauzun (Île St.-Louis)

Begin at Point Zero on the parvis at Notre-Dame to view the cathedral in all its Gothic glory, whether wrapped in fog or washed with sun. **Notre-Dame ❶** (see pp. 48–53) is the city's largest church. Point Zero, dating from 1769 (although the bronze star is new), is the spot from which all road distances throughout the country are gauged.

When you reach the edge of the parvis, follow the Quai du Marché-Neuf, then turn right on Boulevard du Palais to see the glorious **Ste.-Chapelle ❷** (see pp. 56–58), a fine example of high Gothic architecture.

Backtrack and turn right on Quai des Orfèvres, formerly the Île de Galilée until it was attached to the Île de la Cité in 1310. Walk along the quayside for a more scenic route, past the **Palais de Justice** on your right and on past the Pont Neuf, Paris's oldest bridge, to the beautiful **Square du Vert Galant.**

Opposite the statue of Henri IV, take Rue Henri-Robert, which leads to the **Place**

Dauphine ❸. One of the few areas of the islands to have escaped Haussmann's dramatic redevelopment scheme in the 19th century, the square is very central, yet intensely private. The din of cars rushing over the Pont Neuf fades as you step into the secluded Place Dauphine, where actors Yves Montand and Simone Signoret once lived. Turn left onto Rue de Harlay at the end of the square, then right on Quai de l'Horloge. Follow this past the towers of **La Conciergerie ❹** (see p. 60), where Paris's oldest public clock (1370) still runs today.

Now follow the Quai de la Corse to the **Marché aux Fleurs** (Flower Market). Camellias, orchids, jasmine, and bamboo fill shops and stalls. (This is joined by a bird market on Sundays.) Proceed along the Quai aux Fleurs, taking a right onto Rue de la Colombe, then left on Rue des Ursins before rejoining the Quai aux Fleurs.

Continue farther down the quay to the subterranean **Mémorial de la Déportation** (Deportation Memorial) ❺ *(Square de l'Île de France, Métro: Cité),* a stark edifice commemorating the Jewish people who were deported to concentration camps during World War II. It is faced with stone quarried from all the mountain ranges in France. Narrow staircases lead down to a high-walled platform, where the river beyond the iron bars and a portcullis evoke a powerful sense of the loss of freedom. Inside the crypt are two side galleries. Here, a series of small niches in the walls, inscribed with the names of the various concentration camps, contains urns with soil from the camps and ashes from the crematoriums.

A long, dark gallery studded with glass chips symbolizing the tens of thousands of deportees from France holds the remains of an unknown deportee taken from the necropolis of the Struthof concentration camp.

Île St.-Louis

Cross over the Pont St.-Louis to reach the Île St.-Louis. The island was divided in two by a canal (Rue Poulletier) during the 14th century to reinforce the protection of the Charles V Wall. Louis XIII and his mother, Marie de Médicis, undertook the unification of the two islands—called Île Notre-Dame and Île aux Vaches—and the embellishment of the area in the 17th century.

Reunited in 1614, the island underwent massive construction from 1620 to 1650, and was rechristened Île St.-Louis in 1726. The instability of the land hampered building efforts:

Some dwellings lean to the left or right, or have subsided, but in general they support one another.

The views from the island's quays are fabulous, and, if you get hungry, go to **Berthillon** at 31 rue St.-Louis en l'Île to sample some of their marvelous ice creams and sorbets. Other landmarks to look for include the **Hôtel de Jassaud 6** at 19 quai de Bourbon, where French sculptor Camille Claudel lived in a ground-floor studio at the rear of the courtyard; and the **Hôtel de Lauzun 7** at 17 quai d'Anjou, with its gilded dolphin waterspouts. It was here that the poet Charles Baudelaire wrote much of *Les Fleurs du Mal (The Flowers of Evil)*, published in 1857. Baudelaire also first spotted his muse and lover Jeanne Duval—his "Black Venus"—from the window. The **Hôtel Lambert 8** at 2 rue St.-Louis en l'Île is now a private residence.

- See also area map pp. 46–47
- Notre-Dame parvis
- Allow 4 hours
- 2.7 miles (4.3 km)
- Hôtel Lambert

STE.-CHAPELLE

**A true jewel in the heart of Paris, Ste.-Chapelle is a glorious example of the high Gothic style
and is universally recognized as a masterpiece of architecture and stained glass.**

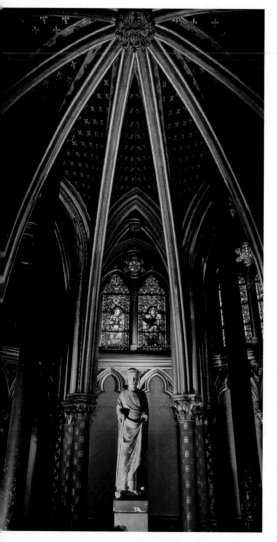

Saint Louis (King Louis IX)
had this luminous chapel
constructed in just six years,
from 1242 to 1248, and it is
generally attributed to Pierre
de Montreuil (who died in
1267). It is essentially an enormous reliquary, built to house
the Crown of Thorns, which
Louis had purchased from the
Emperor of Constantinople,
Baldwin II, in 1239.

Although Louis was undoubt-
edly a religious man—he was
canonized 27 years after his
death—his motives for constructing Ste.-Chapelle were decidedly
political. Louis was just 12 years old
when his father, Louis VIII, died.
His mother, Blanche de Castille,
ruled as regent until his majority. His ascension to the throne
was contested, and in a period
when kings ruled by divine right,
the Crown of Thorns—the most
prized religious relic of all—represented a potent symbol for Louis's
claim to the throne. Indeed, it was
such an important relic (although
never officially recognized by the
Vatican) that it cost three times
more than the construction of
Ste.-Chapelle itself. The crown
was brought to France and placed
in the church in a magnificent
reliquary, which disappeared during the Revolution; most of the
relics, however, were saved, and
are now held in the Treasury of
Notre-Dame (see p. 52).

The sculptures in Ste.-Chapelle depict the 12 Apostles.

Lower Chapel

The spectacular chapel is divided into two levels: the dark, richly decorated lower chapel, reserved for the palace servants, and the stunning upper chapel, used exclusively by the royal family, visiting dignitaries, and heads of state. The vibrant red and blue colors in the lower chapel date from the 19th century when attempts were made to reproduce the original medieval decoration. The windows are small because the lower chapel supports the upper chapel. Unfortunately, the 14th- and 15th-century tombstones on the chapel's floor have been worn almost bare by nearly 900,000 annual visitors.

INSIDER TIP:

Visit Ste.-Chapelle on a bright, sunny day, when the light streams through the stained-glass windows.

—BARBARA A. NOE
*National Geographic Travel Books
senior editor*

Upper Chapel

The effect on entering the upper chapel is breathtaking. The walls are a mosaic of colored light that streams in through the 50-foot-high (15 m) windows. The 15 stained-glass windows in this chapel are the oldest in Paris, with two-thirds

Ste.-Chapelle

- Map p. 46
- 8 boulevard du Palais, Île de la Cité
- 01 53 40 60 80
- Closed Jan. 1, May 1, Dec. 25
- €€
- Métro: Cité, St.-Michel, Châtelet

sainte-chapelle.fr

Stained Glass

In medieval times, as in the present, church leaders were responsible for religious education. During the golden age of stained glass—the 12th and 13th centuries—the church building itself, through its windows and statuary, transmitted this knowledge. The stained-glass windows functioned as immense picture books from which a mostly illiterate population could "read" the biblical stories. The scenes are designed to be read from left to right, and bottom to top.

Stained glass can be traced to ancient times; clear glass was used in Roman baths, and Romans were experts in making colored-glass vases and cups. The technique of using colored glass and lead together appeared later. Stained-glass windows were not an important element of Romanesque architecture; with the development of the Gothic rib-vaulted roof, walls no longer carried the vertical thrust of the building,

allowing builders to create large openings between the pillars that could be filled with stained glass.

The basic techniques for making stained-glass windows have changed little: Colored and clear glass is cut to a pattern, then painted with grisaille (iron oxide) before being baked in a kiln. Then the pieces are assembled with lead strips to create mosaics. In the 12th and 13th centuries, a limited number of colors was used, and glassmakers juxtaposed the bright reds and blues to create jewel-like colors, achieving the unique style seen in many Gothic churches. By the mid-15th century, glassmakers began to imitate paintings by modeling forms, introducing a three-dimensional effect. The glass was still beautiful, but it had lost some of its essential nature; it no longer filtered a mosaic of brilliant colors, but became more like a semi-opaque reproduction of a canvas on glass.

of them dating from the 13th century; together, they include over 1,100 scenes. With the exception of the three windows behind the altar (Saint John the Evangelist, the Passion of Christ, and Saint John the Baptist), and the window immediately to the right on entering the chapel (which recounts the story of the relics), all the others depict scenes from the Old Testament.

The style of the **Rose Window** is markedly different from the other windows; made in 1485 (200 years later than the others), it represents the Apocalypse. It's a good idea to bring along binoculars for viewing the upper windows.

The windows barely escaped destruction during the Revolution, when the church was deconsecrated. For 35 years, from 1802 to 1837, the chapel was converted into a warehouse for archives; the bottom 15 feet (4.5 m) of each window was removed, and filing cabinets rose 25 feet (7.5 m) up the walls. The missing sections of the windows were eventually re-created as exact copies of the originals, but mistakes were inevitably made.

Sculptures

The sculptures in Ste.-Chapelle depict the 12 Apostles, the spiritual pillars of the church, each placed on one of the structural pillars of the chapel. The two alcoves on either side of the chapel were reserved for King Louis (on the left) and his mother (on the right). Louis's wife, Queen Marguerite, overshadowed by her mother-in-law, presumably sat with her husband. The king entered through the main doors, which led directly to the royal apartments in the Conciergerie. ■

■ Ste.-Chapelle's famous Rose Window

EXPERIENCE: Venture On & Off the Beaten Track

Wandering the streets of Paris is always a rewarding experience: You might stumble across a medieval tower in a back street or a charming little square with an old fountain. Even more rewarding are the many walking tours offered throughout the city that allow you to follow your interests while also benefiting from the expertise and insider knowledge of your guide.

Major Sites

Paris Walks (paris-walks .com) offers regular tours of many Paris neighborhoods. Its Monday walk from March to November covers Île de la Cité and Notre-Dame. Participants learn to read the stories embedded in medieval stone and discuss how the cathedral was built. The walk also takes in ancient back streets, the flower market, gardens, hidden courtyards, and the Mémorial de la Déportation on the islands. Other tours cover the major sites and topics, from the Marais and Montmartre to the French Revolution and Hemingway's Paris.

Arty Tours

Paris Muse (parismuse.com) specializes in tours of Paris museums, covering such topics as the Impressionists at the Musée d'Orsay, hidden masterpieces in the Louvre, and medieval masterpieces at the Musée de Cluny. The company also offers neighborhood tours throughout the city, and the "Paris Muse Clues" educational treasure hunt at the Louvre and "Cracking 'The Da Vinci Code'" at the Louvre. "History of Chic: Shopping in Paris" takes a look at how shopping has shaped the city's architecture and urbanism.

African and African-American Sites

Special-interest tours that will take you well off the beaten track are available from **Walking the Spirit** (walkthespirit.com), with tours focusing on the history of African-Americans and Africans in Paris. You might see the theater where Josephine Baker wowed the French, the building James Baldwin lived in, or the café where Richard Wright wrote. Other tours take in the food markets of Little Africa.

INSIDER TIP:

Stroll the Promenade Plantée (starting at Viaduc des Arts): The promenade inspired New York's High Line and other elevated walkways worldwide.

—JUSTIN KAVANAGH
National Geographic Travel Books editor

Wheeling Around

Fat Tire Bike Tours (fattire tours.com/paris) offers not only bicycle or Segway tours of Paris by day or night that are suitable for both adults and kids, but also skip-the-line visits to the Eiffel Tower.

Paris à Vélo, C'est Sympa (parisvelosympa.fr) bikes visitors to parts of town that they might not normally see, such as Belleville or the southern arrondissements, focusing on gardens, architecture, or artists' studios.

For the Gourmand

Context Travel (contexttravel .com) has a full range of high-end specialist tours with such themes as chocolate, Paris art galleries, gardens of Paris, and the Centre Georges-Pompidou, and will arrange custom tours to suit the special interests of visitors. For foodies, its "Baguette to Bistro: Culinary Traditions of Paris" takes small groups to some of Paris's top shops for chocolate, spices, baguettes, cheese, wine, meat, and more.

On the Run

Joggers who don't know where to run in the city or who want to take in the sights while running will appreciate the guidance given by **Paris Running Tour** (parisrunningtour.com). Visitors are accompanied by a coach who is a serious runner and can choose from various scenic areas like the Canal St.-Martin or the Left Bank with runs of varying levels of difficulty.

LA CONCIERGERIE

The Conciergerie was part of the royal palace from the tenth century to 1378, before it became the center of the Paris judicial system. Philippe IV (R.1285–1314) constructed most of the medieval buildings standing today, although they were extensively renovated in the 19th century. After Charles V moved the royal residence to the Louvre Palace (see p. 124), he appointed a concierge, or keeper, to act as his steward, and the complex became a prison.

La Conciergerie

- Map p. 46
- 2 boulevard du Palais, Île de la Cité
- 01 53 40 60 80
- Closed May 1, Dec. 25
- €€
- Métro: Cité, St.-Michel, Châtelet

paris-conciergerie.fr

Medieval Secular Architecture

You will enter the impressive **Salle des Gens d'Armes,** one of the largest—and finest—examples of medieval secular architecture, across the courtyard from the main entrance on Quai de l'Horloge. Its name means "men at arms," and the word *gendarmes* (police) is derived from it. This hall served as the refectory for the palace staff. Rue de Paris, at the far western

Medieval Fireplaces

Thousands ate each day at the Conciergerie. Each of the four fireplaces in the medieval kitchens had a function: One was for soups, another for stews, a third for meat. No one is sure about the fourth.

end of this room, contained prison cells and is named for the executioner, who was traditionally known as Monsieur de Paris. The royal banquet hall upstairs burned down and was reconstructed in 1622 as the **Salle des Pas Perdus.** It is now a lobby for lawyers and clients awaiting their turn in the courts.

The 13th-century crenelated **Tour Bonbec** (meaning "chatter tower") was once used as a torture chamber. Although it is no longer a prison, people are still held in custody here—away from the tourist circuit.

Revolutionary Tribunal

During the Revolution, the Revolutionary Tribunal sentenced more than 2,700 people to die under the so-called democratic blade of the guillotine (previously, the nobility died by the sword; common criminals were whipped, sulfur placed on their open wounds, then they were hanged, drawn, and quartered).

Incarceration here did not follow the new democracy, however. Walk upstairs to see the three reconstructed cells, which illustrate what money could buy: The *pailleux*, or penniless prisoners, slept on straw on the floor; *à la pistole* meant real beds; while prisoners of rank had their own furniture and servants. Queen Marie-Antoinette's cell has been reconstructed, and a chapel of atonement now stands on part of the original cell. Ironically, her accusers, Maximilien Robespierre and Georges Danton, followed her to prison and then the guillotine within a few months. ■

The seat of French university life for centuries, with the Sorbonne and the Collège de France, bookshops, libraries, and cafés

QUARTIER LATIN

Postcards in the Latin Quarter

QUARTIER LATIN

Since the founding of the Sorbonne in the 13th century, the Quartier Latin (Latin Quarter) has been synonymous with university life, and it was once the greatest seat of learning in Europe. The area's very name is derived from medieval university instruction in Low Latin. The area is still in perpetual motion, with students milling about in the streets and cafés or browsing in the Gibert Jeune bookshop.

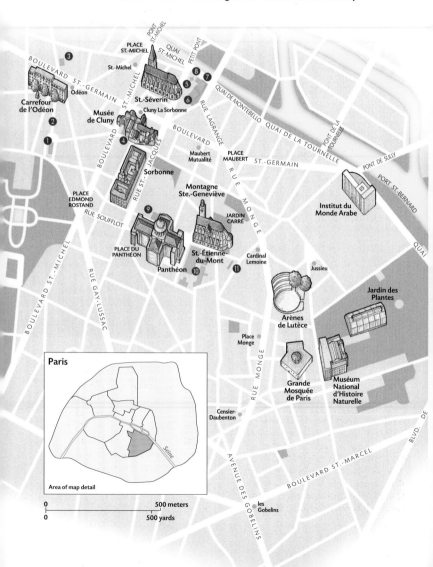

PONT ST.-MICHEL

PLACE ST.-MICHEL

QUAI ST.-MICHEL

PETIT PONT

3

BOULEVARD ST.-GERMAIN

St.-Michel

8 **7**

QUAI DE MONTEBELLO

Odéon

St.-Séverin

5

6

QUAI DE LA TOURNELLE

PONT DE LA TOURNELLE

Carrefour de l'Odéon

Musée de Cluny

Cluny La Sorbonne

RUE LAGRANGE

2

RUE ST.-JACQUES

4

BOULEVARD

PONT DE SULLY

PORT ST.-BERNARD

1

BOULEVARD

Maubert Mutualité

PLACE MAUBERT

ST.-GERMAIN

Sorbonne

PLACE EDMOND ROSTAND

Montagne Ste.-Geneviève

RUE MONGE

Institut du Monde Arabe

BOULEVARD ST.-MICHEL

RUE SOUFFLOT

9

JARDIN CARRÉ

QUAI

PLACE DU PANTHÉON

St.-Étienne-du-Mont

Cardinal Lemoine

RUE GAY-LUSSAC

Panthéon **10**

11

Jussieu

Jardin des Plantes

Arènes de Lutèce

RUE MONGE

Place Monge

Grande Mosquée de Paris

Muséum National d'Histoire Naturelle

Paris

Censier-Daubenton

BLVD. DE

Seine

AVENUE DES GOBELINS

BOULEVARD ST.-MARCEL

Area of map detail

0   500 meters

0   500 yards

les Gobelins

The Latin Quarter encompasses the neighborhoods around St.-Séverin, Montagne Ste.-Geneviève, and Place St.-Michel, with its fountain of the saint slaying a dragon. If it is your first visit to the area, try not to approach the Latin Quarter from the commercial Boulevard St.-Michel, as the fast-food restaurants and clothing outlets detract from the area's mythical status. Instead, enter across the quays from Notre-Dame, through the Square Viviani.

Next to the square is the largely touristy Shakespeare and Company bookstore, not to be confused with the former avant-garde publishing house on Rue de l'Odéon owned by Sylvia Beach (see p. 36), who first published James Joyce's *Ulysses*. Some streets—such as Rue de la Parcheminerie (originally Rue des Escrivains, or Street of Writers)—reflect the literary tradition of the Latin Quarter in their names, although not all do; the nearby Rue de Bièvre, for example, was named for the arm of the river that flowed through the quarter to the Seine.

Historic Area

The Latin Quarter is one of Paris's more historic areas. Here, you can wend your way past Roman ruins, such as the Arènes de Lutèce amphitheater (see p. 74), or the third-century baths (now part of the Musée National du Moyen Âge et des Thermes de Cluny; see

pp. 66–67), up to Montagne Ste.-Geneviève, named after the city's patron saint. Saint Geneviève was instrumental in unifying Paris (see sidebar p. 21), and her importance is reflected in the area, particularly around the St.-Étienne-du-Mont Church, which has the only surviving rood screen in Paris. The church stands where the Basilica of St.-Pierre-St.-Paul, built to commemorate the unity of France, was once located. Next door is the Panthéon (see p. 69), originally a church for Saint Geneviève, but transformed during the Revolution into a temple for "great men" (and a few token women, including Marie Curie).

Down the other side of the hill, to the east, lies the café-lined Place de la Contrescarpe (named after the embankments of Philippe-Auguste's fortifications), and the Rue Mouffetard, one of the oldest streets, which has a great open-air market *(closed Sun. p.m. & Mon.)*.

Few visitors venture farther east, where Paris's principal mosque (see pp. 75) lies opposite the Jardin des Plantes (see pp. 70–71). The intriguing Institut du Monde Arabe (Arab Cultural Institute; see p. 75–76) overlooks the Seine near the open-air Tino Rossi sculpture garden (see p. 205). ∎

JARDIN TINO ROSSI

Seine

ST-BERNARD

PONT D'AUSTERLITZ

PLACE VALHUBERT

Gare d'Austerlitz

L'HOPITAL

---

❶ Odéon-Théâtre de l'Europe ❷ Site of former Sylvia Beach bookstore (Shakespeare and Company), 12 rue de l'Odéon ❸ Café Procope ❹ Gallo-Roman baths ❺ Caveau des Oubliettes ❻ St.-Julien-le-Pauvre ❼ Square Viviani ❽ Shakespeare and Company bookstore, 37 rue de la Bûcherie ❾ Bibliothèque Ste.-Geneviève ❿ Lycée Henri IV ⓫ Philippe-Auguste Wall

ST.-SÉVERIN & MONTAGNE STE.-GENEVIÈVE AREAS

The St.-Séverin and Ste.-Geneviève neighborhoods are among the oldest areas in Paris, with such medieval streets as Rue du Fouarre and Rue Galande. The former was named for the *fouarre*—or hay—on which students would sit while listening to lectures.

■ The asymmetrical interior of St.-Étienne-du-Mont

Caveau des Oubliettes

🗺 Map p. 62

✉ 52 rue Galande

☎ 01 42 02 43 38

🚇 Métro: St.-Michel

caveau-des-oubliettes.com

St.-Séverin Area

One of the most famous historic figures of this area was the 12th-century philosopher and theologian Pierre Abélard (1079–1142). Following his rift with the canons for challenging monastic discipline, Abélard was ousted from the Notre-Dame cloister. He moved to the Left Bank, taking 3,000 students with him. (See p. 114 for an account of his love affair with Héloïse.)

St.-Julien-le-Pauvre: Rue Galande was lined with infamous cabarets during the 18th century. The **Caveau des Oubliettes** was one of the rare spots where only old French songs were featured; now jazz and country have been added to the repertoire, and the bar on the ground floor is a far cry from the old-style cabaret and the guillotine on which Kennedy placed his head when he visited in 1960 (a remnant of the museum of torture that was once here) is no more on display.

Off Rue Galande is St.-Julien-le-Pauvre. One of the three oldest churches in Paris, it was built between 1165 and 1220. Originally a stopping point for travelers en route to the famous pilgrimage site of Santiago de Compostela in Spain, during the later Middle Ages rowdy student assemblies gathered here. Its simple Gothic style bears traces of the Romanesque period, and the beautiful chancel is enclosed by a wooden iconostasis (icon screen) and two beautifully carved pillars.

Square Viviani & Église St.-Séverin: Next door, the lovely Square Viviani has a superb view of Notre-Dame, a contemporary fountain inspired by Saint Julien, and a four-century-old black locust, the oldest tree in Paris. Don't miss the Flamboyant Gothic **St.-Séverin Church,** one of the most beautiful sacred buildings in Paris, with its spiraling vaults, softly lit against brilliant stained glass in the apse.

Montagne Ste.-Geneviève Area

The area around Montagne Ste.-Geneviève, the Roman city mirroring the Gallo-Roman settlement on the Île de la Cité, is filled with winding streets climbing up the hill.

Well-preserved vestiges of the **Gallo-Roman baths** can be found at the corner of Rue des Écoles and Boulevard St.-Michel. Circle around them to the east, up Rue de Cluny and past Square Paul-Painlevé separating the **Musée de Cluny** (see pp. 66–67)

and the **Sorbonne** (see p. 68). On the corner of Rue des Écoles and Rue de la Sorbonne stood a convent, where the great poet and rogue François Villon grew up; he assassinated a priest in 1455 and was subsequently banished from Paris. The name Sorbonne is used interchangeably with the Université de Paris, but is actually the name of the most famous of its colleges. Farther up Rue St.-Jacques is the **Panthéon** (see p. 69), dating from 1754.

On the north side of the Place du Panthéon is the **Bibliothèque Ste.-Geneviève**—the only great monastic library in Paris spared during the Revolution. It has a fine collection of medieval manuscripts. Behind the Panthéon is one of Paris's more intriguing churches, **St.-Étienne-du-Mont** (see p. 76). Across the street is the prestigious **Lycée Henri IV,** the site of the sixth-century basilica built by Clovis following his victory over the Visigoths. Down the street on Rue Clovis is a section of the **Philippe-Auguste Wall** (see p. 21). ∎

Église St.-Séverin

- ⊞ Map p. 62
- ✉ 3 rue des Prêtres St.-Séverin
- ☎ 01 42 34 93 50
- 🚇 Métro: St.-Michel

saint-severin.com

Bibliothèque Ste.-Geneviève

- ⊞ Map p. 62
- ✉ 10 place du Panthéon
- ☎ 01 44 41 97 97
- 🕐 Closed Sun.
- 🚇 Métro: Maubert-Mutualité RER (B): Luxembourg

bsg.univ-paris3.fr

Philippe-Auguste Wall

- ⊞ Map p. 62
- ✉ 3 rue Clovis
- 🚇 Métro: Cardinal Lemoine

EXPERIENCE: Dine on a Parisian Terrace

Few experiences are more Parisian than dining outside in fine weather and watching the parade of people pass along the streets of Paris. Finding a table at a restaurant with a terrace is not easy, however. Try one of the following, but book in advance. Not far from the Jardin des Plantes is **Chez Lena et Mimile** (32 rue Tourenfort, tel 01 47 07 72 47, €€€): It has traditional and fusion dishes and an elevated terrace with a view. Nearby,

Chantairelle (17 rue Laplace, tel 01 46 33 18 59, €€) offers traditional French cuisine and a peaceful, off-street terrace. **Le Pavillon du Lac** (Parc des Buttes-Chaumont, Place Armand Carrel, tel 01 42 00 07 21, €€/€€€), recently renovated, is set in a park. **Le Relais du Parc** (55–57 avenue Raymond Poincaré, tel 01 44 05 66 10, €€€), in the 16th arrondissement, offers refined fare by chef Stéphane Duchiron and a courtyard terrace.

MUSÉE DE CLUNY

The remarkable Musée National du Moyen Âge is actually two museums in one: the 15th-century Hôtel de Cluny, which houses the medieval collections and the world-famous "Lady with the Unicorn" tapestries; and the third-century baths, the oldest and most complete vestiges of the Roman occupation in Paris.

Hôtel de Cluny & Baths

The medieval building, constructed between 1480 and 1510 as a temporary residence for visiting religious dignitaries from the wealthy Abbey of Cluny, is one of the oldest surviving examples of civil architecture in Paris. The building stands around a cobblestone courtyard, and visitors used to enter through the exterior, turreted staircase—a distinguishing feature of well-to-do medieval homes.

What is unique about Cluny is that the abbots chose to build their mansion on land abutting the ruins of a Gallo-Roman bath, one of three that existed during the second and third centuries in what was then Lutetia.

The baths contained three large rooms: the **caldarium** (hot room), now in ruins; the **tepidarium** (warm room), which had bathtubs in various alcoves; and the **frigidarium** (cold room). All were once lined with magnificent mosaics. The walls and floors of the caldarium were heated using a system of lead and terracotta pipes that were fed from furnaces in the cellars.

The 45-foot-high (13.5 m) frigidarium has been restored and is now used as a venue for temporary exhibitions. The room was so well designed that even in the hottest days of summer, this immense hall remains cool. The **underground vaults** once housed the furnaces for heating the baths.

■ **Five of the unicorn tapestries at Cluny may illustrate the senses: in this instance, sight.**

Tapestries

In medieval Europe, tapestries developed as a way to cover cold, drafty stone walls. They were easily transported and served to decorate and capture heat in châteaus and churches. They usually depicted moral, historical, floral, and biblical themes, and displayed a person's wealth through their sumptuous fabrics and elaborate designs.

The earliest surviving tapestry from a Paris workshop is the great set of hangings known as the "Apocalypse of Angers" (circa 1375), on view in the city of Angers. After the French defeat at Agincourt in 1415, Arras became the center of tapestry weaving, largely because of the extravagant patronage of the Burgundian dukes. In the 17th century, the tapestry industry flourished once again in Paris with the Gobelins Manufacture, which produced panels of unprecedented technical perfection.

Medieval Collections

The first few rooms are devoted to tapestries, some splendid stained glass, and chests. These lead to the Roman baths via Room VIII, which houses the spectacular **King's Gallery—** 21 of the 28 heads that once stood atop the figures lining the front of Notre-Dame (see pp. 48–53). Although the sculptures represent biblical figures, during the Revolution they were mistaken for the kings of France, and the heads were severed and left among the debris.

Only in 1977 did they turn up, during excavations under a bank. This gallery is now the highlight of the room, which also displays Romanesque sculptures. The oldest sculpture in Paris, the "Pilier des Nautes" ("Boatmen's Pillar"), dating from the first century A.D., stands in the next room, near the frigidarium.

The upper floor contains a collection of precious metalwork, including the "Golden Rose of Basel," a delicate wrought-iron piece made in 1330, and several exceptional altarpieces.

Room XIII, a specially designed rotunda, displays the museum's most famous works, the "Lady with the Unicorn" tapestries (circa 15th century, southern Netherlands). The unicorn motif, which was popular in medieval imagery, symbolized chastity and purity.

Unfortunately, at present, until the spring of 2021, the hôtel and courtyard are **closed due to work.** However, the museum is partially accessible: The frigidarium can be visited free, the entire complex of Gallo-Roman Baths only with a guided tour. The "Lady with Unicorn" remains on display, together with 70 treasures from the permanent collection, and temporary exhibition installations continue.

The museum's **medieval gardens** take you back in time through the Forest of the Unicorn, representing untamed nature, and gardens symbolic of nature tamed: the kitchen garden, the medicinal plants, the heavenly garden (flowers symbolizing the Virgin Mary), and the love garden (courtly and sensual love). ∎

Musée de Cluny

- Map p. 62
- 6 place Paul Painlevé
- 01 53 73 78 00
- Closed Tues., Jan. 1, May 1, Dec. 25
- €€
- Métro: Maubert-Mutualité, Odéon, Cluny

musee-moyenage.fr

THE SORBONNE &
THE COLLÈGE DE FRANCE

The Sorbonne was like a quasi-state within a state for centuries, playing a major political role, while the Collège de France gave priority to educational freedom.

The Sorbonne

- Map p. 62
- 47 rue des Écoles
- 01 40 46 22 11
- By appt. only
- Métro: Maubert-Mutualité, Cluny RER (B): Luxembourg

sorbonne.fr

Collège de France

- 11 place Marcellin Berthelot
- 01 44 27 12 11
- Métro: Maubert-Mutualité, Cluny

college-de-france.fr

The Sorbonne

The Sorbonne was founded in 1253 as a residence hall for 16 theology students, and eventually became a major center for religious education.

Strikes have been a feature of the Paris university since its earliest days. In 1229 the institution went on strike for two years, demanding (and winning) independence from the bishops of Paris. Some 750 years later, the violence that swept through the Latin Quarter in May 1968 was triggered by the arrest of student leaders from this same institution, protesting against a rigid, repressive, and overcrowded university system. Today, the courtyard is open to the public; the chapel, which houses the tomb of Cardinal Richelieu (see p. 23), can be visited during temporary exhibitions and on December 4, the anniversary of Richelieu's death.

INSIDER TIP:

For a sample of Collège de France lectures, try iTunes, which has hundreds of audio podcasts, many in English.

—NEIL SHEA
National Geographic magazine writer

Collège de France

The Collège de France is an unorthodox institution. An average 5,000 auditors follow the diverse lectures given by one of the 52 professors. Classes are free, there are no prerequisites, no academic credits, and no diplomas. Instead, anyone, from students to the merely curious, can attend lectures on topics ranging from molecular biology to Byzantine civilization. ∎

Victor Hugo

Victor Hugo (1802–1885) was France's greatest 19th-century literary icon. He was the closest France ever came to producing a writer whose stature could be compared to that of Homer, Shakespeare, Dickens, or Dante, and his works were said to have helped trigger revolutions—notably the 1830 Revolution (see p. 28). His plays revolutionized French theater, knocking it out of the fettered forms of Corneille and Racine.

Hugo turned to politics, but politics turned on him—after trying to foil Napoleon III's coup in 1851, he dodged arrest, and was subsequently exiled for 18 years, returning in 1870.

A half million people poured into the streets of Paris to mourn when he died in 1885. His body, after lying in state at the Arc de Triomphe, was taken to the Panthéon in a pauper's hearse as a sign of solidarity with the common man.

THE PANTHÉON

The Panthéon, now a shrine "to distinguished men from a grateful nation," was constructed by Louis XV. In 1744 the king fell ill and vowed to construct a church dedicated to Saint Geneviève, if she would come to his aid. He recovered, and in 1754 commissioned Jacques Germain Soufflot to build a vast church that would "combine Greek beauty with Gothic space and light."

■ The Panthéon is an architectural wonder and a monument to great figures in French culture.

Soufflot's immense structure was an unprecedented feat of engineering. The subsoil was honeycombed with wells and quarries that required considerable shoring up. The first stone was laid in 1764 in the king's presence, although the church was only completed in 1790—the year all monastic orders were abolished. It was then declared to be a "temple to the Nation," and author Voltaire, philosopher Jean-Jacques Rousseau, and politician Honoré Mirabeau were buried there. It became a church again several times during the 19th century, but was finally made into a mortuary for French heroes in 1885 during the state funeral for Victor Hugo (see opposite). You can see the tombs of novelist Émile Zola (1830–1902) and physicist Marie Curie (1859–1906). The remains of author Alexandre Dumas (1802–1870) were moved here in 2002, with four men dressed as the Musketeers flanking the coffin. ■

The Panthéon
- Map p. 62
- Place du Panthéon
- 01 44 32 18 00
- Closed Jan. 1, May 1, & Dec. 25
- €€
- Métro: Cardinal Lemoine RER (B): Luxembourg

paris-pantheon.fr

JARDIN DES PLANTES

The oldest garden in Paris was not designed for the pleasure of its inhabitants, but as a research garden for botanists, doctors, and pharmacists. It was created in 1635 as the royal medicinal garden for Louis XIII, but came into its own in 1739, when naturalist Georges Buffon was appointed director. The garden became the natural history museum in 1793, and over the next 30 years an assortment of animals was introduced.

■ Once medicinal plantings, the gardens of the Jardin des Plantes are now open to the public.

Muséum National d'Histoire Naturelle

🅐 Map p. 62

✉ 36 rue Geoffroy-St.-Hilaire

☎ 01 40 79 56 01

🕐 Closed Tues., Jan. 1, May 1, Dec. 25

💲 €€

🚇 Métro: Austerlitz, Jussieu

mnhn.fr

Muséum National d'Histoire Naturelle

By 1965, the crumbling zoology gallery was closed and remained a dusty hulk until 1994, when it finally reopened after a major renovation project. The results are spectacular: Visitors enter the dramatically lit **Grande Galerie de l'Évolution,** a sort of giant Noah's Ark of mounted animals parading down the center of the building. On the lower floor, marine animals are suspended as if still swimming in the sea; the 54-foot (16.5 m) skeleton of a whale hangs in midair. Two floors of galleries upstairs explore evolution, the environment, and the effects of pollution.

The museum's face-lift retained some of the existing metal-frame structure, which is now brilliantly incorporated into the new design. An engaging discovery room introduces fossils and the natural sciences to children under 12, while older kids can explore displays in the science laboratory.

The Gardens

The handsome greenhouses, the oldest dating to 1714, have been renovated and were reopened to the public in 2010. The new theme is biodiversity, and the first three greenhouses respectively present the flora of a rain forest (in an art deco building), the desert, and New Caledonia. The last one offers an overview of the history of plant life.

Three majestic avenues, lined with trees, lead elegantly away from the museum past a series of meticulously planted flower beds. Elsewhere, the geometric formality gives way to a less rigid layout. To the north lie the Ménagerie and an 18th-century labyrinth, which leads to a bronze gazebo called the **Gloriette de Buffon,** the oldest metallic structure in Paris (circa 1786). Nearby is the

can vary as much as 35°F (19.5°C) from one spot to another. Two thousand different species of plants, classified by region, flourish in this lush environment.

The Ménagerie

One of the oldest zoos in the world, this opened in 1794 with animals from the royal collections, and became so popular by 1827 that the arrival of a giraffe—the first ever on French soil—was a major event of the year, drawing 600,000 Parisians. Today, the rustic quarters have an undeniable charm. Recently, the 12-acre (5 ha) zoo was saved from the claws of real estate developers by being classified a historical monument. The drawback, however, is that nothing can be changed from the original design; even renovations

Jardin des Plantes

- Map pp. 62–63
- 36 rue Geoffroy St.-Hilaire. Main entrance: 57 rue Cuvier
- 01 40 79 56 01
- Métro: Austerlitz, Jussieu

jardindesplantesde paris.fr

Ménagerie

- 57 rue Cuvier
- 01 40 79 56 01
- €€€

mnhn.fr

A Home for Fashion & Design

If you have noticed what looks like a massive green carbuncle stuck to the side of a nondescript concrete building on the Left Bank riverside, about a block from the Jardin des Plantes, do not be alarmed: It is not a mutant giant of the species come to devour Paris, but an architectural addition, designed by in-vogue architects Jakob+MacFarlane, to a hundred-year-old customs warehouse. This is **Docks en Seine/Cité de la Mode et du Design** (34 quai d'Austerlitz, 75013), a site for fairs and concept stores devoted to cutting-edge fashion, design, and the arts. It is also home to the French Fashion Institute. The views from the terraces of its restaurants and clubs have made it a popular hangout, especially in good weather.

Alpine Garden (closed Nov.–Mar.). Not easy to find, this discreet haven is buried almost 10 feet (3 m) lower than the rest of the Jardin des Plantes to provide a more varied terrain. The gardeners have somehow created a microclimate of small valleys and hills in the garden, where the temperature

to bring in more modern zoo-keeping methods are ruled out. This, combined with a lack of funds, means that some of the buildings are sadly dilapidated. The curators have taken this in their stride, specializing instead in smaller primates, reptiles, birds of prey, and snow leopards. ■

SUBTERRANEAN PARIS

Paris has an underground life that is just as active as the one above ground. Although the catacombs are one of the most frequently visited underground sites (see Denfert-Rochereau, p. 201), there are lesser known crypts in unexpected places—for example, beneath the July Column at Place de la Bastille (see p. 119), where victims from the 1830 and 1848 revolutions are buried, or under the St.-Sulpice Church (see p. 83).

■ Many Métro stops, such as Cité, reflect the style of the streets above.

The city also has sewer tours; a nuclear-fallout shelter underneath the Sorbonne; a French Resistance hideout underneath that; and many underground quarries, rivers, canals, and even a lake (beneath Place de l'Opéra). Lastly, there are the streamlined Métro and RER, whose rubber tires whoosh from station to station, sometimes surfacing molelike from underground tunnels into the light, but always returning to the dark recesses beneath the streets.

Quarries, Sewers, Pipes, & Water

Paris was built with gypsum and limestone extracted from its subsoil. The Left Bank alone has 186 miles (299 km) of underground tunnels (not open to the public). However, intensive mining has caused subsidence, and although the quarries are no longer exploited and many buildings are reinforced by pilings, several houses are collapsing in areas like Montmartre. (Ironically, this has helped to spare the area from overdevelopment.) Efforts to shore up the limestone quarries are under way, and an inspection team constantly monitors the limestone for fissures and flaws.

If you take a tour of the sewers, you will enter the most malodorous of Paris's museums. In these tours you will learn about sewer- and water-treatment systems, Monsieur Poubelle (for whom the French garbage can is named), and purification equipment. Sewers (égouts) generally run under the middle of streets, although on broader avenues they run underneath the sidewalks. These tunnels feature plaques with the names of the streets above. Larger mains contain pipes for drinking and industrial-use water; pneumatic tubes once used by the post office to speed the delivery of letters and light packages—two are still in use today; telephone and telegraph cables; traffic-signal cables; and pipes for compressed air.

The city's first springwater-fed public fountain opened in 1184, but it was Baron Haussmann (see pp. 166–167) who introduced the modern system. In 1852 his right-hand man, Eugène Belgrand, began diverting springs that currently supply half the city with its drinking water. Inhabitants also rely on water pumped from the Seine and Marne Rivers. The two-tiered, part subterranean Montsouris Reservoir has a capacity of 3.25 million cubic feet (94 million liters) and supplies some of eastern Paris with water. To ensure that the reservoir supply is fresh enough for consumption, trout swim in the turquoise waters.

The Métro

The Métro is the fastest way to get around the city; its speed and design make Paris seem as if it could fit into the palm of your hand. Its stops function as reference points for the city. When construction on the Métro began during the 19th century, bones, teeth, and tusks of mammoths were found near the Montmartre Cemetery and under Square Montholon. From the start, the Métro was designed for intra muras Paris only, and the trains deliberately traveled on the right so they could never be hooked up to trains that went outside the city.

The Métro has well over 300 stations; the busiest is St.-Lazare, the deepest is Abbesses, and the one with the most intersecting lines is République. In the late 1960s, the Louvre-Rivoli station was transformed with copies of works from the museum, and the vogue for theme-based stations took off.

Don't miss the replicas from the nearby Musée Rodin at the Varenne station; illustrations of the storming of the prison at the Bastille station; exhibits of engineering feats at Arts et Métiers; and the art nouveau entrances at Porte Dauphine and Abbesses.

EXPERIENCE: Stop at the Coolest Métro Stations

You can create your own fascinating tour of Paris simply by visiting some of the city's most fascinating Métro stops.

Not all are alike. Some have been decorated in accordance with their location: **Louvre-Rivoli** is a tasteful mini-museum furnished with reproductions of works from the Louvre, while **Varenne** has statues by Rodin. **Gare de Lyon**, on the newest line, no. 14, has a tropical garden; the **Arts et Métier** stop looks like the inside of a submarine; and the **Concorde** station has the Declaration of the Rights of Man written out on its tiled walls.

Perhaps the coolest of all are the ghost stations. Keep your eyes peeled as the trains on line 8 or 9 pass between **Strasbourg/Saint-Denis** and **République** to see the long-closed St.-Martin station, its tiles now covered in graffiti. ADEMAS (ademas.assoc.free.fr) takes you on tours of the Métro, including a ghost station.

More Places to Visit in the Quartier Latin

Arènes de Lutèce

Hidden away behind the modern buildings of the Jussieu University are the vestiges of the Lutetia Arena, a second-century Roman amphitheater designed to seat 15,000 spectators, the second largest in Gaul. The Romans used the slope of what is now called Montagne Ste.-Geneviève (see p. 65) for the 35 tiers of stone seats and placed the stage to the east, where performers would receive the last rays of the setting sun.

Few of the original stones remain: The theater eroded away after Parisians carted off handy building materials to build the walls of the Île de la Cité, and over the centuries the arena gradually filled in with debris. By the 19th century, most people believed that the ancient arena was more legend than reality, but Baron Haussmann uncovered the substructure of the arena when he extended Rue Monge in 1869. True to form, he dug up and destroyed about two-thirds of the arena so that a bus depot could use the grounds. In 1883, Victor Hugo led a determined campaign to save the remaining ruins, and the site was finally restored in 1917; only about one-third of today's arena, however, is original.

🅰 Map p. 62 ✉ 49 rue Monge 🚇 Métro: Jussieu

INSIDER TIP:

For a great view of Paris, go to the Institut du Monde Arabe in the Latin Quarter and head to its rooftop café/ restaurant for a real visual *délice* (treat).

—ANNE RANDERSON
National Geographic contributor

Scams to Watch Out For

Tourists are the preferred victims of street scammers. A favorite scam often encountered near museums goes like this: A person walking toward you suddenly spies something on the ground and picks it up. The scammer approaches you and shows you a "solid gold" ring, says he or she does not want it and offers to sell it to you for, say, €20. Many scammers, especially around the Centre Georges-Pompidou, carry clipboards and pretend to be collecting for charity. Another trick involves a long, complicated explanation about being robbed or having undergone some other traumatic experience and not having the money to go home. In all of these cases, and anything similar, just say *non*, politely but very firmly, and walk away.

Carrefour de l'Odéon

Near the statue of the revolutionary leader Georges Jacques Danton (marking the site of his former home, from which he was arrested in March 1794 and later guillotined), the Carrefour de l'Odéon is a busy crossroads that stretches south to the **Odéon-Théâtre de l'Europe** and north to the famous **Café Procope**—the oldest café in Paris *(13 rue de l'Ancienne-Comédie, tel 01 40 46 79 00)*. Here, Jean le Rond d'Alembert and Denis Diderot began work on their famous *Encyclopédie* in 1727; it was here too that Benjamin Franklin met with Louis XVI to draw up the agreement for the budding American Republic.

Rue de l'Ancienne-Comédie continues to the bustling Rue St.-André-des-Arts. The beautiful, neoclassical Odéon-Théâtre de l'Europe is best viewed from its entrance at the Place de l'Odéon. It was at the Odéon that Pierre Beaumarchais's *Mariage de Figaro* was first performed in 1784; considered subversive, the play cost Beaumarchais a year's imprisonment.

Down the street, at 12 rue de l'Odéon, was Sylvia Beach's bookstore and lending library, the famous **Shakespeare and Company,** the home of the Left Bank expatriate American literary community after 1920. Beach was the first to publish the complete version of Irish writer James Joyce's *Ulysses* in 1922, launching the literary event of the decade and nearly making her bankrupt in the process. Despite Joyce's subsequent sale of the book to Random House for a $45,000 advance in 1932, he never offered her any of the profits. Gertrude Stein was one of the first to subscribe to Beach's lending library, but was so appalled by the publication of *Ulysses,* which she considered obscene, that she informed Beach that she would thereafter borrow solely from the American Library on the Right Bank. (The current Shakespeare and Company bookstore is at 37 rue de la Bûcherie.)

Map p. 62 Métro: Odéon

Grande Mosquée de Paris

Paris's principal mosque for the Algerian-dominated Muslim community encompasses a religious center, marked by a striking green-and-white minaret jutting 85 feet (26 m) into the air; the Institut d'Études Musulmanes, where Arabo-Islamic language and culture are taught; and the beautiful Moorish tearoom, restaurant, and Turkish baths.

Inaugurated in 1926 to commemorate the Muslim war effort, the mosque was built by Charles Heubès, Robert Fournez, and Maurice Mantout. The most gifted Tunisian, Moroccan, and Algerian craftsmen were summoned to layer the edifice with lovely marble, tiles, mosaics, damask, cedarwood, and fountains made of porphyry. The Grand Patio inside the mosque was inspired by the Alhambra in Granada, Spain, and features woodwork in cedar and eucalyptus, a mosaic frieze bearing verses of the Koran, and a beautiful fountain. The outdoor tearoom, where you can drink mint tea, is perfect on a hot, sunny day.

mosqueedeparis.net

Map p. 62 ✉ Place du Puits de l'Ermite (mosque) or 39 rue Geoffroy-St.-Hilaire (tearoom, Turkish baths, restaurant, boutique) ☎ 01 45 35 97 33 (mosque); 01 43 31 18 14 (tearoom, restaurant, baths, boutique) ⊕ Closed during Muslim holidays (Ramadan varies from year to year, call for information) Métro: Censier-Daubenton

Institut du Monde Arabe

Inaugurated in 1987, the steel-and-glass Institut du Monde Arabe is a joint Franco-Arab project designed to encourage cultural

■ **The Institut du Monde Arabe**

links between the West and the Arab world. Twenty Arab states participated in this building, which includes permanent and temporary exhibition areas, a library, a bookstore, conference rooms, an auditorium, and a spectacular rooftop restaurant and café (the view alone is worth the trip).

The widely acclaimed architecture is meant to symbolize a crossroads: The northern or "Western" side facing the Seine is a sleek, transparent wall, while the inner, enclosed courtyard reflects ancient Arab influence through the innovative, high-tech reinterpretation of the traditional *moucharaby* carved-wood latticework. The 1,600 aluminum prisms open and close electronically to regulate the amount of sunlight streaming into the building. The permanent collection occupies three floors and showcases the many scientific and cultural breakthroughs achieved by Arab scientists and astronomers. *imarabe.org*

🅰 Map p. 62 ✉ 1 rue des Fossés-St.-Bernard ☎ 01 40 51 38 38 🕐 Closed Mon. 💲 €€ 🚇 Métro: Jussieu, Cardinal Lemoine, Sully-Morland

St.-Étienne-du-Mont

St.-Étienne-du-Mont is not one of the best-known churches in Paris, yet it is one of the most monumental and unusual. With its highly original, three-tiered facade and asymmetrical interior, it has the only remaining rood screen (a crucifix supported on a screen separating the nave from the chancel) in Paris; the tombs of Jean Racine and Blaise Pascal; an elaborate organ loft; a baroque pulpit supported by a figure of Samson; and the reliquary of Saint Geneviève in an elaborate chapel.

According to legend, one of Geneviève's miracles included restoring her mother's sight by washing her eyes with well water; this is depicted in one of the church's stained-glass windows. Until the French Revolution (when the relics were melted down and the saint's remains burned on the Place de la

Grève), the jewel-studded reliquary was a source of great veneration. In times of floods and epidemics, it was carried in a flower-strewn procession to Notre-Dame after a day of atonement.

The Renaissance rood screen, flanked by two openwork spiral staircases, is magnificent. The cloister's main gallery, the Chapelle des Catéchismes (through the sacristy), is lined with splendid 16th- and 17th-century stained-glass windows. *saintetiennedumont.fr*

🅰 Map p. 62 ✉ Place Ste.-Geneviève ☎ 01 43 54 11 79 🕐 Closed Mon. a.m., Sat. & Sun. 1 p.m.–2 p.m., & Mon.-Wed. during school holidays 🚇 Métro: Jussieu

Hemingway's Paris

When Ernest Hemingway and his wife moved to Paris in 1921, they lived in a primitive apartment on Rue Cardinal Lemoine. That area later became part of the fond memories of the protagonist of "The Snows of Kilimanjaro." "There never was another part of Paris that he loved like that, the sprawling trees, the old white plastered houses painted brown below, the long green of the autobus in that round square, the purple flower dye upon the paving, the sudden drop down the hill of the Rue Cardinal Lemoine to the River, and the other way the narrow crowded world of the Rue Mouffetard."

Two bustling neighborhoods that were once symbolic of the intelligentsia and artistic communities of Paris

ST.-GERMAIN
& MONTPARNASSE

■ On the Rue de la Gaîté, Montparnasse

ST.-GERMAIN & MONTPARNASSE

Paris's legendary St.-Germain-des-Prés quarter sprang up in the ninth century around a famous Benedictine abbey, and is now an area of boutiques, jazz cellars, bookstores, and bistros. Montparnasse, another literary hub, was also the onetime capital of cubism.

The Église St.-Germain-des-Prés was the heart of an abbey whose agricultural domain stretched east to the Petit Pont, encompassing today's 6th and 7th arrondissements. The Romanesque church—the oldest in Paris—holds the remains of 17th-century philosopher and mathematician René Descartes, the founder of modern philosophy. Appropriately, the 20th-century existentialist philosopher Jean-Paul Sartre—the ubiquitous king of the "*gauche caviar*," or elite leftists—used to come to the nearby Café de Flore to write, vacillate, and chat with novelist Simone de Beauvoir and friends. Other intellectuals, such as Raymond Aron, drank at Les Deux Magots café or ate at the Brasserie Lipp (see Travelwise p. 243), making St.-Germain-des-Prés synonymous with Parisian intellectual life.

Once Bohemian, Now Upscale

Montparnasse was the birthplace of what went on to become the École de Paris. Its effervescent energy lured writers, artists, and bohemians from all over the world. Ernest Hemingway, F. Scott Fitzgerald, John Dos Passos, and Edna St. Vincent Millay frequented the brasseries and bars; James Whistler lived nearby; Lenin played chess at the Closerie des Lilas; American poet Hart Crane was arrested for punching a waiter at Le Select; and Kiki, the exotic 1920s "Queen of Montparnasse," aroused them all with her raspy voice and seductive show.

La Ruche was a refuge for many artists, particularly those from Central Europe, including

Constantin Brancusi, Ossip Zadkine, Chaim Soutine, and Marc Chagall. Some were living in dire poverty and thus spent hours each day in cafés simply to escape the cold. Unfortunately, the advent of central heating killed off much of café life.

The famous late-night bookstore and art gallery La Hune is still open, as are dozens of bookshops scattered through the streets of St.-Germain. This area is also where France's leading publishing houses are located. But today's St.-Germain is ruled more by consumerism, with Right Bank fashion moguls encroaching on the formerly sacrosanct literary hub: Armani has bought out the legendary Drugstore Publicis; Cartier replaced a great classical music shop; Louis Vuitton is at 6 place St.-Germain-des-Prés; and even the Flore has its own accessories boutique. Nevertheless, St.-Germain is still a wonderful area to visit. Don't miss the art galleries that line Rue de Seine, Rue Bonaparte, and Rue des Beaux-Arts, and the Musée Delacroix. And be sure to sit around the octagonal basin in the peaceful Jardin du Luxembourg, and

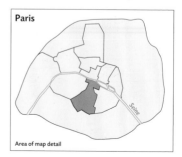

Paris

Area of map detail

to watch the sun slip into the Seine from the Pont des Arts.

Although Montparnasse's heyday is over, you can still get a glimmer of what the excitement was like along the strip at La Coupole (see p. 86) and Closerie des Lilas (see p. 88). ■

❶ Tour Montparnasse ❷ Closerie des Lilas ❸ Marché St.-Germain ❹ École Nationale Supérieure des Beaux-Arts

NOT TO BE MISSED:

Visiting the Église St.-Germain-des-Prés 80

Visiting the graves of the famous at Montparnasse Cemetery 85

A drink at Hemingway's old bar, La Coupole 86

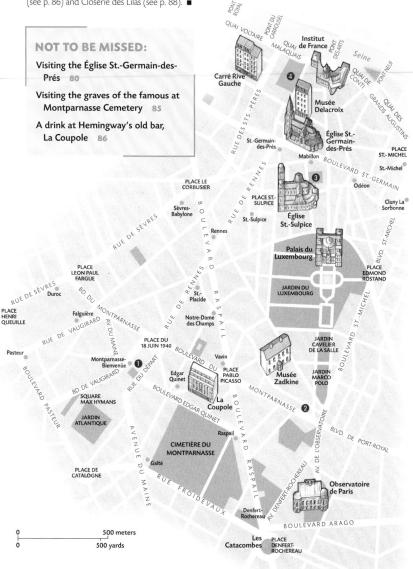

ÉGLISE ST.-GERMAIN-DES-PRÉS

Heeding the advice of Saint Germain, who was soon to be Bishop of Paris, the Merovingian Childebert ordered a basilica and monastery to be built in 543 and dedicated to Saint Vincent (the patron saint of wine growers) and the Holy Cross. The basilica, with its magnificent mosaics and gilded-bronze roof, was nicknamed St.-Germain le Doré (St.-Germain the Gilded).

St.-Germain-des-Prés's 11th-century bell tower

Église St.-Germain-des-Prés

A Map p. 79

✉ Place St.-Germain

☎ 01 55 42 81 18

🚇 Métro: St.-Germain-des-Prés

eglise-saintgermaindespres.fr

The Normans destroyed the abbey, but it was rebuilt as a Romanesque church around 1000; its 11th-century bell tower is the oldest in Paris. The church was consecrated in 1163 by Pope Alexander III. (Maurice de Sully, the Bishop of Paris, was barred from the ceremony to assert the abbey's independence from the bishop.) The church was expanded in 1245 with the Chapelle de la Vièrge and the cloister, vestiges of which can be seen in the small square outside.

Later History

In June 1789, revolutionaries attacked the abbey prison to free soldiers detained for refusing to fire on striking workers in the Faubourg St.-Antoine. The following year, the church was converted into a saltpeter warehouse. The former church prison, along with **St.-Joseph-des-Carmes** *(70 rue de Vaugirard)*, was where the September massacres (see p. 27) began. It was also where Charlotte Corday, who murdered the revolutionary Jean-Paul Marat, was imprisoned during the Terror. In 1794, 15 tons of gunpowder stored in the dining hall exploded, devastating nearly everything.

The church was restored during the 19th century, largely due to efforts by Victor Hugo. Jean Auguste Ingres's student, Hippolyte Flandrin, completed frescoes on the walls of the nave. The columns of the 12th-century chancel are from the Merovingian basilica. In a side chapel to the right of the choir is the **tomb of René Descartes** (who died in 1650). The cloister's small garden has a bronze sculpture of a woman's head by Picasso. ∎

AROUND THE RUE DE SEINE

Two cultural institutions grace the streets near Place Furstenberg, one of Paris's most romantic squares: the Delacroix Museum and the Institut de France, home to the Académie Française.

Musée Delacroix

The Delacroix Museum is housed in the building where the painter lived until his death in 1863. Delacroix moved here in 1857 while painting the murals in the St.-Sulpice Church. The museum provides a more intimate look at the artist. The collection is laid out in Delacroix's apartment and garden studio, with works displayed on a rotating basis. They include the artist's smaller works, religious paintings like the exceptional "Madeleine in the Desert," and portraits. There are also the artist's palettes, and lithographs, engravings, and objects that Delacroix brought back from North Africa.

Institut de France

The Collège des Quatre Nations, the predecessor of the Institut de France, was built by money bequeathed by Cardinal Mazarin in 1661 as a school for provincial children. Its layout—two half-moon wings designed by Louis Le Vau—reflects the influence of Italian architecture. The building, given to the Institut de France in 1806, comprises five academies.

The **Académie Française,** the oldest and the most famous, was founded by Cardinal Richelieu in 1635. Membership is limited to 40 individuals known as *les immortels.*

Orson Welles, Peter Ustinov, and Vaclav Havel have all held positions at the **Académie des Beaux-Arts.** The baroque chapel encloses Mazarin's tomb, and the east wing houses the **Bibliothèque Mazarine,** France's first public library. Nearby is the **École Nationale Supérieure des Beaux-Arts** *(14 rue Bonaparte),* Paris's main fine arts school, housed in the vestiges of the Petits-Augustins convent, commissioned by Marguerite of Valois in 1608; it holds temporary exhibitions *(closed Mon. & Tues.).* ∎

Musée Delacroix

- Map p. 79
- 6 rue de Fürstenberg
- 01 44 41 86 50
- Closed Tues.
- €€
- Métro: St.-Germain-des-Prés

musee-delacroix.fr

Institut de France

- Map p. 79
- 23 quai de Conti
- 01 44 41 44 41
- Métro: St.-Michel

institut-de-france.fr

Love Locks Overload Paris Bridges

Love—in the form of inscribed "love locks" that couples attach to Paris bridges before throwing the key into the Seine to swear undying love—is destroying Paris's beloved Pont des Arts (see pp. 138–139). The thousands of padlocks—inspired by a tradition that originated in Hungary in the 19th century and was taken up in Paris in 2008—burdened the bridge and caused one section of the railing to fall into the river, while other parts are peeling off or have been replaced with graffiti-covered wooden panels, turning the once graceful bridge into an eyesore. The city of Paris has replaced the panels with less aesthetic lock-proof glass, but the locks are beginning to deface the city's other bridges. A plea to lovelorn travelers: Help keep Paris beautiful by finding another way to express your love.

PALAIS DU LUXEMBOURG

Mention Luxembourg to most Parisians, and they will probably describe the elegant 59-acre (24 ha) park, the only real green space in the entire 6th arrondissement, rather than the palace of the same name. For generations, the park has been one of the city's most popular.

■ Backed by the palace, the Jardin du Luxembourg is popular with walkers and families.

Palais du Luxembourg

🗺 Map p. 79

✉ 15 rue de Vaugirard

☎ 01 42 34 20 00

🕐 Interior visits by guided tour only; book through the Direction de l'Accueil et de la Sécurité (tel 01 42 34 20 60). Gardens open daily from dawn to dusk.

🚇 Métro: St.-Sulpice, Odéon RER (B): Luxembourg

senat.fr

Italian-Style Mansion

Both the palace and the gardens were created in the early 17th century by the self-aggrandizing Marie de Médicis after her husband, King Henri IV, was killed. Nostalgic for the Pitti Palace, her childhood home in Florence—and especially the Boboli Gardens—she asked architect Salomon de Brosse to re-create an Italian-style mansion on the property she bought from the Duc de Luxembourg. He retained the smaller building, the Petit Luxembourg (now the official residence of the president of the Senate), and constructed an opulent dwelling for which she commissioned a series of 24 monumental paintings by Rubens depicting the major events of her life (now displayed in the Louvre). In 1630, after only five years in her lavish palace, she was forced into exile by her son, Louis XIII, on the so-called Day of Dupes.

Gardens

Marie de Médicis's devotion to her garden is visible in the 2,000 elm trees, orchards, and formal flower beds she planted. Although the gardens were re-landscaped by Chalgrin in the 19th century, they retain the formal layout; to this day, the park is impeccably maintained, and a gorgeous palette is created by rotating the flower species through the seasons.

The **Médicis Fountain** is one of the prettiest spots in the park, where 100-year-old plane trees shade the long pool. A number of statues dot the park including a small replica of Auguste Bartholdi's "Statue of Liberty." There's no better place to spend an afternoon with small children, as the park has a separate children's play area, with pony rides, swings, slides, and rides; a classic puppet show; and a merry-go-round constructed from plans by Charles Garnier (designer of the Opéra Garnier). ■

ST.-SULPICE & QUARTIER

On a sunny spring day, when the pink-blossomed chestnut trees are in full bloom, the Place St.-Sulpice is one of Paris's loveliest squares. The best place to appreciate the monumental Fountain of Four Bishops (Louis Visconti, 1844) and the imposing Église St.-Sulpice is from one of the tables spilling out on the sidewalk around the Café de la Mairie.

The Church

Église St.-Sulpice is a surprisingly austere yet grandiose structure that took more than 135 years to build (which may explain the two mismatched towers flanking the colonnaded facade). The first stone was laid in 1646 to replace an earlier 13th-century building, but work stopped 20 years later due to lack of funds. Construction started again in the 18th century and proceeded haphazardly until the north tower was completed in 1778. The highlight of St.-Sulpice is Eugène Delacroix's decoration of the **Chapelle des Sts.-Anges,** which took ten years to finish. The tormented scenes of "Jacob Wrestling with the Angel" and "Heliodorus Driven from the Temple" were the artist's last great masterpieces.

Surrounding Streets

A famous *maison close* (brothel) at 36 rue St.-Sulpice once catered to high-class clientele in the very shadow of the church. The brothel is gone, but the colonnaded facade with yellow and green tiles still marks its place.

The streets around **Place St.-Sulpice** are lined with classy clothes shops, florists, lingerie shops, and bookstores. The area—a shopper's paradise—stretches as far as Sèvres-Babylone, where the renovated **Bon Marché** department store has a chic and expensive new look; the food display on the ground floor alone is worth the trip. Just behind the church is the **Marché St.-Germain,** its covered markets filled today with shops and trendy bars that make this a pale version of the famous medieval fair once held here. ■

Église St.-Sulpice

- 🗺 Map p. 79
- ✉ 2 rue Palatine
- ☎ 01 42 34 59 94
- 🕐 Free guided tour every Sun. at 2:30 p.m.
- 🚇 Métro: St.-Sulpice

Edible Jewels

France is home to many a master pastry chef, and you won't walk far in Paris without being tempted into a patisserie by the delicious aroma of baked delicacies. These days, designer pastries presented as edible jewels are all the rage in Paris. Just off the Place St.-Sulpice (three doors north of the corner on Rue Bonaparte) is **Pierre Hermé** *(72 rue Bonaparte, tel 01 43 54 47 77),* who invents such treasures as white-truffle macaroons (in season), while **Pain du Sucre** *(14 rue Rambuteau, tel 01 45 74 68 92)* offers heart-shaped soft-centered chocolate cakes. At Philippe Conticini's **La Pâtisserie des Rêves** *(93 rue du Bac, tel 09 72 60 93 19; 19 rue Poncelet, tel 01 42 67 71 79),* a specialty is a deconstructed Saint Honoré with the whipped cream on the side.

CEMETERIES

For centuries, Parisians buried their dead in the Cimetière des Innocents (Sts.-Innocents Cemetery) next to the teeming marketplace of Les Halles. It was the main cemetery for over 20 parishes in Paris, particularly for those that did not have their own cemeteries, for the destitute, and for those who died in the Hôtel Dieu hospital. Burials were in a common grave that held up to 1,500 bodies; when this was full, another was dug nearby.

The beautiful Cimetière du Père-Lachaise contains a multitude of interesting tombs.

By the late 18th century, the stench had become intolerable, and the grisly contents of the cemetery (the remains of nearly six million people) were transported in convoys to the catacombs near Denfert-Rochereau (see p. 201). The cemeteries within the walls of the city were then closed, replaced by the cemeteries of Père-Lachaise, Montparnasse, and Montmartre.

Cimetière du Père-Lachaise

Père-Lachaise (8 boulevard de Ménilmontant, tel 01 55 25 82 10, Métro: Père-Lachaise,

Philippe-Auguste) attracts more people than any other cemetery in Paris—more than two million visitors every year. It is named after the Jesuit priest de La Chaise, Louis XIV's confessor, who owned the land here between 1665 and 1709. In 1803, architect Alexandre Brongniart redesigned the layout for a cemetery. Drawing his inspiration from English-style gardens, he integrated romantically landscaped paths and exuberant funerary statuary, which nevertheless failed to excite Parisians. The cemetery opened on May 21, 1804, but there were only 2,000 tombs by

1815, partly because it was considered too remote. Ingenious Parisian government officials figured that if they transferred the remains of a few famous people, celebrity-conscious Parisians would soon follow. In 1817 the remains of playwright Molière and poet Jean de La Fontaine, along with Héloïse and Abélard (see p. 114), were brought to the cemetery; by 1828, there were over 33,000 tombs, and several lots were purchased to expand the growing site, creating today's 109-acre (44 ha) cemetery—the largest green area in Paris, with the exception of the Bois de Boulogne and the Bois de Vincennes.

The cemetery is laid out according to numbered divisions. The lower section is a romantic, tangled forest of tombs and sepulchers, arranged along dirt paths and cobblestone lanes. The upper section has a severe, geometric-grid layout. Maps are available at the cemetery's entrance; these indicate the most famous (though not easy to find) tombs—you may have to poke around off the main path. There are a multitude of interesting tombs, and the most intriguing are not always the graves of the famous. Many celebrities are buried here, including Frédéric Chopin and Oscar Wilde. The grave of the late Doors' singer Jim Morrison has become something of a shrine to his fans. A series of monuments near the Mur des Fédérés, or Federalists' Wall, form a moving homage to the French victims who died in Nazi concentration camps, especially the severe bronze monument representing three skeletal figures, a tribute to the dead of Buchenwald-Dora.

Cimetière du Montparnasse

An abbey necropolis has existed on the site of the Montparnasse Cemetery (3 boulevard Edgar-Quinet, tel 01 44 10 86 50, Métro: Edgar-Quinet, Raspail) since 1654, but it became a municipal cemetery only in 1824. Divided into the Petit Cimetière and the Grand Cimetière, it is the smallest of the three Paris cemeteries, and at first sight is less romantic

than Père-Lachaise. Yet along the gridded avenues lie the remains of many of France's intellectual and artistic elite, as well as a profusion of fascinating funerary art. Charles Baudelaire's tomb, for example, features the bust of the 19th-century poet perched above a gigantic bat, contemplating a stone sculpture of his own body below. Constantin Brancusi is also buried here: Several of his sculptures, including "The Kiss," stand atop tombs. Serge Gainsbourg, Jean-Paul Sartre, and Simone de Beauvoir are all interred here.

Cimetière de Montmartre

Montmartre Cemetery (20 avenue Rachel, tel 01 53 42 36 30, Métro: Blanche) was initially a sinister place, where the destitute were thrown into common graves. Redesigned in 1879, it now contains the remains of many in the arts, including Edgar Degas, Émile Zola, and Vaslav Nijinsky.

■ **The famed Cimetière de Montmartre**

LA COUPOLE

In the 1930s, La Coupole was *the* brasserie in which to see and be seen, drawing some of the 20th century's most famous intellectuals. Hemingway and Jean Cocteau were frequent guests. Today, this *bar Américain* par excellence preserves its classic elegance.

La Coupole has been a fashionable hot spot for decades in Montparnasse.

La Coupole
- Map p. 79
- 102 boulevard du Montparnasse
- 01 43 20 14 20
- Métro: Montparnasse-Bienvenüe

www.lacoupole-paris.com

La Coupole has its hours and seasons, though you can eat at any time, day or night. But it is best during oyster season (all months containing the letter "r"). Try to lunch or dine as late as possible; patrons of La Coupole tend to linger. Its fabled bar menu serves up odd blends like the eponymous house concoction (rum, Noilly Prat, grenadine, and Grand Marnier).

The Coupole may have lost some of its soul and its culinary status since it was taken over by the Flo Brasseries chain, but it has retained its marvelous art nouveau and art deco decor, with the stunning cubist-style mosaic floor and the famous 33 columns

painted by neighborhood artists (most of whose names would not be recognized today) in exchange for free drinks. And it still features giant sprays of gladiolas, courtly waiters who seem devoted to treating each customer like a VIP, and a bustling ambience that conjures the ghosts of customers past, among them Samuel Beckett, Ernest Hemingway, and Salvador Dalí.

In the era of the cellphone, you can no longer enjoy the thrill of seeing your name paraded by on a small chalkboard when a phone call comes in for you, but you can still doodle on your place mat, as Swiss sculptor Alberto Giacometti used to do. ■

SOUTHEAST MONTPARNASSE

A short walk from the expanses of the Luxembourg Gardens are two diverse pieces of Parisian culture. The Zadkine Museum honors the sculptor who lived in Paris for decades. Nearby, the Paris Observatory offers a glimpse into the distinguished history of French astronomy.

Musée Zadkine

This small house and flower-filled garden, just a few blocks from the Luxembourg Gardens, is where the Russian-born sculptor Ossip Zadkine lived from 1928 until his death in 1967. Recently restored to its original layout, the house has nearly 70 sculptures scattered around its rooms and in the secluded garden. Several important pieces are on display, including Zadkine's most famous sculpture, "Ville Détruite" ("The Destroyed City").

Observatoire de Paris

The Observatoire de Paris, founded in 1667 and

> **INSIDER TIP:**
>
> On a summer afternoon, join the locals by ordering a kir (chilled white wine with crème de cassis) at a traditional bistro.
>
> —ANNE RANDERSON
> *National Geographic contributor*

completed in 1672, is the oldest observatory in the world still operating. Constructed by Claude Perrault (older brother of the fairy-tale author, Charles Perrault, who published the original *Cinderella*), the building's conception and architectural layout mirrors the cosmos: The main body of the edifice is oriented toward the four cardinal points, and the walls of the two octagonal towers on the southern facade indicate the sun's position during the summer and winter solstices.

Here the moon's surface was charted (1679), the metric weights and measures system devised (1791), Neptune discovered by Leverrier (1846), and the speed of light determined (18th century). The observatory remains a research center for astronomy and related services, but the building's interior can no longer be visited by outsiders. ∎

Musée Zadkine

- Map p. 79
- 100 bis rue d'Assas
- 01 55 42 77 20
- Closed Mon.
- Métro: Vavin, Notre-Dame des Champs RER (B): Port-Royal

zadkine.paris.fr

Observatoire de Paris

- Map p. 79
- 61 avenue de l'Observatoire
- RER (B): Port-Royal

obspm.fr

Tour Montparnasse

- Map p. 79
- 33 avenue du Maine
- 01 45 38 52 56
- €€€
- Métro: Montparnasse-Bienvenüe

tourmontparnasse 56.com

Tour Montparnasse

Don't miss the 58-floor, 688-foot-high (210 m) Montparnasse Tower, the highest steel-and-glass monstrosity in Europe. It grew out of the old Montparnasse railway station, where the German army signed its surrender of Paris on August 25, 1944. The top of the tower has a panoramic restaurant and terrace, with a terrific view over Paris.

A WALK THROUGH MONTPARNASSE

You can still find traces of historic Montparnasse in some of its most famous establishments, such as the Closerie des Lilas and La Coupole, although it is no longer the vivacious center of art and literature it was in the early part of the 20th century.

Rue de la Gaîté, in Montparnasse, is known for its theaters.

Begin your walk at the Raspail Métro, turning down **Rue Campagne Première ❶**. At No. 31 is Atelier 17, decorated with tall windows and ceramic tiles. American photographer Man Ray rented a studio here, then moved with his mistress "Queen" Kiki to the Istria Hotel next door. The Istria was home to numerous artists and writers, including Francis Picabia, Austrian poet Rainer Maria Rilke, Marcel Duchamp, and composer Erik Satie. Poet Paul Verlaine lived across the street at No. 14 (the house is no longer standing); when he moved out, he passed his room on to his companion, poet Arthur Rimbaud.

At No. 9, go through the door leading to another group of artists' studios at the back of a cobbled courtyard. Before World War I, many artists left Montmartre for Montparnasse, seeking lower rents and inspiration in the Boulevard du Montparnasse cafés. Italian artists Giorgio de Chirico and Amedeo Modigliani and painter

NOT TO BE MISSED:

Closerie des Lilas • Rodin's "Balzac" • La Coupole • Le Select

James Whistler were among those who lived in this building.

Turn right on the Boulevard du Montparnasse and head for the lavender sign of the **Closerie des Lilas ❷** (see Travelwise p. 243), a favorite haunt of artists and writers such as Ernest Hemingway. Arriving in Paris in 1921, Hemingway soon settled in at the Closerie, where he wrote *Big Two-Hearted River*, part of *The Sun Also Rises*, and many of his short stories. Its Cuban mahogany bar (where a plaque marks Hemingway's spot), red lamps, mirrored decor, and leather seats are just as inviting today as they were back then.

Outside the Closerie stands a statue of Marshal Ney, a hero of the French Revolutionary and Napoleonic Wars. Hemingway lived nearby at 113 rue Notre-Dame des Champs (turn left from the Closerie to continue the walk) above a sawmill, which no longer exists (even the street number has disappeared; the numbers jump from 111 to 115).

Turn left off Rue Notre-Dame des Champs on Rue de Chevreuse. At the intersection with Boulevard du Montparnasse (where the Le Boa restaurant is found), stood Le Jockey—the 1920s haunt presided over by the legendary singer and artist's model "Queen" Kiki.

Turn right on Boulevard du Montparnasse. At the Carrefour Vavin stands Rodin's famous statue **"Balzac"** (see p. 178). Cross Boulevard du Montparnasse and turn down Rue Delambre. At No. 10 is the **Auberge de Venise,** called Le Dingo in the 1920s; another expatriate hangout, it was where Hemingway first met fellow American F. Scott Fitzgerald.

Turn right on Rue du Montparnasse. The **Falstaff** (now a tacky beer bar) is on the left toward the end; it was once a favorite drinking spot for Samuel Beckett, Kiki, Man Ray, Fitzgerald, and Hemingway.

Turn right on Boulevard du Montparnasse. Ahead lies the Vavin Métro and four of the most famous cafés in the world—Le Select, La Rotonde, Le Dôme (now an upscale fish restaurant; see Travelwise p. 244), and **La Coupole ③** (see p. 86 & Travelwise p. 244). American critic and editor Malcolm Cowley described the first three as the "heart and nervous system of the . . . literary colony." Russian revolutionary Leon Trotsky often met up with Mexican painter Diego Rivera at La Rotonde. **Le Select,** the first café in Paris to stay open all night long, was where American poet Hart Crane picked a fight that landed him in jail for a week.

🗺 See also area map
pp. 78–79
▶ Raspail Métro
🕐 Allow 2 hours
🔁 1.3 miles (2.1 km)
▶ Vavin Métro

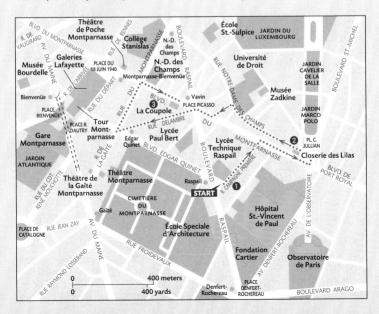

More Places to Visit in St.-Germain & Montparnasse

Carré Rive Gauche

The cream of the Paris antique trade is clustered within a few prestigious blocks of the 6th arrondissement. Bordered by the Quai Voltaire, Rue des St.-Pères, Rue de l'Université, and Rue du Bac, the Carré Rive Gauche offers shops with high-quality furniture, objets d'art, and paintings. Each of the 30 or so associated shops showcases an exceptional object relating to a theme that is selected annually for a special one-week show in mid-May. carrerivegauche.com

🅰 Map p. 79 🚇 Métro: Rue du Bac, Solférino

Institut Pasteur

The research institute was founded in 1888 by the great scientist Louis Pasteur, to whom we owe, among other things, the invention of the pasteurization process (which takes its name from him) and the development of the first vaccine of history, the anti-rabies one. The structure includes a museum, set up in what was Pasteur's home for the last seven years of his life. The domestic spaces retain the furnishings of the time, and in a room a laboratory has been reconstructed, with tools which trace the precious research work of the scientist. The basement houses Pasteur's tomb in a crypt with Byzantine-style mosaics inspired by his discoveries. The museum is currently only accessible with a group guided tour, to be booked at least three months in advance (see website). pasteur.fr

✉ 25 rue du Docteur Roux ☎ 01 45 68 82 83 🕐 Closed Sat., Sun., Aug., & public holidays 💲 €€€ 🚇 Métro: Pasteur.

La Ruche

Just outside Montparnasse, but of interest to students of art, is La Ruche ("the beehive"), which celebrated its centenary in 2002–2003. It is one of the oldest artists' colonies still operating today. Sculptor Alfred Boucher salvaged the wine pavilion built by Gustave Eiffel for the Paris Universal Exposition of 1900 and converted it into La Ruche, thus baptized because the beehive-shaped rotunda's main stairway leads to ateliers (studios) where artists paint, sculpt, and write.

The polygonal building was divided into 24 triangular ateliers, each nicknamed *quart de brie* (slice of brie). It provided a refuge for artists like Amedeo Modigliani, Marc Chagall, and Constantin Brancusi, and writers such as Apollinaire, Max Jacob, and Blaise Cendrars, many of whom lived and worked here in dire poverty. It was also near the cafés of Montparnasse. The building, once nearly demolished, was saved by a committee headed by Chagall; it is now a classified monument and a thriving artistic hub. laruche-artistes.fr

✉ 2 passage de Dantzig 🕐 Some studios may be visited at the discretion of their occupants. 🚇 Métro: Convention

---

EXPERIENCE:
Practice Your French

A good way not only to meet French people, but also to improve your French, is through language exchanges. Usually, the deal is that you meet up with a French speaker who wants to practice his or her English, and the two of you spend half the time speaking each language. (There's no reason you could not speak English the whole time, however.) You can get started online before you even leave home by finding partners at *mylanguageexchange.com* or the French/English Language Exchange on Facebook, or go to informal language exchanges like the **Polyglot Club,** which holds gatherings every Saturday from 8 p.m. to midnight at the **Café Le Basile** (*34 rue Grenelle, Métro: St-Germain-des-Prés*).

The former market at Les Halles, now an underground shopping complex, but still, as Zola described it, the "belly of Paris"

CHÂTELET & LES HALLES

Henri de Miller's modern head-and-hand sculpture, named "L'Écoute" ("listen"), outside the Église St.-Eustache

CHÂTELET & LES HALLES

The area around Châtelet and Les Halles, particularly the narrow back alleys and roads, is reminiscent of the cobbled streets of old Paris—bustling, crime-ridden, and foul-smelling, but vibrant.

Life and death coexisted in many medieval Parisian squares, where markets and fairs often sprang up in cemeteries because of the available free space, bringing together mime artists, jugglers, musicians, the homeless, and thieves amid the mixed smells of newly slaughtered meat and the freshest farm produce.

❶ Théâtre du Châtelet ❷ Tour St.-Jacques ❸ Théâtre de la Ville

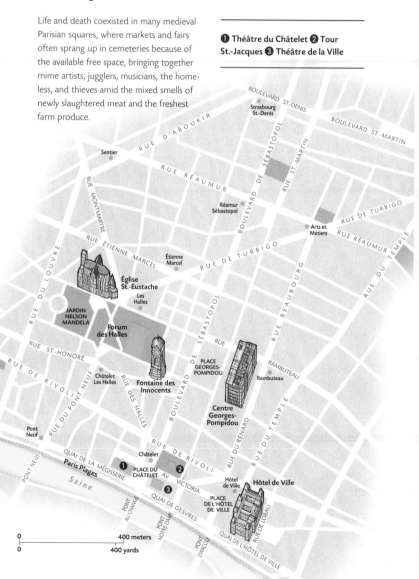

Paris

Area of map detail

Les Halles

Les Halles (see pp. 98–99), a market for French produce for 800 years, continues to draw in the crowds—especially around the Fontaine des Innocents (see p. 102); the surrounding gardens, terraces, and sculptures; the seedy Rue St.-Denis; and the Église St.-Eustache (see p. 102)—although the actual market was transferred south of Paris to Rungis in 1969 to ease traffic problems.

The sterile, largely subterranean modern commercial and cultural complex at Forum des Halles that replaced the marketplace has been revamped into a more attractive, upscale shopping center. It remains to be seen how the transformation of Les Halles will affect its surroundings. To the east are the modern Centre Georges-Pompidou (also called Beaubourg; see pp. 96–97) and the neo-Renaissance Hôtel de Ville (City Hall; see p. 94). Beaubourg, originally a 12th-century village, retains a touch of medieval atmosphere, particularly in its narrow side streets. The former 17th-century Cour des Miracles (see sidebar p. 25), once a byword for vice in the red-light area of the 2nd arrondissement, is now a fun place to browse shops, enjoy street performers, and watch the world go by from terrace cafés. ∎

République

PLACE DE LA RÉPUBLIQUE

Temple

Châtelet

The area around the Place du Châtelet (see p. 95) was associated with the powerful butchers' guilds, the tanneries, and the sinister Grand Châtelet Prison. With its twin theaters and Châtelet Fountain decorated with sphinxes around the base, it is difficult to imagine the square as it once was.

The nearby Tour St.-Jacques—the Flamboyant Gothic bell tower of the church of St.-Jacques la Boucherie—was built for the powerful 16th-century butchers' guild and served as a landmark for pilgrims en route to Santiago de Compostela in Spain. The scallop shells (coquilles) with which the pilgrims decorated their hats and capes became a symbol of the pilgrims—hence the famous dish, Coquilles St.-Jacques. In 1648, Blaise Pascal used the tower to repeat the barometric experiments he had carried out in Puy-de-Dôme, and the tower, standing in a small park, is now open to the public in summer.

Rue St.-Denis was once the path of the kings of France. Today it is lined with fast-food joints, clothing outlets, and sex shops. Its northern end, still a seedy red-light district, is gradually being gentrified.

HÔTEL DE VILLE

Although the current building is fairly recent, the site of the Hôtel de Ville (City Hall) has always played an essential role in the history of the capital.

■ The Hôtel de Ville: location of Paris's municipality since 1357

Hôtel de Ville

- ⓐ Map p. 92
- ✉ Place de l'Hôtel de Ville (public entrance: 29 rue de Rivoli)
- ☎ Individual visits suspended until further notice; for group tours, call 01 42 76 54 04 (Protocol Department) two months in advance.
- Ⓜ Métro: Hôtel de Ville, Châtelet

Water was vital in the development of the city's municipal administration, which originated with the powerful water merchants' guild that controlled and administered trade on the Seine, Oise, Yonne, and Marne Rivers. In the mid-13th century, Saint Louis introduced a municipal government composed of leading *échevins* (guildsmen), headed by the *prévôt des marchands* (equivalent to aldermen and a mayor) who were elected by the Parisian bourgeoisie to form the Parloir aux Bourgeois. The seal of the water merchants (an emblem depicting a boat on the river) became the symbol of Paris.

The site of municipal administration shifted from the Place du Châtelet in 1357, when the provost Étienne Marcel bought the Maison des Piliers on the Place de la Grève (*grève* means shore), the name given to the Place de l'Hôtel de Ville until 1830. This first Hôtel de Ville was the site of revolutions, celebrations, and executions from 1310 to 1830. Louis XVI was forced to kiss the tricolor cockade here in 1789, and revolutionaries Danton, Marat, and Robespierre used the hôtel as their headquarters during the Terror (see p. 27).

Water is still present in François-Xavier Lalanne's 1980s fountains flanking the busy, bright white edifice, which is frequently the home of temporary exhibitions. A lavish nativity scene is set up outside the building each Christmas. The interior has a series of beautiful reception halls, glittering chandeliers, gilding, ornate woodwork (note the seven different types of wood in the Salon Bertrand), a sumptuous grand staircase with murals of "Summer" and "Winter" by Puvis de Chavannes, and triumphant Third Republic ceiling murals.

Burned down to a stone shell in May 1871, the Hôtel de Ville was rebuilt between 1874 and 1882, its exterior replicating the French Renaissance style. ■

PLACE DU CHÂTELET

With its elegant twin theaters, monumental fountain, and great view of the river, the Place du Châtelet bears little trace of its notorious former prison and the crime-ridden streets around it. It does, however, retain the names of the streets where the activities of the butchers and tanneries were carried out—Rue de la Tuerie (killing) and Rue de l'Ecorcherie (skinning).

The square is named for the Grand Châtelet fortress, constructed by Louis VI le Gros (circa 1130) to defend the Île de la Cité. The fortress stood at the entrance to the Pont au Change (Money Changing Bridge), then the city's main access.

Later the area became the seat of the courts, provostship, and prison. In 1808, Napoleon razed the fortress, replacing it with a fountain. A column was also built to commemorate the emperor's victories.

Until the Revolution, the Quai de la Mégisserie was the site of the slaughterhouse; today, the attractive riverfront is lined with florists and shops selling caged animals, although these traditional businesses are now being replaced by home-decoration stores.

Between 1860 and 1862, at the request of Baron Haussmann,

INSIDER TIP:

Walk around Fontaine du Palmier and admire the figures of Prudence, Temperance, Justice, and Strength, on each side.

—TOM O'NEILL
National Geographic magazine writer

architect Jean-Antoine-Gabriel Davioud built two identical theaters on the square's opposite sides: the Théâtre du Châtelet (officially the **Théâtre Musical de Paris**) and the **Théâtre de la Ville,** once owned by the actress Sarah Bernhardt. Today, with the bustling Châtelet Métro/RER stop far beneath its streets, the square has become one of the busiest crossroads in Paris. ∎

Place du Châtelet

🅰 Map p. 92

✉ Métro: Châtelet

Café Nuts & Bolts

After a day on your feet, nothing is more welcome than a stop at a café. Some are low-profile local places where working people eat a quick snack at lunchtime and residents meet in the evening. In general, cafés open early in the morning, in time to serve the traditional *grand crème* (large cup of coffee with milk) with croissants to people on their way to work.

Throughout the day they also serve wine, beer, pastis—a strong aniseed spirit diluted with water—and, of course, espresso (Parisians traditionally add milk to their coffee only in the morning). Drinks are cheaper *au bar* (standing at the bar) than *en salle* (sitting at a table inside). They are even more expensive if you sit at a table outside, but this never seems to worry anyone who is intent on soaking up the atmosphere or smoking a cigarette.

CENTRE GEORGES-POMPIDOU

The Pompidou Center, renovated extensively between 1997 and 2000, is one of the city's most popular sites. Standing in the midst of Paris like a slumbering giant, its blue, green, yellow, and red pipes and ducts coiled against the gray rooftops and cityscape, Richard Rogers and Renzo Piano's arts complex spearheaded contemporary architecture in Paris in 1977, injecting an avant-garde tone into one of the city's oldest neighborhoods and causing great controversy.

■ The architecture of the Centre Georges-Pompidou is distinctive if not universally admired.

Since the spectacular $90 million renovation of the center (called Beaubourg by Parisians), the main foyer has been redesigned; exhibition space nearly doubled; disabled access improved; and the library (now with its own entrance) expanded and equipped with 370 computers. Drama, dance, and cinema theaters have opened on the lower level; and a museum gallery, graphic arts gallery, and media collection

have been added. A trendy (if overblown) restaurant (Georges)—where you'll at least get a great view—is found at the top of the six-level center.

The center still houses the **Center of Industrial Creation** (CCI), specializing in architecture, urbanization, and visual communications; the **Institute for Research and Acoustical/Musical Coordination** (IRCAM) for contemporary music; and the **Cinema,** featuring film festivals and rare movies. It also hosts a **Children's Workshop** to foster touch, color, and artistic expression in 6- to 12-year-olds, and conferences, seminars, lectures, and debates.

On the other hand, the renovation has made for a less-democratic building: In a plan that was highly criticized by both architects, visitors now have to pay to take the escalators up for the splendid panoramic view. (If you are lucky enough to be there on the first Sunday of the month, escalator admission is free.) But the ticket gives access to the Musée National d'Art Moderne and its extraordinary collection of 20th-century works. The focus of the center now is to direct attention to the museum.

Musée National d'Art Moderne

The MNAM's extensive collection is second only to that of New York's Metropolitan Museum of Modern Art, housing some 60,000 works from the early 20th century to the present. The renovation expanded the exhibition space by 50 percent, and the contemporary and modern collections are now rehung every year or two.

Visitors enter through the contemporary art section on the fourth level, which has rooms devoted to pop art, *arte povera,* and other major movements, as well as to individual artists such as Yves Klein and Jean Dubuffet. Visitors then proceed upstairs to the modern section (1905–1960),

featuring movements such as fauvism and cubism and works by Picasso, Kandinsky, Rouault, Chagall, and Matisse, among others. New acquisitions include Francis Picabia's "Dresseur d'Animaux." In general, there is more sculpture (Giacometti, in particular) and contemporary French art, and the

Brancusi's Sculpture Studio

When the Romanian-born sculptor Constantin Brancusi died in 1957, he left his studio to the French government, on condition that it be fully reconstituted. Originally on the Impasse Ronsin in the 15th arrondissement, the atelier was rebuilt at the Palais de Tokyo before being moved to the Pompidou Center in 1977, where it is now located on the plaza. On view are the artist's sketches, original plasters, bronze sculptures, stone and marble sculptures, bed, wardrobe, tools, and maquettes. Temporary exhibitions are held in the studio as well.

collections now include furniture, design, and graphic arts. It is easier for visitors to circulate on both levels of the museum, and the ceilings have been opened up to reveal the pipes and ducts painted white, creating the impression of higher ceilings and brighter space. There are also video lounges, installation areas, and performance art spaces. ∎

Centre Georges-Pompidou

🅰 Map p. 92

✉ Place Georges-Pompidou (until fall 2020, entrance on rue Beaubourg for renovation work)

♿ IRCAM: entrance on Place Igor Stravinsky. For comprehensive information visit www.handicap.centrepompidou.fr

☎ 01 44 78 12 33

🕐 Closed Tues. Museum & exhibitions open at 11 a.m.; Atelier Brancusi opens at 2 p.m.

💲 €€€

Ⓜ Métro: Hôtel de Ville, Rambuteau

centrepompidou.fr

LES HALLES

The forum at Les Halles is but a pale shadow of the legendary "belly of Paris" described by Émile Zola, where fishwives and market porters worked through the night to load the pavilions with the gleaming produce of rural France by dawn.

■ The Bourse de Commerce (Commodity Exchange) reflects Les Halles' historic economic role in Paris.

Les Halles

🅰 Map p. 92

🚇 Métro: Les
Halles, Châtelet
RER: Châtelet
Les Halles

Philippe-Auguste built Les Halles between 1181 and 1183, financing it partially by using property confiscated from the Jewish residents he expelled in 1182. When the two large 13th-century warehouses for drapers and weavers that formed the primitive market at Champeaux closed on Saturdays, the merchants and craftsmen set up their shops at Les Halles. By the mid-14th century, merchants were present three times a week. In 1851, Napoleon III instructed the architect Victor Baltard to construct cast-iron "umbrellas," and ten pavilions with cast-iron frames were built in Les Halles between 1854 and 1912. In 1936 two more were added, but by 1969, the market's popularity and resultant traffic problems forced authorities to move it south of the city to Rungis. All but two of the pavilions were destroyed, and for nearly a decade a gaping hole remained where the market once stood.

Beginning in 2020, the old grain exchange, converted into

Late-Night Restaurants

Paris may be an international metropolis, but surprisingly few restaurants stay open late at night. If you do not know where to find a meal after 10:30 or 11 p.m., you may find yourself going to bed hungry after the theater or a film. Your best chances will be found around Les Halles, where a number of traditional restaurants stay open until the wee hours: **La Tour Montlhéry** (a.k.a. Chez Denise, 5 rue des Prouvaires, tel 01 42 36 21 82), **La Poule au Pot** (9 rue Vauvilliers, tel 01 42 36 32 96), **Au Pied de Cochon** (6 rue Coquillière, tel 01 40 13 77 00). In the Marais, **Les Philosophes** (28 rue Vieille-du-Temple, tel 01 48 87 49 64) serves until 1 a.m. Around the Champs-Élysées: **L'Alsace** (39 avenue Champs-Élysées, tel. 01 53 93 97 00), specializing in choucroute, is open 24/7, and the **Maison de l'Aubrac** (37 rue Marbeuf, tel 01 43 59 05 14) is open round-the-clock Wed.–Sat. Near the Opéra: **Le Grand Café Capucines** (4 boulevard des Capucines, tel 01 43 12 19 00) serves all day and night.

the Bourse de Commerce in 1889, houses the contemporary art exhibition spaces of the collection Pinault designed by Tadao Ando. The platform on the 16th-century column next to it, once part of Catherine de Médicis's palace, was used by her astrologer for purposes of divination.

In 1979, the new Les Halles took form, resulting in a commercial and cultural boom. Today, the sprawling Métro-RER station at Châtelet Les Halles acts as a high-speed crossroads for commuters and shoppers. Crowds from all walks of life mill around in this vast, four-level, subterranean shopping complex, which includes a photo exhibition space, gymnasium, pool, tropical greenhouse, movie complex, center for films on Paris, music library, film library, dance center, and billiards hall.

The Renovation

Now, just 40 years after the building of the controversial Forum des Halles, with its mirrored "upside-down-umbrella"

aboveground structures, all this has changed. In 2010, beginning with the gardens, a massive renovation project started. After several years of architectural competitions, heated consultations with the public, and refinements of the winning project, the new Les Halles took shape under architect David Mangin's direction. The renovation, completed in 2018, included a reorganization of the Métro-RER transport hub, a new garden with two playgrounds, and a roof, known as "La Canopée," which covers the shopping center. The gently undulating greenish-yellow roof, designed by Patrick Berger and Jacques Anziutti, incorporates solar panels and rainwater tanks, and at night it resembles a giant glowing spaceship that has landed in the center of Paris.

Besides being the most visited shopping center in the whole of France, the present Forum des Halles also includes a public library, an elegant conservatory, and two cafés overlooking the park. ■

NEIGHBORHOOD MARKETS

For local color, nothing beats a morning at one of the many food markets scattered throughout Paris. You will be tempted by the brilliant displays of red and yellow peppers, slithering stacks of mysterious sea creatures, and countless different cheeses; extra encouragement comes from the boisterous sellers hawking their produce.

The market on Rue Mouffetard attracts locals and visitors to the Latin Quarter.

Every neighborhood has its own market. A few are still housed in old, covered buildings and, while some are permanent, others are set up for only two or three mornings a week. Although the markets are less crowded and the food is fresher early in the morning, there are good bargains at the end of the day, when vendors sell off their last few pounds of fruit cheap. Don't pick up the food yourself, however; point out what you want and tell the vendors, and let them handle their merchandise themselves.

Permanent & Temporary Markets

The permanent (regular) markets are closed on Sunday afternoons, Mondays, and also during several hours at lunchtime. The Marché d'Aligre, on Place d'Aligre, is one of the cheapest in Paris. It has lots of exotic goods, like North African spices, as well as many secondhand clothes stalls. The covered Marché des Enfants Rouges, the city's oldest (1615), is also a popular lunch spot, offering shoppers a choice of French, Italian, and Moroccan specialties.

Another colorful market extends along the lower end of Rue Mouffetard; it would look like a film set if it weren't for all the tourists.

For true Left Bank chic, try the Buci Market on Rue de Seine and Rue de Buci, where a quintessentially Parisian clientele crowds the busy (and expensive) stands on Sunday morning. And for organic Left Bank chic, the Sunday Marché Biologique on Boulevard Raspail offers high-priced free-range poultry and chemical-free produce. Other permanent market streets include Rue Montorgueil, a holdover from Les Halles; Rue du Poteau, a great, little known food market; and Rue Poncelet.

The largest temporary market stretches along Boulevard Richard Lenoir near the Bastille on Thursday and Sunday mornings. As with most neighborhood markets, locals usually return to the same vendors, but as prices and quality vary, take time to shop around. Afternoon markets include Saint Eustache–Les Halles market (*Thursday p.m.*) and Place Baudoyer (*Wednesday p.m.*).

Specialty Markets

Paris also has its share of specialty markets. In the shadow of the Paris law courts on the Île de la Cité is the flower market (see p. 54).

On Sunday a bird market also takes place here, and the air is filled with their trilling and squawking.

If you want antique or secondhand books, try the book market on Rue Brancion, near the Parc Georges Brassens, on Saturday and Sunday. The serious book collectors arrive early to browse through the weekly selection.

INSIDER TIP:

Visit the vast Saint-Ouen Puces Antiques Market [*marcheaux puces-saintouen.com*] for all kinds of vintage treasures.

—NEIL SHEA
National Geographic magazine writer

The area at the base of Montmartre is the place to find fabrics. There are two main stores. Marché St.-Pierre (*2 rue Charles Nodier*), a four-floor free-for-all, has the best prices for silks, wools, and furnishing fabrics. Across the street is the more sedate and expensive Reine (*5 place St.-Pierre*). All around are smaller fabric outlets, selling everything from buttons to bolts of exotic African and Middle Eastern fabrics.

EXPERIENCE: Finding the Markets

Join the Parisians in shopping for produce, cheese, or charcuterie at one of Paris's many neighborhood markets. For hours and closing days, check *paris.fr*.

Markets

Marché d'Aligre (*Métro: Ledru-Rollin*)
Rue Mouffetard market (*Métro: Censier-Daubenton*)
Marché Biologique (*Sun. a.m., Métro: Sèvres-Babylone*)
Rue Montorgueil market (*Métro: Les Halles, Étienne-Marcel*)
Rue du Poteau market (*Métro: Jules Joffrin*)

Rue Poncelet market (*Métro: Ternes*)
Boulevard Richard Lenoir market (*Thurs. & Sun. a.m., Métro: Bastille, Richard Lenoir*)
Place Baudoyer (*Wed. p.m., Sat. a.m., Métro: Hôtel de Ville*)
Marché des Enfants Rouges (*Métro: Temple*)
Rue Brancion (*Sat. & Sun., Métro: Porte de Vanves*)
Marché St.-Pierre and **Reine** (*Métro: Barbès-Rochechouart, Anvers*)
Saint Eustache–Les Halles (*Thurs. p.m. & Sun. a.m., Métro: Les Halles*)

More Places to Visit in Châtelet & Les Halles

Église St.-Eustache

Gothic and classical in plan and layout and Renaissance in decoration, this 16th-century church is second in size in Paris only to Notre-Dame. It was named for a Roman general who was said to have converted to Christianity after seeing a cross between a stag's antlers. (Note the stag's head beneath the gable point on the beautiful Renaissance transept facade.) During the Revolution, the church was converted into a secular Temple of Agriculture—a fitting transformation given its proximity to the former food market.

Many famous historical figures have made their mark on St.-Eustache. For example, it is where Molière was baptized (1622); Louis XIV made his first Communion (1649); and Jean Colbert, Minister of Finance to Louis XIV, is buried (see his tomb, with statues of a kneeling Colbert and allegorical figures by Antoine Coysevox). The funeral service for poet Jean de La Fontaine was held here (1695).

Many notable musicians are associated with the church. Here, Hector Berlioz attended the performance by 950 musicians of his massive choral/symphonic work *Te Deum* (1855); Franz Liszt's *Grand Mass* premiered here (1866); and Charles Gounod directed the choir. The church's fine acoustics have ensured a long history of organ and choral music; concerts are still held regularly on the premises (check *Pariscope* for information).

Antoine Soulignac's 17th-century stained-glass windows are remarkable. There are also paintings by the school of Rubens ("Disciples at Emmaüs") and Simon Vouet ("Saint Eustache the Martyr"), and a somewhat jarringly naive sculpture by Raymond Mason.

Next to the church, on Rue Montorgueil, garden stalls, butchers' shops, and boutiques give a hint of the former, bustling Les Halles market quarter. Rue du Jour has been usurped by Agnès B. and other fashionable boutiques, although the magnificent portal of the **Hôtel des Abbés de Royaumont** on this street is worth a detour.

Nighthawks gather at nearby **Au Pied de Cochon** at 6 rue Coquillère for hearty food, served until dawn (see sidebar p. 99).

saint-eustache.org

🗺 Map p. 92 ✉ Rue du Jour
🚇 Métro: Les Halles, Châtelet

Where to Buy a Handmade Hat

Here's an original idea for a souvenir of a trip to Paris: a handmade hat. Drop by the Les Halles shop of Anthony Peto (*56 rue Tiquetonne, tel 01 40 26 60 68, anthonypeto.com*), a British haberdasher with a sense of humor (from his website's FAQ section: "Are your hats for men or women?" "Yes"; "Will hats ever come back into fashion?" "No"), for a fitting and to choose your preferred style and fabric. The *chapeau* can be as eccentric or traditional as you wish. Your new headgear will be ready in one week for between €80 and €180.

Fontaine des Innocents

Completed by Jean Goujon in 1549, this is Paris's only Renaissance fountain (where the Cimetière des Innocents was once located; see p. 84). With its delicate bas-reliefs of nymphs and angels, the fountain is a great meeting place for lovers, skateboarders, punks, and bums alike. Although the surrounding square has suffered encroachment by fast-food and clothing chains and other eyesores, it still offers proof of human creativity through performing musicians and entrancing mime artists.

🗺 Map p. 92 ✉ Rue des Innocents
🚇 Métro: Les Halles, Châtelet

A vast outdoor museum, with well-groomed squares, quiet gardens, and elaborate architectural designs

LE MARAIS
& BASTILLE

■ The historic Marais neighborhood preserves many old decorative details.

LE MARAIS & BASTILLE

Until the 13th century, the area around Rue St.-Antoine was a marsh, giving the Marais (meaning "swamp") its name. Fed by the flooding of the Seine, it was used for market gardening. The quarter was gradually converted into a residential area; several convents were established, followed by lords' country homes, or *courtilles*, and royal residences.

The religious orders, who subsisted on the market gardens in the 14th century, sold their properties to members of the nobility who were seeking land outside the city walls. By the late 15th century, the old nobility, or *noblesse d'épée,* was firmly implanted in the quarter.

In the 16th century, there was an influx of newly ennobled financial and intellectual bourgeoisie—the *noblesse de robe*—which supplied the crown with much required funds by purchasing expensive titles. The royalty left after Henri II's death in 1559, but the aristocracy remained, erecting a number of superb mansions. In the late 17th century, after the court moved to Versailles, Le Marais began to fall into decline because of its remote eastern location, and by 1815, the area had become more synonymous with the *petite bourgeoisie.*

The square of the Place des Vosges (see pp. 106–107) replaced the Maison Royale des Tournelles, long the residence of the kings of France, encompassing a huge house and gardens surrounded by a wall and many small *tournelles,* or towers. Formerly called the Place Royale, the Place des Vosges was built by Henri IV in 1605. It spearheaded the development of the elegant Marais area, filled with sumptuous *hôtels particuliers* reminiscent of tiny, individual castles, including the Hôtel de Sully (see p. 116), the Hôtels de Rohan et de Soubise (see pp. 117–118), the Hôtel de Sens (see p. 120), the Hôtel Salé (home of the Musée Picasso; see pp. 110–111), and the Hôtel Carnavalet (see p. 113).

Architectural Tradition

Le Marais escaped the major urbanization overhaul during the 1960s, as Culture Minister André Malraux decreed that it be restored, given its historic value. The architectural traditions were successfully preserved, and the area is dense with elaborate doorways, windows, inner courtyards, bas-reliefs (such as the "Horses of Apollo" at the Hôtel de Rohan), and original street names carved in stone. Historic landmarks include vestiges of the Philippe-Auguste Wall, the Porte Clisson, and the nearby Place de la Bastille. However, fashion designers and yuppies have moved into the neighborhood, and the resulting gentrification has glazed over much of the area's charm.

The conversion of the former *hammam* (Turkish baths) on Rue des Rosiers in the old Jewish quarter into a clothing store is a potent illustration of the area's changing character. ■

NOT TO BE MISSED:

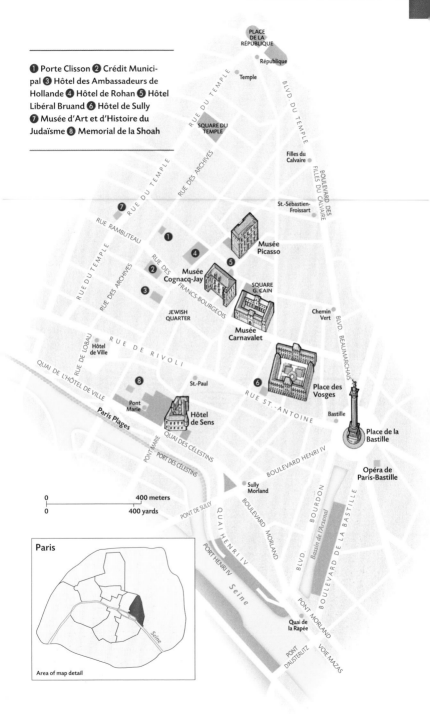

❶ Porte Clisson ❷ Crédit Municipal ❸ Hôtel des Ambassadeurs de Hollande ❹ Hôtel de Rohan ❺ Hôtel Libéral Bruand ❻ Hôtel de Sully ❼ Musée d'Art et d'Histoire du Judaïsme ❽ Memorial de la Shoah

PLACE DE LA RÉPUBLIQUE

République

Temple

RUE DU TEMPLE

BLVD DU TEMPLE

SQUARE DU TEMPLE

Filles du Calvaire

BOULEVARD DES FILLES DU CALVAIRE

RUE DES ARCHIVES

St.-Sébastien-Froissart

RUE RAMBUTEAU

Musée Picasso

RUE DU TEMPLE

RUE DES ARCHIVES

RUE DES FRANCS-BOURGEOIS

Musée Cognacq-Jay

SQUARE G. CAIN

Chemin Vert

JEWISH QUARTER

Musée Carnavalet

BLVD BEAUMARCHAIS

RUE DE LOBAU

RUE DE RIVOLI

Hôtel de Ville

Place des Vosges

QUAI DE L'HÔTEL DE VILLE

St-Paul

RUE ST-ANTOINE

Bastille

Place de la Bastille

Pont Marie

Paris Plages

Hôtel de Sens

QUAI DES CELESTINS

PONT MARIE

PORT DES CELESTINS

BOULEVARD HENRI IV

Opéra de Paris-Bastille

BLVD BOURDON

Bassin de l'Arsenal

BOULEVARD DE LA BASTILLE

0 ——————— 400 meters
0 ——————— 400 yards

PONT DE SULLY

Sully Morland

QUAI HENRI IV

BOULEVARD MORLAND

BLVD

PORT HENRI IV

Seine

PONT MORLAND

Quai de la Rapée

PONT D'AUSTERLITZ

VOIE MAZAS

Paris

Seine

Area of map detail

PLACE DES VOSGES

The Place des Vosges (originally the Place Royale, but rebaptized in 1800) was Paris's first open-air square, with a striking, redbrick symmetry of 36 pavilions, 9 on a side, each with 4 arcades and steeply pitched slate roofs. Following Louis d'Orléans's death in 1407, it became Crown property. When Charles VI moved there the Place was expanded to include dwellings, chapels, parks, and meadows (hence the nearby Rue du Foin, meaning "hay").

Striking redbrick buildings surround the open-air Place des Vosges.

Place des Vosges

Map p. 105

Métro: Bastille, Chemin Vert, St.-Paul

Charles VII, Louis XI, Charles VIII, Louis XII, François I, and Henri II all resided here. Four years after Henri II's death in a jousting accident on the Cours St.-Antoine (near the current Place des Vosges) in 1559, his wife, Catherine de Médicis, moved the royal residence to the Louvre and ordered the Hôtel des Tournelles to be torn down. The square subsequently became a horse market.

Although Henri IV originally intended to convert the square into silk workshops to ease France's dependence on Italian imports, he decided instead in 1605 to build the Place Royale

there, providing a square for public festivities that was otherwise lacking in Paris. The large southern pavilion, the **Pavillon du Roi,** served as a model for the others, with the **Pavillon de la Reine** opposite on the north side.

Henri IV was assassinated in 1610 before the square's inauguration in 1612. The inauguration celebrated a fantastic double wedding between Louis XIII (Henri IV's successor, whose statue stands in the square) and Anne of Austria, and between Princess Elisabeth of France and the future Philippe IV. Thirteen hundred horsemen paraded to the sounds of 150 trumpets and 80 musettes, oboes, and violins; torchbearers streamed through the streets of Paris at night, while fireworks were fired over the Bastille.

Thereafter, the square became a stopping-off spot for foreign envoys en route to the Louvre and a hub for luminaries such as the financier Maximilien Sully and the Princesses de Rohan and de Guéménée.

Each of the numbered residences has its own story. No. 1: Built with Crown money, the Pavillon du Roi was never a royal residence, but was rented out. No. 1B: The famous literary hostess Madame de Sévigné was born here in 1626. No. 4: The Marquis de Favras, who was accused of having plotted the kidnapping of Louis XVI and the murder of Lafayette, Commander of the National Guard, lived here in 1789. No. 6: Victor Hugo lived here from 1832 to 1848, writing *Les Chants du Crépuscule* and *Ruy Blas*. In the early 20th century, the building was converted into a museum, the **Maison de Victor Hugo** *(tel 01 42 72 10 16, maisonsvictorhugo.paris.fr, closed Mon.)*, containing the four-poster bed in which he died. No. 7: The entrance to the Petit Hôtel Sully, used by its owner, the Duc de Sully in the 17th century to reach the Place Royale. No. 8: The writers Théophile Gautier and Alphonse Daudet lived on the second floor in the mid-19th century. No. 9: The 19th-century tragedian Rachel (Élisa Félix) lived here in 1857; it is now the Ambroisie restaurant. No. 21: Cardinal Richelieu lived here from 1615 to 1623.

The equestrian statue of Louis XIII that Cardinal Richelieu erected in the square in 1639 was destroyed in the Revolution; it was replaced in 1825. Today, the square is trimmed with linden trees, and you can stretch out on the grass. Sunday afternoons are great for strolling around the arcades, listening to a variety of street musicians, browsing in the shops, and people-watching. ■

EXPERIENCE: Brunch à la Française

The French idea of brunch bears little resemblance to the American original. In most Paris restaurants offering brunch, customers are served a bewildering overload of dishes all at once: salad, eggs, pastries, French toast and/or pancakes, smoked salmon or ham, sometimes followed by a main course and usually by dessert. Arrive with an appetite, because you'll need it.

Some popular Sunday brunch spots—which are sure to be packed, usually with a lively crowd of youngish bobo (bourgeois-bohemian) types—are **Des Gars dans la Cuisine** *(72 rue Vieille-du-Temple, tel 01 42 74 88 26)*, a few blocks west of the Place des Vosges, and **Café Charlot** *(38 rue de Bretagne, tel 01 44 54 03 30)*, also in the Marais. For those who love retro atmospheres, the ideal place for brunch is **Pamela Popo** *(15 rue François Miron, tel 01 42 74 14 65)*. For a wonderful English-style brunch, try the **Rose Bakery** *(46 rue des Martyrs, tel 01 42 82 12 80)*, but be prepared to wait for a table.

For an excellent Moroccan brunch, try **404** *(69 rue des Gravilliers, tel 01 42 74 57 81)*, also in the Marais.

STREETS OF PARIS

For centuries, travel was arduous through Paris's dark, muddy streets, then unmarked and unnumbered. Store signs came into use by the 15th century, and these served as addresses. At first they were unwieldy sheet-metal plaques suspended on a long iron arm. By the mid-18th century, signs were smaller and fixed above the stores. Some wonderful store signs can be seen at the Musée Carnavalet (see p. 113).

The streets of Paris, such as Rue Mouffetard, are filled with eye-catching details.

Street Names

In 1728, street names were ordered to appear on corners; plaques went up all over the city, with names also carved into stone on street corner buildings. In 1844, the blue, enameled iron plaques currently in use began to appear. Many streets have been named and renamed—after noted merchants or residents, such as Galande; surrounding villages, like Belleville or Charonne; churches; professions (Coutellerie for the knifemaking area); landmarks like fountains or horse markets (Cul-de-sac du Ha! Ha!, now Impasse Guéménée); store signs (Chat Qui Pêche, Pot-de-Fer); historic milestones and events (Rue du Quatre-Septembre); heroes; victories; leaders; and even Métro stations. The new streets around the Bibliothèque Nationale de France in 1994 were named after writers such as François Mauriac and Raymond Aron.

In certain areas, such as Le Marais, you can still see the stone street name underneath the blue plaque. Political upheavals would sometimes upend street names: Rue de Berlin became Rue de Liège after World War I, for example. Sometimes, the names shocked residents—for example, Rue du Pélican was originally a den of iniquity called Rue du Poil-au-Con (a coarse reference to hairy buttocks); others merely evolved through wordplay (Rue de la Croix became Rue Eugène-Delacroix in 1868).

Lighting the City of Light

In 1318, only three public lanterns lit Paris at night, one at the Grand Châtelet fortress-prison; another at the Nesle Tower to guide sailors; and the last at the Cimetière des Innocents—the "lantern of the dead." In the first half of the 16th century, Louis XII, François I, and Henri II ordered candles to be placed in one window of each home—yet 15 people on average were murdered in the streets each night. In 1662 a mobile lighting system was adopted for those wishing to move about town at night. Porters bearing wax torches (and charging per layer of wax consumed) or oil lamps accompanied people to their doors, even if they lived several flights up.

Under Louis XIV (R.1643–1715), 3,000 lanterns were placed in the streets; these in turn were gradually replaced by oil-fueled, reflecting street lamps. There were 13,000 by 1837, and 240 lamplighters lit them as night approached, taking only three-quarters of an hour. Gas lighting spread quickly during the Restoration, with 8,000 gas lamps by 1845. Electricity first lit the Place de l'Opéra in 1878.

More recently, high-tech lighting systems using halogen lamps to bring out sculpture and details have upgraded bridges. The Eiffel Tower, in contrast to more traditional floodlighting, now glows from the inside and sparkles every hour after dark.

What to Look For

Paris is best seen at a slow stroll—as you go along, look up at the rooftop gardens, pilasters, caryatids, and mosaics. You'll also

■ The blue enameled plaque of the Place des Victoires is typical of Paris's old street signs.

find a series of cityscape frescoes scattered throughout Paris. The idea for frescoes stemmed from 1930s ads painted onto walls billing the aperitif "Dubo Dubon Dubonnet"—still visible on some streets in the city—or the chocolate drink Banania. In the 1970s, artists were commissioned to decorate walls with trompe l'oeil frescoes or figures. The murals come and go over the years, with new ones being added throughout the city—like the man climbing stairs accompanied by a pianist and violinist at Métro Etienne Marcel, and the blue-and-purple greenhouse at 60 rue de Reuilly in the 12th arrondissement.

Wolves & Bad Boys

One of the pleasures of sign-spotting in Paris is finding some of the more eccentric street names, such as:

Rue de l'Arbre Sec (Dry Tree St., 1st arrondissement) from tales of Marco Polo

Rue des Deux Boules (Two Balls St., 1st arrondissement) probably named after a shop sign

Rue des Mauvais Garçons (Bad Boys St., 4th arrondissement)

Rue Dieu (God St., 10th arrondissement) named after General Dieu

Rue Brèche aux Loups (Wolf Gap St., 12th arrondissement)

Rue Vineuse (Winey St., 16th arrondissement) King Louis XIII was known to stop by and drink the fine wine made by the convent there

Rue Poulet (Chicken Street, 18th arrondissement)

MUSÉE PICASSO

With its sphinx-guarded entrance, the Musée Picasso has the largest collection of works by Picasso in the world and gives a strong sense of the freshness and inventiveness that permeated every medium he touched. It reopened in 2014 after extensive renovations.

Musée Picasso

🗺 Map p. 105

✉ Hôtel Salé, 5 rue de Thorigny

☎ 01 85 56 00 36

🕐 Closed Mon., Dec. 25, Jan. 1, May 1

🚇 Métro: St.-Sébastian-Froissart, Chemin Vert

museepicassoparis.fr

Hôtel Salé

The Musée Picasso is located in the Hôtel Salé, built by Jean Boullier in 1656 for a salt-tax collector named Pierre Aubert de Fontenay. (*Salé* means "salty," but it also means "very expensive"—probably because salted meat was considered more valuable than poorly salted meat.) Aubert, a nouveau riche who made his fortune as a tax collector, displayed his ostentatious taste in the grandiose ironwork

staircase, encompassed by winged figures bearing garlands of fruit framing medallions, and the Salon de Jupiter, with its cherubs, garlands, and two medallions with reclining gods. The decoration is the work of the sculptor Martin Desjardins.

Following Aubert's death, the hôtel was rented out to various parties, including the Venetian Embassy and Leclerc de Juigné. The last archbishop of Paris before the Revolution, de Juigné covered up the nude sculptures on the walls. The hôtel was pillaged during the Revolution, then sold and rented to two art schools, the École Centrale des Arts et Manufactures and the École des Métiers d'Art. The City of Paris acquired the mansion in 1964 and leased it to the State. Picasso's death in 1973 prompted a search for a proper museum to display his works, and the Hôtel Salé was selected in 1976.

Picasso's Legacy

Picasso liked to joke that he was the world's greatest collector of Picassos, and indeed he kept much of his own output during his nearly 80 years of artistic production. Born in Málaga in 1881, Picasso left Spain at the age of 23 for France. Due to his close affinity with France, he lived most of his life here. After a 1934 visit to Spain, he vowed never to

■ "Dora Maar Seated" (1937), one of Picasso's singular portraits

return because of his opposition to Franco.

After Picasso's death in Mougins, his heirs donated his artworks in lieu of paying estate duties, and this allowed the State to have first choice in selecting the works that now form the bulk of the museum's collection.

The Art

After a five-year renovation, the museum, now accessible to the disabled, reopened in 2014 with additional exhibition space allowing the presentation of some 400 works.

A chronological visit begins with works showing off the artist's precocious talents as a boy in Spain, quickly moving on to the turn of the 20th century, when Picasso was traveling between Paris and Spain, and painted "The Death of Casagemas" (1901, Room 0.1) in honor of a friend who committed suicide. His blue period is represented by "Self-Portrait" (1901, Room 0.2), showing him as a gaunt, intense young man.

Subsequent rooms on the ground floor take visitors through works demonstrating the influence of African sculpture on his work, notably in a number of studies for "Les Demoiselles d'Avignon" (1906–07, Room 0.4), soon to be followed by groundbreaking cubist works like "Man with a Guitar" (1911–13, Room 0.6).

Take the grand staircase to the second floor, noticing the wrought-iron light fixtures by Diego Giacometti. Don't miss

---

EXPERIENCE:
Join the Vintage Craze

Don't pay top dollar for high fashion. Do as the Parisians do—pick up last year's Saint Laurent and Dior fashions at the city's many *dépôts-ventes*, consignment shops. Or join a younger crowd at trendy vintage shops, many of them located in the Marais. For those who love a little rummaging around the racks Free'p'star (52 & 61 rue de la Verrerie, tel 01 42 78 03 48) **is a good place to hunt for hidden gems, while the more far-out (both stylistically and geographically) GoldyMama** (99 Rue Orfila, tel 01 40 30 08 00, goldymama.com) **offers selected vintage designer clothing and embellished used garments.**

"Head of a Bull" (1942) high on a wall in Room 1.7, one of many sculptures made from found objects, in this case a bicycle seat and handlebars.

With the end of World War I, Picasso returned to classicism, exemplified in his work by the massive yet sprightly figures in "Two Women Running on the Beach" (1922, Room 1.4).

The next floor is arranged by such themes as war paintings and assemblages, including the sculpture "The Goat" (1950, Room 2.6). The artist's reworkings of Manet's "Déjeuner sur l'Herbe" are in Room 2.7.

The top floor intersperses Picasso's personal collection, including art by Cézanne, Modigliani, and Miró, with his own works to show their influence. The basement presents Picasso's ceramics and offers a photographic tour of his studios. ■

JEWISH QUARTER

Jewish people have lived in Paris since the sixth century, as recorded by Gregory of Tours. They were believed to have come with the Romans as merchants or craftsmen. The first Jewish quarter in Paris was not created, however, until 1119 along Rue de la Juiverie (now Rue de la Cité).

The bustling Rue des Rosiers offers stores with traditional Jewish food.

Jewish Quarter

🗺 Map p. 105

🚇 Métro: St.-Paul

Musée d'Art et d'Histoire du Judaïsme

✉ Hôtel de Saint-Aignan, 71 rue du Temple

☎ 01 53 01 86 60

🕐 Closed Mon., Jan. 1, some Jewish holidays

💲 €€

🚇 Métro: Rambuteau, Hôtel de Ville

mahj.org

Following Philippe-Auguste's expulsion of the Jews in 1182, there was a new influx in 1198, with some returning to the Left Bank, and others gravitating toward the Right Bank and Rue St.-Bon. Over the centuries, Jews were repeatedly expelled and then allowed to return. They were granted citizenship in 1791 during the Revolution. In 1871 the Jewish community numbered 25,000.

In the late 19th century, an influx of Jews from Central and Eastern Europe settled in and around **Rue des Rosiers.** Sephardic Jews from Egypt, Algeria, Tunisia, and Morocco, arriving between 1950 and 1962, spread the community far beyond this initial area. Today, the more traditional section of the quarter has been squeezed down to the western end of Rue des Rosiers.

The old **Jewish grammar school** (École des Hospitalières, 10 rue des Hospitalières-St.-Gervais), where 165 students were rounded up and sent to death camps, is adjacent; N'OUBLIEZ PAS ("Do not forget") is engraved on the wall.

The **Musée d'Art et d'Histoire du Judaïsme** explores Jewish heritage. A Holocaust Memorial, **Memorial de la Shoah** (17 rue Geoffroy l'Asnier, memorial delashoah.org), remembers those killed on a "Wall of Names" and has a documentation center. ∎

MUSÉE CARNAVALET

This Renaissance-style museum devoted to Parisian history is housed in the Hôtel Carnavalet, where celebrated letter-writer Madame de Sévigné once lived. Originally built for the president of the parliament in 1548, it was acquired by the widow of Henri III's tutor, Kernevenoy, who was nicknamed Carnavalet (a corruption of his name).

The Museum

As he was razing Paris and pushing the poor out toward the suburbs, Baron Haussmann (see pp. 166–167) asked the City of Paris in 1866 to acquire the Musée Carnavalet for storing the interiors of buildings he dismantled. The mansion was expanded, Renaissance-style galleries were built, and architectural elements, such as the Nazareth archway (from the old Palais de la Cité), were added. The museum's collection is displayed in two buildings—the remodeled Hôtel Carnavalet has collections dating from the origins of Paris to the Revolution; and the adjacent Hôtel Le Peletier de St.-Fargeau has the world's largest collection of portraits, objects, and memorabilia from the Revolutionary period and after.

The Collections

The rooms are arranged chronologically to illustrate the changing face of Paris. Exhibitions range from the city's origins to the 16th-century Renaissance influence; 17th-century decorative ensembles; the French Revolution; the Second Empire; and the belle époque. You'll also find such curiosities as Marcel Proust's bedroom, a scale model of a guillotine, and objects belonging to Voltaire and Rousseau. Don't miss Charles Le Brun's painted ceiling in the Hôtel de la Rivière, the Louis XV Bouvier collection, and Demarteau's salon by Boucher and Fragonard. The Orangerie houses Neolithic canoes and other Gallo-Roman finds and hosts temporary exhibits as well as concerts. ∎

Musée Carnavalet

- Map p. 105
- 16 rue des Francs-Bourgeois
- 01 44 59 58 58
- Closed Mon. & public holidays
- €€ for special exhibitions
- Métro: St.-Paul, Chemin Vert

carnavalet.paris.fr

■ The secluded gardens of the Musée Carnavalet

FAMOUS PARISIAN LOVE AFFAIRS

Time seems to stand still for lovers in Paris. Passion—as intangible and ephemeral as the charms of the city itself—has created such timeless pairs as sculptors Auguste Rodin and Camille Claudel (see sidebar p. 179) and writers Anaïs Nin and Henry Miller. The fame of these historic liaisons is such that for many the capital is synonymous with love itself.

Jacques-Louis David's painting highlights the moment in 1804 when Napoleon made an empress of his beloved wife, Josephine.

Love United in Death: Héloïse & Abélard

One of the earliest recorded pairs of lovers reposes in the Père-Lachaise Cemetery. Sometime around 1118, a man named Fulbert offered scholar Pierre Abélard (1079–1142) hospitality in his home on the Île de la Cité in exchange for ensuring Héloïse's (his 17-year-old niece) education. Despite their age difference (Abélard was 39), the two fell in love and married secretly. Outraged, Fulbert laid a trap for Abélard and had him castrated. Héloïse, who died 24 years after her lover, had arranged for the two to be united in death by being buried in the same coffin; a disapproving nun thwarted her plans

and placed them in separate coffins. Héloïse's wish was finally granted in 1817, when their remains were united in the neo-Gothic tomb at Père-Lachaise (see pp. 84–85).

Royal Mistress: Henri II & Diane de Poitiers

Although the initials of Henri II (1519–1559) and Catherine de Médicis carved throughout the south wing of the Cour Carrée in the Louvre seem to imply a great devotion between the monarchs, the intertwined letters "H" and "C" were actually an expression of Henri's deep attachment to his mistress, Diane de Poitiers, who was 20 years his senior. The insignia was therefore meant to be read as a double "D" for Diane, not "C" for Catherine. When Henri granted Diane the revenue from a tax on church bells, Rabelais famously quipped: "The king hung the bells of the realm around the neck of his mare." The queen was relegated to near obscurity until the king died, at which time she took her revenge by ousting Diane from her beloved Château de Chenonceau in the Loire Valley.

Unrequited Love:
Napoleon & Josephine

Napoleon Bonaparte, the man who conquered most of Europe, had trouble conquering the woman he loved. On March 9, 1796, he married Josephine de Beauharnais in a simple civil ceremony. What began as a marriage of convenience for Josephine—a widowed aristocrat seeking security in the troubled years after the Revolution—was a true affair of the heart for the future emperor of France, who was passionately in love with his wife. He ended one of his many ardent letters to her with these words: "I shall see you in three hours. Until then, *mio dolce amor,* a thousand kisses; but give me none in return, for they set my blood on fire." They spent their happiest moments together at the Château de Malmaison (see p. 232), but he divorced her in 1809 when she could not produce an heir. Napoleon continued to bankroll her extravagant lifestyle, however, while pleading with her to limit her spending. Despite his support, she owed three million francs at her death in 1814.

The Romantics:
George Sand & Frédéric Chopin

The 19th century was the era of the Romantics. A leading figure of the times, writer George Sand (born Amandine-Aurore-Lucie Dupin in 1804) led a wild, bohemian life in Paris after leaving her oafish husband in the countryside. She embarked on a tempestuous, short-lived love affair with French poet Alfred de Musset, followed by her most famous liaison with Polish composer Frédéric Chopin.

The two were part of the community of Romantic artists and writers who lived in the area known as La Nouvelle Athènes, just south of Montmartre. They broke off their affair in 1847 when he fell ill with tuberculosis and grew impatient with her hovering maternal solicitude. Traces of this famous couple are visible at the Musée de la Vie Romantique *(16 rue Chaptal, tel 01 55 31 95 67, vie-romantique.paris.fr, closed Mon., Métro: St.-Georges, Pigalle),* with Chopin memorabilia and a re-creation of Sand's drawing room.

The Eroticists:
Henry Miller & Anaïs Nin

The film *Henry and June* (1990) shows something of the stormy ménage à trois between American writer Henry Miller, his wife June, and the French erotic writer, Anaïs Nin, during the 1930s. The three of them embarked on an exploration of sexual libertinism that gave birth to a new form of literature, resulting in Miller's *Tropic of Cancer,* published in the 1930s in France but not until 1961 in the United States, and Nin's *Diaries* (in which she chronicled her sexual experiences) and *Delta of Venus.* Miller rented a house at 18 Villa Seurat, which he sometimes shared with Nin.

The Jilted First Lady:
François Hollande & Valérie Trierweiler

A sitting president's extracurricular shenanigans reached new heights of silliness when President François Hollande was snapped by a paparazzo in January 2014 sitting on the back of a motor scooter while paying a visit to his lover, actress Julie Gayet. This came as a great shock to France's First Lady, Hollande's live-in partner Valérie Trierweiler, who checked into a hospital to recover and was soon separated from the president. She quickly sought revenge, however, by publishing a memoir, *Thank You for This Moment,* in which she painted a portrait of Hollande as a petty, prevaricating snob.

A WALK AROUND THE OLD MARAIS

The sheer density of the historical and architectural wealth in Paris's best preserved quarter is overwhelming, requiring several days to visit all of its museums, *hôtels particuliers*, squares, and various sites.

Begin at Place de la Bastille and walk down Rue St.-Antoine, past Beaumarchais's statue on your right. Turn right on Rue de Birague to enter **Place des Vosges ❶** (see pp. 106–107) via the king's pavilion, and right again under the arcades to visit the

NOT TO BE MISSED:

Place des Vosges • Place du Marché Ste.-Catherine • Musée Carnavalet • Square Georges Cain • Musée Picasso • Rue des Rosiers

stores and galleries, noting the illustrious residences. Exit at No. 7 through the passageway into the beautiful French-style gardens and Renaissance building of **Hôtel de Sully,** which organizes regular photography exhibitions. The passageway may be closed at night; if so, return to Rue de Birague to reach Rue St.-Antoine.

Turn right on Rue St.-Antoine and right again on Rue Caron. Continue to **Place du Marché Ste.-Catherine,** once a 13th-century Augustinian priory. Cross the square and turn left on the tranquil Rue de Jarente. No. 6 leads to a charming, villagelike wing off the street. From there, turn right onto Rue de Sévigné, and then left onto Rue des Francs-Bourgeois. No. 23, now a chic clothing store, was a former belle époque *boulangerie.*

Be sure to visit the **Musée Carnavalet ❷** (see p. 113) before continuing down Rue des Francs-Bourgeois. Stop at the corner of Rue Pavée and Rue des Francs-Bourgeois to admire the lovely quadrangular watchtower bearing the letters S. C. on its base. This marks the limits of the estates of the Convent of Ste.-Catherine-du-Val-des-Écoliers from which the land was bought. It is part of one of the Marais' oldest mansions, the **Hôtel de Lamoignon** (now the Bibliothèque Historique de la Ville de Paris—the History Library of Paris). Hector Guimard built

The elegant older buildings and squares of the Marais make it ideal for walking.

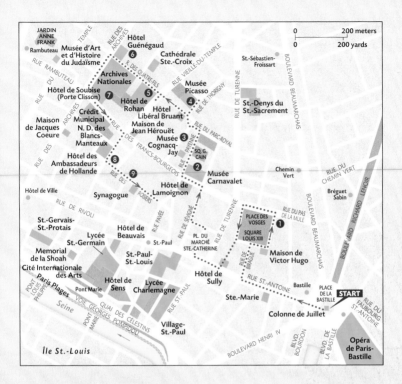

the synagogue at 10 rue Pavée; he fled to the United States with his American-Jewish wife during the rise of Nazism in Europe.

Turn right on Rue Payenne. The **Square Georges Cain,** a splendid small park with ruins and monuments, holds the **Musée Lapidaire de Paris** (Stone Museum of Paris), a cemetery for old stones. Look through the fence of **Musée Cognacq-Jay** ❸ (see p. 120) at No. 11 on the left side of the street; note the keel-shaped roof of the Swedish Cultural Center next door, where the governess of Marie-Antoinette's children once lived. The courtyard of No. 13 is particularly exquisite in summer.

Take a left on Rue du Parc-Royal, opposite Square Léopold Achille, and continue to Place de Thorigny. The **Hôtel Libéral Bruant** at 1 rue de la Perle used to have a lock museum with locks, door handles, and metal fastenings from Roman times to the belle époque. It now hosts

- ⊠ See also area map p. 105
- ▶ Place de la Bastille
- ⏱ Allow 3 hours
- ⟺ 1.5 miles (2.4 km)
- ▶ Rue des Rosiers

a contemporary art center. Take a right onto Rue de Thorigny for the **Musée Picasso** ❹ (see pp. 110–111). Backtrack and continue down Rue de la Perle, taking a detour onto Rue Vieille-du-Temple (left) to see the 18th-century **Hôtel de Rohan** ❺, home to part of the National Archives. Walk along Rue des Quatre-Fils (the continuation of Rue de la Perle after the Vieille-du-Temple intersection) toward the **Hôtel Guénégaud** ❻ on the right. This 17th-century mansion, now the Musée de la Chasse et de la Nature–Museum of Hunting and Nature *(62 rue des Archives, tel 01 53 01 92 40, chassenature.*

org, closed Mon., Métro: Rambuteau), with its small, beautiful formal garden, is the only Mansart-designed *hôtel particulier* still fully intact. It is due to reopen in October 2020, after renovation.

Gateway to Rue des Rosiers

Turn left on Rue des Archives—No. 58 is the great **Porte Clisson** ❼ (built between 1372 and 1375), flanked by two Gothic turrets. Built on Templar grounds, it was the gateway to the manor house of Olivier de Clisson, Constable of France and companion-in-arms to the warrior Du Guesclin, and it is one of the city's oldest remaining structures. The Guise family, the most powerful in the Marais, obtained the mansion in the 16th century, using it as their headquarters during the Wars of Religion; the St. Bartholomew's Day Massacre (see p. 22) was probably plotted here. The mansion was reconstructed by François de Rohan, Prince of Soubise, and the Clisson gateway was incorporated. In the early 19th century, the mansion became state

---

Housing the History of France

Former French president Nicolas Sarkozy wanted to turn the stately Hôtel de Rohan, home to part of the Archives Nationales, into a museum on the history of France. But virulent debate among historians about which version of French history to present delayed its opening, and the idea was quietly dropped by the new Socialist government. Luckily for visitors, the gardens in the center of this block of aristocratic mansions have been renovated and opened to the public. Each of the four gardens is different, with many romantic nooks and crannies, and even an artificial stream to provide soothing sound effects. Enter to the right of the entrance to the National Archives in the Hôtel de Soubise.

INSIDER TIP:

L'As du Falafel on Rue des Rosiers has the best falafel sandwiches in town, including chickpea fritters, hummus, pickled cabbage, and harissa.

—BARBARA A. NOE
National Geographic Travel Books senior editor

---

property, and Napoleon annexed Rue des Quatre-Fils and Rue des Archives to store the national archives in 1808.

Take a left on Rue des Francs-Bourgeois. On the right at No. 55 is the Mont de Piété or **Crédit Municipal,** a government-run pawnshop, auction house, and bank created in 1777. Enter the courtyard on the right to see one of Philippe-Auguste's 20 towers from the 800-year-old wall, preserved thanks to Victor Hugo's intervention. Continue to the graceful Renaissance-style tower on the corner of Rue Vieille-du-Temple and Rue des Francs-Bourgeois, home of Jehan Hérouet, Louis XII's treasurer.

Turn right onto Rue Vieille-du-Temple, which has a stupendous door facade (No. 47) with Renaudin's Medusa head, the entrance to the Hôtel Amelot de Bisseuil, also known as the **Hôtel des Ambassadeurs de Hollande** ❽, where Beaumarchais lived and wrote *The Marriage of Figaro.* Although never an embassy, it was from 1720 to 1727 home to a Protestant chaplain from the Dutch embassy, who held services after the Edict of Nantes was revoked. One of Benjamin Franklin's relatives was wed here, and Madame Necker, the future Madame de Staël, a Protestant, was baptized here in 1766. Knock and you may be permitted inside to see a 1660 bas-relief of "Romulus and Remus" and four large sundials on the walls.

As you exit, turn right and then left onto **Rue des Rosiers** ❾ (see p. 112), the heart of the medieval Jewish Quarter. Traces of the Philippe-Auguste Wall can be found at Nos. 8, 10, and 14.

PLACE DE LA BASTILLE

The golden spirit of liberty gleams in the sun by day, and the illuminated July Column (Colonne de Juillet) shines beaconlike at night. Place de la Bastille is not significant for what stands here today—cafés, movie theaters, and an opera house (Opéra Bastille) that looks like a beached silver whale—but for its history. Intended as a square for the people, it is still the scene of many political and social demonstrations and it has just been redesigned to include a large walking area.

Every year, on July 14, the entire city celebrates Bastille Day, with major fireworks held on the 13th and street dances and a military parade along the Champs-Élysées on the 14th.

The original eight-towered fortress, now destroyed, with its moat, drawbridge, and crenellated walls, was built during the 14th century to ward off English attacks from the east and protect the Hôtel St.-Pol (Charles V's residence). The Café Français *(3 place de la Bastille)* now stands where the medieval gate was. Pinkish cobblestones indicate the precise location of the Bastille, which never played a military role except during the Fronde (see p. 24); instead, it was a State prison from the days of Cardinal Richelieu.

A series of illustrious figures were imprisoned here in the 17th and 18th centuries, in surprisingly comfortable conditions—the Cardinal de Rohan hosted a dinner party for 20 here; the Marquis de Sade had his own wine brought in from Provence; and Voltaire praised the food upon his release. Because the prison was expensive to run, Necker, Minister of Finance to Louis XVI, planned to tear down the Bastille (and replace it with Place Louis XVI), but Revolutionary fervor did it for him.

■ **The July Column stands in front of the opera house.**

The July Column

The July Column was inspired by Trajan's column in Rome and commemorates those who died during the July 1830 revolution. Beneath the column is a gallery where victims' remains from the 1830 and 1848 revolutions lie. ■

Place de la Bastille

🅼 Map p. 105
🚇 Métro: Bastille

More Places to Visit in Le Marais & Bastille

Bassin de l'Arsenal

Leisure boats are docked in a basin that occupies what used to be part of the ancient moats of the Bastille. The southern extremity of Canal St.-Martin (see sidebar p. 210) rises from underneath Place de la Bastille, flanked by a lovely garden on the eastern bank.

▲ Map p. 105 ✉ Between Boulevards Bourdon & de la Bastille 🚇 Métro: Bastille

---

INSIDER TIP:

Take a canal ride with Canauxrama [*canauxrama.com*] beneath the Place de la Bastille to Parc de la Villete.

—BARBARA A. NOE
National Geographic Travel Books senior editor

Hôtel de Sens

One of the few great medieval private residences in Paris, this beautiful, half-civilian, half-military mansion (circa 1475) overlooking the Seine provides a fine example of the transitional period between Gothic and Renaissance styles. The architect remains unknown, although it was possibly a joint project of Tristan de Salazar, Archbishop of Sens at the time, and Martin Chambiges, who designed the transept for Sens

cathedral. In 1605 Henri IV housed his former wife, Queen Margot, here. The gable next to the tower on the left still holds the orange-size shell that was lobbed at the mansion during the 1830 Revolution.

The City of Paris purchased the Hôtel de Sens in 1911 and began to restore it in 1929. In 1961 it was turned into the Forney Library of Decorative and Fine Arts; its stunning reading room is open to the public. *paris.fr*

▲ Map p. 105 ✉ 1 rue du Figuier
☎ 01 42 78 14 60 🕒 Closed Sun.–Mon.
💲 Free; special exhibits € 🚇 Métro: St.-Paul, Pont Marie

Musée Cognacq-Jay

The museum, with its collection of 18th-century European paintings and furniture, was assembled by Ernest Cognacq and his wife, Louise Jay (founders of the Samaritaine department store). All of the objects were part of Cognacq's personal collection, which was bequeathed to the City of Paris in 1928 and includes works by Fragonard, Boucher, Chardin, Reynolds, Guardi, Canaletto, and Watteau. There is also an extremely rare collection of jeweled and enameled snuffboxes. *museecognacqjay.paris.fr*

▲ Map p. 105 ✉ Hôtel Donon, 8 rue Elzévir ☎ 01 40 27 07 21 🕒 Closed Mon.
💲 Free; special exhibits € 🚇 Métro: St.-Paul

EXPERIENCE: Dancing at the Firehouse

The traditional thing to do in Paris on Bastille Day is to go to a *bal des pompiers* (firemen's ball), which are held in firehouse courtyards on the evenings of July 13 and 14. The most popular are held in the *casernes* (firehouses) at 21 rue du Jour (near Les Halles), 7 rue de Sévigné (in the Marais), and 28 rue Blanche (near Pigalle). Most of these balls are like big open-air clubs with music provided by

DJs, rather than the corny accordion bands of the firemen's balls of the past. Go early (around 8 p.m.) to avoid waiting in long lines. The firemen ask for a small entry donation and sell drinks at reasonable prices.

If you manage to last the pace and stay until closing time at 4 a.m., you may well see a few spontaneous stripteases, both male and female.

One of the world's largest museums, and the premier attraction
in a stately neighborhood built up through centuries of royal rule

THE LOUVRE &
PALAIS-ROYAL

■ Detail of the Pont Alexandre III

THE LOUVRE & PALAIS-ROYAL

The monarchy may be long gone, but almost everything in this neighborhood is a reminder of centuries of royal rule. Although the Louvre is now a museum, it was originally constructed as a fortress to protect Paris from foreign invaders. For nearly 600 years it was the royal residence; each king (and emperor, for that matter) altered, expanded, and renovated the work of his predecessors.

As the palace expanded, so did its surrounding streets. The gardens were extended westward; the Tuileries Palace was constructed outside the old city walls, then linked to the Louvre; the Palais-Royal, a former royal residence (see p. 141), was built; and Rue de Rivoli (see p. 142) was laid out.

As the Louvre museum was formed from royal collections, so the Bibliothèque Nationale (see p. 165) began as a royal library, when Charles V brought his personal library of 973 works to the palace in 1373. After being stored in a lavish palace on Rue de Richelieu, the library outgrew its original premises; the books have been transferred to the new Bibliothèque de France (on Quai de la Gare), which opened in 1997, while prints, photographs, maps, and musical scores remain in the older building.

During the 19th century, France wavered between royal rule and revolution, and much of the action was staged in and around the Louvre. Louis XVI was held captive in the Tuileries Palace before being beheaded, and revolutionaries gathered in the Palais-Royal gardens, where the first call to arms was sounded. During the Commune of 1870–71, the Tuileries Palace, the symbol of royal oppression, was burned down. Afterward, a relative peace settled over Paris, and this neighborhood once again attracted the rich and fashionable.

Although the streets are now lined with tourist shops, a few exclusive establishments remain. It is easy to escape the noise of the nearby streets in the Jardin des Tuileries (see p. 137), or the even more discreet gardens of the Palais-Royal, which are completely shut off from traffic.

The Louvre has been revived both above and below ground. I. M. Pei's controversial 1989 pyramid was the first of many manifestations of this major face-lift. An entire subterranean city stretches out beyond the museum, with the Carrousel du Louvre—a vast, elegant, underground complex, complete with shops, parking, and a food court. An inverted glass

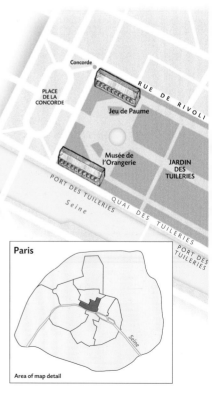

pyramid echoes Pei's main entrance, providing light to the entire underground area.

The Tuileries gardens lie west of the Louvre toward the Place de la Concorde and the 8th arrondissement. Two museums flank the gardens, overlooking the Concorde: the Jeu de Paume, now an exhibition center for photography; and the Orangerie (see p. 140), which houses Monet's famous water lilies paintings and a range of other Impressionist artworks. ■

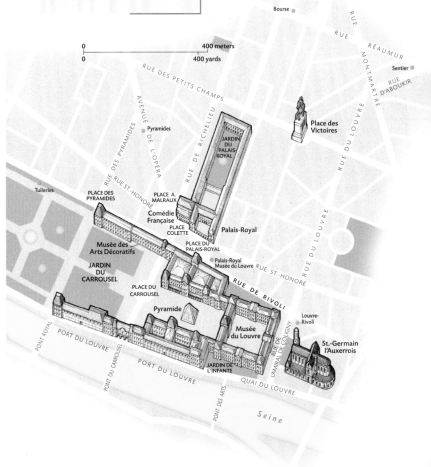

MUSÉE DU LOUVRE

The huge "Grand Louvre" modernization project, initiated by President François Mitterrand in 1981, has transformed this magnificent museum both inside and out. The first step was I. M. Pei's glass pyramid, which created space, light, and a much needed main entrance; the next steps reorganized the collections and exhibition spaces.

■ I. M. Pei's once controversial glass pyramid marks the main entrance to the Louvre museum.

The Louvre began in 1190, when King Philippe-Auguste built a massive fortress surrounded by a wall and towers on the western edge of Paris before setting out on a crusade. In the 14th century, Charles V commissioned Raymond du Temple to turn the medieval keep into a royal residence. It expanded under two visionary Renaissance builders: Kings François I, who tore down the medieval keep; and Henri IV, who constructed the immense gallery bordering the Seine, thus linking the Louvre to the Tuileries Palace, begun in 1564 by Catherine de Médicis. The Louvre consisted of a string of buildings that stretched over a quarter of a mile along the Seine—a long passageway linking the city palace to the country home. (At that time the Tuileries lay beyond the city walls.)

In 1608, Henri IV opened up the palace to artists, granting them studio space, living quarters, and the status of official recognition. When Louis XIV moved his court to Versailles in 1682, the Louvre was overrun by sculptors, painters, and architects who left the palace in a pathetic state by the mid-18th century. Among them were Jean Honoré Fragonard, Jean Chardin, François Boucher, and Guillaume Coustou, who, along with Antoine Coysevox, sculpted the famous "Horses of Marly," now wonderfully displayed in the glass-covered Cour Marly.

In 1793 the Musée Central des Arts was inaugurated at the Louvre, which then opened as a museum, marking a turning point in its history. Napoleon III realized Henri IV's dream of constructing the Richelieu Wing to mirror the Galerie du Bord de l'Eau.

The Louvre had finally achieved a state of architectural symmetry, but it didn't last long: The Tuileries Palace enclosing its western edge was burned to the ground in 1871 by the Commune.

The Louvre and its collection of royal artwork survived, the latter growing through donations and acquisitions. The museum's antiquities departments flourished in the 19th century, as excavations sponsored by the government unearthed treasures in Egypt and the Middle East. Under questionable terms, the archaeological finds were divided between the various countries involved. This form of looting was justified by the argument that without outside intervention, these prized works faced almost certain destruction.

I. M. Pei's controversial pyramid shocked many when it was unveiled in 1989 as the new main entrance to the museum, yet it is in keeping with a long tradition—architects have always been faced with the problem of integrating the palace's disparate elements.

INSIDER TIP:

Keep kids from melting down by following one of the "thematic trails" outlined on the activities section of the Louvre's website.

—PATRICIA DANIELS
National Geographic contributor

The Collections

The Louvre's collections are divided into seven departments, displayed in three main sections: Sully (the Cour Carrée); Richelieu (enclosing the wing parallel to Rue de Rivoli); and Denon (the wing along the Seine), each accessible from the main entrance beneath the pyramid.

Despite the organization, the Louvre can be a daunting and tiring experience. On a first visit, pick up one of the free maps or the guidebook "Louvre First Visit" in the main hall and choose a few works of art or periods before setting out (for example, the "Winged Victory of Samothrace" and the "Mona Lisa").

Start in the Sully Wing, at the foundations of Philippe-Auguste's medieval keep—it's in the heart of the Louvre, kids love it, and it leads straight to the Egyptian rooms.

Musée du Louvre

🗺 Map p. 123

✉ Main entrance: Pyramide du Louvre, Cour Napoléon. Other entrances: Galerie du Carrousel, Porte des Lions (often closed; call first)

☎ 01 40 20 53 17

🕐 Open 9 a.m.–6 p.m. Closed Tues., Jan. 1, May 1, Dec. 25. Open until 9:45 p.m. Wed., Fri., & first Sat. of each month. Rooms closed on a rotating basis (check before visiting).

💲 €€€. Free 1st Sat. of each month 6 p.m.–9:45 p.m., always for under 18 & EU residents under 26, Fri. from 6 p.m. for all under 26. Guided tour: €€€. Audio guide: €€. To avoid long lines, purchase tickets in advance online (ticketlouvre.fr) or at FNAC sales outlets in France.

🚇 Métro: Palais-Royal Musée du Louvre

louvre.fr

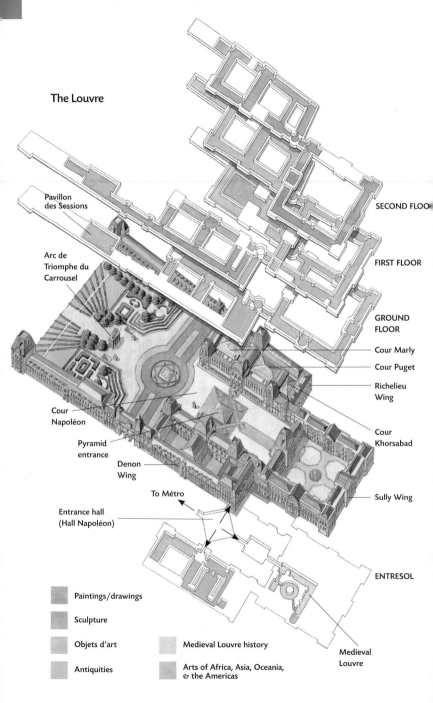

The Louvre

Pavillon des Sessions

Arc de Triomphe du Carrousel

SECOND FLOOR

FIRST FLOOR

GROUND FLOOR

Cour Marly

Cour Puget

Richelieu Wing

Cour Napoléon

Cour Khorsabad

Pyramid entrance

Denon Wing

Sully Wing

To Métro

Entrance hall (Hall Napoléon)

ENTRESOL

Medieval Louvre

Paintings/drawings

Sculpture

Objets d'art

Medieval Louvre history

Antiquities

Arts of Africa, Asia, Oceania, & the Americas

■ Sphinx-like statues are part of the Louvre's enormous Egyptian collection.

Antiquities

The Louvre's Egyptian treasures are displayed in the Denon Wing and in Rooms 1–30 of the Sully Wing. Greek, Etruscan, and Roman antiquities are found on the entresol and ground floors of Denon and on the ground and first floors of Sully (Rooms A, B, and 1–44).

Egyptian Department: For years, this collection of nearly 55,000 objects (of which about one-tenth is exhibited), the largest collection of Egyptian antiquities after the Cairo Museum, was cramped for space. The renovated and expanded section is now worthy of these masterpieces, which are so rich that curators have created a twofold display. The ground floor (Rooms 1–19) is arranged thematically and the upper floor (Rooms 20–30) is organized chronologically,

from prehistory to the Roman conquest.

The first few rooms are devoted to specific aspects of Egyptian life—writing, fishing, farming, music, games, jewelry, and funeral rituals. A spectacular room follows, with a row of 20-foot-high (7 m) palm- and papyrus-shaped columns of pink granite and huge statues of

French Father of Egyptology

Jean François Champollion (1790–1832) is considered the French father of Egyptology. He played a major role in deciphering the hieroglyphic text of the Rosetta Stone, thereby unlocking the mysteries of the Egyptian language. He was appointed the Louvre Egyptian Department's first curator in 1826.

Ramses II (Room 12). This room contains one of the loveliest of the many friezes of the collection, a limestone relief of Ramses II among the gods (1275 B.C., 19th dynasty). The world of the dead is displayed in the dramatic Crypt of Osiris (Room 13), providing an informative overview of Egyptian religious practices. The exhibits on this floor also include animal mummies—from an 8-foot (3 m) crocodile to a tiny, mummified scarab.

INSIDER TIP:

In the Louvre basement, you'll find the remains of the original royal castle—including the dungeon—dating from 1190 to the 16th century.

—BARBARA A. NOE
National Geographic Travel Books
senior editor

The collection continues in chronological order on the first floor. The first object is one of the oldest: a predynastic ivory dagger from Gebel El-Arak. This sophisticated ceremonial knife was sculpted more than 5,000 years ago. The following rooms trace the rise of the First Kingdom, the era in which the pyramids were built, the cult of the pharaoh grew, and a centralized government developed. "The Seated Scribe" is in this section (Room 22), as well as a radiant, surprisingly tender, wooden sculpture, "Anonymous

Couple." The famous Amarna period is illustrated by a colossal statue of Akhenaten (Room 25). Although his reign lasted only 16 years, and his capital Amarna was destroyed, the pharaoh's influence can be seen in the more lifelike, expressive art of later dynasties. The New Kingdom (1554–1075 B.C.) was a golden age for the arts in ancient Egypt, especially during the reigns of the Tuthmoses, Amenophis, and Ramsesid kings, as illustrated by the painted limestone relief of Seti I and the goddess Hathor (Room 27).

The Greco-Roman period began in 332 B.C. with the conquest by Alexander the Great, ending a period of Egyptian rule that lasted over 3,000 years. Room 29 contains one of the last masterpieces of Egyptian art, a magnificent gold jewel representing the triad of Osiris (god of the dead), Isis (goddess of the throne), and Horus (god in the form of a falcon), their son.

To continue this chronological tour, visit the sections devoted to Egypt under Roman control and to Coptic art on the entresol level in the Denon Wing. There are a number of funerary statues and mummies, as well as the striking funerary portraits from Faiyum. On the opposite side of the Cour Visconti is the collection of Coptic art, dating from the early centuries of the Christian era.

Among the Louvre's most obscure treasures are the Coptic fabrics that date from the second century A.D. and include the brilliantly colored, complex "Sabine Shawl." The Bawit Room contains

Etymology of "Louvre"

No one knows the origin of the word "Louvre," or *Lupara* in Latin. Theories suggest it came from the words for leper house, watchtower, or Saxon fortress, or that it was named for a pack of wolves *(loups)* that lurked in the area.

a reconstruction of the Coptic Church of Bawit (sixth–seventh centuries A.D.), discovered in 1900, and now believed to represent only a small part of the original monastery's structure.

Greek Antiquities: Two lovely women reign over this department: the "Venus de Milo" and the "Winged Victory of Samothrace." The former may be more famous, but the latter is quite simply breathtaking. She stands ready to take flight from the top of the monumental staircase in the Denon Wing, looking as though she had been sculpted by the wind.

The Louvre's collection stretches from preclassical Greece to the final years of the Roman Empire. The section devoted to the preclassical era has several remarkable examples from the Geometric (650–480 B.C.) and Archaic (circa 900 B.C.) periods. The Cycladic sculptures are especially striking: The pared-down, almost abstract idols look like sculptures from our own century.

Antiquities from the classical and Hellenistic periods are on the ground floor of the Sully Wing (Rooms 7–17). During the classical period, the reputation of Greek artists spread, and they were in demand from Persia to Rome. Figures came to life—for example, in the Frieze of the Panathenaic Procession, 447–406 B.C. (Room 6), as artists explored ideals of beauty, form, and emotional expression.

The Hellenistic period began with the death of Alexander the Great and the breakup of his immense empire. This period ushered in a more experimental style, and sculptors worked to capture a broader range of human experience and movement. The "Winged Victory of Samothrace," which commemorated a naval victory, is an incomparable example

■ The Louvre's "Venus de Milo" is almost as famous for what she lacks (arms) as for what she has (grace and beauty).

of this command of motion. It is dated at 190 B.C., but was discovered in 1863. The sensuality, dignity, and simplicity of the "Venus de Milo" (Room 16), circa 100 B.C., on the other hand, echoes the ideals of the earlier classical era.

The Greek collection continues on the first floor, with displays of bronzes and stoneware (Rooms 32–44). Among the fine works is a cache of 109 pieces of silver and

Treasures in Wartime

Evacuated during World Wars I and II, the Louvre's treasures were packed up in unmarked crates and moved to safety (many works went to the Château de Chambord in the Loire Valley). During World War II, almost all the works had left Paris by September 1, 1939.

gold found at Boscoreale, near Pompeii (Room 33), as well as the collection of Greek ceramics in the Campana Gallery (Rooms 39–44). No examples of Greek painting have survived, but these vases, from the geometric-style funerary urns and amphorae of the eighth century B.C. to the classical masterpieces, give some indication of what it may have looked like. The golden age of Greek pottery was from the mid-sixth to the mid-fifth century B.C., with the development of the so-called red-figure technique (replacing the earlier black-figure technique). A krater (bowl for mixing wine and

water) illustrated by Euphronios (510 B.C.) in Room 43 shows the refinement in painting at this time, with attention to anatomical detail and emotional expression.

Etruscan Antiquities:
There's something intriguing about the distant, cheerful smiles on the faces of many Etruscan sculptures, and their civilization remains a compelling mystery. It thrived for ten centuries, from about 1000 B.C. to the early years of the Christian era, and was the most sophisticated culture in pre-Roman Italy. Although the Etruscans thrived at the same time as the Greeks, they developed a unique artistic style. This was revealed in their skill with bronze- and metalworking, and is best seen in their delicate jewelry and elegant bronze mirrors.

The painted terra-cotta "Sarcophagus of a Married Couple" (Denon Wing, Room 18) is another of the Louvre's masterpieces; equality between husband and wife was one of the more extraordinary aspects of Etruscan society; women had more independence than anywhere else in classical antiquity.

Roman Antiquities:
Although Roman artists constantly copied Greek sculptures, their art was more than just a watered-down version of Hellenistic Greek art. The Roman Empire encompassed many different countries and cultures, and Rome itself was filled with foreign artists. They integrated

elements from both the Etruscan and Greek cultures, adapting the styles to their own more factual concerns, namely the glorification of the State and the great patrician families.

Portraiture took on a new dimension in Roman art, as the classical ideal of abstract beauty was replaced by more realistic and representative images. Portraits were so popular that the heads were often sculpted separately and placed on a kind of standard-issue body (for example, the statue of "Augustus," Room 23).

Wealthy Romans decorated their homes with lavish frescoes and mosaics. The fourth-century mosaic on the floor of Room 31 once decorated the Constantine Villa near Antioch.

Near Eastern Antiquities:
Covering northern Africa to the borders of India, the Near Eastern antiquities encompass the world's earliest known civilizations. From these societies sprang many technological and philosophical inventions—wheeled vehicles, astronomical models, musical systems, and the birth of writing. Of special interest is the set of laws (recorded in the Code of Hammurabi exhibit in the Cour Khorsabad, Room 3) that formed the basis of the Greek and Roman legal systems.

The Louvre's collection covers four distinct regions and periods: Mesopotamia; ancient Iran; the Levant (all located on the ground floor in the Richelieu and Sully Wings; Rooms A–D and 1–21); and the Islamic arts (which now

■ The "Mona Lisa" holds court in the newly renovated Salle de la Joconde (Salle des États).

have their own space in the Cour Visconti in the Denon Wing). Most of the displays came from 19th-century French excavations that unearthed long-lost palaces and cities, including the winged bulls from the palace of King Sargon II of Assyria (720 B.C.) and the winged archers and bull-headed capitals from the palace of Darius in Susa (late sixth century B.C.).

Painting

The Louvre's paintings are divided into four sections: French works from the 14th through the 19th centuries, Italian, Northern European, and other European paintings.

EXPERIENCE: To Your Brushes!

Visitors to Paris often have the urge to do what the Impressionists did: set up an easel *en plein air* and paint the passersby, the bridges over the Seine, and the city's famous pearly gray light. For those who would like some guidance, a number of specialist schools offer both indoor and outdoor courses in the arts.

Painting in the Place du Tertre, Montmartre

Artist and French teacher **Brigitte Isaeff** *(tel 06 73 54 07 52, brigitte-isaeff-language-learning.blogspot.com, €€€)* has had the bright idea of killing two birds with one stone by teaching French through art study. After a presentation and discussion of the work of a few French artists, students do their own artworks and discuss them in six half-day classes.

The **Atelier Alupi** *(18 rue Pernety, tel 06 78 26 82 94, atelieralupi.com, €€€€)* has ongoing courses in drawing and painting, but visitors can attend as few or as many sessions as they like. Its one-day or one-week Paris Cityscape Art Workshop takes students into the streets to paint in the city's food markets, for example, or on bridges over the Seine. Both beginners and established artists of all ages are welcome to join the small groups.

The **Paris American Academy** *(275 rue St. Jacques, tel 01 44 41 99 20, parisamericanacademy.fr, €€€€)* offers an intensive four-week summer workshop in fine arts (painting and drawing), with both studio courses and sketching sessions in museums, parks, markets, and the streets to allow students to copy famous artworks and draw from life.

For experienced artists who want an atmospheric place to draw from a life model and meet other artists, the **Académie de la Grande Chaumière** *(14 rue de la Grande Chaumière, tel 01 43 26 13 72, academie grandechaumiere.com)* is an open studio in Montparnasse where Modigliani and Gauguin once sat on the same wooden stools still used today. Just show up with your materials *(check website or call for hours, €€€€).*

Visitors who prefer to see the sights through a lens might want to improve their photography skills at the **Spéos Paris Photographic Institute** *(8 rue Jules-Vallès, tel 01 40 09 18 58, speos.fr, €€€€€),* which offers a variety of summer workshops suitable for visitors, with courses on portrait, studio, and commercial photography and more.

Those who want to learn more about art but aren't interested in practicing themselves can choose from the lectures and museum visits offered by **Paris Art Studies** *(14 boulevard Saint-Martin, tel 06 86 58 98 09, parisartstudies. com, €€€)* and given by art historian Chris Boïcos, who has garnered a loyal following of Anglophones who admire his inspired lectures.

French Painting: The French paintings on the first floor of the Denon Wing and the second floor of the Sully and Richelieu Wings cover every major period, from the early medieval and Renaissance periods through the mid-19th century. (Works after this date are found in the Musée d'Orsay; see pp. 180–184.) The collection starts with the oldest surviving easel painting, "Portrait of Jean le Bon" (circa 1350; Richelieu, Room 1). The Renaissance came to France via King Charles VIII and King François I (portrait of François I by Jean Clouet, Room 7). Although Italy and France battled incessantly, the French kings easily admitted the superiority of Italian culture, bringing both its art and artists (such as Leonardo da Vinci) back to France. French painting in the 17th century moved toward realism, illustrated especially in Room 24 (Sully) with Georges de la Tour's "The Cheat."

Rooms 50–73 concentrate on the first half of the 19th century. The last few rooms (63–73) contain landscapes by painters like Jean-Baptiste Corot, who prefigured the Impressionists.

The French collection does not end with this chronological sequence, however; large-format paintings hanging in two adjoining rooms (75 and 77) in the Denon Wing (first floor) illustrate the two conflicting schools of painting in the 19th century—Neoclassicism and Romanticism. Painters clashed over the merits of the two: the idealized, cold, and rational beauty of the first (represented by Jacques-Louis David, the court chronicler for the Napoleonic era, in "The Oath of the Horatii," 1784, and "The Coronation of Napoleon I," 1804), and the emotion and individualism of the latter (as spearheaded by Eugène Delacroix in "The Death of Sardanapalus," 1827). The Romantics sought their subjects from contemporary events: Théodore Géricault created a scandal by illustrating an actual shipwreck in "Raft of the Medusa" (Room 77), with its themes of treachery and cannibalism.

INSIDER TIP:

Stop in Magasin Sennelier *[3 quai Voltaire]* to buy art supplies where Cézanne, Gauguin, Monet, and Picasso got their brushes and paints.

—JUSTIN KAVANAGH
*National Geographic
Travel Books editor*

European Painting: Northern European painting is exhibited in the Richelieu Wing, and includes 15th-century Dutch works by Jan van Eyck. The Galerie Médicis contains a rather overwhelming series of canvases (nearly 330 square yards, or 275 square meters) by Peter Paul Rubens, created for the Luxembourg Palace, ordered by Marie de Médicis. There are also works by Rembrandt van Rijn, including the lovely "Bathsheba," and two masterpieces by Jan Vermeer, "The Lacemaker" and "The Astronomer."

The Italian collection (Denon Wing, first floor, Rooms 1–13) begins with the painters Giovanni Cimabue and Giotto (Room 3), whose work profoundly influenced the development of the Renaissance. Thirty years after Cimabue's "Virgin and Child," Giotto's "Saint Francis of Assisi Receiving the Stigmata" created a new style, placing more realistic figures within space and using basic notions of perspective (defined by Filippo Brunelleschi in the 1420s). The collection continues with the Quattrocento artists: Paolo Uccello, Andrea Mantegna, and Domenico Ghirlandaio.

There are several paintings by Leonardo da Vinci in the Grande Galerie: "The Virgin of the Rocks" and "Saint John the Baptist," for example, that are just as intriguing as the "Mona Lisa" (the first has gained much attention since it was featured in the *The Da Vinci Code*). One room is dedicated entirely to the "Mona Lisa" (typically barricaded by crowds) and Veronese's colossal work "Marriage Feast at Cana," surrounded by other Italian Renaissance masterpieces.

Sculpture

Even on a gloomy day, the Marly and Puget courtyards, covered by skylights, create an ideal setting for outdoor sculpture. Those in the Cour Marly were created for Louis XIV's private château at Marly. During the Revolution, the "Horses of Marly" were placed on the Place de la Concorde, but they were moved to the Louvre in 1984; cast models now stand in their original setting.

French sculpture begins in rooms around the Cour Marly with works from the 12th century and continues through the

French sculpture adorns the luminous Marly courtyard.

Romanesque and Gothic eras; many pieces came from French churches. One of the oddest is the actual-size funeral cortege of the 15th-century "Tomb of Philippe Pot" (Room 10), with eight hooded mourners bearing the deceased.

The Denon Wing houses a smaller collection of sculpture from Italy, Germany, the Netherlands, and Spain, including Michelangelo's two "Slaves" and other celebrated Italian works from the 16th and 17th centuries, such as Antonio Canova's "Psyche Revived by Cupid's Kiss."

Objets d'Art

The objets d'art collection contains works ranging from the Middle Ages through the 19th century. This includes everything from religious relics and enamels to tapestries, jewels, and furniture—the everyday items of the aristocracy. All are located on the first floor of the Richelieu and Sully Wings. The glittering Galerie d'Apollon has magnificent painted ceilings, and the rooms covering the reigns of Louis XIV, XV, and XVI have been beautifully renovated.

Among the Louvre's more obscure objets d'art are the Napoleon III apartments, which were opened to the public when the Finance Ministry moved to the Quai de Bercy.

Arts of Africa, Asia, Oceania, & the Americas

While most of the national collection of non-Western art is now in the Musée du Quai

Louvre Staff

A staff of 2,000—curators, guards, and technical specialists, among others—keeps the Louvre running. Sixty curators watch over the 460,000 works of art, of which only about 38,000 are on display at any one time.

Branly, the crème de la crème is in the Louvre's little-visited Pavillon des Sessions (enter through the Porte des Lions if open). Its 108 magnificent sculptures are a reminder of the importance of "primitive" art, with such masterpieces as a carved ivory horn from the Sapi culture in Sierra Leone (15th or 16th century); a long, spindly Zulu wooden spoon with a highly abstracted human form (19th or early 20th century); and a monumental sculpted totem pole of the cannibal ogress Dzonoqwa from a Kwakiutl house in British Columbia (late 19th century).

Prints & Drawings

Temporary displays draw on this collection located on the first floor of the Denon Wing (Rooms 9–11), which has some 120,000 works—treasures such as illuminated manuscripts, drawings by Leonardo da Vinci, Delacroix's Moroccan sketchbook, and studies by Rembrandt. The Chalcographie shop, which sells engravings made from original copper plates, is located under the pyramid. ■

MUSÉE DES ARTS DÉCORATIFS

Le Musée des Arts Décoratifs, housed in the Rohan and Marsan Wings of the Louvre, is administered by Les Arts Décoratifs (formerly Union Centrale des Arts). Along with the rest of the Louvre, this museum has been redesigned to add more space; the new arrangement integrates the former Musée de la Mode et du Textile and Musée de la Pubilcité, now two of its seven thematic sections.

Rohan & Marsan Wings of the Louvre

🅰 Map p. 123
✉ Palais du Louvre, 107 rue de Rivoli
☎ 01 40 20 53 17
🕐 Closed Mon., Jan. 1, May 1, Dec. 25
💲 €€
🚇 Métro: Palais-Royal Musée du Louvre, Tuileries, Pyramides

madparis.fr

The Decorative Arts Museum, part of the Louvre since 1905, presents an extraordinarily rich collection of some 220,000 works—including ceramics and glassware, jewelry, wallpaper, drawings, and toys. Best of all is the Galerie des Bijoux, a dramatic glass bridge between two rooms; but don't miss the toy collection and chair display. The exhibition is arranged both thematically and chronologically, with five sections covering the Middle Ages and the Renaissance, the 17th-18th centuries, the 19th century, Art Nouveau and Art Deco, and the modern-contemporary period.

The former Fashion and Textile Museum's permanent collection, now making up one of the main departments of the Musée des Arts Décoratifs, explores major trends in fashion through the ages. Clothing from the 17th to the 19th centuries, fashion accessories, and rare fabrics are on display, as are major contributions from 20th-century haute couture artists and contemporary fashion designers. The curators rotate the collection with two thematic displays that are changed each year and a half.

The former Advertising Museum was created in 1978. Its collection comprises nearly 50,000 posters from around the world, ranging from the mid-18th century to 1949; in addition, it has 50,000 contemporary posters donated by agencies and designers, and 20,000 contemporary publicity films. The works are displayed through temporary exhibitions. ∎

EXPERIENCE: Spot Paris's Feathered Inhabitants

Bird-watchers do not have to leave Paris to give their binoculars a workout. The some 60 species that nest in the City of Light, including kingfishers and sparrow hawks, can be spotted everywhere from stadiums to urban parks of all sizes (such as the Tuileries gardens and the Bois de Vincennes), cemeteries, and vacant lots.

Over 150 species, including migrators, can be seen throughout the city. Many of them enjoy the same sites as tourists: The common kestrel (*Falco tinnunculus*), for example, prefers high-end real estate and builds nests in niches in Notre-Dame (you can often see them soaring around the spires), the Eiffel Tower, and Sacré-Coeur. One couple has even famously nested on the balcony of an apartment.

The most active of several local birders' associations, the **Délégation LPO Île-de-France** (*tel 01 53 58 58 38, www.lpo-idf.fr*), organizes numerous tours in and around Paris. Reservations are required. Website and tours are in French, but bird names are international!

JARDIN DES TUILERIES

The view west from the Louvre encompasses one of the most impressive alignments of monuments in any city. This symmetry starts with the Arc de Triomphe du Carrousel, framed by the two wings of the Louvre, and continues past the Luxor Obelisk at the Place de la Concorde to the Arc de Triomphe and the Grande Arche de La Défense, 5 miles (8 km) beyond.

■ The Jardin des Tuileries links the Louvre to the Place de la Concorde.

When the Tuileries was created by André Le Nôtre in 1666, it was outside the city walls—a place where aristocrats came to see and be seen and enjoy royal festivities and fireworks. As part of the Grand Louvre project, completed in late 1997, the adjoining gardens were given a face-lift to emphasize the east–west axis and link the new Louvre parvis (square) to the gardens on the west.

The original design, which called for a more formal garden near the Louvre, gradually becoming more wooded toward Place de la Concorde, was reinstated. The beginning of the gardens' eastern edge, marked by the Arc de Triomphe du Carrousel added by Napoleon, is enclosed within the long wings of the Louvre. Seen through this arch, the Luxor Obelisk (see p. 147) and the Arc de Triomphe are perfectly aligned. Replanting has restored Le Nôtre's original design, and cafés, pony rides, and a summer fair create a pleasure garden atmosphere.

Hidden away among hedges of yew near the Louvre is a sculpture garden with 20 bronzes by Aristide Maillol. ■

Jardin des Tuileries

🅰 Map pp. 122–123

🚇 Métro: Palais-Royal Musée du Louvre, Tuileries, Pyramides, Concorde

BRIDGES & QUAYS OF PARIS

Stand on the Pont de la Concorde at night, with the Assemblée Nationale illuminated at one end and the imposing Madeleine Church in the distance at the other, and you can see why Paris is called the City of Light. Or wander along the quays to explore the 36 other bridges spanning the Seine, where lovers, traffic, history, politics, and art all converge. The city's splendor and its traditions are reflected, quite literally, in the waters of the Seine.

The exuberant, ornate Pont Alexandre III was built in the late 19th century.

Paris's two islands, the Île de la Cité and the Île St.-Louis, are connected to the rest of the city by eight and five bridges respectively, with one footbridge—the Pont St.-Louis—joining the two islands behind Notre-Dame. The Pont de Sully, at the quaint eastern tip of the Île St.-Louis, took its name from the celebrated duke, minister, and friend of Henri IV, who masterfully directed the royal finances in the late 16th century.

Majestic Pont Neuf

Just west of the Latin Quarter, between the Quai des Grands Augustins and the Quai de la Mégisserie, sits the Pont Neuf with its 12 perfect arches. One of Paris's loveliest bridges, it is also the oldest remaining one—despite its name, which means "new bridge." It was inaugurated in 1607 under the direction of Henri IV, who is immortalized in bronze on horseback on the bridge. The Pont Neuf was the first bridge to be lined with sidewalks rather than dwellings, and became a fashionable strolling place. It has inspired countless artists: Auguste Renoir and Paul Signac painted it; Christo wrapped it in golden fabric; and Leos Carax made it the star of his film *Les Amants du Pont Neuf*.

Unusual & Artistic Bridges

The Pont des Arts, to the west, is a wooden footbridge that attracts the city's romantics, who have lately been defacing it with "love locks" (see sidebar p. 81).

The 348-foot-long (106 m) Passerelle Léopold-Sédar-Senghor links the Louvre complex with the Musée d'Orsay via the Jardin des Tuileries. The metal arched-suspension bridge includes a two-tiered walkway built from exotic wood; it is the only Parisian bridge accessible from both the river and street levels.

Winged horses, cherubs, nymphs, gold-leaf swords (regilded for the 1989 bicentennial and repainted in gold in 1997), and other art nouveau details grace the Pont Alexandre III, Paris's most celebrated and photographed bridge. It was named after Tsar Alexander III, whose son laid the first stone in 1896 (see p. 149).

Cult Bridges: Pont de l'Alma & Pont de Bir-Hakeim

The area around the Pont de l'Alma and the tunnel that passes underneath it is heavily visited by tourists drawn to the site where Diana, Princess of Wales, was killed in 1997. The Pont de l'Alma has a sculpture of a Second Empire soldier, known as the Zouave, which is used to measure the level of the Seine. During the major flood of 1910, the water reached as high as his beard.

At the foot of the bridge on the Right Bank sits the gold-encrusted Statue of Liberty flame, cast from the original mold. A scale replica of the entire statue now greets river visitors to

■ Gilded details brighten the Pont Alexandre III, a highlight of boat trips on the Seine.

Paris as they sail under the Pont de Grenelle.

Farther west, the Seine is straddled by the gray-metal stanchions of the Pont de Bir-Hakeim. In the 1970s, it gained cultlike status with the movie *Last Tango in Paris*.

The sleek Charles de Gaulle bridge spans the Seine between the Pont d'Austerlitz and the Pont de Bercy, and the Passerelle Simone-de-Beauvoir footbridge links the Bibliothèque François Mitterrand with the Parc de Bercy.

EXPERIENCE: Getting Married in Paris

What could be more romantic than exchanging vows in the City of Light? French red tape and residency requirements make a civil ceremony difficult, so it is wise to have legal requirements taken care of at home and then arrange a church wedding (at the American Church, for example, or the American Cathedral) or a symbolic ceremony in Paris. A number of wedding planners can help organize weddings in spectacular settings, among them **Dreams in Paris**

(*dreams-in-paris.com*), **Fête in France** (run by two bilingual American women, *fetein france.com*), or **Perfect Paris Wedding** (*perfectpariswedding.com*). Or be creative and organize your own ceremony: For those on a tight budget, say "I do" on the Pont des Arts at sunset or on a Bateau-Mouche as it cruises the Seine, for example; for those on a bigger budget, rent out the **Musée Jacquemart-André** (*tel 01 45 62 16 40*), housed in an elegant 19th-century mansion.

AROUND THE TUILERIES

Flanking the Tuileries gardens are two small but important museums: the Musée de l'Orangerie, containing Impressionist masterpieces, and the Jeu de Paume, once tennis courts and now a center for photography exhibitions.

Musée de l'Orangerie

▲ Map p. 122

✉ Jardin des Tuileries, Place de la Concorde

☎ 01 44 77 80 07

🕐 Closed Tues.

💲 €€

🚇 Métro: Concorde

musee-orangerie.fr

Jeu de Paume

▲ Map p. 122

✉ Jardin des Tuileries, Place de la Concorde

☎ 01 47 03 12 50

🕐 Closed Mon.

💲 €€

🚇 Métro: Concorde

jeudepaume.org

Musée de l'Orangerie

Claude Monet's "Water Lilies" have made the Musée de l'Orangerie famous. However, this small gem of a museum also boasts 144 masterpieces by other School of Paris artists —from the Impressionists to artists of the 1930s.

The Orangerie building was constructed in 1852 as a winter shelter for the orange trees lining the Tuileries walkways. It now houses the remarkable Walter-Guillaume Collection. Paul Guillaume amassed this collection of works by the School of Paris

---

INSIDER TIP:

Rent a toy sailboat from one of the vendors and join in the fun of pushing it around the water of the Tuileries fountain.

—KENNY LING
National Geographic contributor

---

painters and opened a gallery in 1914 in Paris, enthusiastically supporting such avant-garde painters as Chaim Soutine and Maurice Utrillo. The exhibit reflects his pioneering stance as a collector and supporter of modern art, with 22 works by Soutine, and others by Cézanne, Matisse, Modigliani,

and Picasso. Guillaume's wife, Domenica, donated the works to the government in 1977 on condition that the paintings remain together.

Monet's "Water Lilies," in beautifully restored oval rooms, are the highlight. The French politician Georges Clemenceau helped Monet get the commission to paint these enormous murals in 1914 as a gift to France. Throughout World War I, Monet remained absorbed by the elusive patterns and luminous colors of this theme. The specially designed oval rooms containing the murals, often referred to as the Sistine Chapel of Impressionism, were inaugurated in 1927, less than a year after the painter's death.

Jeu de Paume

Napoleon III constructed the Jeu de Paume between 1861 and 1862 as an indoor tennis court. Used as an exhibition space in 1909, it was co-opted by the Nazis as a temporary storehouse for plundered art. Immediately after the war, it became one of the world's finest Impressionist museums. In 1986 the collection was moved to the Musée d'Orsay (see pp. 180–184), and its light, spacious rooms now house a photography and media arts center, with a range of exhibitions, previously the Galerie Nationale du Jeu de Paume. ■

PALAIS-ROYAL

The Palais-Royal was indeed a royal palace at one time. The original structure (not the gardens behind) was built by Cardinal Richelieu in 1636 and thus named the Palais Cardinal. Today it holds government offices and surrounds a quiet park.

■ Daniel Buren's black-and-white columns were added to the Palais-Royal in the 1980s.

Louis XIV lived here as a child for some time, before fleeing to escape the Fronde (see p. 24). He was never fond of Paris and was happy to hand over the city property to his brother, Philippe d'Orléans. Much to the disdain of Philippe's aristocratic kin, his deeply debt-ridden son (also named Philippe) went on to construct 180 arcades and shops on the site.

This new Palais-Royal opened with great fanfare in 1784 and soon drew merchants, intellectuals, and houses of ill repute. When the puritanically minded Louis-Philippe was crowned in 1830, he closed down this hotbed of vice, causing fashionable Parisians to move to other neighborhoods.

By the time Colette and Jean Cocteau had become residents (at 9 rue de Beaujolais and 36 rue de Montpensier, respectively), the gardens had become an island of serenity in the heart of Paris. The former palace, burned during the Commune and restored, is now home to government institutions.

The Palais-Royal's most recent controversy was the installation of Daniel Buren's black-and-white striped columns at the south end of the gardens. At the other end is one of Paris's loveliest restaurants, the elegant 18th-century Grand Véfour (see Travelwise p. 247). Between these, today's gardens form one of the city's most peaceful public parks, surrounded by quaint arcaded shops. ■

Palais-Royal

▲ Map p. 123

✉ Place du Palais-Royal

🚇 Métro: Palais-Royal Musée du Louvre

More Places to Visit in the Louvre & Palais-Royal

Comédie Française

The theater troupe inspired by the playwright Molière found a home in the 1790s next to the Palais-Royal and has remained there ever since, making it one of the world's oldest established theaters. Created in 1680 by Louis XIV, this state-subsidized company performs primarily classic and modern French plays, such as those by Molière, Racine, and Feydeau. However, in recent years newer playwrights, including Tennessee Williams, have taken their place among the classics (see Travelwise p. 262). *comedie-francaise.fr*

The St.-Germain l'Auxerrois church contains original Gothic structures.

Map p. 123 ✉ Place Colette
☎ 01 44 58 15 15 🚇 Métro: Palais-Royal Musée du Louvre

Place des Victoires

The Maréchal de la Feuillade, a fawning court follower, created this square solely as a backdrop for a gilded statue of Louis XIV. Melted down during the Revolution, the statue was replaced in 1822. Now mainly a quiet shopping area, the square's boutiques have been colonized by various Japanese designers, including Kenzo.

Map p. 123 🚇 Métro: Louvre-Rivoli, Bourse

Rue de Rivoli

Always packed with tourists because of its proximity to the Louvre, Rue de Rivoli was built by Napoleon to provide the city with another east–west axis to ease the traffic along the existing Rue St.-Honoré. The covered arcades, completed in 1835, were an innovation at the time, providing pedestrians with protection from both the weather and carriages. Today, souvenir shops share the elegant facades with old-time luxury hotels like Le Meurice. Two English bookshops, W. H. Smith and Galignani, are also here, as well as the Angelina tearoom at No. 226, famous in particular for its hot chocolate.

Map pp. 122–123 🚇 Métro: Concorde, Tuileries, Palais-Royal Musée du Louvre

St.-Germain l'Auxerrois

This church, opposite the eastern end of the Louvre, was the royal parish for the Valois kings while they resided in the palace across the street. Most of the original decoration has disappeared, with the exception of the superb Flamboyant Gothic porch (circa 1435), the only original one left in Paris.

Map p. 123 ✉ Place du Louvre
☎ 01 42 60 13 96 🚇 Métro: Louvre-Rivoli

The fabled avenue, long called the Triumphal Way, and its well-heeled neighbors

CHAMPS-ÉLYSÉES & 16TH ARRONDISSEMENT

Carvings from the Musée National des Arts Asiatiques-Guimet

CHAMPS-ÉLYSÉES &
16TH ARRONDISSEMENT

No first-time visitor to Paris wants to miss the mythical Champs-Élysées, the famous Arc de Triomphe, or the glitter of lights around the Place de la Concorde, which symbolize the French sense of grandeur in the most ostentatious way. A stroll through the nearby 16th arrondissement (see pp. 154–157) takes you to some handsome buildings and museums.

The Champs-Élysées area is a relatively recent neighborhood, developed mostly during the Second Empire (1852–1870). Under Napoleon III, Adolphe Alphand's gardens and parks (such as the Parc Monceau; see p. 158) transformed the western edge of Paris into a respectable, residential neighborhood.

The international heart of haute couture was created in Paris's 8th arrondissement by Englishman Charles Worth during the Second Empire, and is still firmly clustered around the Champs-Élysées.

The Rue du Faubourg St.-Honoré, running parallel to the Champs-Élysées to the north, is lined with art galleries and fine shops, including Hermès at No. 24 (leather goods, silk scarves, and clothes). At No. 55 is the Palais de l'Élysée, the official presidential residence since 1873. It is open to the public during the Journées des Patrimoine (National Heritage Weekend), usually around the third weekend of September.

16th Arrondissement

Much of the 16th arrondissement, especially near the Champs-Élysées, is occupied by banks, multinationals, overpriced hotels, and fashion designers. The southern part of this arrondissement, including the former villages of Passy and Auteuil, is just as snooty but still has a neighborly feel, however exclusive. Connoisseurs of art will enjoy the area's wealth of art nouveau and art deco buildings as well as the fabulous Impressionist collection at the Musée Marmottan-Monet. ∎

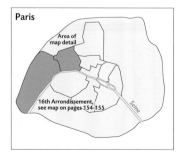

Paris

Area of map detail

16th Arrondissement, see map on pages 154–155

1 Théâtre des Champs-Élysées
2 Théâtre du Rond-Point **3** Théâtre
Marigny **4** Palais de l'Élysée
5 Musée Cernuschi

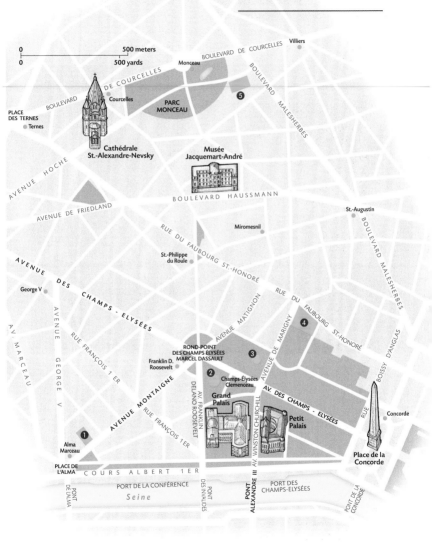

0   500 meters
0   500 yards

Villiers

BOULEVARD DE COURCELLES

Monceau

BOULEVARD DE COURCELLES

BOULEVARD

PLACE
DES TERNES

Courcelles

PARC
MONCEAU

5

BOULEVARD MALESHERBES

Ternes

Cathédrale
St.-Alexandre-Nevsky

Musée
Jacquemart-André

AVENUE HOCHE

BOULEVARD HAUSSMANN

St.-Augustin

AVENUE DE FRIEDLAND

Miromesnil

BOULEVARD MALESHERBES

RUE DU FAUBOURG ST-HONORÉ

St.-Philippe
du Roule

AVENUE DES CHAMPS - ELYSÉES

George V

RUE DU FAUBOURG ST-HONORÉ

AVENUE MATIGNON

AVENUE DE MARIGNY

4

RUE FRANÇOIS 1ER

AV. MARCEAU

AVENUE GEORGE V

ROND-POINT
DES CHAMPS ÉLYSÉES
MARCEL DASSAULT

3

BOISSY D'ANGLAS

Franklin D.
Roosevelt

2

Champs-Élysées
Clemenceau

AV. DES CHAMPS - ÉLYSÉES

Concorde

AVENUE MONTAIGNE

RUE FRANÇOIS 1ER

AV. FRANKLIN DELANO ROOSEVELT

Grand
Palais

Petit
Palais

RUE

1

AV. WINSTON CHURCHILL

Place de la
Concorde

Alma
Marceau

PLACE DE
L'ALMA

COURS ALBERT 1ER

PORT DE LA CONFÉRENCE

PORT DES
CHAMPS-ELYSÉES

Seine

PONT
DE L'ALMA

PONT
DES INVALIDES

PONT
ALEXANDRE III

PONT DE LA
CONCORDE

CHAMPS-ÉLYSÉES

Napoleon III returned from London determined to bring the space and greenery of British gardens to the French capital; employing Adolphe Alphand, he overhauled the Champs-Élysées. Once the promenade of elegant aristocrats and the bourgeoisie, its buildings today range from an elegant mansion, now the home of an auction house, to movie theaters, fast-food emporiums, airline agencies, and megastores.

■ A fountain at the Place de la Concorde frames a distant view of the Eiffel Tower.

Place de la Concorde

🗺 Map p. 145

Ⓜ Métro: Concorde

Place de la Concorde

Once the site of Revolutionary bloodbaths, today's Place de la Concorde is framed by the American Embassy and the luxurious Hôtel Crillon, and offers a breathtaking view up the Champs-Élysées toward the Arc de Triomphe.

The Place de la Concorde was laid out in 1757 by the royal architect Jacques-Ange Gabriel as a backdrop for an equestrian statue

of Louis XV. Paris's other royal squares (Place des Victoires and Place Dauphine, for example) were enclosed, but Gabriel constructed buildings on one side only, leaving intact the view from the Tuileries Palace up the Champs-Élysées to the Rond-Point. His two colonnaded buildings—now the Crillon hotel and the Hôtel de la Marine (where Marie-Antoinette once kept a secret apartment; reopened to the public in June

2020)—mirror the facade of the National Assembly across the river. Louis's statue was pulled down during the Revolution, and the Place Louis XV was rebaptized the Place de la Révolution. During the Terror, more than 1,200 people were guillotined here, including Louis XVI, Maximilien Robespierre, and Marie-Antoinette.

The Obelisk: After a series of name changes, the square was renamed the Place de la Con-corde in 1795. Louis-Philippe erected statues and fountains representing the great cities of France and placed a central monument in the square—a 3,300-year-old obelisk, a twin of the one that stands in front of the Temple of Luxor, given to France in 1829 by Egyptian viceroy Muhammad Ali.

Some 200,000 Parisians cheered as the engineer Le Bas and his 120-strong team raised the obelisk in 1836. Their exploit is recorded on the obelisk's base, which is the best place to appreciate the square's sweeping view of the Louvre's pyramid (to the east), and the Champs-Élysées extending west toward La Défense, framed by copies of the "Horses of Marly." The originals are now in the Louvre (see p. 125).

Champs-Élysées

When it was created by André Le Nôtre in 1667 for Louis XIV, the Champs-Élysées was meant to be a visual extension of the Tuileries gardens. It was not yet the classy neighborhood it was to become, and the fields and undergrowth served as a meet-ing place for the city's riffraff. The Champs-Élysées is divided into two sections: the pretty, garden-lined avenue that leads from Place de la Concorde to the Rond-Point, and the com-mercial area from the Rond-Point to the Arc de Triomphe.

In the 1830s, architect Jacques Hittorff began to transform this unpopulated area of Paris. Over 1,200 gas lamps were installed, and the area became a giant

Champs-Élysées

⬛ Map pp. 144–145

▦ Métro: Concorde, Champs-Élysées Clemenceau, Franklin D. Roosevelt, George V, Charles de Gaulle Étoile

Where to Slunch

Traditionally, the French are rigid in their eating habits: breakfast in the morning, lunch at 1 p.m., and supper (dinner) between 8 p.m. and 10:30 p.m. Trying to eat in a restaurant outside of those times has always been difficult. Those rules are breaking down in Paris, however, as outside influences change eating habits (American-style hamburgers are now ubiquitous). The latest trend is slunch (between supper and lunch, at around 5 p.m.), which comes in the form of a trayful of small dishes, all served at the same time for diners to choose from.

Just off the Champs-Élysées in the Grand Palais, the **Mini Palais** (*Avenue Winston Churchill, tel 01 42 56 42 42*), with a menu by superstar chef Eric Frechon, offers a gourmet slunch. For those who crave a real, high-quality American hamburger and/or who want to eat at anytime they feel like it between noon and 12:30 a.m. (1 a.m. on week-ends), that old faithful **Joe Allen** (*30 rue Pierre Lescot, tel 01 42 36 70 13*) is the best bet.

Grand Palais

▲ Map p. 145

✉ 3 avenue Général Eisenhower

☎ 01 40 13 48 00

🕐 Closed Tues.

$ €€€

Ⓜ Métro: Champs-Élysées Clemenceau

grandpalais.fr

Palais de la Découverte

✉ Avenue Franklin D. Roosevelt

☎ 01 56 43 20 20

🕐 Closed Mon., Jan. 1, May 1, July 14, Dec. 24

$ €€

Ⓜ Métro: Champs-Élysées Clemenceau, Franklin D. Roosevelt

palais-decouverte.fr

playground, filled with gardens, fountains, and restaurants. All that remains of these former pleasure pavilions are two expensive restaurants, Ledoyen (see Travelwise p. 250) and Laurent. The gardens of the **Palais de l'Élysée** (the presidential residence) border the northern edge of Avenue Gabriel.

During the 1914 Occupation of Paris, Russian troops set up camp along the Champs-Élysées, devastating the area; it took the city two years to repair the damage.

INSIDER TIP:

Time your ascent of the Arc de Triomphe with the illumination of the Eiffel Tower: The view is truly magical.

—NEIL SHEA
National Geographic magazine writer

West of the Rond-Point stretches what the French like to call the most beautiful avenue in the world, still considered the obligatory route for all important gatherings, departures, and returns. For example, the July 14 military parades, with their low-flying jets, pass here; it marks the finish line of the annual Tour de France bicycle race and the starting point of the Paris Marathon.

However, the Champs-Élysées' reputation tends to outshine its reality. Despite a face-lift in the 1990s that removed parking and expanded sidewalks, in recent times it has been invaded by flashy car dealerships, fast-food

restaurants, and giant movie complexes.

Universal Exposition Monuments

These three legacies of the 1900 Universal Exposition were conceived as monuments to French art. The 1889 Universal Exposition was so successful that immediately after it closed, plans were laid for another in 1900. This time, the city decided to build permanent structures.

Grand Palais: The Grand Palais, which replaced the Palais de l'Industrie of 1885, is a huge iron-and-glass structure with a neoclassical stone facade. Exuberant ironwork, the colossal bronze statues of Apollo's chariot drawn by flying horses, and a seemingly endless glass roof are characteristic of the art nouveau style of its time.

The Grand Palais has hosted many major exhibitions, including the 1905 Salon d'Automne that launched the Fauves group of artists. The Grand Palais's exhibition space reopened in 2005, with its magnificent glass roof restored.

The **Galeries Nationales du Grand Palais** host international art exhibitions. At the **Palais de la Découverte,** the Grand Palais science museum, interactive exhibits explore such diverse topics as animal communication, Earth's origins, and meteorology. They will both be closed for renovation and upgrade from December 2021 to 2024, during which time the Grand Palais Éphémère, a provisional building on Champ de Mars, will host art, fashion, and sports events.

Petit Palais: The Petit Palais was also built for the 1900 exposition; it now belongs to the City of Paris and houses a mixed collection that ranges from Chinese porcelain to 19th-century paintings. The beautifully renovated building has an interior garden and fountains.

Pont Alexandre III: Another vestige of the 1900 exposition is the Pont Alexandre III, an extravagant structure with gilded statues dedicated to friendship between Russia and France. Tsar Nicholas II laid the first stone on October 7, 1896, and it was completed two years later.

Avenue Montaigne

Branching off from the Champs-Élysées and home to one of the most famous *bals populaires* (dance halls) in the mid-1800s, the ultra-chic Avenue Montaigne is lined with luxury shops, palatial hotels, and the haute couture houses of some of France's leading fashion names, including Chanel, Givenchy, and Christian Dior.

Arc de Triomphe

Parisians still call the square surrounding the Arc de Triomphe "*l'Étoile*" ("the star"), despite its name changing in 1970 to the Place Charles de Gaulle. It gets its name from the 12 avenues radiating from it. At its center stands the Arc de Triomphe, a striking landmark in the middle of Paris's longest vista.

■ **French soccer fans celebrate a victory on the Champs-Élysées near the Arc de Triomphe.**

In 1806, Napoleon commissioned a monument from the architect Jean-François Chalgrin to honor his Grande Armée and the victory of Austerlitz. In keeping with the Napoleonic sense of grandeur, the Arc de Triomphe is 164 feet high (50 m) and 147 feet wide (45 m)—the largest arch of its kind ever built. It was finally completed in 1836.

Its bas-relief sculptures include the famous "Départ des Volontaires," or "La Marseillaise," a winged figure leading soldiers into battle, by François Rude; and its friezes depict the departure of the French armies (eastern side) and their return (western side).

(continued on p. 152)

Petit Palais

🗺 Map p. 145

✉ Avenue Winston Churchill

☎ 01 53 43 40 00

🕐 Closed Mon. & public holidays

Ⓜ Métro: Champs-Élysées Clemenceau

petitpalais.paris.fr

Arc de Triomphe

🗺 Map p. 144

✉ Place Charles de Gaulle

☎ 01 55 37 73 77

💲 €€ (includes museum)

Ⓜ Métro: Charles de Gaulle Étoile

paris-arc-de-triomphe.fr

PARIS, CAPITAL OF CHIC

France's reputation as the world's luxury capital remains untarnished. New York, London, and Milan may have their own unique styles, but Paris is the only true center of classic haute couture.

■ Models sashay down the runway during a Christian Dior spring show in Paris.

Fashion for the New Millennium

The new buzzwords: luxury and functionality. Women are no longer afraid to wear clothes at work that would previously have been considered more suitable for the opera than the office. Meanwhile, the invasion of foreign designers continues unabated: For instance, London-schooled Italian designer Ricardo Tisci reigned for 12 years at Givenchy, whose creative director is now the British Clare Waight Keller. Why do top designers flock to Paris? They are given creative freedom and can rely on a network of incomparable craftsmen to give form to their visions.

Parisian Haute Couture

Designers' dazzling collections may seem remote and dauntingly priced—few can afford extravagances such as handmade designs that sell for $10,000 and higher—but their inspiration will inevitably trickle down into ready-to-wear and accessories in boutiques around the world.

The haute couture collections unveiled in January and July demonstrate the pivotal role Paris plays as the center of creative fashion. Expression is at its peak, with designers choosing eccentric locations to play up the clothes on view. What counts? Virtuosity in technique,

detail, and color, and—most of all—the "theater
of the moment"—the *spectacle.*

The great couture tradition was founded
in the mid-20th century by the likes of Coco
Chanel, Christian Dior, Hubert de Givenchy,
and Pierre Cardin, names that convey the difference between what is French and what is
the Rest of the World. (The master of them
all, the late Yves Saint Laurent, retired in 2002
with a retrospective of his 40-year contribution
to the field.)

New York fashion is about practicality,

■ Brocade shoes in a shop window

featuring clothing that travels from office to
evening; London fashion is more eccentric; and
in Milan, the focus is on the beauty, quality, and
salability of fabrics. That leaves the out-and-out
sheer romantic glamour to Paris.

Less Is More

French style—the much admired way
French women have of carrying themselves, wearing a scarf, and pulling a look
together in a seemingly effortless, innate
manner—is the subject of much study and
imitation; it can sometimes be learned,
but it can never be bought.

As with many other nationalities,
the French have embraced the American
fashion influence, but their approach to
style as an art form can be seen as much
on Parisian streets as on the catwalks at
fashion houses. Designers may throw
sportswear elements into the mix, but
they are statements or quotations, not
the whole story. Unlike her Anglo-Saxon
counterpart—whose buying habits
tend toward quantity and all-purpose
wear—the Frenchwoman (particularly the
Parisian) usually buys fewer, higher-ticket
items, such as an excellent pair of shoes,

a top-quality handbag, or a colorful silk
scarf, and has no qualms about wearing the same thing twice or more in one
week, as a designer piece will look just as
chic on the hundredth wearing. Accessories do not have to match, and the
sharpest dressers adhere to the no-more-
than-two-colors rule. Handbags by such
Paris-based designers as Vuitton, Hermès,
Longchamp, and Lancel are always highly
desirable purchases.

France is not a country where dressing for success has become politicized.
Most Frenchwomen dress to accent
their femininity, even playing it to their
advantage in a business context: They
don't worry that high hemlines or figure-
revealing clothes might interfere with
being taken seriously, any more than the
average Frenchman worries about offering a compliment.

Cathedrale St.-Alexandre-Nevsky

- 🗺 Map pp. 144–145
- ✉ 12 rue Daru
- ☎ 01 42 27 37 34
- 🕐 Open for visits 3–6 p.m. Tues., Thurs., Fri., & Sun.
- Ⓜ Métro: Courcelles

cathedrale-orthodoxe.com

The 12 avenues radiating out from the Arc and the 12 matching *hôtels* (residences) surrounding the Place were not part of the original design, but were introduced by Baron Haussmann (see pp. 166–167). The result is perhaps monumental in a way he never intended: The streets converging at the Étoile now create a huge traffic jam.

Over the years, the Arc de Triomphe has symbolized all that is great and glorious in France: Napoleon's ashes passed under the arch on their way to Les Invalides, as did Victor Hugo's funeral cortege. The conquering armies—the Prussians in 1871 and the Germans in 1940—that marched here were succeeded by France's heroic liberators, such as General Charles de Gaulle, who led the Allied victory march along the avenue before thousands of jubilant Parisians on August 26, 1944 (see p. 33).

An unknown soldier's tomb

was placed here in 1920, and every evening at 6:30 veterans relight the flame. An underground walkway at the end of the Champs-Élysées leading underneath the Place Charles de Gaulle provides a safe passage to the Arc de Triomphe, where the view from the top overlooks Haussmann's design.

Beneath the viewing platform is a small museum with an exhibition on the history of the building of the monument and mementos of Napoleon and World War I.

Cathédrale St.-Alexandre-Nevsky

The heart of Little Russia, this onion-domed, Russian Orthodox cathedral was constructed in 1861 and is based on a Greek-cross floor plan. The inside is lined with impressive frescoes and icons, and the tympanum is covered with mosaics on a gilded background. ∎

■ Parisians relax in the sun in the Parc Monceau, near the Cathédrale St.-Alexandre-Nevsky.

EXPERIENCE: Learning La Cuisine Française

Where better to learn to cook than in Paris? Other national cuisines may have their advocates, and rightly so, but French cooking techniques remain the gold standard for chefs around the world. And, in the past 20 years or so, French chefs have become far less rigid and are experimenting with international influences of all sorts, reviving and enriching their national cuisine.

In Paris, there are dozens of options for learning to cook, from one-off demonstrations or hands-on classes for the amateur to serious professional programs, almost all of them available in English. Best of all, participants get to eat the results. Choose one that suits your interests and time constraints.

Cordon Bleu & Escoffier

The granddaddy of them all is the **Cordon Bleu** (*13–15 quai André Citroën, tel 01 85 65 15 00, cordonbleu.edu*), which offers a variety of diplomas and certificates for those who wish to become career chefs or sommeliers, with the possibility of internships in Parisian restaurants. The school also offers short-term cooking and wine-tasting demonstrations and courses for amateurs.

The **Ritz Escoffier School** (*15 place Vendôme, tel 01 43 16 30 50, ritzescoffier.com*) was named after Auguste Escoffier, who laid down many of the rules for French cooking in his *Le Guide Culinaire* and was the first head chef of the Ritz Paris. Located in a nicely decorated room in the basement of the Ritz, near the

■ Few dishes are more quint-essentially French than garlicky *escargots* (snails).

kitchen, this school offers diploma courses for professionals and individual workshops for foodies.

Ducasse & Others

Internationally renowned chef Alain Ducasse may be the Escoffier of today, but only time will tell. He is passing on his expertise through the **École de Cuisine Alain Ducasse** (*64 rue du Ranelagh, tel 01 44 90 91 00, ecole cuisine-alainducasse.com*), which offers classes with chefs trained by Ducasse in different cooking styles and

by guest chefs who share their skills in such varied cuisines as Indian or Basque. Most courses are in French, but translation can be arranged on request.

For a quick, fun cooking class, ranging from 30 minutes to 4 hours, on a wide range of topics, try the **Atelier des Chefs** (*several locations, tel 01 53 30 05 82, atelierdeschefs.fr*). It offers a wide variety of classes to choose from and is easy to book online.

To Market, To Market

Cook'n With Class (*6 rue Baudelique, tel 01 42 57 22 84, cooknwithclass.com*) offers classes that begin with a visit to a street market with a chef, who explains how to choose the best products and introduces participants to some of the vendors. They then return to the school with their purchases to cook up a three-course meal and sit down to eat it together, accompanied by wine and cheese from the market. More specialized classes on such topics as making *macarons* or holiday meals are also available, as well as workshops featuring a cheese and wine tasting or wine and food pairings.

16TH ARRONDISSEMENT

Despite its reputation as a refuge for the rich and as an opulent but boring neighborhood, the 16th arrondissement has a wealth of museums, a few remaining traces of its former village life, and the most concentrated number of art nouveau and art deco buildings in Paris. Comfortably wedged between the Seine on one side and the Bois de Boulogne on the other, the 16th arrondissement is the neighborhood favored by both old and new money.

■ The view from the Palais de Chaillot

This part of Paris has lured the upper classes for centuries. Catherine de Médicis often stopped on Chaillot Hill (the present-day Trocadéro, a semicircular plaza in front of the Palais de Chaillot) on her way from St.-Germain-en-Laye to Paris, gradually expanding the lodge that stood on the site. The wine produced by the Abbey of Passy and the Minimes de Chaillot was famous throughout the region, and vineyards lined the hills sloping toward the Seine. In the 17th century, the curative powers of Passy's spring brought upper-crust clientele to its thermal spa; today, its source still provides crystal-clear water.

Architectural Gems

More than half of Hector Guimard's art nouveau buildings are in the 16th arrondissement, particularly in Auteuil. Best known for his superb glass-and-iron Métro entrances (especially the one at Porte Dauphine), Guimard also designed the flamboyant Castel Béranger, an art nouveau masterpiece, and several other buildings along Rue La Fontaine. The streamlined art deco style followed in the 1920s and '30s; its chief Parisian proponent, Robert Mallet-Stevens, designed a series of town houses on an Auteuil street that now bears his name. Several small alleyways off Rue Boileau (*Métro: Exelmans*), including the Villa Cheysson and the Villa Mulhouse—originally built to house millworkers—are lined with charming houses and gardens.

The villages of Passy, Auteuil, and Chaillot were annexed to the City of Paris in

Porte
d'Auteuil

BLVD. D'AUTEUIL

MURAT

BOULEVARD

Porte de
St.-Cloud

AV. DE LA PORTE
DE ST.-CLOUD

PLACE DE
LA PORTE
ST.-CLOUD

1 Porte Dauphine Métro **2** Castel Béranger **3** Rue Boileau

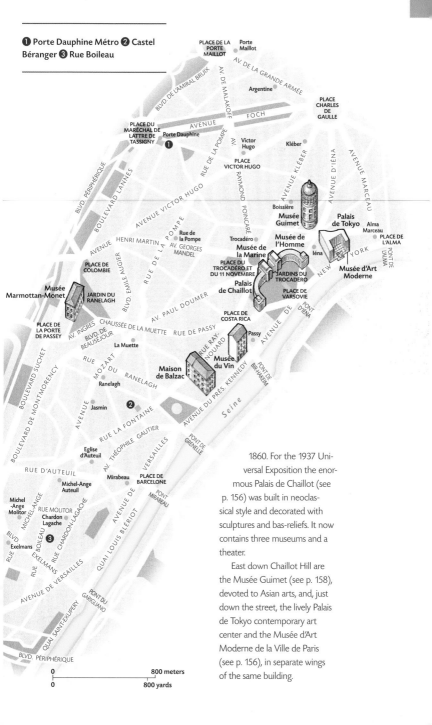

PLACE DE LA PORTE MAILLOT
Porte Maillot
AV. DE LA GRANDE ARMÉE
BLVD. DE L'AMIRAL BRUIX
AV. DE MALAKOFF
Argentine
PLACE CHARLES DE GAULLE
AVENUE
FOCH
PLACE DU MARÉCHAL DE LATTRE DE TASSIGNY
Porte Dauphine
1
RUE DE LA POMPE
AV. RAYMOND POINCARÉ
Victor Hugo
PLACE VICTOR HUGO
Kléber
AVENUE KLÉBER
AVENUE D'IÉNA
AVENUE MARCEAU
BLVD. PÉRIPHÉRIQUE
BOULEVARD LANNES
AVENUE VICTOR HUGO
AVENUE HENRI MARTIN
RUE DE LA POMPE
Rue de la Pompe
AV. GEORGES MANDEL
Boissière
Trocadéro
Musée Guimet
Palais de Tokyo
Alma Marceau
PLACE DE L'ALMA
Musée de l'Homme
PONT DE L'ALMA
PLACE DE COLOMBIE
BLVD. ÉMILE AUGIER
Musée de la Marine
PLACE DU TROCADÉRO ET DU 11 NOVEMBRE
Iéna
NEW YORK
Musée d'Art Moderne
Musée Marmottan-Monet
JARDIN DU RANELAGH
AV. INGRES
CHAUSSÉE DE LA MUETTE
AV. PAUL DOUMER
JARDINS DU TROCADÉRO
Palais de Chaillot
PLACE DE VARSOVIE
PONT D'IÉNA
PLACE DE LA PORTE DE PASSEY
BLVD. DE BEAUSÉJOUR
RUE DE PASSY
La Muette
PLACE DE COSTA RICA
RUE RAYNOUARD
Passy
AVENUE DE
RUE MOZART DU RANELAGH
Ranelagh
Maison de Balzac
Musée du Vin
PONT DE BIR-HAKEIM
BOULEVARD SUCHET
BOULEVARD DE MONTMORENCY
AVENUE
Jasmin
2
RUE LA FONTAINE
AV. THÉOPHILE GAUTIER
AVENUE DU PRÉS. KENNEDY
Seine
Eglise d'Auteuil
AV. VERSAILLES
PONT DE GRENELLE
RUE D'AUTEUIL
Mirabeau
PLACE DE BARCELONE
Michel-Ange Auteuil
AVENUE DE VERSAILLES
PONT MIRABEAU
Michel-Ange Molitor
RUE MOLITOR
Chardon Lagache
RUE CHARDON-LAGACHE
QUAI LOUIS BLÉRIOT
BLVD EXELMANS
Exelmans
3
RUE BOILEAU
BLVD
RUE EXELMANS
AVENUE DE VERSAILLES
PONT DU GARIGLIANO
QUAI SAINT-EXUPERY
BLVD. PÉRIPHÉRIQUE

| 0 | 800 meters |
| 0 | 800 yards |

1860. For the 1937 Universal Exposition the enormous Palais de Chaillot (see p. 156) was built in neoclassical style and decorated with sculptures and bas-reliefs. It now contains three museums and a theater.

East down Chaillot Hill are the Musée Guimet (see p. 158), devoted to Asian arts, and, just down the street, the lively Palais de Tokyo contemporary art center and the Musée d'Art Moderne de la Ville de Paris (see p. 156), in separate wings of the same building.

Palais de Chaillot

🗺 Map p. 155

✉ 17 place du Trocadéro

☎ Cité de l'Architecture et du Patrimoine: 01 58 51 52 00
Musée de l'Homme: 01 44 05 72 72
Musée de la Marine: 01 53 65 69 69

🕐 Closed Tues., Jan. 1, May 1, Dec. 25

💲 €€

🚇 Métro: Trocadéro

citedelarchitecture.fr
museedelhomme.fr
musee-marine.fr

Musée d'Art Moderne de la Ville de Paris

✉ 11 avenue du Président Wilson

☎ 01 53 67 40 00

🕐 Closed Mon. & public holidays

💲 €€–€€€

🚇 Métro: Iéna

mam.paris.fr

Palais de Tokyo

✉ 13 avenue du Président Wilson

☎ 01 81 97 35 88

🕐 Closed Tues., Jan. 1, May 1, Dec. 25

💲 €€

🚇 Métro: Iéna

palaisdetokyo.com

Palais de Chaillot & Trocadéro Museums

The view from the terrace of the Palais de Chaillot across the river is one of the best in Paris. The museums inside this monument, however, are less well known—the Musée de

---

INSIDER TIP:

Don't miss Patrick Roger's chocolate boutique [45 avenue Victor Hugo], which features fantastical chocolate sculptures.

—PATRICIA DANIELS
National Geographic contributor

---

l'Homme, Musée de la Marine, and the Cité de l'Architecture et du Patrimoine, which includes the Musée des Monuments Français, a huge architecture museum. Down the hill, the Palais de Tokyo houses the Musée d'Art Moderne de la Ville de Paris and the Site de Création Contemporaine.

Cité de l'Architecture et du Patrimoine: This

revamped institution brings together the Institut Français de l'Architecture, focusing on modern architecture, and the Musée des Monuments Français, with its various models of French monuments.

Musée de l'Homme: The

Musée de l'Homme, an ethnology and anthropology museum,

reopened in 2015 after six years of renovation work.

Musée de la Marine:

Created in 1748, this establishment is one of the oldest marine museums in the world. It contains intricate scale models of warships dating from the 17th century to the present and splendid examples of the famous tall sailing ships. Currently closed for renovation, it will reopen in 2022.

Musée d'Art Moderne de la Ville de Paris: This museum

in the Palais de Tokyo's east wing represents many artists of the school of Paris as well as a rich collection of fauvist and cubist works—including pieces by Matisse and Dufy and the École de Paris artists Soutine, Modigliani, and van Dongen. The Contemporary Art Department continues its ambitious temporary shows of young international artists and current art trends.

Palais de Tokyo: In the west

wing of the Palais de Tokyo, this "laboratory of contemporary art" presents cutting-edge exhibitions, installments, and performances.

Musée du Vin

On the other side of Palais de Chaillot is a 15th-century hideaway enclosing the wine cellars of the former Minimes de Chaillot monastery, which distilled one of Louis XIII's favorite vintages. Most of the buildings were destroyed during the Revolution, and the cellars were forgotten until the 1950s. In 1984 they were made into a wine museum *(5 square Charles Dickens, tel 01 45 25 63 26, museeeduvin-paris.com, closed Sun., Mon., & Dec. 25, €€)*. Visitors can explore the former limestone quarries that house objects used in the making and drinking of wine and sign up for classes. Entry to the museum is free if you eat in the restaurant. (Reserve for theme dinners.)

Musée Marmottan-Monet

Although the Musée Marmottan-Monet is now famous throughout the world for its Impressionist paint-ings, the museum was initially devoted to an entirely different theme: the Napoleonic era.

Jules and Paul Marmottan, father and son, were responsible for this collection, housed in a former hunting lodge, which was entirely remodeled by Marmottan senior. At the turn of the 19th century both men were interested in Napoleonic memorabilia, and they amassed a superb collection of Empire furnishings. After his father's death made him a wealthy man, Paul Marmottan became a recognized expert on Empire art. When he died in 1932, he left his mansion and entire art collection to the Institut de France.

Several later bequests trans-formed the Marmottan into a world-renowned Impression-ist museum. The first bequest included Monet's "Impression: Sunrise," while a second in 1966,

from his son Michel, brought 65 works by the painter, including some of his best paintings.

A number of the "Water Lilies" paintings are exhibited downstairs, along with the images of smoke-filled train stations and brilliant fields of flowers and other works such as Alfred Sisley's "Spring in the Environs of Paris" and Paul Gauguin's "Bouquet of Flowers."

The ground-floor room contains a collection of medieval illuminated manuscripts from the Georges Wildenstein collection. ∎

Musée Marmottan-Monet

- Map p. 155
- 2 rue Louis Boilly
- 01 44 96 50 33
- Closed Mon., Jan. 1, May 1, Dec. 25
- €€
- Métro: La Muette

marmottan.fr

■ **The Jardins du Trocadéro front the Palais de Chaillot.**

More Places to Visit Near the Champs-Élysées & in the 16th Arrondissement

Maison de Balzac

In 1840, Honoré de Balzac, writer of La Comédie Humaine (The Human Comedy), was on the brink of financial ruin. He moved to this house in Passy, where he lived under the pseudonym of Monsieur de Breugnol. A museum since 1960, it displays many of his personal objects, including his writing desk, where he sometimes worked for 24 hours at a stretch. As he wrote to Madame Hanska, whom he married just before his death at the age of 51, this desk "witnessed my anguish, my miseries, my distress, my joys, my everything." Raised in Paris, Balzac set many of his works in the French capital. maisondebalzac.paris.fr

🗺 Map p. 155 ✉ 47 rue Raynouard
☎ 01 55 74 41 80 🕐 Closed Mon. & public holidays 🚇 Métro: Passy

---

INSIDER TIP:

Try classic Guerlain fragrances (including Shalimar) at the company's 68 Champs-Élysées flagship shop.

—SHEILA BUCKMASTER
National Geographic Traveler magazine
editor at large

Musée Jacquemart-André

This museum in the home of Edouard André and his wife, Nélie Jacquemart, reflects the couple's lifetime devotion to building their art collection. Famous for its Italian Renaissance works, the collection includes a rare fresco ceiling by Tiepolo, "Henri III Received in Venice by the Doge Cantarini," and Uccello's "Saint George Slaying the Dragon." There are also French and Flemish paintings (with Rembrandt's "Pilgrims of Emmaus,"

"Amalia von Sohms," and "Doctor Tholinx"). musee-jacquemart-andre.com

🗺 Map p. 145 ✉ 158 boulevard Haussmann ☎ 01 45 62 11 59 💲 €€ 🚇 Métro: Miromesnil, St.-Philippe du Roule

Musée National des Arts Asiatique-Guimet

The museum's original collection came from Lyon industrialist Émile Guimet, who gathered a fantastic number of objects during his trips around the world in the late 19th century. His Egyptian collection eventually went to the Louvre, but works from the Far East remained here. A national museum since 1928, it exhibits Guimet's collection, which ranges from Afghan to Japanese works and spans eras from 2000 B.C. to the 19th century, including examples of Khmer artwork, bronze statues from India, and antique jade and porcelain from China. The galleries of the Buddhist pantheon at 19 avenue d'Iéna are devoted to the history of Far Eastern religions. www.guimet.fr

🗺 Map p. 155 ✉ 6 place d'Iéna
☎ 01 56 52 54 33 🕐 Closed Tues., Jan. 1, May 1, Dec. 25 💲 €€ 🚇 Métro: Iéna

Parc Monceau

This park is farther afield but is linked in spirit to the Second Empire, when it and much of the area surrounding the Champs-Élysées became a fashionable neighborhood. It retains something of its former 19th-century bourgeois aura, with its picturesque park, grottoes, and rock garden, along with several extravagant follies (decorative constructions). The **Musée Cernuschi** (7 avenue Vélasquez, tel 01 53 96 21 50, cernuschi.paris .fr, closed Mon., Jan. 1, May 1, Dec. 25), with its wonderful collection of Asian art, is located next to the park. 🗺 Map p. 145 ✉ Boulevard de Courcelles 🚇 Métro: Monceau

Created in the 19th century for the up-and-coming bourgeoisie, encompassing the Opéra, department stores, and theaters

LES GRANDS BOULEVARDS

Covered passages link parts of the boulevards.

LES GRANDS BOULEVARDS

Les Grands Boulevards begin near the Madeleine Quarter and run eastward as far as the Bastille. These wide thoroughfares form a shopping and cultural hub, including the ostentatious Opéra Garnier, luxury food stores and designer boutiques, fashion houses, cafés, theaters, and galleries.

"Là est la vie!" ("That's where life is!") proclaimed Honoré de Balzac, referring to Les Grands Boulevards. Created by Louis XIV in the 1670s, they became the center of entertainment in the 19th century after the prudish Louis-Philippe closed down the bordellos and gambling dens at the Palais-Royal. Crowds flocked to the boulevards, the wealthy to the west of Rue Montmartre, the poor to the east.

The Boulevard des Capucines, Boulevard des Italiens, and Avenue de l'Opéra converge at the Opéra Garnier (see p. 163) in the Place de l'Opéra designed by Baron Haussmann (see pp. 166–167). It is one of Paris's most brilliant illustrations of the Napoleon III style. Napoleon III crowned the Colonne d'Austerlitz on Place Vendôme (see p. 162) with an imperial effigy of his uncle (Napoleon I) dressed as Julius Caesar. Ancient Greece inspired the series of temples previously commissioned by Napoleon I as well: La Madeleine church, a temple of glory to the Grande Armée, and La Bourse, or Paris stock exchange, a temple to finance.

The Madeleine Quarter, where Les Grands Boulevards begin, is also a modern-day temple to luxury. Rue de la Paix and Place Vendôme were tranquil bourgeois

corners of Paris until the late 19th century, when the lavish boutiques of jewelers and fashionable tailors, including the *maison de couture* of Englishman Charles Frederick Worth, moved in.

Artists were drawn to the area: The first Impressionist exhibition was held at 35 boulevard des Capucines, and the first showing of the Lumière brothers' film shorts was at No. 14 (now the Scribe hotel) in 1895. Musicians such

as Lully (the 17th-century court composer) gravitated to the area around the now vanished Opera House of Paris.

The elegant Square Louvois, near the Bibliothèque Nationale (see p. 165), with its magnificent Labrouste Reading Room, now stands in place of the old Opera House. Behind it are the Vivienne and Colbert Galleries, in one of the area's remaining 19th-century covered arcades. Today, the Galerie Vivienne has stores and cafes, while the Galerie Colbert belongs to the Bibliothèque Nationale.

Place Vendôme is studded with the world's leading jewelers, the Ritz Hotel, and the Justice Ministry. Luxury shops, such as Fauchon and Hédiard, are scattered around the Madeleine, along with the famous flower market. ■

NOT TO BE MISSED:

A concert at La Madeleine 162

Window-shopping for luxuries on Place Vendôme 162, 164

A tour of the Opéra Garnier 163

Indulging in a Mona Lisa chocolate éclair at Fauchon 164

Taking in an exhibition at the Bibliothèque Nationale 165

Tea and shopping in the Galerie Vivienne 165

Exploring the arcades off the Passage des Panoramas 168

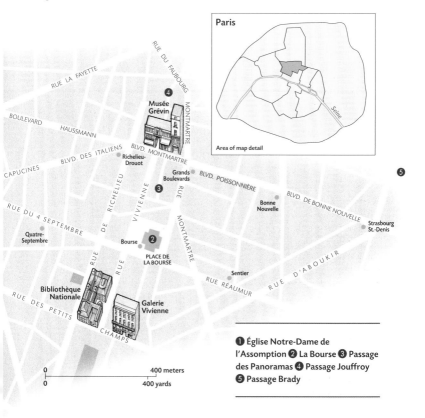

Paris

Area of map detail

❶ Église Notre-Dame de l'Assomption ❷ La Bourse ❸ Passage des Panoramas ❹ Passage Jouffroy ❺ Passage Brady

LA MADELEINE & PLACE VENDÔME

The contrasting influences of the royal family and Napoleon I both shaped two iconic locations among the Grand Boulevards: the imposing church of La Madeleine (formally the church of Saint Mary Magdalene) and Place Vendôme.

La Madeleine

Map p. 160

Place de la Madeleine

01 44 51 69 00

Métro: Madeleine

eglise-lamadeleine.com

Place Vendôme

Map p. 160

Métro: Opéra, Madeleine

La Madeleine

La Madeleine is one of the most famous monuments in Paris, particularly interesting for its colossal exterior and 64-foot-high (20 m) Corinthian columns. The interior is dark and lugubrious, with light coming from three domed skylights in the nave and a semicircular apse. Here celebrity weddings, funerals, and memorial services (as well as regular religious services) are held. In the vestibule is the "Baptism of Christ" (far left), a masterpiece by François Rude.

INSIDER TIP:

The roof of the Galeries Lafayette [40 boulevard Haussmann] offers stunning views of the city.

—GILLES MINGASSON
National Geographic photographer

The church was planned as part of J. A. Gabriel's layout for the Place Louis XV (today's Place de la Concorde). The original construction, begun in 1764, was razed in favor of a building modeled on the Panthéon until work was halted by the French Revolution. In 1806, Napoleon commissioned a temple to his Grande Armée, and the existing structure was once more razed. However, in 1814 Louis XVIII confirmed that it should be a church and devoted the building to his guillotined brother, Louis XVI.

Place Vendôme

Place Vendôme is superlatively spacious and luminous at night, with an imposing, imperial air. The square (called Place Louis-le-Grand until the Revolution) was originally created by Louis XIV to rival Place des Vosges. In 1792, the square's statue of Louis XIV was destroyed. It was replaced in 1810 by the Colonne d'Austerlitz to glorify Napoleon's military campaigns. The bronze spiral wrapped around the stone column—inspired by Trajan's column in Rome—was made from the 1,200 cannon captured at the Battle of Austerlitz (1805).

Opened in 1898 overlooking the square, the Ritz was the first hotel to have private bathtubs. Scott and Zelda Fitzgerald lived here in the 1920s. Ernest Hemingway claimed to have "liberated" the hotel with Allied soldiers in August 1944, and Coco Chanel died here. ■

OPÉRA GARNIER

The Opéra Garnier, built under Napoleon III, features both ballet and opera, as does the Opéra Bastille. Following an attempt on Napoleon III's life near the old opera house on Rue Le Peletier, the emperor moved the Opéra to a more secure site. Architect Charles Garnier resolved the dilemma of building the Opéra over a lake—it still lies underneath, and the fountains and pools in the basement are said to have inspired *The Phantom of the Opera.*

The over-the-top style of the Opéra Garnier is typical of Napoleon III's era.

Despite Baron Haussmann's approval of Garnier's project in 1861, Empress Eugénie asked: "What is this style? It is no style at all, neither Greek nor Louis XVI." To which Garnier reportedly replied: "Those styles have had their day. It is Napoleon III, and for this you complain?"

The Opéra indeed epitomizes Napoleon III style: baroque, eclectic, and ridiculously extravagant, with its Apollo-crowned dome and statues of music and dance, including a copy of Carpeaux's "La Danse." The bacchanalian sculpture to the right of the entrance was branded an "ignoble saturnalia" and an "offense to public morals" (the original work

is now in the Musée d'Orsay). The Emperor's Pavilion on Rue Scribe, which once featured a ramp to allow the king to enter the royal box directly from his carriage, now provides access to a museum of props and scores.

The Opéra's interior is filled with gold leaf, precious stones, frescoes, marble, and a grandiose foyer and staircase. The five-tier auditorium has only 2,131 seats, some with no visibility, but the huge stage can accommodate up to 450 performers. The false ceiling painted by Chagall in 1964 can be seen when performances or rehearsals are not in progress.

Honey made in beehives on the roof is sold in the boutique. ∎

Opéra Garnier
- Map p. 160
- Place de l'Opéra
- Tour info/museum: 08 25 05 44 05
- Closed May 1 & Dec. 25. Closed for visits on days when there is a matinée performance or special event. Guided tours by prior arrangement.
- €€ (for tour)
- Métro: Opéra

operadeparis.fr

A WALK ALONG LES GRANDS BOULEVARDS

As you stroll along Les Grands Boulevards, originally laid out as tree-lined promenades in the 17th century, you can still get an impression of what the area looked like in its heyday.

Local passages are a shopper's paradise.

NOT TO BE MISSED:

Opéra Garnier • Hédiard • Rue de la Paix • Bibliothèque Nationale • Galerie Vivienne

Begin your walk at the 19th-century **Café de la Paix** on the Place de l'Opéra, once frequented by Émile Zola and Guy de Maupassant. Next, visit the landmark **Opéra Garnier ❶** (see p. 163).

Exiting the Opéra, turn right down Boulevard des Capucines. The Hôtel Scribe at No. 14 is where, in 1895, the Lumière brothers first showed film shorts. The refurbished **Olympia** concert hall, at No. 28, is where Edith Piaf, Jacques Brel, and the Beatles once performed.

Continue straight on Boulevard des Capucines to **La Madeleine ❷** (see p. 162). Visit the flower market (circa 1834) and continue to **Fauchon** at 26 place de la Madeleine—Paris's most extravagant food store—then on to the more discreet **Hédiard** at 21 place de la Madeleine, on the opposite side of the church. Hédiard is renowned for miniature and exotic fruits and vegetables. Also on Place de la Madeleine are the Maison de la Truffe (No. 19) and Caviar Kaspia (No. 17) for caviar and pepper vodka.

Circle back in front of the church; Marcel Proust lived at 9 place de la Madeleine, where the restaurant Lucas Carton is located. Head down **Rue Royale ❸** and within a few paces take a short detour into the Village Royal, or Cité Berryer, which has a few interesting boutiques and a brasserie. You're in the lap of luxury on the Rue Royale, with the Ladurée tea salon and pastry shop, Maxim's restaurant, Lalique crystal, and Christofle flatware all nearby.

Turn left on Rue St.-Honoré. On the right is the 17th-century **Église Notre-Dame de l'Assomption ❹**, the former chapel of the Convent of the Sisters of the Assumption (now the Polish Church in Paris). Continue until you reach a passage just before Rue de Castiglione, and cut left through the passage to Place Vendôme (famed for its many fine jewelers, including Cartier), leading to **Rue de la Paix,** the 19th-century's most glamorous shopping street.

Past the north side of the square, turn right on Rue Danielle Casanova (which becomes Rue des Petits Champs). Look to the right toward **Rue du Marché St.-Honoré** to see the glass-and-steel Marché St.-Honoré–part of BNP Paribas (a bank), it houses offices, galleries, and upscale shops, and is surrounded by lively cafés and restaurants. At 40 rue des Petits Champs, turn left into the **Passage Choiseul ⑤**. Built in 1825 by Bertrand Tavernier, it has an attractive glass roof and has recently been revamped.

Turn right down perpendicular Passage Ste.-Anne at the Lavrut art supplies store, which leads to Rue Cherubini and Square Louvois. Cross Rue de Richelieu and enter the courtyard of the **Bibliothèque Nationale ⑥** (*58 rue de Richelieu, tel 01 53 79 59 59, closed Sun., Métro: Bourse*). Temporary exhibitions display some of the treasures of this library, initially founded with royal collections in 1666. The books have been transferred to the Bibliothèque Nationale de France–Site Tolbiac, located in the 13th arrondissement, but the maps, musical scores, medals, prints, and photographs remain here.

Turn right and enter the main building to see the spectacular **Labrouste Reading Room** created by Henri Labrouste in 1868; it's not open to the public, but you can peek through the glass doors. The building is undergoing renovation in stages until 2021, so some sections may be inaccessible. Continue down the corridor of the main building and exit right through the gardens. Directly opposite is the entrance to the 19th-century arcade of **Galerie Vivienne ⑦**; the Galerie Colbert is perpendicular to the right. The belle époque Grand Colbert restaurant is located here, and the Galerie Vivienne makes for a nice coffee spot away from the road.

⛰ See also area map pp. 160–161
➤ Café de la Paix, Place de l'Opéra
🕐 3 hours
🔁 1.6 miles (2.6 km)
➤ Galerie Vivienne, Rue Vivienne
Take this walk during the day, as it explores several passageways that close around 7 p.m.

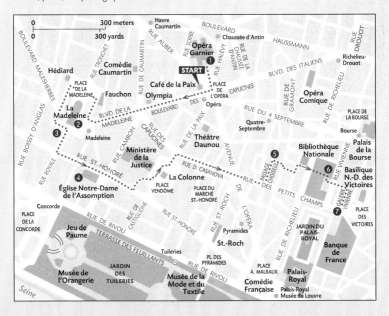

FROM MEDIEVAL TO MODERN: HAUSSMANN'S PARIS

At the turn of the 19th century, France was coming to terms with the Revolution and the end of the monarchy, and was about to embark on an industrial revolution that would transform its society and alter the city almost beyond recognition.

Impact of the Industrial Revolution

The development of steam-powered trains, iron wheels, and tracks in the early 19th century created a railway network that linked cities. Suddenly, architects had to find a way to integrate train stations—vast, industrial buildings—into the heart of the city. New materials, including cast iron and sheet glass, solved the problem. Metal was lightweight, strong, and flexible, and glass created uniform, overhead lighting. Glass-and-iron structures were therefore perfect for museums, stations, and marketplaces. The first passageways in Paris used this type of design, as did the marketplace at Les Halles.

■ **Georges-Eugène Haussmann studied law before entering the civil service.**

As industry thrived in the mid-19th century, workers from the provinces poured into the capital looking for work. Land seized from the Church and the aristocracy during the Revolution was divided up by speculators and developers, and a building boom was soon under way. By the time Louis-Napoleon Bonaparte came to power in 1848, Paris's population had doubled, and the congested city had serious housing, water supply, sanitation, and transportation problems. Inspired by the large parks and wide avenues of London, where he had lived in exile, Napoleon envisaged a new Paris. This was to be created by his prefect of the Seine, the Alsatian Baron Georges-Eugène

Haussmann—the grandson of a Napleonic general and a longtime civil servant. Political concerns also motivated Louis-Napoleon's decision. Just a few years earlier, barricades set up in the city center by rebellious Parisians had led to the downfall of his predecessors Charles X and Louis-Philippe. Haussmann's intention was to rid the capital of the ancient, intricate warren of tiny streets and replace them with broad, clean avenues, which were much easier to control and patrol.

Haussmann's Transformations

Haussmann's plan to link the great train stations with wide avenues coincided with a changing view of the city. The newly created bourgeois classes wanted to live, work, and play in the center of the city, to enjoy the wealthy classes' privileges of theaters, museums, libraries, and department stores. Haussmann gave them what they wanted, and more. The entire urban structure was ripped apart and remodeled. The social ramifications of this upheaval were even more brutal. Those not wealthy enough to afford apartments in the lavish new neighborhoods—political troublemakers in Napoleon's eyes—were banished to outlying areas in Paris or to the suburbs.

A major aim was to facilitate traffic flow,

which Haussmann did by opening up the area and slicing wide boulevards straight through the city (including Avenue de l'Opéra, Boulevard St.-Germain, and Boulevard Haussmann) and creating large squares, such as Place de la République. These new avenues were often designed to showcase a monument, for example, the exuberant Opéra Garnier at the end of Avenue de l'Opéra. Haussmann's sweeping vision of urban renewal was contested as Paris became a gigantic, muddy construction site.

Destruction & Renewal

With the exception of the major monuments, most of the Île de la Cité was destroyed. Entire blocks of centuries-old buildings collapsed under Haussmann's demolition crews. His methods were brutal—even unscrupulous—yet his ability to see the entire city as interlinking elements was

a revolutionary new approach to city planning. Nearly 25,000 houses were destroyed, replaced by 50 boulevards and streets, 75,000 new buildings, and 3 new parks: Parc Monceau, Parc Montsouris, and Parc des Buttes-Chaumont. Sewers, sidewalks, schools, hospitals, markets, and new parks went in. The new streets were lined with Haussmannian buildings, distinguished by their coherence and architectural unity (a result of strict building codes that defined every architectural element from overhangs to door widths). Haussmann also reorganized the political structure of the city, creating a town hall for each arrondissement. In just 17 years, he remodeled the entire city—a phenomenally expensive project that, for better or for worse, transformed Paris from a filthy warren of medieval streets to a modern, functioning metropolis.

■ **Haussmann's encompassing vision of a city of broad avenues is particularly clear from above.**

More Places to Visit on Les Grands Boulevards

Musée Grévin

The Musée Grévin (wax museum) had a great impact in 1882—an age devoid of television or media images—as it enabled people to discover what celebrities looked like.

Figures now include French musicians such as Serge Gainsbourg and Johnny Hallyday, former president Barack Obama, and historic figures such as Charlemagne, Napoleon III, and Marat, whose stabbed effigy lies in the actual bathtub in which he was killed. Don't miss the Palais des Mirages sound-and-light show (held at regular intervals throughout the day), first featured at the Paris Universal Exposition of 1900. It's a kaleidoscope of images, music, and sound effects. *grevin-paris.com*

🗺 Map p. 161 ✉ 10 boulevard Montmartre ☎ 01 47 70 85 05; 💲 €€€ 🚇 Métro: Grands Boulevards

Other Passages & Galleries

Described as "human aquariums," the glass-roofed passages and galleries of Paris run from north to south off Les Grands Boulevards, linking one area to the next.

The arcades allowed shoppers to browse without fear of being splashed by mud from passing vehicles. Although there are now only about 20 left, more than 100 existed in the early 19th century.

Passage Brady: Passage Brady is a passage to India and South Asia, featuring exotic spices, fruits, vegetables, and a variety of inexpensive restaurants.

🗺 Map p. 161 ✉ Between 46 rue du Faubourg St.-Denis and 43 rue du Faubourg St.-Martin 🚇 Métro: Château d'Eau

Passage des Panoramas: This is the first gaslit passage and second oldest arcade in Paris. (The Passage du Caire, with its three heads of Hathor reflecting the Egyptomania following Napoleon's Egyptian campaigns, is the oldest.) Opened in 1800, the Passage des Panoramas is named after the giant, circular trompe l'oeil "panorama" paintings (such as those by the American Robert Fulton) of Rome, London, and other world capitals, which once decorated the entrance. It branches off into a labyrinth of arcades—Galerie St.-Marc, Galerie des Variétés, and Galerie Feydeau. Note the Stern Engraving Company's (founded 1840) impressive store sign (No. 47) and the Napoleon III decor of the L'Arbre à Cannelle tea salon.

🗺 Map p. 161 ✉ Entrances at 11 boulevard Montmartre and 10 rue St.-Marc 🚇 Métro: Grands Boulevards

Passage Jouffroy: Adjacent to the Musée Grévin, this busy passage has storefronts containing miniatures, handcrafted toys, collector walking canes with ivory heads of dogs and lions, tea salons, and bistros; the continuing Passage Verdeau has books and lithographs.

🗺 Map p. 161 ✉ 12 boulevard Montmartre 🚇 Métro: Grands Boulevards

---

EXPERIENCE: Spend a Night at the Ballet

Fine wine, fine food, and fine clothing may all be hallmarks of Parisian culture, but for the full cultural experience, visitors should not pass up a trip to the **Paris Opera Ballet** *(operadeparis.fr)* at the glittering Opéra Garnier (see p. 163). This is the company, after all, that invented the five basic ballet positions. With more than 150 dancers and a big budget, the ballet puts on a lavish show, presenting not only traditional ballets but works by such newer choreographers as Wayne McGregor and its former director, Benjamin Millepied.

Where monuments, museums, and ministries occupy former aristocratic mansions with a quiet elegance

TOUR EIFFEL &
LES INVALIDES

The Musée du Quai Branly

TOUR EIFFEL & LES INVALIDES

Extending west of St.-Germain-des-Prés, the elegant 7th arrondissement—a former haven of aristocratic mansions, many of which are now government buildings and embassies—prides itself on its wealth of museums and on the greatest tourist site of them all, the Eiffel Tower.

In the early 17th century, this area was a large expanse of mostly empty land; it was far from the city center and very hard to reach. The Pont Royal, constructed in 1689 to replace the 1632 Pont Rouge footbridge, linked Rue du Bac on the Left Bank to the Jardin des Tuileries (see p. 137), thus providing easier access to the Right Bank.

The 18th century ushered in a new era of development for this neighborhood as nobles returned to Paris. Many of their former mansions are now embassies and government ministries, including the magnificent Palais-Bourbon, built for the Duchesse du Bourbon and now the home of the Assemblée Nationale (see p. 176); and the beautiful Hôtel Matignon at 57 rue de Varenne, the official residence of the prime minister. The former Hôtel Biron at 77 rue de Varenne is today the Musée Rodin (see pp. 178–179), where you can visit the artist's former studio or enjoy a stroll through the gardens.

The other major museum is the Musée d'Orsay (see pp. 180–184), which is devoted to 19th-century art and holds some of the world's best known Impressionist paintings. Next door to the Orsay is the little known Musée de la Légion d'Honneur, displaying a collection of the red-rosette decorations instituted by Napoleon. France's famous emperor is forever linked to the district, as his ashes are enthroned under the gilded dome of Les Invalides, originally built by Louis XIV (see p. 177). The world's most famous monument, the Eiffel Tower (see pp. 172–173), soars 1,051 feet (320 m) above the grassy expanse of the Champ de Mars (see p. 174), on the western edge of the neighborhood.

The Y-shaped UNESCO Building behind the École Militaire (see p. 174) was considered revolutionary when inaugurated in 1958. A giant Calder mobile and a Henry Moore sculpture, "Silhouette," adorn the esplanade outside, while works by Karel Appel, Jean Arp, Matta, and Picasso are inside. Isamu Noguchi designed the lovely Japanese Zen garden, restored in 1998.

There are a few places with a more human scale—for example, the street

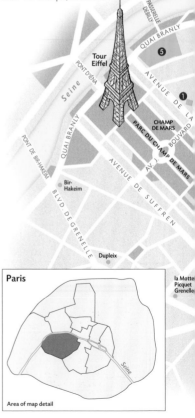

market on Rue Cler is lined with upscale shops, and the entrance to 29 avenue Rapp nearby is one of Paris's best examples of art nouveau architecture. For a subterranean view of the city, visit the famous *égouts* (sewers; see pp. 72–73), the entrance to which is on Place de la Résistance, opposite the Pont de l'Alma.

The Musée du Quai Branly (see p. 175), specializing in tribal arts, opened in 2006 and displays a huge collection of works moved from the Musée de l'Homme and the Musée des Arts d'Afrique et d'Océanie. ∎

NOT TO BE MISSED:

Watching the Tour Eiffel sparkle at night (on the hour, after dark until 1 a.m.) 172–173

Enjoying a picnic on the Champ de Mars 174

Unusual art at the Musée du Quai Branly 175

A visit to the Musée Rodin and its exquisite garden 178–179

Impressionist artworks at the Musée d'Orsay 180–184

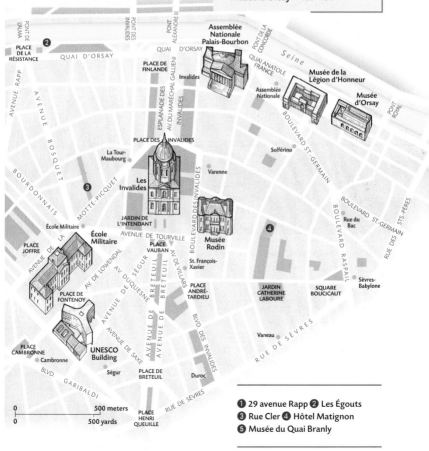

0	500 meters
0	500 yards

❶ 29 avenue Rapp ❷ Les Égouts
❸ Rue Cler ❹ Hôtel Matignon
❺ Musée du Quai Branly

TOUR EIFFEL

Parisians typically greet any new monument in their urban landscape with a mixture of horror, criticism, and public dismay for a few years, after which it becomes a cherished national symbol. The Eiffel Tower is a perfect example.

■ Brilliantly lit at night, the once reviled Tour Eiffel is now the international symbol of Paris.

Tour Eiffel

🅰 Map p. 170

✉ Champ de Mars

☎ 08 92 70 12 39

💲 €€–€€€

🚇 Métro: Bir-Hakeim
RER (C):
Champs de
Mars–Tour Eiffel

toureiffel.paris.fr

In 1887, Gustave Eiffel's cast-iron monument design was selected to showcase the 1889 Universal Exposition celebrating the centennial of the French Revolution. He used the same techniques for construction that he had used for his bridges in France and abroad: All 15,000 metal parts were prefabricated and numbered for assembly, and most of the 2.5 million rivets were already in place before the tower went up. His well-laid plans and technological wizardry ensured that, with 300 steel-workers toiling 7 days a week for 26 consecutive months (and without a single fatal accident), the world's tallest building was completed just 7 days before the exhibition opened.

The Eiffel Tower was the largest and most innovative structure of its time, sending a clear message that France and French engineers intended to lead the world into the 20th century. Some critics, however, were less than enthusiastic, calling it "the hollow candlestick" and "a disgusting column of bolts and sheet metal." Guy de Maupassant was so distressed at the sight of it that he ate in its second-floor Le Jules Verne restaurant, claiming it was the only place in town he couldn't see it. Although it was slated for demolition 20 years after the exposition closed, it was unexpectedly saved by the invention of radio (or wireless) transmission, as its height made it an unrivaled setting for an antenna.

The tower offers a magnificent view that extends up to 45 miles (73 km) on a clear day. Ticket price varies, depending on how high you want to go and whether you take the elevator: You can walk up to the second platform. You can save time by buying tickets online, up to a day in advance, but be prepared for lines even for ticket holders. If you're willing to take the stairs to the first or second platforms, you won't have as long to wait (but

INSIDER TIP:

The best time to take in the view from the Eiffel Tower is late afternoon or sunset. Bring a windbreaker in spring and fall—it gets chilly on top.

—GILLES MINGASSON
*National Geographic
photographer*

you'll need to be in decent physical shape to make it up the 704 steps to the second level). To go to the top, pick up a second elevator at the second level.

The tower's nearly seven million annual visitors rarely include Parisians, who often snub it as the ultimate in kitsch, but the one-star Le Jules Verne restaurant (see sidebar below) is gradually luring them back. It's expensive, but has a wonderful view and excellent cuisine. ■

Restaurants Open on Sunday

Parisian chefs like to relax on the weekend, so getting a good meal on a Sunday night can be a problem. Here are a few exceptions to the rule: In the Eiffel Tower itself, the pricey but stunning **Le Jules Verne** (€€€€€, tel 01 83 77 34 34, restaurants-toureiffel.com); close to the Champ de Mars, **La Fontaine de Mars** (€€€, 129 rue St.-Dominique, tel 01 47 05 46 44), a high-quality traditional bistro where former President Barack Obama and his wife, Michelle, ate on a visit to Paris in 2009; in St.-Germain-des-Prés,

top chef Yves Camdeborde's excellent **Comptoir du Relais** (€€€, 9 carrefour de l'Odéon, tel 01 44 27 07 97); in the Marais, **Les Chouettes** (€, 32 rue de Picardie, tel 01 44 61 73 21), with fine food in a spacious setting with designer decor, or **Glou** (€€€, 101 rue Vieille-du-Temple, tel 01 42 74 44 32), a trendy restaurant popular with young people; and in the 11th arrondissement, **Astier** (€€, 44 rue Jean Pierre Timbaud, tel 01 43 57 16 35), a well-loved bistro with a wood-paneled interior and tasty food.

CHAMP DE MARS
& ÉCOLE MILITAIRE

The Champ de Mars spreads out like an immense green carpet to the base of the Eiffel Tower, but it actually predates the tower by 140 years. Today, it is a pleasant expanse of open grass, where children play soccer and throw frisbees, and families relax.

The Champ de Mars stretches down to the École Militaire.

École Militaire

Map p. 171

École Militaire, Place Joffre

Métro: École Militaire RER (C): Champ de Mars–Tour Eiffel

The Champ de Mars was initially laid out as a parade ground for the École Militaire, a military school founded to educate members of the impoverished nobility. Young Napoleon Bonaparte spent a year at the school (1784–1785).

The first Bastille Day was celebrated here on July 14, 1790, when crowds gathered to watch Louis XVI pay allegiance to the new constitution (see pp. 26–28). In the late 18th century, the half-mile-long (0.6 km) Champ de Mars was transformed from parade ground to playground when the sport of horse racing was introduced from England, and it remained a racecourse until 1855.

French city planners have always had a penchant for majestic vistas, and one of the best is from the École Militaire (not open to the public), across the Champ de Mars toward the Eiffel Tower, with the outstretched wings of the Palais de Chaillot in the background. The well-manicured lawns also make a good spot for a picnic after climbing the Eiffel Tower. ■

Festival of the Supreme Being

In June 1794, the Champ de Mars was the site for one of the Revolutionary era's spectacles, the Festival of the Supreme Being. The festival was the brainchild of Maximilien de Robespierre, who opposed the more extreme "cult of reason" movement of the Revolution. In a speech at the Festival, Robespierre declared: "The Author of Nature has bound all mortals by a boundless chain of love and happiness." The following month, he and his comrades were guillotined by a populace that blamed him for the bloody Reign of Terror.

MUSÉE DU QUAI BRANLY

The Musée du Quai Branly, located on the Seine, opened in June 2006. Its vast collection, comprising 3,500 pieces from the Musée de l'Homme and the Musée National des Arts d'Afrique et d'Océanie, showcases ethnic art from all over the world. Jean Nouvel designed the glass-fronted structure, which echoes the shadow of the neighboring Eiffel Tower and is surrounded by a park of paths, a pool, and 200 trees.

The collection, much of it gathered by 19th-century travelers, includes stone sculptures from Sumatra, artifacts connected with initiation rites and ancestor worship from New Guinea, and aboriginal art from

INSIDER TIP:

Visit in spring to admire the Musée du Quai Branly's unique and beautiful garden.

—CHRISTEL CHERQAOUI
*National Geographic Books
promotion director*

Australia. In the large collection of **African arts,** you'll find furniture, embroidery, wooden vessels, pottery, and jewelry. The **French-Indochina collection** explores farming, Buddhism, and popular religious cults.

In the **textiles collection** are pre-Columbian weavings from Paracas, painted skins from the North American plains, Bengal embroidery, and other sumptuous examples of ethnographic materials. Elsewhere, a huge number of **musical instruments,** including drums and idiophones—rigid bodies made to vibrate by concussion, shaking, scraping—are housed

in a transparent Glass Tower. A multimedia system plays the songs of the nomads of Niger, the vocal polyphonies of the Pygmies of Cameroon, the processional music of Nepal, and more.

Adding to the richness of the displays, the stories behind the artifacts are evoked by paintings, sculptures, travelers' notebooks, and watercolors painted by sailors at the turn of the 19th century (including Paul Gauguin). ∎

Musée du Quai Branly

🗺 Map p. 170
✉ Rue de l'Université or Quai Branly
☎ 01 56 61 70 00
🕐 Closed Mon. (except during school holidays), May 1, Dec. 25
💲 €€
🚇 Métro: Iéna, Alma-Marceau

quaibranly.fr

▪ Carvings at the Musée du Quai Branly

ASSEMBLÉE NATIONALE

After Louis XIV's death in 1715, the many nobles who had followed the king to Versailles were delighted to return to Paris at the end of his 72-year-long rule, and several moved to this area, building ornate mansions and palaces, including one that became the Assemblée Nationale.

Assemblée Nationale

- Map p. 171
- 36 quai d'Orsay
- 01 40 63 60 00
- Individuals can visit at certain times; call or reserve online.
- Métro: Assemblée Nationale

assemblee-nationale.fr

The lower house of the French Parlement (Assemblée Nationale) is housed in the Palais-Bourbon; the Upper House (Sénat) is in the Palais du Luxembourg (see p. 82). Visitors can view the Hémisphère (where political debates take place) and the library, decorated by Delacroix's "History of Civilization."

The Palais-Bourbon, which houses the 577 elected deputies of the Assemblée Nationale (the government's legislative body), was built between 1722 and 1728 for the Duchesse de Bourbon; she ceded part of her property to her lover, the Marquis de Lassay, who constructed the magnificent Hôtel de Lassay next door.

The government confiscated the buildings in 1795, making them the seat of the elected assembly. Such extensive remodeling was done, including adding a neoclassical facade and a semicircular Council Chamber to replace the formal reception rooms, that only the courtyard of the original gracious mansion remains. The Assemblée can be visited during the Journées du Patrimoine (Heritage Days, in September) and by appointment. ∎

INSIDER TIP:

In Paris, what you're holding in your hands isn't a menu, it's called *la carte*. A *menu* is a set lunch or dinner.

—ANNE RANDERSON
National Geographic contributor

The Assemblée's Inner Workings

The political leanings of a deputy in the French National Assembly can be read in a glance at the "hémicycle," as their chamber is called: Ever since the French Revolution, the left-wing deputies have sat to the left (from the vantage point of the president, who sits facing them) and the right-wing to the right.

The Assembly, located in the Palais-Bourbon facing the Seine, is the lower house of the French Parliament. The upper house, the Senate, is located in the Palais du Luxembourg. The Assembly's 577 deputies are elected for five-year terms from metropolitan France and the French overseas departments and territories through a two-round system (if no candidate has a majority, the two top vote-winners face off in a second round of elections).

Each constituency is represented by one deputy. The French president has the power to dissolve the Assembly and call new elections (if he has not done this in the past year), but rarely does so. The Assembly, in turn, has the right to censure the government, but it has done so only once since 1958.

LES INVALIDES

The shining dome of the Église St.-Louis-des-Invalides is visible from all over Paris, marking the expansive collection of military museums and monuments that stands just off the Champ de Mars. Most famously, it denotes the final resting place of Napoleon I.

Originally built by Louis XIV as a hospital for his veterans, Les Invalides comprises the largest single complex of monuments in Paris, including the Musée de l'Armée, the Musée des Plans-Reliefs, the Musée de l'Ordre de la Libération, and the Église St.-Louis-des-Invalides.

After Versailles, Les Invalides ranks as the most important architectural project of Louis XIV's reign. In 1670 the king commissioned Libéral Bruant to build a military hospice on the far western edge of the Faubourg St.-Germain for poor, infirm soldiers and aging veterans. Originally intended for 1,500 invalids, by 1690 some 6,000 men were clamoring to enter, and monarchs throughout Europe began modeling their own military hospitals on it.

■ **The dome of Les Invalides looms over military museums.**

Napoleon's Tomb

The dome of the church at Les Invalides, designed by Jules Hardouin-Mansart and completed in 1706, is a gleaming landmark in the Parisian landscape. What was designed as a royal chapel became an imperial mausoleum in 1840 when the body of Napoleon I was returned to France from Saint Helena. In 1861, his ashes were laid to rest in a porphyry tomb, inside a glass-topped crypt in the center of the dome. Others interred in Les Invalides include Claude Rouget de Lisle, composer of *La Marseillaise*.

Military Museums

Three museums are housed within the grounds of Les Invalides. The **Musée de l'Armée** is one of the most complete military museums in the world. Its collection ranges from antiquity to World War II, including Napoleonic souvenirs. The **Musée des Plans-Reliefs** is an intriguing museum of three-dimensional scale models of fortified towns, a collection that began in 1668. The **Musée de l'Ordre de la Libération** honors those who fought for France during World War II. ■

Les Invalides

🗺 Map p. 171

✉ Esplanade des Invalides

☎ Musée de l'Armée 01 44 42 38 77; Musée des Plans-Reliefs 01 45 51 95 05; Musée de l'Ordre de la Libération 01 80 05 90 81

🕐 Closed Jan. 1, May 1, Nov. 1, Dec. 25

💲 €€ (one ticket provides access to all sites)

🚇 Métro: Varenne, La Tour-Maubourg

musee-armee.fr

museedesplans reliefs.culture.fr

ordredelaliberation .fr

MUSÉE RODIN

Auguste Rodin's sculptures fill the luxurious gardens and interiors of the 18th-century Hôtel Biron, the most charming and intimate spot in this otherwise grandiose neighborhood on the Rue de Varenne.

■ Rodin's "The Thinker" holds a place of honor in the gardens.

Rodin is generally credited as the founding father of modern sculpture. A self-taught artist, he vehemently rejected academic conventions throughout his life.

Born into poverty, Rodin worked in obscurity on public monuments for years. He was almost 38 when his first important work, "The Age of Bronze," was exhibited in 1878 amid great controversy. It was so perfectly sculpted that critics accused him of taking plaster casts directly from his model. He was finally vindicated, and the ensuing publicity catapulted him into the public eye.

Two years later he received a commission for "The Gates of Hell" (a work never completed in his lifetime), and by the time he had reached his mid-40s, he had achieved international fame. Yet nearly all of his major works created controversy, from "The Burghers of Calais" (1895) to his statue of Victor Hugo (1909), shocking his patrons with their realism, power, and emotional content. His statue of Balzac, wearing his legendary dressing gown, was considered so inappropriate that it was initially refused by the Société des Gens de Lettres (an institution of literary figures), and remained hidden from public view for 41 years. In 1939, "Balzac" was finally placed on Boulevard Raspail near the intersection with Boulevard Montpanasse, where it now stands.

Camille Claudel

Rodin said of Camille Claudel: "I showed her where to find gold, but the gold she found was truly hers." She came to Rodin's studio as a student in 1883 and soon became his model and lover. Her face appears in some of Rodin's best work, including "The Kiss," "The Gates of Hell," and "Fugit Amor." Their liaison lasted through 1898, when it became clear that Rodin would never break his long-term relationship with Rose Beuret.

Claudel retreated into madness, living alone in her studio on the Île St.-Louis. She was interned in a mental institution in 1913, where she remained until her death in 1943. In his will, Rodin stipulated that her work be exhibited in his museum, which has such intensely emotional pieces as "Sakountala" (perhaps her most important work), "Waltz," and "L'Age Mûr," created during her separation from Rodin.

Hôtel Biron

The rococo-style Hôtel Biron was completed in 1730, and, after the Revolution, it housed the Russian Embassy and then a religious school. By 1905, it was in a dilapidated state, and its future uncertain.

INSIDER TIP:

The Musée Rodin's gardens are a destination in themselves, a place of respite for visitors with tired feet.

—PATRICIA DANIELS
*National Geographic
contributor*

During negotiations, a few artists were allowed to use the building as a temporary studio—Austrian poet Rainer Maria Rilke (Rodin's secretary at the time), Henri Matisse, Jean Cocteau, and lastly, Rodin, who moved there in 1908. This situation became permanent when the State purchased the property in 1911. In the early

20th century, at the height of his career, Rodin's dream of creating a museum of his work in the Hôtel Biron was approved by the State, but he died before his museum was officially inaugurated.

Rodin donated all of his own work to the State, as well as his collection of paintings and Greek and Roman sculptures. All of his major pieces are represented here—"The Thinker," "The Walking Man," "The Burghers of Calais," and others, plus a number of studies. (Rodin's home and studio, in Meudon, also contain thousands of his terra-cotta and plaster models.)

Gardens

No fewer than 27 bronzes and 40 marbles by Rodin are scattered around the Hôtel Biron's lovely grounds. The 7-acre (3 ha) gardens are divided into a rose garden to the north (including the Rodin rose) and other plantings to the south. The café and restaurant in the gardens are currently closed for renovation. ∎

Musée Rodin

- 🗺 Map p. 171
- ✉ 79 rue de Varenne
- ☎ 01 44 18 61 10
- 🕐 Closed Mon., Jan. 1, May 1, Dec. 25
- 💲 €€
- 🚇 Métro: Varenne, Invalides

musee-rodin.fr

Rodin's Home & Studio

- ✉ Villa des Brillants, 19 avenue Auguste Rodin, Meudon (on the southern edge of Paris)
- ☎ 01 41 14 35 00
- 🕐 Open Fri.–Sun.
- 💲 €
- 🚆 RER (C): Meudon-Val-Fleury

MUSÉE D'ORSAY

Although the Impressionist paintings are probably the greatest draw for visitors to the Musée d'Orsay, the museum also features decorative arts, photography, and the performing arts.

The grand Musée d'Orsay began its existence as a train station.

Musée d'Orsay

- Map p. 171
- 1 rue de la Légion d'Honneur
- 01 40 49 48 14
- Closed Mon., May 1, Dec. 25
- €€. Free 1st Sun. of each month, always for under 18 & EU residents under 26.
- Métro: Solférino RER (C): Musée d'Orsay

musee-orsay.fr

The Musée d'Orsay's building rose from a pile of ashes. The former Palais d'Orsay, home of the Conseil d'État and the Cour des Comptes, was burned during the Commune in 1871 (see pp. 30–31). Émile Zola described the scene: "The four buildings, which surrounded the great inner courtyard, had caught fire at once; and then the oil poured down the stairs to the four corners, streaming along the steps like torrents from hell." The blackened ruins were left standing for nearly 30 years. On the eve of the Paris Universal Exposition of 1900, the government agreed to allow the Orléans Railway Company to construct a train station on the site of the ruins, providing a station that was more central than the remote Austerlitz.

The problem of integrating the train terminus with its aristocratic environment was solved in 1898 by Victor Laloux, who suggested hiding the cast-iron structure under finely cut stone. He incorporated the most up-to-date technology inside the building—elevators, ramps, luggage elevators, electric traction, and even a 370-room hotel surrounding the station along the length of Rue de Bellechasse, Rue de Lille, and part of the quay.

The station and hotel were inaugurated on July 14, 1900, and their lobby was so luxurious that the painter Edouard Detaille called it—prophetically—a "Palace of Fine Arts." Train stations around the world were modeled after Orsay, including Grand Central Terminal in New York and Union Station in Washington, D.C. For nearly 40 years, the Orsay station was the hub for traffic bound for southwest France. By 1939, however, long-distance trains no longer stopped here, as the platforms were too short for the longer modern trains.

The building was then put to a number of different uses, becoming a mailing center during World War II, a holding center for returning prisoners of war, a film set (featured in Orson Welles's adaptation of Kafka's *Trial* in 1962), and a temporary auction house. In the 1960s, plans to destroy the building and replace it with a modern hotel complex had already been approved when critics lobbied to have it classified as a historical monument. It was saved in 1977 when President Valéry Giscard d'Estaing proposed transforming it into a museum devoted to all forms of 19th-century art (from 1848 to 1915), thus filling a historical gap between the collections of the Louvre museum and the Centre Georges-Pompidou.

The ACT architecture group transformed the building itself, and a team of architects under Italian Gae Aulenti worked on its interiors. The masterful result incorporates Laloux's original cast-iron pillars and stucco decoration in a space suitable for the museum's requirements. The huge, luminous central entrance hall is divided by stone partitions and lined with galleries.

The Musée d'Orsay was officially inaugurated on December 1, 1986, by President François Mitterrand and it became the new home for Impressionist works that had been displayed at the Jeu de Paume. The Louvre transferred Salon paintings and works by artists born after 1820, and Post-Impressionist works came from the Musée National d'Art Moderne.

The Collections

The period covered by the Musée d'Orsay is important in the history of contemporary art. Academic conventions were overturned, new themes were introduced, and a radical approach to painting and

---

EXPERIENCE: Enjoy Kids' Stuff at Museums

Many Paris museums have special activities for children, and even spaces where the kids can be parked while the parents visit an exhibition. The **Musée en Herbe** (musee-en-herbe.com) specializes in exhibitions for kids that are enjoyable for adults as well. The **Centre Georges-Pompidou** (see pp. 96–97) has a children's gallery and special workshops. Its Studio 13/16 offers teenagers a space where they can participate in workshops or just hang out with friends. **Paris Tours with Kids** (paristourswithkids.com) offers cultural tours in English especially designed for children and families.

photography regarding color and composition appeared. The museum is organized in broad chronological sequences.

Ground Floor: The period represented here, from 1848 to 1870, is less familiar than that of the Impressionists, yet it was these artists who broke new ground for the generations to come. At that time, the yearly Salon (an official exhibition of art sponsored by the French government), with its staid and predictable historical and mythological paintings, was the standard by which artists were measured.

Ingres and Delacroix, who belonged to the earlier years of the century, continued as leading figures, and several of their later works illustrate the transition in academic painting. Thomas Couture and Alexandre Cabanel exemplified the languid, classical, and uncontroversial subjects of the *pompiers* (as in "pomp" and "pompous"), although they were highly regarded in their day. To the left of the entrance are landscapes from the Barbizon school (Jean-Baptiste Camille Corot, Charles Daubigny, and Théodore Rousseau), whose work was based on an idealization of nature and a rejection of academic convention. Jean-François Millet's painting "Gleaners" perhaps best represents this humanistic spirit.

Honoré Daumier was a major figure in realism, the movement that opposed the *pompier* style. Although better known as a cartoonist, his real masterpieces (on display) are the 26 painted clay busts that ruthlessly caricatured contemporary politicians. The Realist leader was Gustave Courbet, who portrayed scenes from contemporary life with an unsentimental yet sympathetic eye (as in his "Burial at Ornans"). His most sensational painting, the sexually explicit "Origins of the World," only acquired in 1995, was so realistic that it had never before been shown in public.

This floor also exhibits works painted before 1870 by Impressionist artists, including Édouard Manet, whose "Olympia" caused a scandal at the 1865 Salon des Refusés (created for those turned down by the official Salon). However, it was his subject matter—criticized as an obscene portrayal of a prostitute—that shocked the critics, not his technique, and although sympathetic to other

"Bathers" is one of many Cézanne paintings in the museum.

Impressionists, Manet remained aloof from them. Works by Monet, Degas, and Fréderic Bazille illustrate their early experiments in solving the problems of light and shadow, and their work pioneered a new vision of painting. Luminous works by Nabi painters Pierre Bonnard, Édouard Vuillard, Maurice Denis, and Félix Vallotton are shown in Room 8.

The central aisle emphasizes 19th-century sculpture in the neoclassical tradition; the most interesting are those by Jean-Baptiste Carpeaux, whose risqué "Dance" for the facade of the Opéra Garnier was called "an offense to public morals."

Top Floor: For a chronological overview of the development of Impressionism, take the elevator or escalator to the top (fifth) floor. The beautifully renovated Galerie des Impressionistes opens with pre-Impressionist works, mostly by Cézanne, Monet, and Manet, notably the former's "Poppy Field" and the latter's famed "Déjeuner sur l'Herbe." "Arrangement in Grey and Black No. 1," better known as "Whistler's Mother," also makes an appearance here.

After the Prussian Wars (1870–1871), Renoir, Monet, and Pissarro, along with Berthe Morisot and Alfred Sisley, banded together in opposition to the official Salons. The first exhibition by the Impressionist painters, held in 1874, was where the term "Impressionism" was coined, when critic Louis Leroy used it to mock Monet's painting,

"Impression: Sunrise" (now in the Musée Marmottan-Monet, see p. 157). The artists proudly adopted the name themselves, continuing to exhibit until 1886.

The following rooms contain a true feast of Impressionist painting, including Renoir's "Bal du Moulin de la Galette," and shimmering works by Sisley, Pissarro, Monet, Renoir, and Caillebotte.

INSIDER TIP:

After the Impressionist Gallery, stop into Café Campana—an aquatically inspired, art nouveau masterpiece designed by the Campana brothers.

—NEIL SHEA
*National Geographic
magazine writer*

Paul Cézanne's works are also displayed here. Note especially "The Card Players" and "The Bathers." He was less interested in the Impressionist experiments with light, working instead on structure, color, and composition. Ridiculed by critics, Cézanne was ultimately vindicated as the forerunner of 20th-century painting; both Picasso and Matisse were heavily influenced by his work.

Some of Monet's water lilies, haystacks, and views of the cathedral of Rouen, all vibrant experiments in portraying the changing effects of light, can be found in Room 34.

The innovative tendencies of

the next generation—Gauguin and the Pont-Aven painters Paul Sérusier, Émile Bernard, and others—are exhibited in the Rooms 38–40, and works by neo-Impressionists such as Paul Signac, Henri-Edmond Cross, and Georges Seurat in Room 36.

Gauguin's Tahiti paintings can be found in the Galerie Bellechasse, alongside masterpieces by van Gogh including "Van Gogh's Bedroom in Arles," "The Church in Auvers-sur-Oise, View from the Chevet," "Dr. Paul Gachet," and the artist's 1889 "Self-Portrait."

Middle Floor: While Room 6 hosts a few works by Henri de Toulouse-Lautrec, most of this level is devoted to decorative arts and sculptures, with nearly a quarter of the sculpture terrace devoted to Rodin. Several works are on loan from the nearby Musée Rodin (see pp. 178–179), including the plaster versions of "The Gates of Hell" and "Balzac." Commissioned for a museum that was never built, "The Gates of Hell" is based on Dante's "Divine Comedy."

Several rooms are also dedicated to the art nouveau movement that spread through Europe under various names—Modern Style, Jugendstil, and Stile Liberty—in the late 19th century. Objects range from chairs to furniture, glassware, and stained glass, illustrating what was a radically new approach to design at the time. One of the most beautiful examples is the Charpentier Dining Room (circa 1900), a luscious interior of mahogany, oak, and poplar, with the characteristic floral decoration.

Photography

The museum also has several thousand images from the earliest days of photography. Interesting temporary exhibitions offer retrospectives of little-known 19th-century artists.

The museum hosts films, lectures, and lunchtime concerts in its auditorium. Special joint tickets give discounted access to the Musée de l'Orangerie or the Musée Rodin; the Orsay ticket will also give you reduced rates at the Opéra Garnier or the Gustave Moreau Museum. ■

Salon des Refusés

Today, crowds flock to the Musée d'Orsay to see the works of Édouard Manet, Claude Monet, Vincent van Gogh, and dozens of other artists whose works are worth multiple millions. It is well known that van Gogh only sold one painting in his lifetime, but he was not the only one who struggled. At the beginning of their creators' careers, works by Manet, Whistler, Monet, and many other now famous artists were rejected by the jurors of the official Salon, the gateway to success for artists at the time. In reaction, some of them staged Salons des Refusés. One was even sponsored by the French government in 1863. Monet and other Impressionists also held alternative salons to show their work.

A neighborhood of narrow, sinuous streets snaking downward toward Pigalle and, in the heart of it all, the dome of Sacré-Coeur

MONTMARTRE

Sculpture at the Musée de Montmartre

MONTMARTRE

There is no other place in Paris quite like Montmartre. High on a hill (known to Parisians as the "Butte"), it has a unique village atmosphere, encompassing both Pigalle's neon lights and the lyrical, winding streets and charming houses just steps away. Music, art, and wine—along with a touch of the licentious and an irreverence for authority and tradition—have all contributed to the myth of Montmartre.

The Butte Montmartre has been a place of worship since earliest history: The Druids celebrated their priestly rites here, and it was also the site of a Roman temple, probably dedicated to Mercury. This area has escaped real estate development largely because the ground is riddled with tunnels from old quarries, where gypsum and limestone have been mined since Roman times.

Montmartre's hill was also punctuated with Christian edifices, such as the Royal Abbey of St.-Denis, constructed in 1136 by Louis VI and his wife, Adelaide de Savoy, in honor of the martyred saint (see p. 19). Its lands extended south into the present-day 9th arrondissement and north toward the abbey. After the Revolution, the abbey's lands were sold and its buildings dismantled, except the Romanesque St.-Pierre de Montmartre Church (see p. 190), which continued to be the villagers' favored place of worship even after work on the Basilica of Sacré-Coeur (see p. 190) began in 1876. The villagers' long history of independence was demonstrated when, infuriated by Thiers's capitulation to the Prussians in 1871, they refused to hand over the cannon guarding the city, setting off a series of events that produced the Commune (see pp. 30–31). The generals dispatched by Thiers to recover the cannon were killed, an act that would be commemorated on a plaque behind the basilica (on Rue Chevalier-de-la-Barre).

Montmartre's social structure was transformed when trainloads of people from the provinces came to the capital during the industrial revolution to look for work and ended up living in this inexpensive neighborhood. The

> **NOT TO BE MISSED:**
>
> **Catching a show at the Lapin Agile** 188
>
> **The windmill of the Moulin de la Galette** 189
>
> **Shopping on Rue des Abbesses** 189
>
> **The view from Sacré-Coeur** 190
>
> **The medieval interior of St.-Pierre de Montmartre** 190
>
> **Having your portrait drawn by a Place du Tertre artist** 191
>
> **The fascinating mansion of the Musée Gustave Moreau** 194

wall of the Fermiers Généraux, or toll road, where the present-day Place Pigalle is, effectively cut Montmartre off from the city. Incoming goods were levied on Pigalle's tollgate; therefore, outside the walls, wine—produced in abundance on the hills of Montmartre—was cheaper and the demand was heavy. The village was incorporated into the City of Paris in 1860 as the 18th arrondissement.

By the late 19th century, the area's numerous cabarets, brothels, and nefarious underworld activities had earned Montmartre an enduring reputation for depravity that inevitably attracted artists, writers, and bourgeois Parisians in search of new thrills. Artists of all types, from Eugène Delacroix, Hector Berlioz, and Vincent van Gogh to contemporary painters, have come to the Butte for its charm, light, and, in the past, low rents.

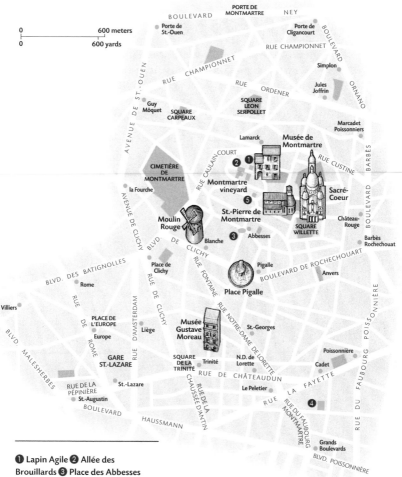

0 | 600 meters
0 | 600 yards

❶ Lapin Agile ❷ Allée des
Brouillards ❸ Place des Abbesses
❹ Folies Bergère ❺ Place du Tertre

Montmartre today is much as it has always
been: a heady mix of romance, poetry, sex,
and commercialism. The Moulin Rouge (see
pp. 192–193) is packed every night, and Place
du Tertre (see p. 191) is inundated with portrait
painters and the smell of crêpes from food
stands. But glimpses of a more lyrical era survive in the labyrinth of steep, tree-lined streets
encircling the Butte. From its vantage point, the
busy capital below seems miles away. ■

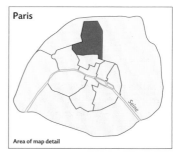

Paris

Area of map detail

A WALK THROUGH MONTMARTRE

This bohemian area of Paris may have lost some of its romantic appeal, but there are times when a stroll around the quaint old streets can take you back a hundred years or more to an age when it was a renowned artists' quarter.

Sacré-Coeur rises over a Montmartre street.

NOT TO BE MISSED:

Place Pigalle • Sacré-Coeur • Place du Tertre • St.-Pierre de Montmartre Church • Allée des Brouillards

As the steps and steep streets may make this rather a strenuous walk, another option is to take the small train that leaves Place Blanche or Place du Tertre every 30–45 minutes for a 35-minute guided tour of the Butte, although some of the sites below can only be reached on foot.

Begin at the **Place Pigalle** (*Métro: Pigalle*), whose late 19th-century dance halls and cabarets lured Parisians in search of flash and flesh. A less classy ambience still reigns among the garish, neon-lit sex shops and seedy boulevards.

Walk east on Boulevard de Clichy and turn left up Rue des Martyrs, the street once climbed by many illustrious Christian pilgrims on their way to the Basilica of Sacré-Coeur. Turn right to reach 9 rue Yvonne Le Tac. Here Saint Denis was supposedly beheaded in the third century

(see p. 19) and Ignatius of Loyola founded the order of the Jesuits in 1534. At the end of Rue Yvonne Le Tac, turn right on Rue des Trois Frères, then left at the Place Charles Dullin, past the **Théâtre de l'Atelier** (1822).

Continue to Rue de Steinkerque, over which Sacré-Coeur looms, and turn left up the street. The streets and the nearby Place St.-Pierre are lined with shops offering the best prices and widest selection of fabrics in Paris. From here, the only way to go is up—climb the steps that zigzag up the middle or the set of steps just past the funicular, or if you prefer to ride, take the funicular off to the left side (fare: one Métro ticket).

After enjoying the view and visiting **Sacré-Coeur** Basilica ❶ (see p. 190), follow the tourists heading up Rue Azais to **Place du Tertre** (see p. 191), an unavoidable tourist stop on any tour of Montmartre. Take the time to explore the church of **St.-Pierre de Montmartre** ❷ (see p. 190), one of Paris's few remaining Romanesque churches.

Walk past the church down Rue du Mont Cenis (past Rue St.-Rustique) to explore the real charms of old Montmartre. Turn left on Rue Cortot to reach the **Musée de Montmartre** ❸ at No. 12 (see p. 191). Turn right on Rue des Saules to see Montmartre's last remaining vineyard, whose harvest festival takes place on the first Saturday in October. Straight ahead is the legendary **Lapin Agile** ❹ (*22 rue des Saules, tel 01 46 06 85 87*), the cabaret whose regulars once included Picasso and Modigliani.

Backtrack up the hill and turn right onto Rue de l'Abreuvoir. The postcard-perfect, pink house at No. 2 was immortalized by the painter Maurice Utrillo. Continue down the mysterious **Allée des Brouillards,** across the street from Renoir's onetime residence. The fountain in the nearby Square Suzanne-Buisson is reputedly where Saint Denis stopped to wash off his severed head. Go to **Avenue Junot** ⑤ and turn left. At No. 25 is the **Villa Léandre,** a row of impeccable houses built in 1926.

Go through the gate at No. 23 and walk down the steps to Rue Lepic. Turn left here to see one of the two remaining windmills on the Butte Montmartre—the **Moulin de la Galette** ⑥ of Renoir's famous painting is now a restaurant. Turn right down Rue d'Orchampt to reach **Place Émile Goudeau** ⑦. Here Picasso, Max Jacob, and others lived in the Bateau-Lavoir, an old wooden warehouse, during the early 1900s.

The original building was replaced by a block of studios at 6 rue Durantin (to the right).

Turn left and continue along Rue Durantin to Rue Tholozé and turn left down the hill to No. 10. The Studio 28 Cinema made headlines in 1930 when shocked spectators pelted the screen with eggs and ink during the premiere of Luis Buñuel's classic surrealist film *L'Age d'Or;* Buñuel's and Jean Cocteau's footprints are embedded in the hall of the cinema.

Turn left on Rue des Abbesses, where you can end the walk and rest your legs at any one of the local cafés. Or go on to the Métro at **Place des Abbesses** ⑧.

> ◩ See also area map pp. 186–187
> ▶ Place Pigalle (Métro: Pigalle)
> ⏱ Allow 2 1/2–3 hours
> ↔ 3 miles (4.8 km)
> ▶ Place des Abbesses (Métro: Abbesses)

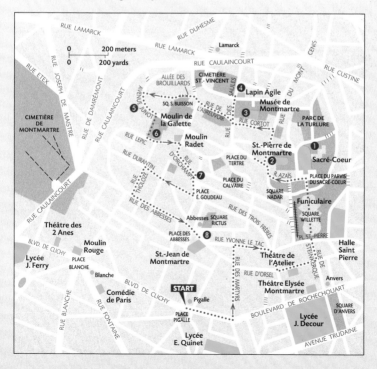

SACRÉ-COEUR

Rising like a giant wedding cake in northern Paris, the Basilica of Sacré-Coeur stands on the highest point of the city and is thus the most visible of Montmartre's monuments, though one of its most recent. One of Sacré-Coeur's most striking aspects is its perpetually sparkling white stone, despite the dirt and grime of city pollution. The stone, from the Seine and Marne regions, produces a white-lime deposit when it rains.

Sacré-Coeur
- 🅰 Map p. 187
- ✉ Place du Parvis du Sacré-Coeur
- ☎ 01 53 41 89 00
- 💲 Basilica: Free. Crypt/dome: €€
- 🚇 Métro: Anvers, Abbesses, Lamarck

sacre-coeur-montmartre.com

St.-Pierre de Montmartre
- 🅰 Map p. 187
- ✉ 2 rue du Mont-Cenis
- ☎ 01 46 06 57 63
- 🚇 Métro: Anvers, Abbesses, Lamarck

The Basilica

The impetus for the construction of this Romano-Byzantine church came from the French Catholics' vow to build a basilica devoted to the Sacred Heart of Jesus after the country's humiliating defeat in the Franco-Prussian War of 1870.

Work began in 1876. The architect, Paul Abadie (a student of Eugène Viollet-le-Duc), died in 1884, and the project was completed by Lucien Magne, who added the 275-foot (84 m) campanile. Preparation of the foundations alone was an enormous engineering feat: 83 wells were dug 147 feet (45 m) deep and filled with masonry, then connected by a series of underground arches to stabilize the subsoil and compensate for quarried tunnels riddling the hillside. Twenty-eight horses were needed to draw the wagon carrying the Savoyarde bell up Montmartre's hill; one of the world's largest bells, it resonates at a high C note. Today, visitors can climb to the stained-glass gallery in the dome for a view of the church's interior.

INSIDER TIP:

Ideal for a picnic lunch, the Square Marcel-Bleustein-Blanchet has a magnificent view of the basilica.

—CHRISTEL CHERQAOUI
*National Geographic Books
promotion director*

St.-Pierre de Montmartre

Residents of Montmartre continued to worship in the Church of St.-Pierre. Situated between the basilica and the Place du Tertre, this is one of the oldest churches in Paris. Open the doors of the 18th-century facade to discover the beauty of its 12th-century, Romanesque-style nave within. ∎

■ The white domes of Sacré-Coeur mark Paris's highest point.

PLACE DU TERTRE

The Place du Tertre and its surrounding streets are lined with souvenir shops, overpriced cafés, and portrait painters, all vying for your euros.

In the morning, before the crowds arrive, you can see traces of old Montmartre in this village square, which once housed the post-Revolution town hall. At La Mère Catherine restaurant, the culinary use of the word "bistro" was coined when Russian soldiers during the 1814 occupation banged on the table, shouting "*Bistro!*"— Russian for "quick."

Musée de Montmartre

The Musée de Montmartre *(12 rue Cortot, tel 01 49 25 89 39, €€, Métro: Lamarck, museede montmartre.fr)* is just behind the Place du Tertre. In the late 19th century, a number of French artists lived in this 17th-century building, including Dufy and Renoir. The museum re-creates the unique atmosphere of Montmartre's past.

Don't miss the reproduction of one of the great artistic jokes

■ Stalls and tourists can't erase the charm of Place du Tertre.

played on the Montmartre art scene when the author Roland Dorgelès—who despised modern art—attached a paintbrush to the tail of the donkey that belonged to the owner of the Lapin Agile cabaret. The resulting canvas, "Sunset over the Adriatic," received critical acclaim. ■

Place du Tertre
Ⓜ Map p. 187

EXPERIENCE: Connecting on the Web

For younger people (20s to 30s), who might be somewhat shy about striking up a conversation at a bistro, a great way to meet the French is to go to one of the many Thursday-night after-work parties, usually held in clubs. For an entry fee of €15–€20, you get a buffet and champagne if you arrive early, followed by dancing. Visit their websites to sign up and to get a password for reduced fees:

afterwork-paris.fr. To find like-minded French people to go out with to a film, concert, or dance class, for example, you can suggest an outing or sign up for one on *paris.onvasortir.com* (click on the British flag for English). Or try *meetup. com/cities/fr/paris* to join events ranging from language exchanges to *apéros* (drinks parties) to outings to hidden corners of Paris.

CABARET

Paris has continually invented and reinvented new forms of entertainment. The *cafés chantants* or *goguettes* popular during the Revolution gave way during the Second Empire and belle époque to concert-cafés, the forerunners to the 20th-century music halls and irreverent *cabarets artistiques* launched in Montmartre at the turn of the century.

A Fine French Tradition

Talents such as balladeers Léo Ferré and Georges Brassens debuted in cabarets during the 1950s. In the 1960s, a new form of expression surfaced in the *café-théâtres*, which combined comedy and satire performed in close-quartered cafés (initiated by Le Royal in Montparnasse and La Vieille Grille in the Latin Quarter). The café-théâtre was responsible for launching such diverse talents as the late comedian Coluche, Gérard Depardieu, and the Théâtre du Splendide troupe (featuring Anémone and Gérard Jugnot). The tradition is alive and well today.

INSIDER TIP:

Be careful when ordering your meals in Paris: An entrée is the first course, not the main dish, called *plat principal.*

—ANNE RANDERSON
National Geographic contributor

However, the most typically French tradition in this hub of hedonism is the legendary music hall revue—a throwback to the champagne nights of the belle époque era. The Crazy Horse saloon *(tel 01 47 23 32 32, lecrazyhorse paris.com)* on Avenue George V evolved from a Wild West–style barroom, with swinging doors and signs like "Check Your Guns Here," into a theater flaunting the wildest of risqué apparel, with features such as Betty Buttocks and Nouka Bazooka. (During the 1950s, one routine featured blond dominatrix Dodo d'Hambourg and Bertha Von Paraboum—clad merely in boots,

helmet, and a swastika G-string. This made a negative impression on Parisians who remembered the German occupation.)

Exoticism & Extravagance

On the Champs-Élysées, the Lido *(tel 01 40 76 56 10, lido.fr)* and its glittering Bluebell Girls are the closest you'll get to Las Vegas this side of the Atlantic, with extravagant megaproductions featuring lasers, video, fountains, and fire-breathing dragons. The Paradis Latin *(tel 01 43 25 28 28, paradislatin.com),* staged in a theater designed by Gustave Eiffel, supposedly offers a traditional Parisian cabaret, driven by a feathered Latin beat.

The Folies Bergère *(tel 08 92 68 16 50, www. foliesbergere.com),* inaugurated in 1869, no longer has its own cabaret show, but hosts various concerts and musical comedies. It's worth going to see the historic interior. The Folies are closely associated with the legendary cabaret *artiste* Josephine Baker, but she debuted in *La Revue Nègre* at the Théâtre des Champs-Élysées in 1925. Born in St. Louis, Missouri, she was the star attraction of the Folies. Baker became a French citizen and remained in France until her death in 1975.

Moulin Rouge

We couldn't fail to mention the kitschy Moulin Rouge *(tel 01 53 09 82 82, moulin rouge.com),* where today only the red windmill is original, but the feathered Doriss Girls still offer up a cancan or two. The Moulin is usually associated with the cancan (which originated in Montparnasse) due to Toulouse-Lautrec's paintings, but it is believed that it was the striptease that

■ The unsubtle Moulin Rouge is a staple of the Montmartre neighborhood.

actually originated here in 1893. Supposedly, during a contest between artists' models at the yearly Bal des Quat'z Arts held by the Fine Arts School students at the cabaret, one of them leaped up on a table and threw off her clothes. Outraged upon learning of this new phenomenon, the president of the Ligue Contre la Licence des Rues—the league in charge of cleaning up the streets—took the case to court. The model was arrested, sparking protests by students demanding the right to "artistic nudity." The publicity surrounding the case led to risqué sketches in neighboring cabarets as well.

Check *Pariscope* for information on cabarets, addresses, and current shows.

More Places to Visit in Montmartre

Montmartre Vineyard

The Butte was once covered with vineyards, but by the 1920s grapes were no longer harvested here. In 1929, when a vacant lot opposite the Lapin Agile was earmarked for real estate development, a group of drinking buddies came up with a plan to save the property by creating a park.

Again threatened with a building project five years later, the plotters proposed replanting the hill with vines. However, they didn't realize that the vines needed to mature for four years before producing fruit, so they gaily made plans for a harvest festival the first year. With the vines bare and the festival approaching, the good-natured but visibly incompetent group was saved when French wine growers shipped in more than 30 tons (27 tonnes) of grapes.

Today, the vineyard produces about 75 gallons (284 L) of wine each year (reputedly of dubious quality), which are auctioned off along with a painting by a local artist, with the proceeds going to charity.

🅰 Map p. 187 ✉ 14 rue des Saules
🚇 Métro: Lamarck

Musée Gustave Moreau

Situated south of Montmartre, the Musée Gustave Moreau offers a rare glimpse into the intimate world of an artist and his workplace. It was created by and for the artist, who planned the layout and collections before his death. Considered a precursor of the surrealist movement, Moreau was a shy, financially independent painter who shunned exhibitions of his own work, instead teaching at the Fine Arts School. Among his most celebrated pupils were Georges Rouault and Henri Matisse. A marvelous clutter hangs on the museum's walls and fills the rooms of the meticulously organized family mansion. The ornate, double-spiral staircase is one of its more interesting features; the nearly 6,000 drawings and paintings include watercolors and large, mythological themes, such as "Apollo and Pegasus," "The Unicorns," and "The Descent from the Cross."
musee-moreau.fr

🅰 Map p. 187 ✉ 14 rue de la Rochefoucauld
☎ 01 48 74 38 50 🕐 Closed Tues., Jan 1, May 1, July 14, Dec. 25 💲 € 🚇 Métro: Trinité

■ The Montmartre vineyard slopes downhill from the Lapin Agile.

Containing two vast landscaped parks, former outlying villages, and the ambitious urban project La Défense

AROUND THE PÉRIPHÉRIQUE

■ The Château de Vincennes

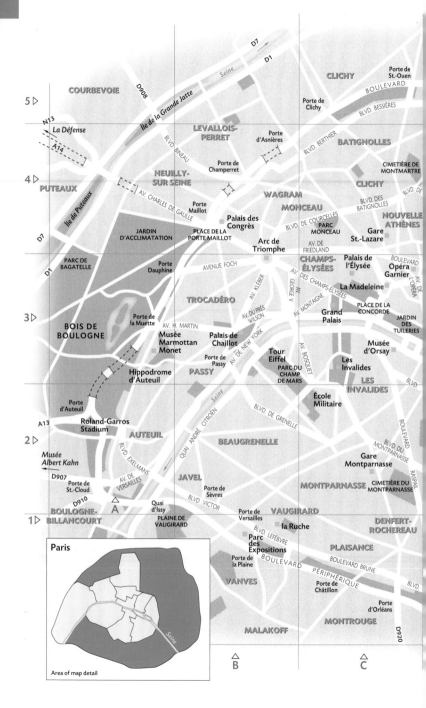

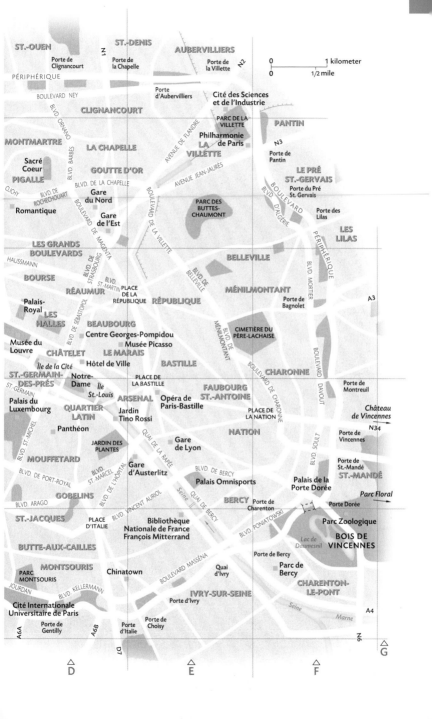

ST.-OUEN

ST.-DENIS

AUBERVILLIERS

N1

Porte de
Clignancourt

Porte de
la Chapelle

Porte de
la Villette

N2

PÉRIPHÉRIQUE

0   1 kilometer
0   1/2 mile

BOULEVARD NEY

Porte
d'Aubervilliers

Cité des Sciences
et de l'Industrie

BLVD. ORNANO

CLIGNANCOURT

PARC DE LA
VILLETTE

PANTIN

AVENUE DE FLANDRE

MONTMARTRE

LA CHAPELLE

Philharmonie
de Paris

LA
VILLETTE

N3

Sacré
Coeur

BLVD. BARBÈS

GOUTTE D'OR

Porte de
Pantin

LE PRÉ
ST.-GERVAIS

PIGALLE

CLICHY

BLVD. DE
ROCHECHOUART

BLVD. DE LA CHAPELLE

AVENUE JEAN-JAURÈS

BOULEVARD

BLVD. D'ALGÉRIE

Porte du Pré
St. Gervais

Gare
du Nord

Porte des
Lilas

Romantique

BOULEVARD DE MAGENTA

Gare
de l'Est

PARC DES
BUTTES-
CHAUMONT

LES
LILAS

BOULEVARD DE LA VILLETTE

PÉRIPHÉRIQUE

HAUSSMANN

LES GRANDS
BOULEVARDS

BLVD. DE STRASBOURG

BELLEVILLE

BOURSE

BLVD. DE BELLEVILLE

BLVD. MORTIER

RÉAUMUR

ST.-MARTIN

PLACE
DE LA
RÉPUBLIQUE

MÉNILMONTANT

A3

Palais-
Royal

LES
HALLES

BEAUBOURG

RÉPUBLIQUE

Porte de
Bagnolet

BLVD. DE SÉBASTOPOL

Centre Georges-Pompidou

Musée du
Louvre

CHÂTELET

LE MARAIS

Musée Picasso

BLVD. DE MÉNILMONTANT

CIMETIÈRE DU
PÈRE-LACHAISE

BOULEVARD

Île de la Cité

Hôtel de Ville

BASTILLE

CHARONNE

ST.-GERMAIN-
DES-PRÉS

Notre-
Dame

PLACE DE
LA BASTILLE

BOULEVARD DE CHARONNE

DAVOUT

Porte de
Montreuil

ST.-GERMAIN

Île
St.-Louis

ARSENAL

FAUBOURG
ST.-ANTOINE

Palais du
Luxembourg

QUARTIER
LATIN

Opéra de
Paris-Bastille

Jardin
Tino Rossi

PLACE DE
LA NATION

Château
de Vincennes

BLVD. ST.-MICHEL

Panthéon

NATION

N34

Porte de
Vincennes

JARDIN DES
PLANTES

Gare
de Lyon

BLVD. SOULT

MOUFFETARD

BLVD. DE PORT-ROYAL

BLVD. ST.-MARCEL

Gare
d'Austerlitz

BLVD. DE BERCY

Porte de
St.-Mandé

ST.-MANDÉ

GOBELINS

QUAI DE LA RAPÉE

BLVD. DE L'HÔPITAL

Palais Omnisports

Palais de la
Porte Dorée

Parc Floral

BLVD. ARAGO

Seine

BERCY

Porte de
Charenton

Porte Dorée

ST.-JACQUES

PLACE
D'ITALIE

BLVD. VINCENT AURIOL

Bibliothèque
Nationale de France
François Mitterrand

QUAI DE BERCY

BLVD. PONIATOWSKI

Parc Zoologique

BOIS DE
VINCENNES

BUTTE-AUX-CAILLES

Lac de
Daumesnil

MONTSOURIS

Chinatown

Porte de Bercy

Parc de
Bercy

PARC
MONTSOURIS

BOULEVARD MASSÉNA

Quai
d'Ivry

CHARENTON-
LE-PONT

JOURDAN

BLVD. KELLERMANN

IVRY-SUR-SEINE

Seine

Cité Internationale
Universitaire de Paris

Porte d'Ivry

A4

A6A

A6B

Porte de
Gentilly

Porte
d'Italie

Porte de
Choisy

Marne

D7

N6

G

D

E

F

AROUND THE PÉRIPHÉRIQUE

The Périphérique ring road that encloses Paris sharply defines the city's limits. Many areas of the arrondissements bordering the Périphérique are somewhat off the beaten track, but form entities in and of themselves, with a degree of independence that survives to this day. If you have enough time, they are well worth a visit.

Walkers enjoy the paths of the Parc de Belleville.

Butte-aux-Cailles (see p. 202), for instance, is typical of old Paris with its narrow cobbled streets, obscure passageways, and small vine-covered town houses. Belleville, with its hamlet Ménilmontant (see pp. 206–207), served as the vineyard for the great abbeys of Paris and as a place for Parisians to go on Sundays to drink a glass of *guinguet* (a sour-tasting wine). Both were active during the Commune (see pp. 30–31), and have been bastions of working-class agitation. Belleville has traditionally drawn waves of immigrants from the world over, and its population is the most diverse and cosmopolitan in the city, with Chinese, Arabic, African, and Turkish quarters, and colorful, ethnic markets.

The former slaughterhouses at La Villette are now part of a huge park (see pp. 208–209), a recent addition to the vast city-park system that includes the great Bois de Vincennes (see p. 203) and Bois de Boulogne (see opposite) flanking eastern and western Paris respectively. ■

NOT TO BE MISSED:

A walk through the Bagatelle Garden in the Bois de Boulogne 199

The view from the Grande Arche de La Défense 200

Exploring the catacombs 201

Boating in the Bois de Vincennes 203

The entertaining museums of Parc de la Villette 208–209

BOIS DE BOULOGNE

An immense park of 2,132 acres (863 ha), the Bois de Boulogne draws people from all over the city. The two lakes (Lac Supérieur and Lac Inférieur) within the park are at different levels, connected by a superb waterfall.

The Bois de Boulogne was commissioned by Napoleon III. The elegant world met there during the day, while a more dubious underworld congregated at night—and still does, so certain areas are best avoided after sunset.

INSIDER TIP:

Visit the Bois de Boulogne in the early mornings, when the park is quiet and feels like the countryside.

—GILLES MINGASSON
National Geographic photographer

Graceful avenues and paths lead to the lakes through a pine forest and several oak groves. The **Jardin d'Acclimatation** has rides, miniature golf, and other activities, and is also home to the new **Louis Vuitton Foundation for Creation** (*8 avenue du Mahatma Gandhi, tel 01 40 69 96 00, €–€€, fondationlouisvuitton.fr*), housed in a spectacular glass building designed by Frank Gehry.

The **Jardin Shakespeare** (*Route de Suresnes*) encompasses a small, 300-seat open-air theater (performances in English and French). Nearby is the romantic (and expensive) **Le Pré Catelan** restaurant (see Travelwise p. 254).

The **Bagatelle Garden** (*Route de Sèvres à Neuilly, €*) is a spectacular showcase in the spring and summer with nearly 9,000 rosebushes. The gardens also contain an impressive water lily and iris garden.

At the southern edge of the Bois, near the **Roland-Garros Stadium** (venue of tennis's French Open; *2 avenue Gordon Bennett*), is an unexpected haven: the greenhouses of **Auteuil**, which contain exotic plants, a tropical greenhouse, and a palmarium under the light of the central dome. ■

Bois de Boulogne

 Map p. 196 A2–4

Jardin d'Acclimatation

✉ Carrefour des Sablons, Bois de Boulogne

☎ 01 40 67 90 85

$ €

Ⓜ Métro: Les Sablons

jardindacclimatation .fr

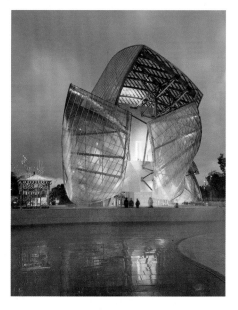

■ **The Louis Vuitton Foundation in the Bois de Boulogne**

LA DÉFENSE

La Défense, with its Grande Arche completing the monumental east–west axis cutting through Paris, is the French response to the Manhattan skyline.

La Défense
🔺 Map p. 196 A4

Conceived in 1950 and begun in the early 1960s, this commercial district was designed on an American model as a functional and modern international business center for Paris.

In the early 1970s, it became a symbol of the inhumanity of modern architecture; companies snubbed the project, yet the 1980s brought a recovery with the construction of the gigantic Quatre-Temps shopping center

◼ The Grande Arche de La Défense

as well as a new IMAX theater.

Some berate La Défense as inhuman and sprawling; others praise it as innovative and futuristic. But it remains one of the most ambitious urban developments in Europe. Designers initially modeled their plan on similar structures in U.S. cities such as Manhattan and Chicago, but went further by eliminating traffic. The result is a two-tiered development, with the aboveground commercial and residential buildings linked by an immense esplanade, and a network of roads, trains, parking lots, and Métros below.

One of the first structures was the CNIT building, with a record-breaking 759-foot (230 m) roof span. Major trade fairs used to be held here, before moving to the Porte de Versailles. It now houses smaller shows, a hotel, and various stores and restaurants.

Concrete, glass, and steel are the rule here, but the esplanade has been brightened up with works of art that include a gigantic sculpture by Alexander Calder, a piece by Nikki de Saint-Phalle, and several playful fountains.

The crowning work, however, is **La Grande Arche,** which opened in 1989. Its rooftop, at 300 feet (91.5 m), is open to the public, alongside a photography exhibition space (€€, *lagrandearche.fr*). Faced with glass and Carrara marble, this vast, empty cube is large enough to frame Notre-Dame. ◼

DENFERT-ROCHEREAU

The 14th arrondissement is a good place to get a feel for everyday Parisian life by exploring the streets, markets, parks (particularly Montsouris), and the nearby Montparnasse Cemetery.

Paris's catacombs are literally lined with bones.

In the center of Place Denfert-Rochereau stands the "Lion of Belfort," a copy of a lion sculpted by Frédéric Auguste Bartholdi as a tribute to Alsatians during the Franco-Prussian War. North of the place, at 261 boulevard Raspail, stands the **Fondation Cartier** *(€€, fondationcartier.com, closed Mon.).* Constructed in 1994, the sleek glass-and-steel structure stands in a beautiful garden and hosts art shows.

The strangest necropolis in all of Paris is the **catacombs** (entrance on Place Denfert-Rochereau), the resting place for more than six million skeletons (and parts thereof) moved from inner-city cemeteries in the 18th and 19th centuries because of crowding and stench. Stacks of bones line miles of corridors under the city streets. ■

Catacombs

✉ Place Denfert-Rochereau

☎ 01 43 22 47 63

🕐 Closed Mon. & public holidays

💲 €€

Ⓜ Métro or RER (B): Denfert-Rochereau

catacombes.paris.fr

Wallace Fountains

The elegant, green cast-iron drinking fountain that graces Place Denfert-Rochereau is one of 66 Wallace fountains scattered around Paris. Designed by Sir Richard Wallace as public hygiene became a prime concern under the Second Empire and Third Republic, they were placed around the city, with the first inaugurated in 1871 on Boulevard de la Villette.

The fountains are easily recognizable by their four caryatids of Simplicity, Charity, Sobriety, and Abundance, which support a dolphin-topped dome. The fountains are typical of the 19th-century style of street furniture, including benches, street lamps, and columns.

BUTTE-AUX-CAILLES

Past and present coexist in this workers' quarter, which was one of the city's many outlying villages. Locals were called *pieds mouillés* or "wet feet" as they waded barefoot across the Bièvre River (now channeled under the Rue Corvisart) into Paris to avoid paying tolls.

■ The streets of Butte-aux-Cailles have an old-fashioned feel.

Butte-aux-Cailles

🄰 Map p. 197 D1

✉ Between Rue de la Butte-aux-Cailles & Rue des Cinq Diamants

🚇 Métro: Corvisart

The Butte-aux-Cailles became famous on November 21, 1783, when physicist Pilâtre de Rozier landed his hot-air balloon between the Moulin des Merveilles and Moulin Vieux windmills, having left the Château de La Muette 25 minutes earlier. It was the first manned free flight in a hot-air balloon, reaching an altitude of roughly 3,100 feet (945 m). The butte was a marvelous natural belvedere, overlooking the swamps, prairies, and water mills of the Bièvre Valley and the steeples of Paris.

This working-class neighborhood was one of the first to rebel during the Commune, and it still has a strong independent streak, represented by Le Temps des Cerises restaurant (one of the rare anarchist establishments in Paris until the 1980s) and Le Merle Moqueur (dating from the Commune). The area served as a refuge for Communards, and even today the Association des Amis de la Commune holds regular meetings, selling books and documents that revive the spirit of the period.

In addition to being one of the bastions of the Paris Commune, the Butte-aux-Cailles also became famous for having the last cows in Paris; there was a farm and cows near the Passage Barrault well into the first half of the 20th century. Small houses, cobbled streets, and winding lanes stand next to apartment buildings against the ultramodern backdrop of high-rises in Paris's premier **Chinatown** and the Place d'Italie, which used to be an ancient Roman crossroads.

Explore the charming, picturesque Rues Buot, Michal, de la Butte-aux-Cailles, and des Cinq Diamants, as well as the Villa Daviel, with its scenic miniature villas and cottages, and farther away, the town-house-lined Square des Peupliers.

Near Place Verlaine is an indoor-outdoor public swimming pool *(tel 01 45 89 60 05, closed Mon. & public holidays)*. Built in 1924 in the art nuoveau style, it is fed by an artesian well of sulfurous water at 82°F (28°C). ■

BOIS DE VINCENNES & CHÂTEAU

This park is still the most popular in the eastern section of Paris. Like the Bois de Boulogne, it has a racetrack. In addition, a highly colorful Buddhist temple is located on park grounds, as well as a lake, zoo, museum, children's play area, and, of course, a château.

Once the Bois de Boulogne had been painstakingly landscaped and given to the city in 1852, Napoleon III decided to make a grand gesture in 1860 for "the workers of the 11th and 12th arrondissements," by commissioning a matching park to the east, the Bois de Vincennes. Four lakes were created, complete with romantic islands dotted with restaurants and secret grottoes.

The park's main attractions include the large **Daumesnil Lake** and the recently renovated **Parc**

Where to Run in Paris

Serious runners should find a hotel near the Bois de Vincennes, the Bois de Boulogne, the Jardin du Luxembourg, the Parc des Buttes-Chaumont (warning: very hilly), the Parc Montsouris, or the Parc de Villette. While a jog along the Seine is beautiful, it is not ideal, since it is not always possible to avoid running alongside heavy traffic, except on Sundays, when the highways at water level are closed to traffic during the day. Ditto for running along the Canal St.-Martin, pleasant only on Sunday.

INSIDER TIP:
Find the bargains—or the interesting junk—of Paris early in the morning at the Porte-de-Montreuil flea market, west of the Bois de Vincennes.

—PATRICIA DANIELS
National Geographic contributor

Zoologique de Paris *(Avenue Daumesnil, tel 0811 224 122, parczoologiquedeparis.fr)*. The imposing walled **Château de Vincennes,** ringed by a moat, was a royal abode for centuries. Its 14th-century keep, once a State prison, is now a museum and recently underwent a 12-year restoration. The 16th-century chapel still has its beautiful 17th-century stained glass. Less well-known is the **Parc Floral,** a magnificently landscaped park within the park. A separate children's play area includes rides, climbing frames, Ping-Pong, and minigolf, while pavilions house special exhibitions and concerts.

To their delight, children can still experience country life at the **Ferme de Paris** *(1 route du Pesage),* a model organic working farm founded in 1860 where kids can milk cows and groom animals. ∎

Bois de Vincennes

⊠ Map p. 197 F1
✉ Avenue Daumesnil or Avenue de Gravelle

paris.fr

Tibetan Temple (Kagyu Dzong)

✉ Route de la Ceinture du Lac Daumesnil
☎ 01 40 04 98 06
⏱ Closed Mon.
🚇 Métro: Porte Dorée

kagyu-dzong.org

Château de Vincennes

⊠ Map p. 197 G2
✉ Avenue de Paris
☎ 01 43 28 15 48
💲 €€
🚇 Métro: Château de Vincennes

chateau-de-vincennes.fr

Parc Floral

⊠ Map p. 197 G2
✉ Route de la Pyramide
☎ 01 49 57 24 84
💲 €
🚇 Métro: Château de Vincennes

parcfloraldeparis.com

PARKS & GARDENS OF PARIS

Parisians often complain about the lack of open space in this dense city, yet more than 400 parks, gardens, and squares dot the urban landscape, ranging from André Le Nôtre's formal French design for the Tuileries in the 17th century to the color-coded, postmodern André Citroën Garden at the edge of the 15th arrondissement.

The Parc des Buttes-Chaumont offers great views of the city.

Great Parisian Parks

Until the 19th century, the great gardens—Luxembourg, Palais-Royal, Tuileries—were part of royal domains. But under the Second Empire, enormous parks and small neighborhood squares began to appear all over Paris, under the impetus of Jean-Charles Alphand, Baron Georges-Eugène Haussmann's chief park director. He transformed what remained of the Rouvre Forest into the Bois de Boulogne and created the Bois de Vincennes, along with the Parc des Buttes-Chaumont and Parc Montsouris.

By the early 20th century, planners were using available land for housing, and few new parks were opened up. It wasn't until the 1980s that the authorities shifted their attention back toward open spaces. In the last 20 years alone, nearly 250 acres (101 ha) of new parks have been opened, affording plenty of places to escape the noise and congestion of the city.

Lesser Known Parks

Created by Jean-Charles Alphand during the Second Empire from a dismal gypsum quarry, the Buttes-Chaumont (*Rues Botzaris, Manin, and de Crimée, Métro: Simon Bolivar, Buttes-Chaumont*) in northeast Paris is a romantic park with steep slopes and intertwining paths, grottoes, and a famous belvedere perched at the top of a hill. There is a small lake, a bandstand for summer concerts, children's activities, and a spectacular view of the city.

A Pick of Paris's Best Gardens

Formal French gardens: Tuileries (see p. 137), Luxembourg (see p. 82)
Botanical gardens: Parc Floral de Vincennes (see p. 203), Auteuil greenhouses (see p. 199), Jardin des Plantes (see pp. 70–71)
Romantic gardens: Parc Monceau (see p. 158), Buttes-Chaumont, Parc Montsouris, Parc de Bagatelle (see p. 199), Musée Rodin (see pp. 178–179)
Contemporary gardens: Jardin Tino Rossi, Parc de Bercy, Parc de Belleville (see p. 207), Parc de la Villette (see pp. 208–209)
The giants: Bois de Vincennes (see p. 203), Bois de Boulogne (see p. 199)

Parc Montsouris *(Avenue Reille/Boulevard Jourdan, RER B: Cité Universitaire),* in the southern part of the city, is another of Alphand's creations, meant to mirror Buttes-Chaumont. Although it doesn't occupy as dramatic a site, it is equally romantic, with weeping willows and a lake dotted with swans. Alphand solved the problem of disguising the train lines running through the park by transforming their trenches into ravines lined with pine trees. It is a popular site with the students who live across the street at the Cité Internationale Universitaire.

A more recent addition to the Paris park system is the unusual Promenade Plantée, created from a former railway viaduct. It leads from Place de la Bastille as far as the Bois de Vincennes to the east; the first part used to be a raised rail track on the viaduct and is now a landscaped footpath that crosses through several parks and an overhead bridge. Bikes are allowed in the second section, from the Jardin de Reuilly in the 12th arrondissement to the Bois de Vincennes. A classy shopping arcade called the Viaduc des Arts occupies the former arches below the viaduct.

Not far away is the Parc de Bercy, on the site of the former wine warehouses near the Bercy Stadium and the fortresslike Ministry of Finance. Fortunately, some of the hundred-year-old trees were saved along with some 18th-century ruins. The gardens include a canal, an orchard, vegetable garden, and gardens created around the four seasons.

A fine place to enjoy the Seine is at the Jardin Tino Rossi in the 5th arrondissement, an open-air sculpture garden where tango and salsa dancers gather on warm evenings.

One of the most interesting parks in the Paris region is the Albert-Kahn Gardens *(11 rue des Abondances, Boulogne-Billancourt, tel 01 55 19 28 00, closed Mon. & Dec. 24–Jan. 1),* located on the western outskirts of the city. The grounds include a beautiful Japanese garden.

■ **The green refuge of the Parc des Buttes-Chaumont**

BELLEVILLE/MÉNILMONTANT

While Belleville isn't as picturesque a butte as Montmartre, it is certainly more multicultural and dynamic—and definitely more radical. The area's population is one of the most diverse and cosmopolitan in Paris, given the successive layers of immigration. Neighboring Ménilmontant is a curious mixture of modern housing and older residences that are becoming increasingly gentrified, making the area a thriving center of alternative Paris.

The friendly Café Aux Folies in the Belleville/Ménilmontant neighborhood

Then & Now

Incorporated into the rapidly expanding city of Paris in 1860, the former village of Belleville was a hotbed of opposition to the Empire and the last quarter to surrender its arms during the Commune. Various attempts were made to quell working-class protests, such as splitting the Belleville area up into the 11th, 19th, and 20th arrondissements.

For a long time, the butte—419 feet high (128 m)—maintained its 1930s look, a typically Parisian quarter with traditionally proletarian leanings. Yet it is continually changing, with the influx of immigrants and with countless rebuilding and renovation projects, which sometimes seem to be killing off the soul of old Belleville—some high-rise complexes have no ground floor markets or stores, for example. Sinuous side streets slope down past shops, ateliers, period bistros, and villas, and hushed gardens hide behind ornate doorways.

Belleville and its neighbor, Ménilmontant, bear traces of their rural and working-class past, when craftsmen and workers exploiting the local gypsum quarries lived at the foot of the butte. Founded in the 15th century around the vineyards run by the great abbeys of Paris, Belleville was known for its *guinguettes* (open-air cafés), and Parisians would come on Sundays to drink a sourish wine called *guinguet*. Working-class people ousted from the city by Haussmann's 19th-century upheavals sought new residences here.

Until 1914, Belleville and Ménilmontant rivaled Montmartre with their cafés, cabarets, and *bals-musettes* (dance halls with traditional French music). The Élysée Ménilmontant (no longer standing) was one of the most famous of these; Maurice Chevalier debuted here. Edith Piaf was born at 72 rue de Belleville; the La Java nightclub features the original *bal-musette* setting. Rue des Envierges, lined with restaurants, bistros, and *cafés chantants*, comes alive each night.

What to See

One of the great panoramic views of the city can be found where Rue Piat, Rue du Transvaal, and Rue des Envierges converge, at the highest point of Belleville, with the Belleville Gardens below. Rue Piat led to two windmills in the last century; it now opens onto the **Parc de Belleville,** which has a spectacular view over Paris and a great children's play area.

Villa Castel off Rue du Transvaal is a beautiful alley with fabulous houses, where François Truffaut shot scenes for his film *Jules et Jim* in 1962. An open house organized by local painters is held once a year (usually in the spring), revealing magnificent courtyards, studios, and hidden gardens.

The intertwining side streets and passages between Rue de Belleville and Rue de Ménilmontant are mostly paths that once linked vineyards. Today, Rue de Ménilmontant is becoming fashionable again, particularly along the lower end near Oberkampf, where trendy bars and cafés—like Café Charbon, with the Nouveau Casino concert and club venue next door, and the intimate La Mercerie—are burgeoning. ■

Belleville/Ménilmontant

🅰 Map p. 197 F3

✉ Belleville: centered on Rue de Belleville. Ménilmontant: centered on Rue de Ménilmontant

Ⓜ Métro: Belleville: Belleville or Pyrénées; Ménilmontant: Ménilmontant

---

Back to the 18th Century

Near the Rue de Belleville lingers a remnant of a more elegant corner of the area. The chic **Manoir de Beauregard** (*43 rue des Lilas, tel 01 42 03 10 20, manoirde beauregard.free.fr, €€€–€€€€*), set in a converted 18th-century hunting lodge decorated with period furniture, is something of an anomaly in this working-class neighborhood. Hostess Mary-Rose Girard welcomes her guests with tea and cake served in fine porcelain in a wood-paneled dining room. The B&B is not far from the **Parc des Buttes-Chaumont** (*Map p. 197 E4*)—itself worth a visit for its trees, lake, and clifftop temple.

PARC DE LA VILLETTE

One of the largest recent redevelopment projects in Paris has also been among its most successful. Just a few decades ago, the former slaughterhouses of La Villette stood in a gigantic no-man's-land in the northeast corner of Paris. Today, the 89-acre (35 ha) park contains the Cité des Sciences et de l'Industrie (Science Museum), the Philharmonie de Paris, the Zénith—a popular venue for pop and rock concerts—and the Grande Halle, a temporary exhibition space.

■ The gleaming Géode at the Cité des Sciences et de l'Industrie houses an IMAX theater.

Parc de la Villette

🅐 Map p. 197 E4

✉ 211 avenue Jean-Juarès

☎ 01 40 03 75 75

🚇 Métro: Porte de Pantin, Porte de la Villette

lavillette.com

Zénith

✉ 211 avenue Jean-Jaurès

🚇 Métro: Porte de Pantin

le-zenith.com

Cité des Sciences et de l'Industrie

With around three million visitors per year, the Science Museum is the park's most popular attraction. As opposed to the traditional style of French museum, which tends to be heavy on text and description, the Science Museum has plenty of interactive, hands-on exhibitions in its giant, five-level glass-and-steel building. *Explora*, the core permanent exhibits, lets visitors discover the brain, outer space, and the history of trans-portation through a multitude of innovative displays, while popular, ground-breaking temporary exhibitions explain such subjects as robotics, the birds, and the bees.

Opened in 1986, the museum also has a planetarium for trips to outer space, a Géode sphere (a 100-seat IMAX theater, which has become the symbol of the futuristic park and will reopen in 2021 after renovation), and the *Argonaute* full-scale submarine. Two sections are reserved for kids in the

Cité des Enfants, a science village where children can play with interactive exhibits, with one area for 2- to 7-year-olds and another for 5- to 12-year-olds. Reserve one of the 90-minute sessions when you purchase your entrance ticket.

Philharmonie de Paris

A major addition to the park, the Philharmonie de Paris, with a flamboyant design by architect Jean Nouvel, opened in January 2015. Home to the Orchestre de Paris, it boasts the latest acoustic technology and a 2,400-seat concert hall. The former Cité de la Musique, with its Music Museum, smaller concert hall (Philharmonie 2), research center, and conservatory, is now part of the Philharmonie complex. Free and low-cost events are planned for weekends.

Other Features

Besides the museums, the vast park, designed by Swiss Bernard Tschumi, features a magical bamboo forest; wacky 20th-century, red-metal structures known as "follies" (one of which houses an information center); a children's playground with a huge dragon slide; and ten different thematic gardens. Don't miss the gargantuan half-buried bicycle sculpture by Claes Oldenburg. During the summer, a giant screen is set up in the park for open-air movies, and concerts are scheduled regularly.

The one remaining feature from its days as a slaughterhouse and cattle market is the **Grande Halle** *(221 avenue Jean-Jaurès, Métro: Porte de Pantin),* one of the most beautiful examples of glass-and-cast-iron architecture in Paris. Built in 1867, it originally was little more than a metal shelter for the cattle sold here. It has since been renovated to accommodate temporary exhibitions and concerts. ∎

Cité des Sciences et de l'Industrie

- Map p. 197 E5
- 30 avenue Corentin Cariou
- ☎ 01 85 53 99 74
- Closed Mon., Jan. 1, May 1, Dec. 25
- €€
- Métro: Porte de la Villette

cite-sciences.fr

Philharmonie de Paris

- Map p. 197 E4
- 221 avenue Jean-Jaurès
- ☎ 01 44 84 44 84
- Closed Mon., Dec. 25
- €€
- Métro: Porte de Pantin

philharmoniede
paris.fr

EXPERIENCE: Picnicking With the Locals

Take a break from churches and museums and relax Parisian style, with an open-air picnic. Although many people picnic along the quays of the Seine in fine weather, this venue has two main drawbacks: a lack of comfortable seating and a dearth of toilets. The Parc de Villette and Parc de Vincennes, with their expansive lawns, are better bets. Popular spots for picnicking include the banks of the Canal St.-Martin, though they have the same drawbacks as the quays of the Seine. Gardens such as the Tuileries or the Luxembourg are often crowded, while more intimate options for your *déjeuner sur l'herbe* are certainly the Parc Monceau and Parc de Bercy.

More Places to Visit Around the Périphérique

Chinatown

At first sight, the stark high-rise buildings in the 13th arrondissement—known as the Choisy Triangle—form a depressing complex. Yet this is the heart of the city's colorful Chinatown, with an estimated 30,000 Asian residents and entire, transplanted cultures, complete with pagoda-fronted shops and martial arts centers. Don't miss the Tang Frères on Avenue d'Ivry (the largest Asian supermarket in France), and the restaurants offering every type of Asian cuisine.
Map p. 197 D1 Métro: Tolbiac, Porte d'Ivry

Goutte d'Or

East of Pigalle and Montmartre is the Goutte d'Or (Drop of Gold) district, named for the once highly prized wine produced on its hillsides. Since the 19th century, however, it has offered some of the cheapest housing in Paris. In the last few decades it has become mostly an Arab and African neighborhood, teeming with a multitude of languages, dress, spicy foods, and Kabyl cafés.

Browse through the crowded and ultra-cheap Tati Department Store and on to the Dejean Market *(near the Château-Rouge Métro)* or the open-air market on Boulevard de la Chapelle *(Wed. & Sat.)*. Every summer, the Goutte d'Or en Fête music festival features local musicians along with big names in *rai* (North African rock 'n' roll), rap, and hip hop.
Map p. 197 D4 Métro: Barbès-Rochechouart

Nouvelle Athènes

Tucked into the area between Pigalle and Les Grands Boulevards is Nouvelle Athènes, where a number of 19th-century artists, including Theodore Géricault, Eugène Delacroix, and Frédéric Chopin, congregated. The fascinating **Musée Gustave Moreau** is here (see p. 194), as is the **Musée de la Vie Romantique** (see p. 115). Installed in the studio and home of painter Ary Scheffer, this museum is a tribute to the Romantic period, with memorabilia of George Sand and others. The prettiest spot, however, is the **Place St.-Georges,** featuring the gorgeous facades of the neo-Renaissance Hôtel de la Païva and the Hôtel Dosne-Thiers, which organizes temporary exhibitions and houses the **Masson Fund'**s Napoleonic memorabilia *(Bibliothèque Thiers, 27 place St.-Georges, tel 01 48 78 92 90, open Thurs. & Fri. 12 p.m.–6 p.m. and by appt.).* Map p. 196 C4 Métro: St.-Georges, Pigalle

Romantic Parisian Canals

With the opening of La Villette park (see pp. 208–209) to the north, visitors who want to see the less traveled reaches of Paris near the Périphérique can do so via the city's canals. For example, a trip down the **Canal St.-Martin** leading to the Bassin de la Villette and the Canal de l'Ourcq passes through a series of eight locks, two swing bridges, and some graceful wrought-iron footbridges.

Although pleasure boats ply this 3-mile (5 km) route, the most romantic way to explore the area is on foot. The building that inspired Marcel Carné's great film *Hôtel du Nord* (1938) is at 102 quai de Jemmapes. The building's facade was saved from destruction in the 1980s and it now houses a popular restaurant.

Boat cruises along the Canal St.-Martin to the Bassin de la Villette and the Canal de l'Ourcq provide a relaxing way to view the city and are operated by several companies (see p. 236); reservations are recommended.

Abbeys, castles, forests, and towns that have fed the inspiration of artists—all within easy reach of the capital

EXCURSIONS

A fountain at Versailles

EXCURSIONS

A trip away from hectic, urban Paris is a welcome break in any season (but try to avoid traveling on weekends from mid-July to the end of August, as the French tend to leave en masse for vacations then). For many first-time visitors to Paris, Versailles is a must-see. Outside of Paris the rest of the Île de France region is also studded with châteaus, such as the Italian-style Fontainebleau and Rambouillet, a residence of the French presidents for over a century.

The beautiful château at Vaux-le-Vicomte (see p. 222) was not a royal palace, but it was so luxurious that Louis XIV's crooked finance minister, Nicolas Fouquet, was imprisoned for embezzling state funds to build it. The Château de Chantilly's collection of artistic treasures includes paintings by Raphael and the stunning, medieval miniatures from the "Très Riches Heures du Duc de Berry" (see p. 232), not to mention the imposing stables built

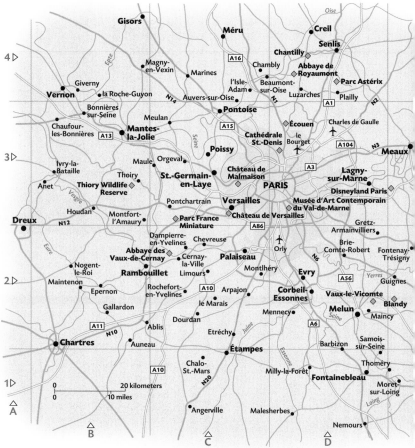

■ Donald, Mickey, and Minnie welcome visitors to Disneyland Paris.

in the 18th century to house the prince of Condé's 240 horses (now a museum).

There are a few excursions within a reasonable distance of Paris that offer a unique glimpse into medieval French life: for example, the last remaining fortress at Blandy (see p. 222), near Vaux-le-Vicomte; and the hilltop town of Provins (see p. 223), which hosts annual fairs with

costumed actors reenacting some of the more colorful aspects of medieval life. And in the suburb of St.-Denis is the 13th-century cathedral of the same name (see p. 220), the first large Gothic building in Europe.

Monet's home and gardens at Giverny (see pp. 230–231) and the town of Auvers-sur-Oise (see p. 227) are both landmarks for art lovers. The Abbaye de Vaux-de-Cernay (see sidebar p. 226), a 12th-century abbey turned luxury hotel, is a haven in the middle of the vast Rambouillet Forest. The original refectory is still standing, as is the roofless cathedral.

Lastly, Chartres Cathedral (see pp. 228–229), the jewel of medieval France, has the most brilliant collection of 13th-century stained glass anywhere in the world. ■

Map labels

Ourcq · Marne · la Ferté-sous-Jouarre · A4 · Grand Morin · la Ferté-Gaucher · Coulommiers · Béton-Bazoches · Esternay · N4 · N19 · Provins · Nangis · Nogent-sur-Seine · Seine · A5 · Montereau-Faut-Yonne · Bray-sur-Seine · F · E

NOT TO BE MISSED:

The fabled Château de Versailles and its grand gardens 214–219

The Gothic architecture of Cathédrale St.-Denis 220

Celebrating at a medieval festival in Provins 223

The 13th-century windows of Chartres Cathedral 228–229

Seeing the inspiration for Monet's "Water Lilies" at Giverny 230–231

CHÂTEAU DE VERSAILLES

For sheer glitter, nothing beats Versailles. An extravagant palace built during Louis XIV's reign, it is not the oldest or largest of the French châteaus, but it illustrates the essence of a royal palace. Although Louis XIV (known as the Sun King) constructed the château and the famous gardens, the property had originally belonged to his father, Louis XIII. An enthusiastic hunter, Louis XIII built a lodge in 1623 in the forest; he built more spacious quarters in 1634.

■ The grounds of Versailles have 32 pools and fountains.

When he died nine years later, his son Louis XIV was only five years old. The boy loved the small château, but his reasons for later spending so much time and money—and ultimately moving the court to Versailles—had more to do with the turbulent politics of the day than the château's bucolic attractions. As a child, Louis XIV had witnessed the uprising of the Fronde (see p. 24), and he remained distrustful of Parisians throughout his life. By forcing the nobles to

follow him to the more isolated Château de Versailles, he could keep a close watch on them, curtailing their capacity for independent political action.

Throughout his 72-year reign, Louis XIV spent lavishly to build the château, hiring the best designers France had to offer: the architect Louis Le Vau (succeeded by Jules Hardouin-Mansart), the landscape designer André Le Nôtre, and the painter Charles Le Brun, all of whom had worked previously on the sumptuous, but ill-fated Château de Vaux-le-Vicomte (see p. 222).

The Château of Versailles is inseparable from the personality of the king. (His great-grandson Louis XV and great-great-great-grandson Louis XVI made only minor alterations to his grand plan.) The finished château perfectly mirrored the ambitions of the Sun King, whose reign typified the absolutism of the monarchy, guided by the principle of *la gloire* (glory). When Versailles became the seat of government in 1682, it had to be expanded even further to house the entire court, along with all the civil servants.

Interior

The **State Apartments** give some idea of Louis XIV's practical interpretation of *la gloire*: The rooms were decorated throughout with gold and marble (quarried from every corner of his kingdom) and organized around the theme of the planets gravitating around the sun (the king's emblem). No sooner had these apartments been built than Louis XIV decided he needed more intimate quarters, so from 1684 on these rooms were designated for official functions and royal audiences, while the king resided in the old part of the château facing the Marble Court.

Everything at Versailles was ruled by protocol and etiquette—even in the king's private quarters. Courtiers fought jealously for the privilege of being received there, especially for the "Rising" and "Setting" ceremonies of the Royal Heavenly Body. The gilt-and-crimson **King's Bedchamber** is

Château de Versailles

- Map p. 212 C3
- 12 miles (19 km) southwest of Paris
- 01 30 83 78 00
- Closed Mon., Jan. 1, May 1, Dec. 25
- €€€. Free 1st Sun. of each month, always for under 18 & EU residents under 26.
- By car: A13 to exit "Versailles-Château," then follow signs. By train: from Paris-Montparnasse to Versailles Chantiers; from Paris-St.-Lazare to Versailles-Rive Droite. RER (C) to Versailles–Rive Gauche

chateauversailles.fr

EXPERIENCE: Become a French Royal for a Night

The Château de Versailles now offers the public many of the divertissements that were once the exclusive province of its royal residents and their fawning courtiers: operas and concerts by baroque composers like Jean-Baptiste de Lully and Henry Purcell in the Royal Opera House, strolls in the park, lavish fireworks displays, and more.

There is one big event that Louis XIV missed out on, however: **Les Grandes Eaux Nocturnes.** While Louis was behind the major engineering feat required to create the multiple fountains on the grounds of the château, he certainly never witnessed them in this way, lit by spectacular light installations and complete with aquatic effects, laser shows, and musical accompaniment.

Gently guided by park staff and a map, visitors are free to wander the grounds in the dark from one magical fountain spectacle to another, all of them different and surprising, and many of them hidden behind walls of greenery. The evening ends with a brilliant fireworks display over the Grand Bassin at 11 p.m., leaving just enough time to catch a train back to Paris.

Early arrivals can enjoy a **"Royal Serenade,"** a re-creation of a French ball with musicians and dancers, in the gorgeous Hall of Mirrors between 6:30 p.m. and 8 p.m., or picnic on the grounds before the gates to the Grandes Eaux Nocturnes open (*8:30 p.m. Sat. nights mid-June–mid Sept., chateauversailles-spectacles. fr, €€€*).

now restored exactly as it was on September 1, 1715, the day the king died.

The gilded splendor of the **Queen's Room** is even more lavish, though she and the other women who lived there (two queens, two dauphines, and the wife of the king's eldest son) had even less privacy. These women gave birth to a total of 19 children, always a public affair to ensure that there were no substitutes for the royal offspring.

Nowhere is Louis XIV's quest for grandeur more evident than in the gilded, slightly gaudy **Hall of Mirrors,** a 240-foot-long (73 m) room constructed by Hardouin-Mansart that runs the entire length of the central part of the château and faces the huge gardens outside. The 17 tall, arched windows are matched on the opposite wall by 17 tall French mirrors, while the coffered ceiling (decorated by Charles Le Brun) immortalizes the diplomatic and military conquests of the king over such foreign powers as Spain and Holland. More recently, during World War I, Versailles was used by the Allied War Council, and the Treaty of Versailles was signed in the Hall of Mirrors on June 28, 1919.

■ Versailles's Hall of Mirrors exemplifies the palace's glittering grandeur.

Château de Versailles

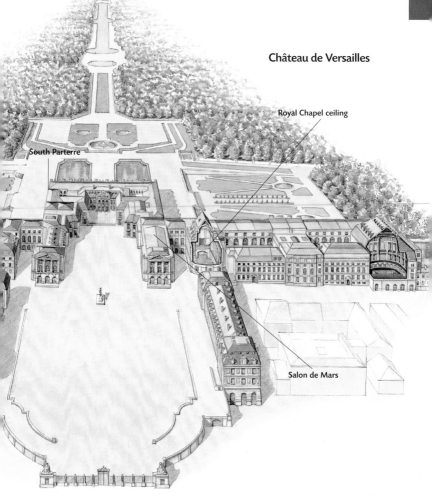

Royal Chapel ceiling

South Parterre

Salon de Mars

Gardens

Making the most of the steep, marshy ground, André Le Nôtre designed what has been called the most perfect example of a formal French garden. In an era that believed that nature was to be mastered by man, Le Nôtre undertook immense drainage work, shifting masses of earth to form the terraces that begin with the **Parterre d'Eau** (two symmetrical pools) just below the windows of the Hall of Mirrors and lead down to the **Bassin d'Apollon** and the **Grand Canal.**

The king was so proud of his gardens that he wrote a detailed description of the best way to visit them. Although formal in design and organized around two main axes—one running east to west, the other north to south— the gardens contain charming groves, fountains, and labyrinths

The King's Composer

Although he was Italian, Jean-Baptiste Lully (né Giovanni Battista Lulli in 1632) is considered the leading composer of French Baroque music. He started his career as a scullery boy for the Duchess of Montpensier, a fabulously rich cousin of Louis XIV, but eventually worked his way to the court as a dancer and later became the king's favorite composer. Today you can hear his music and that of other Baroque composers in the lavish Royal Opera in the Château de Versailles, designed by architect Ange-Jacques Gabriel and decorated with multiple crystal chandeliers by Augustin Pajou. Performers include top international artists such as Jordi Savall, Cecilia Bartoli, and Nathalie Dessay. (Chateau de Versailles Spectacles: *chateauversailles-spectacles.fr*)

INSIDER TIP:

Save your visit to the grounds for late afternoon, when the setting sun transforms the palace's gardens, statues, and walls.

—GILLES MINGASSON
National Geographic photographer

with names like "Bacchus Basin," "Apollo Baths," and "Room of Chestnut Trees."

The groves were equipped with a sophisticated system of fountains, created to accompany the festivities organized by Louis XIV. The most famous of these, held in 1664, was dedicated ostensibly to his wife, Marie-Thérèse, but was actually in honor of his favorite mistress, Mademoiselle de La Vallière. The playwright Molière wrote several plays, including *Tartuffe*, for the week-long celebration, and the entire château and gardens were turned into a backdrop for ballets, fireworks, tournaments, waterworks, and ornate banquets. Today, the Grandes Eaux celebrations (see sidebar p. 215), held every weekend from mid-June through mid-September, re-create something of the ambience of these events.

Louis demanded that the flowers in his gardens flourish all year long. Through the ingenuity of Jean-Baptiste de La Quintinye, the king ate strawberries in March and lettuce in January. The **King's Kitchen Garden,** which has produced fruit and vegetables continuously for three centuries, is also open to the public.

Grand & Petit Trianons

Versailles was sometimes too large and too public, even for Louis XIV. With nearly 10,000 people occupying the palace, there was no way to escape the jostling courtiers. The king, therefore, asked Hardouin-Mansart to build the Grand Trianon, a pink marble mini-palace, in his gardens. Only slightly less magnificent than Versailles, the Grand Trianon became a getaway for several royal families. The building was renovated under General de Gaulle and used as the official residence for foreign heads of state.

After Louis XIV's death, Louis XV continued to live at Versailles, where he constructed the Petit Trianon in 1769 as a place where he could meet his mistress, Madame de Pompadour. When Marie-Antoinette became queen, she created an English-style garden and a miniature mock-hamlet, complete with farm animals.

Visiting the Château

Several different tickets are available, depending on what you want (or have the energy) to see. The basic "Palace" ticket, which includes an audio guide, admits you to the Hall of Mirrors, King and Queen's Grand Apartments, the King's Bedchamber, the Dauphin's apartments, the gardens, the park, and the Coach Gallery. The more costly "Passport" ticket includes all of the above, plus the Trianon Palaces and Marie-Antoinette's Estate, temporary exhibitions, and musical fountains (when they are in operation). A less expensive ticket admits you only to the Trianon Palaces, their gardens, and Marie-Antoinette's Estate. Other tickets include the Academy of Equestrian Arts and dressage demonstrations.

Buy your ticket online to avoid standing in two separate lines at the always crowded château. Plan on spending at least two hours visiting the château, and about the same for the Trianon Palaces. It takes about half an hour to walk through the park to Marie-Antoinette's Estate, but a little train can take you there faster.

The gardens are free, except during the Grandes Eaux performances, when the 32 pools and fountains are turned on as part of a musical display. ■

Versailles's formal gardens were intended to show the mastery of the human hand over nature.

CATHÉDRALE ST.-DENIS

St.-Denis, the cathedral that inspired Gothic architecture in France, stands in an unlikely setting in the working-class suburb of St.-Denis, 5 miles (8 km) north of Paris. More than 800
years separate the two monuments for which the town is famous: the cathedral, a landmark
in the evolution of Gothic architecture; and the Stade de France, a major sports stadium.

■ The Cathédral St.-Denis was a pioneer of Gothic style.

St.-Denis

🅼 Map p. 212 D3

**Cathédrale
St.-Denis**

✉ 1 rue de
la Légion
d'Honneur

☎ 01 48 09 83 54

💲 €€

🚇 Métro: Line 13
to St.-Denis-
Basilique.
By car: via A1

**saint-denis.
monuments-
nationaux.fr**

The official burial site for French
monarchs since 1122, St.-Denis
represents a turning point in
the history of architecture. The
Abbey of St.-Denis, built around
475, was already powerful when
Abbot Suger improved the
existing Merovingian basilica by
adding intersecting ribbed vaults
on a large scale throughout the
church—an innovation for the
time. The master builders of the
other great cathedrals that followed (including Chartres and
Senlis) drew their inspiration
from this prototype. Unfortunately, the church was badly damaged during the Revolution, and
most of its treasures are now in
the Louvre.

Royal Monuments

The crypt represents a fascinating
chronology of the French monarchy. Sometime around 1260,
Saint Louis commissioned images
of his predecessors, starting with
the seventh century. From the
14th century on, the heart and
viscera of deceased royals were
removed and dispersed to separate monuments, while the bodies were buried at St.-Denis.

For centuries, almost every
king, queen, and royal child was bur-
ied here, from Dagobert through
Louis XVIII. The most interesting
funerary monuments are those of
Dagobert, Henri II, Catherine de
Médicis, Pépin the Short, Charles
Martel, Louis XII, and François I. ■

DISNEYLAND PARIS

Disneyland Resort Paris has expanded beyond the original Disneyland theme park opened in 1992 and now features the Disney Village, a golf course, La Vallée outlet shopping center, and the much hyped new attraction, the Walt Disney Studios Park. Visitors will find the same beaming "cast members," attractions similar to the U.S. versions, and the same turreted Sleeping Beauty's Castle—a somewhat hollow edifice in a country overrun with real châteaus.

If you're traveling with children who balk at visiting one more museum, Disneyland can provide an entertaining break from Paris. The youngest kids love **Fantasyland,** where Disney habitués will recognize such rides as "It's a Small World" and the "Alice in Wonderland" maze, complete with trick fountains. Older kids and adults head straight for **Discoveryland** and "Star Wars Hyperspace Mountain," a heart-stopping roller coaster that literally shoots you off the starting line. The nearby "Star Tours" is a popular simulator ride. **Frontierland** offers a few other thrills, notably the "Big Thunder Mountain" roller coaster. One small pocket of calm is the "Pocahontas Indian Village," a parent-free playground.

Somewhere between the gentle Fantasyland and the other looping rides is **Adventureland,** with "Indiana Jones and the Temple of Peril," another wild attraction, and the "Pirates of the Caribbean" boat trip. There are lots of restaurants—where, at least in some establishments, among them the Auberge de Cendrillon, Disney has taken into account French culture by allowing wine to be served.

Outside the park itself is the **Disney Village,** a complex with restaurants, a disco, and shops. And finally, the most recent addition is the **Walt Disney Studios Park**, where the secrets of Hollywood come alive in a studio-like setting, with attractions such as the "Moteurs...Action! Stunt Show Spectacular" (a big favorite). ∎

Disneyland Paris
- Map p. 212 E3
- 20 miles (32 km) east of Paris in Marne-la-Vallée
- 01 60 30 60 53
- €€€€€
- By car: A4 toward Nancy-Metz, exit 14. By train: RER (A), exit Marne-la-Vallée-Chessy. Shuttles from Roissy & Orly airports

disneylandparis.com

The City of Little Lights—Paris for Kids

Aside from Disneyland Paris, there are other local options for kids. At the **Thoiry Wildlife Reserve** (tel 01 34 87 40 67, thoiry.net, €€€, closed in winter) west of Paris on the D11, animals roam free as you drive through the park; there is also a traditional zoo.

North of Paris on the A1 at Plailly is an entire theme park devoted to a French favorite, the plucky comic hero Astérix. **Parc Astérix** (tel 09 86 86 86 87 parcasterix.

fr, closed Jan.–Mar. [check website], shuttle buses leave from the Carrousel du Louvre shopping center, Metro: Palais-Royal, €€€€) comes complete with rides and attractions.

Parc France Miniature (tel 01 30 16 16 30 franceminiature.fr, closed Nov.–Mar., €€€) is a little known attraction beyond Versailles. More than 150 of France's famous monuments have been reconstructed at a tiny fraction of their size at a 12.3-acre (5 ha) park.

VAUX-LE-VICOMTE & BLANDY

Vaux-le-Vicomte is one of the best examples of the Louis XIV style. If you can schedule a visit on Saturday night, don't miss the special Candlelight Evenings, when 2,000 candles illuminate the castle and gardens.

The magnificent Vaux-le-Vicomte is protected by a moat.

Vaux-le-Vicomte
- Map p. 212 D2
- 30 miles (50 km) southeast of Paris
- 01 64 14 41 90
- Open daily mid-Mar.–Nov. & some days at Christmas
- €€
- By train: Gare de Lyon to Melun, then taxi or shuttle bus

vaux-le-vicomte.com

Château Forteresse de Blandy-les-Tours
- 30 miles (50 km) southeast of Paris
- 01 60 59 17 80
- Closed Tues., May 1, Dec. 25
- €

chateau-blandy.fr

Vaux-le-Vicomte was built for Nicolas Fouquet by the greatest 17th-century French architects and designers—Louis Le Vau, Charles Le Brun, and André Le Nôtre. However, Fouquet's fatal mistake was to create a palace even more radiant than the Sun King's, with most of the building funds embezzled from the French government.

Fouquet was one of the most powerful men in the kingdom when he began work on Vaux-le-Vicomte in 1653. For six years, he spent lavishly to create his splendid château and landscaped gardens. In 1661, fearful that he had fallen from the king's favor, Fouquet invited Louis XIV to a celebration that included 6,000 guests, fireworks, and complex waterworks.

A jealous Louis had him arrested that month and thrown into prison, where he remained until his death 15 years later. The king then requisitioned the furniture, statuary, tapestries, and the same architect to build Versailles.

Highlights include the oval salon, Le Brun's painted ceilings in the Salon des Muses, the restored kitchen, and the terraced gardens.

Blandy's Fortress

A few miles to the east of Vaux-le-Vicomte *(Map p. 213 E2)* is Blandy-les-Tours, the last remaining medieval fortress in the Île de France. The ruins lie in a valley, their stone towers lacking only colorful banners to make you believe you have stumbled into the Middle Ages. ■

PROVINS

Every spring and summer, this hilltop town, a World Heritage site, transports visitors 800 years into the past, with knights in armor astride charging steeds, catapults assaulting ancient stone ramparts, falconry shows, and costumed actors.

Provins was an economic capital of the Champagne region as early as the tenth century; it traded in expensive silks, exotic spices, and wool during its twice-annual fair, which brought traders from all over Europe. A good place to discover the past is at the **Grange aux Dîmes,** a wax museum on Rue St.-Jean.

INSIDER TIP:

When in this village of yore, be sure to catch the fascinating equestrian falconry show.

—BARBARA A. NOE
*National Geographic Travel
Books senior editor*

The ancient upper town has been restored and now has 58 historical monuments that form the backdrop for colorful reenactments of medieval life *(Apr.–Oct.).* A jousting tournament re-creates a battle in 1230, when Comte Thibaud de Champagne saved Provins from besieging armies. Every summer nearly 80 birds of prey swoop over the crowds in a demonstration of falconry.

A self-guided walking tour of the town (brochure available from the tourist office) explores the 11th-century ramparts that extend nearly a mile around the old town. The César Tower stands high above the town, offering a fine view over the Brie region.

The town is honeycombed with nearly 6 miles (9.6 km) of ancient tunnels linking dozens of vaulted cellars. The walls bear the mysterious marks of various secret societies (including the Freemasons), who once used these underground galleries for their meetings.

A medieval feast is held every Saturday mid-Mar.–Oct., and other events, including concerts and a sound-and-light show, are scheduled throughout the summer. ■

Provins

⚐ Map p. 213 F2

✉ 50 miles (80 km) east of Paris

🚗 By car: A4 toward exit 13 at Serris, follow signs to Provins (D231). By train: Paris Gare de l'Est to Provins

Visitor Information

✉ 4 chemin de Villecran

☎ 01 64 60 26 26

provins.net

■ **The César Tower in medieval Provins**

FONTAINEBLEAU & NEARBY

Fontainebleau is one of the most popular weekend destinations for Parisians, who flock to the forest to enjoy hiking, rock climbing, and riding. While Versailles reflects a single monarch's glory (Louis XIV), the royal abode of Fontainebleau has evolved constantly during the reigns of 30 different rulers of France, and much of its charm is due to the disparate elements and odd series of buildings they created. Like Versailles, however, it is immense.

■ The Château of Fontainebleau housed generations of French rulers, beginning in 1137.

The Château

Drawn by the abundant game in the forest, Louis VII began building here in 1137. Subsequent kings, similarly attracted to hunting, remodeled and expanded the property. The first major work was undertaken in 1530 by François I, who preferred Fontainebleau to his other royal palaces. He brought Italian artists (including Leonardo da Vinci, whose "Mona Lisa" hung on the walls at Fontainebleau before being transferred to the Louvre) and craftsmen to construct a magnificent mannerist palace to replace the existing modest hunting lodge; the frescoes and stucco work in the François I Gallery remain from this period.

Henri II continued his father's projects, including the 98-foot-long (30 m) ballroom—a dazzling display of Renaissance style, with a coffered ceiling by architect Philibert Delorme and frescoes by Italian artist Francesco Primaticcio. The exterior horseshoe staircase was constructed by Louis XIII; it is where Napoleon I famously addressed his men in 1814 before being sent into exile.

The emblems of various rulers can be spotted in different rooms: the interlaced "H" and "C," for Henri II and Catherine de Médicis (intended to be interpreted as a "D," for his mistress, Diane de Poitiers); Napoleon's insignia of golden bees, emblazoned on red velvet in the throne room; and François I's salamander. There is also a museum of Chinese works collected by Empress Eugénie as well as a Napoleon Museum.

Fontainebleau Forest

Covering 61,750 acres (25,009 ha), the forest is crisscrossed with roads, 200 miles (320 km) of marked paths, and countless lanes. The Fontainebleau tourist office provides maps of the forest and information for excursions. Although the elevation never climbs above 482 feet (127 m), the forest is popular with rock climbers. Bicycles can also be rented. Some of the more popular sites include the Apremont Gorges, the Franchard Gorges, and the Béatrix Grotto.

Other Places Nearby

The area around Fontainebleau is legendary in the history of painting. The village of **Barbizon** nearby *(Map p. 212 D2, tel 01 60 66 41 87)* was a mecca for 19th-century landscape painters including Daubigny, Corot, and Millet. The single main street is lined with antique dealers and art galleries, as well as a couple of museums: the **Auberge Ganne,** and the house-studios of both Millet and Théodore Rousseau.

Thoméry *(Map p. 212 E1, visitor information available at Fontainebleau),* nestled in a loop of the Seine, has long been famous for its Chasselas Doré grapes. The fortified town of **Moret-sur-Loing** *(Map p. 212 E1, tel 01 60 70 41 66),* immortalized by painters such as Camille Pissarro, hosts a sound-and-light show on Saturday nights from mid-June through mid-September. And **Samois-sur-Seine** *(Map p. 212 D1),* in the middle of Fontainebleau Forest, hosts the annual summer Django Reinhardt Jazz Festival. ∎

Fontainebleau

- Map p. 212 D1
- 40 miles (60 km) southeast of Paris near Melun

Visitor Information

- 4 bis place de la République, Fontainebleau
- 01 60 74 99 99

fontainebleau-tourisme.com

Château de Fontainebleau

- 01 60 71 50 70
- Closed Tues., Jan. 1, May 1, Dec. 25
- €€. Free 1st Sun. of each month, always for EU residents under 26.
- By car: A6 south, exit at Fontainebleau. By train: Paris Gare de Lyon to Fontainebleau-Avon, then take bus 1 to château

chateaude fontainebleau.fr

EXPERIENCE: Enjoy a Walk in the Royal Forest

Art, history, nature, and photography lovers—not to mention rock-climbing enthusiasts—all owe themselves a walk through the **Fontainebleau Forest** *(fontainebleau-tourisme.com).* Pathways lead you through the trees of this surprisingly large woodland, popular with weekend visitors from Paris and beyond.

In the 19th century, this was the favorite spot for painting *en plein air* for Barbizon School artists Camille Corot, Gustave Courbet, Théodore Rousseau, and others. Don't forget to bring a sketchbook or a camera—you are sure to be inspired by the surrealistic rock formations, carved by the sands of an ancient sea, and by the wealth of vegetation (some 5,000 plant species).

Don't be surprised if a family of roe deer, one of 6,600 animal species living in the forest, goes leaping by. The occasional poetry-inscribed 19th-century fountain or grotto in the middle of the forest adds to the romantic atmosphere.

RAMBOUILLET & AROUND

Although not the most beautiful château in the Île de France region, Rambouillet a royal, imperial, and presidential retreat, sits in the middle of a magnificent forest, with plenty of nearby excursions.

■ Once a lodge for Louis XVI, Rambouillet hosted the first G6 summit in 1975.

Château de Rambouillet

- Map p. 212 B2
- 30 miles (50 km) southwest of Paris
- 01 34 83 00 25
- Closed Tues., Jan. 1, May 1, Dec. 25
- €. Free 1st Sun. Mar.–Nov., always for under 18 & EU residents under 26.

chateau-rambouillet.fr

Rochefort-en-Yvelines

- Map p. 212 C2
- 10 miles (16 km) southeast of Rambouillet

Montfort-l'Amaury

- Map p. 212 B3
- 16 miles (26 km) north of Rambouillet

The Château

Rambouillet was renovated and modified by successive owners. Louis XVI, a frequent guest on hunting expeditions, acquired the long-coveted property in 1784, adding several rustic features for Queen Marie-Antoinette—including a dairy and sheepfold. Between 1897 and 2009, the château was used by France's heads of state.

Visitors can tour the château, apartments, queen's dairy and National Sheepfold, and magnificent French-style water gardens with their large artificial lakes. One of the château's most famous rooms is the Napoleon I bathroom decorated with a mock ancient fresco in 1807. There is also a cottage adorned inside with seashells, mother of pearl, and marble.

Nearby Places

Southeast of Rambouillet, **Rochefort-en-Yvelines** has hardly changed for centuries. An 11th-century village, **Montfort-l'Amaury** is one of the prettiest in the area, its château visible atop the hillside. ■

Abbaye des Vaux-de-Cernay

Founded in 1148, the Abbaye des Vaux-de-Cernay (Map p. 212 C2, tel 01 34 85 23 00), 6 miles (10 km) northeast of Rambouillet, is spectacular, with vaulted ceilings and stone walls. It functioned as a prosperous Cistercian abbey until the Revolution and is now a luxury hotel.

AUVERS-SUR-OISE

Auvers is something of a pilgrimage site for people seeking traces of Van Gogh. A series of panels representing famous paintings by van Gogh, Cézanne, and others have been placed all over town on the exact sites where they were painted. The tourist office has suggestions for walks, taking in the Auberge Ravoux, where van Gogh died after a self-inflicted bullet wound on July 29, 1890, and the church and cornfields immortalized by the painter.

Van Gogh lived here for only 70 days, under the care of close friend Dr. Gachet (homeopathic doctor to the artists of Auvers-sur-Oise), but he worked frenetically, producing 70 paintings and numerous drawings. He is buried in the local cemetery next to his brother.

INSIDER TIP:

If you favor the taste of anise, try some modern absinthe, prepared in the traditional way with cold sugary water.

—PATRICIA DANIELS
National Geographic contributor

Before van Gogh arrived, Auvers was already a favorite destination of 19th-century landscape painters. Charles Daubigny, a member of the Barbizon school, moored a houseboat here in 1857 and was soon followed by many other artists, who used his **studio** *(61 rue Daubigny, tel 01 34 48 03 03, atelier-daubigny.com, €)*, established in 1861 on what is now Rue Daubigny, as a meeting place. Daubigny campaigned for younger painters like Renoir,

Monet, and Cézanne, who also visited him, along with Corot and Daumier. Daubigny's paintings and memorabilia are in the **Daubigny Museum** *(Colombières Manor, Rue de la Sansonne, tel 01 30 36 80 20, museedaubigny.com, €)*.

Two other museums are worth visiting in Auvers: The **Absinthe Museum** *(44 rue Alphonse Callé, tel 01 30 36 83 26, musee-absinthe.com, €–€€)* explores the elixir known as "the green peril"; and the 17th-century **Château d'Auvers** *(Rue Léry, tel 01 34 48 48 48, chateau-auvers.fr, €€)* offers a presentation on the Impressionists and lovely terraced gardens, complete with an orangerie and a hedge maze. ■

Auvers-sur-Oise

🅐 Map p. 212 C4

✉ 22 miles (35 km) north of Paris

🚉 By train: Paris Gare du Nord to Auvers-sur-Oise (via Pontoise) Apr.–Nov.; direct train on weekends

ville-auverssuroise.fr

Auberge Ravoux

✉ Place de la Mairie

☎ 01 30 36 60 60

🕐 Closed Mon. & Tues. & Dec.–Feb.

💲 €€ (restaurant)

maisondevangogh.fr

■ Van Gogh painted cottages in Auvers in 1890, shortly before his death.

CHARTRES CATHEDRAL

For nearly 800 years, Chartres Cathedral has stood like a beacon, seemingly alone amid the flat fields of the Beauce region. Despite fires, revolutions, and two world wars, the church has remained almost intact from the day it was consecrated in 1260, although the current restoration program, which involves some repainting of the interior, is sparking controversy.

■ The glowing beauty of Chartres has remained intact since the Middle Ages.

Chartres

🅰 Map p. 212 B2

✉ 52 miles (83 km) southwest of Paris

🚘 By car: Take the A6, then A10, then A11 toward Le Mans & follow signs to Chartres. By train: Paris Gare Montparnasse to Chartres. Train information: sncf.com

The present cathedral stands on the site of earlier churches dating from the eighth century. The most important event in its history was the gift of the "Sancta Camisia," a priceless relic presented by Charles the Bald, Charlemagne's grandson. This was the tunic supposedly worn by Mary as she gave birth to Christ, and it transformed Chartres into one of the most popular pilgrimage shrines in Europe (the relic is still stored in the Treasury). In the tenth century, the School of Chartres was one of the most prestigious centers of learning in Europe.

A series of fires destroyed the successive churches, but the most serious one was in 1194, when the entire city went up in flames, destroying everything but the Royal Portal and the western towers of the church. The local townspeople were mortified to think that the precious relic had been lost. Three days later, as the church lay smoldering, a procession appeared holding the relic. This miracle was seen as a sign from Mary that Chartres would be an ever greater church, and the rebuilding project was begun immediately with great zeal. The result is this breathtaking Gothic cathedral. Its architectural and sculptural unity is chiefly due to the fact that it was constructed almost entirely in less than 30 years.

"Chartres Blue" Stained Glass

The cathedral's stained-glass windows, with the unique "Chartres blue" color, are famous throughout the world. They form the most complete collection of medieval glass anywhere. The 12th-century Royal Portal survived the great fire, as did its glass and the spectacular window known as "the Blue Virgin." The 13th-century windows in the rest of the church form radiant illustrations of biblical and historical scenes, peopled with knights, peasants, kings, noble ladies in furs, and craftsmen at work, providing a fascinating record of religion and daily life in medieval times. Each panel tells a story to be read from left to right, and bottom to top.

Statuary & Maze

The statuary on the three main portals completes the iconography of the church. The North Porch shows the story of Creation (on the left side), leading to the Fall of Adam and Eve (right), followed by Old Testament figures, and a nativity scene. The South Porch depicts scenes of the Last Judgment.

Unfortunately, the rows of chairs now in the nave hide the best-preserved stone labyrinth in France, where pilgrims used to make their way through the 953-foot-long (291 m) maze on their knees.

What to See & Do

Take a tour (in English) by resident historian Malcolm Miller, who offers a look at the glass, sculptures, and history of the cathedral. Check times with the tourist office.

If you have a few extra hours, the old town is worth exploring. The tourist office provides maps

---

INSIDER TIP:

As you gaze at the cathedral's stained glass, think of how advanced it must have seemed to pilgrims in the Middle Ages.

—DIANA PARSELL
National Geographic contributor

---

of a Circuit Touristique that takes you to the former **Episcopal Palace** and the **Fine Arts Museum** and down to the river, which winds past an old mill and half-timbered Renaissance houses and over stone bridges. A small train runs during the tourist season and follows much the same itinerary through the town.

Don't miss the **St.-Pierre Church** nearby at Place St.-Pierre. Usually overshadowed by the more famous cathedral, it also contains some fine 13th- and 14th-century stained glass. ∎

Cathédrale Notre-Dame de Chartres

✉ 16 cloître Notre-Dame, Chartres

☎ 02 37 21 59 08

🕓 Open every day 8:30 a.m.–7:30 p.m.; Tues., Fri., & Sun. in Jul. & Aug. until 10 p.m.

cathedrale-chartres.org

Visitor Information

✉ 8 rue de la Poissonnerie

☎ 02 37 18 26 26

chartres-tourisme.com

GIVERNY

In 1883, Claude Monet moved with his family to this house, where he remained until his death in 1926. The house and gardens were an unceasing source of inspiration for the painter. Wherever he lived, Monet always had a garden, but at Giverny it became his life's work: There he created in nature the motifs that became his obsession, transposing the water lilies, boats, and bridges of his garden onto his canvases.

Monet's carefully tended gardens at Giverny are reflected in his art.

Giverny

🗺 Map p. 212 B4

✉ 49 miles (78 km) northwest of Paris

🚗 By car: Autoroute de l'Ouest (A13/ E05) from Pont de St.-Cloud, toward Rouen. Exit at Bonnières, follow the D201 to Giverny. By train: from Paris-Gare St.- Lazare on the Rouen line, get off at Vernon, & take a shuttle bus or a taxi, or walk the 3 miles (4.8 km)

By 1966, when his son Michel donated Giverny to the Acadé- mie des Beaux-Arts, the floors and ceiling beams had rotted away. It took ten years to restore the house and the gardens; the museum eventually opened in 1980, and now hosts around 500,000 visitors every year.

Gardens

Whatever season you arrive, the garden is as much a profusion of color as it was in Monet's lifetime. When the family first moved here, the garden was a modest orchard of about

2 acres (0.8 ha), enclosed within high stone walls. The painter transformed it, creating patterns and perspectives by planting clumps and shapes of color that changed with every month. Monet detested the formal French garden and instead cre- ated rose-covered archways entwined with trailing nastur- tiums, dividing the garden into brilliant flower beds filled with hollyhocks and annuals.

Ten years after he moved to Giverny, Monet bought the land on the other side of the railroad tracks, intending to divert the Epte

River to create a pond and water garden. He had an artificial lake dug and then created an exotic garden with bamboo plants, wisteria, willows, and, of course, the famous water lilies. A local craftsman built the graceful Japanese bridge; a wooden boat still floats at one end of the pond.

House & Studio

The house, with its pink, roughcast facade and green shutters, was the scene of entertaining for Monet's many guests. Friends such as Sacha Guitry, Stéphane Mallarmé, and Pierre-Auguste Rodin gathered in the blue-tiled kitchen and sunny yellow dining room.

Monet loved Japanese engravings, and his precious collection (which inspired his design of the water garden) is displayed in several of the rooms. On the walls of the modest living room hung Monet's personal collection of works he particularly admired, including a dozen Cézannes, a few Renoirs, eight Manets, a couple of Degases, and two bronzes by Rodin. Now

dispersed to collections around the world, these works have been reproduced to re-create the interior in Monet's day.

The huge Nymphéas studio was constructed in 1916 to give Monet the room and light he needed to paint the giant "Water Lilies," which were commissioned by his friend Georges Clemenceau for the Musée de l'Orangerie in Paris (see p. 140). Today, the studio exhibits reproductions of his work and also houses a souvenir shop.

To avoid the crowds, come on a weekday. (Wednesdays can also be busy.) Tour buses often leave around 4 p.m., but the gardens stay open until 6 p.m., which is a lovely time to enjoy them.

Musée des Impressionismes

Also worth seeing is the Musée des Impressionismes. Devoted to Impressionism and its evolution in the 20th century, the museum holds exhibitions and has a minimalist modern garden that is a nice contrast to Monet's. ◾

La Maison de Monet (museum)

✉ 84 rue Claude Monet

☎ 02 32 51 28 21

🕑 Open Apr.–Oct.

💲 €

fondation-monet.com

Musée des Impressionismes

✉ 99 rue Claude Monet

☎ 02 32 51 94 65

🕑 Open Apr.–Oct.

💲 €

mdig.fr

EXPERIENCE: Take Art Classes *en Plein Air*

Learn to paint in Monet's garden and around the artist's beloved village of Giverny. English-language artistic retreats are run by **Art Colony-Giverny** (*artcolony-giverny.com*), with hands-on workshops taught by professional artists. In seven-day sessions, painters and photographers at every level of skill have an opportunity to capture the *en plein air* spirit at sites made famous by French and

American Impressionist painters.

Participants, who are housed near Monet's home in a charming B&B, Les Moulin des Chennevières, have the special privilege of being allowed to work in Monet's gardens when they are closed to the public, in addition to other sites. Classes are limited to eight students, each of whom will receive personalized instruction.

More Places to Visit Around Paris

Château de Chantilly & Forest

Set in the middle of a romantic moat in the heart of the forest, Chantilly is one of the most beautiful châteaus around Paris. It was destroyed during the Revolution but has been re-created and is now home to the **Condé Museum,** an excellent art collection put together by the Duc d'Aumale in the 19th century.

What sets Chantilly off from other châteaus, however, are the **Museum of the Horse** and the **Great Stables** (circa 1719–1735), housed in a monumental stone building that at its height held 240 horses and 300 hounds. The public can attend dressage demonstrations and equestrian shows. Chantilly is also the site of one of France's major horse-racing tracks.

Other sites nearby include the Cistercian **Abbaye de Royaumont** *(Map p. 212 D4, Asnières-sur-Oise, tel 01 30 35 59 00)* and the ancient royal town of **Senlis** *(Map p. 212 D4)*. *domainedechantilly.com*
🅰 Map p. 212 D4 ✉ Chantilly, 25 miles (40 km) north of Paris ☎ 03 44 27 31 80 🕐 Closed Tues. in winter 💲 €€–€€€ 🚘 Car: Take the A1 to the Chantilly exit, then the D924A to Chantilly. Train: Gare du Nord or RER (D) to Chantilly-Gouvieux, then a short walk

Château de Malmaison

Josephine purchased this property when Napoleon was still the First Consul. He found his official residence, the Tuileries Palace, too depressing and retreated to Malmaison whenever he could. Josephine kept the château after Napoleon divorced her, and she devoted considerable sums to the house and gardens, creating the first great collection of roses here. The house is now a museum devoted to Napoleonic history and Empire memorabilia. *chateau-malmaison.fr*
🅰 Map p. 212 C3 ✉ 1 avenue du Château de Malmaison, Rueil-Malmaison ☎ 01 41 29 05 55 🕐 Closed Tues., Jan. 1, & Dec. 25 💲 € 🚇 Métro or RER (A) to Grande Arche de La Défense, then bus 258

Écouen Château & Museum

Many of the works in the collection of this Renaissance museum came from the Musée de Cluny in Paris. The magnificent 16th-century château was constructed by some of the most famous artists of the time, including Le Rosso and Jean Clouet; the south wing has remained nearly intact since that time. The collection includes a series of 16th-century tapestries depicting the story of David and Bathsheba. *musee-renaissance.fr*
🅰 Map p. 212 D3 ✉ Écouen, 12 miles (19 km) north of Paris off N16 ☎ 01 34 38 38 50 🕐 Closed Tues., Jan. 1, & Dec. 25 💲 € 🚇 Train: Gare du Nord to Écouen-Ézanville, then bus 269

Château de St.-Germain-en-Laye

This magnificent pile of medieval and Renaissance architecture stands on a plateau in the center of the town of St.-Germain-en-Laye *(Map p. 212 C3)*, about 25 minutes from Paris by train *(RER A to St.-Germain-en-Laye)*. The royal château, which now houses the **National Museum of Archaeology** *(tel 01 39 10 13 00, musee-archeologie nationale.fr, closed Tues., Jan. 1, May 1 & Dec. 25, €)*, is a stunning sight. The 13th-century chapel was the work of Pierre de Montreuil, architect of Ste.-Chapelle in Paris, and is a smaller model of that church. Louis XIV was born at St.-Germain-en-Laye and turned it into a luxurious residence, complete with terraced gardens. The chapel and the gardens, with their lovely views over the valley of the Seine, with Paris in the distance, can be visited for free.

TRAVELWISE

A parking spot is a rarity in Paris.

TRAVELWISE

PLANNING YOUR TRIP
When to Go

If you visit in late summer, when many residents are vacationing, you'll find that some stores and restaurants are closed. However, Paris has a special, sometimes villagelike quality in summer. The city has less traffic and pollution, and offers free activities like Paris Plages, concerts in the parks, and outdoor movies at La Villette. Another advantage of the summer months is that it is low season for the hotels, and many offer reduced rates. Reservations are also easier to obtain, as there are no major conventions or events being held.

In fall, the Parisians return, the weather is good, and the city bustles again. Winter and spring are often cold and rainy, but the Christmas holidays can light up the city.

Climate

Paris has moderately cold winters, with little snow; cool springs and falls; and moderately hot, humid summers.

What to Take

Be prepared for rain in any season, and always pack a sweater, even in the summer. Other necessities: comfortable walking shoes, a dressy outfit for evenings out, and a major credit card with an international PIN number (check with your bank) so you can withdraw cash from money machines. Don't forget the essentials: passport, driver's license, and insurance documentation.

Insurance

Make sure you have adequate coverage for medical treatment and expenses, including repatriation, and baggage and money loss.

Passports

For U.S. and Canadian citizens only a passport is needed to enter France for a stay of up to 90 days. No visa is required. Your passport must be valid for at least three months before your intended date of departure.

HOW TO GET TO PARIS
Airports

Roissy–Charles de Gaulle (north of Paris), tel 3950
Orly (south of Paris), tel 3950
Airport information:
parisaeroport.fr
Direct flights to Paris are available from most major cities via Air France *(tel 800 237 2747)* and many other international airlines. Paris has two airports: Roissy–Charles de Gaulle and Orly. To get into town from Roissy–Charles de Gaulle, take a taxi (around €50); Le Bus Direct (Line 2 stops at Porte Maillot, Étoile; Line 4 at Gare Montparnasse, Gare de Lyon); the Roissybus (stops at Opéra); or the RER, the regional mass-transport train (Line B stops at Gare du Nord, Châtelet, St.-Michel, Luxembourg, Port-Royal, and Denfert-Rochereau). From Orly, take a taxi (around €45); the Orlybus (stops at Denfert-Rochereau); Le Bus Direct (stops at Gare Montparnasse, Trocadéro, Étoile); or the Orlyval train (connects with RER at Antony station).

You can arrange for a door-to-door shuttle:
Paris Limousine Service (tel 07 55 72 84 88, paris-limousine-service.com, chauffeured car €50–€795, depending on type of car and service)
Super Shuttle Paris (tel 800 258 3826, supershuttle.com, €27 for Roissy; €20 for Orly in shared vehicle)
Blue Airport Shuttle Paris (tel 01 43 327 081, paris-blue-airport-shuttle.fr, from €30 per person, Charles de Gaulle)

GETTING AROUND
By Car
Car Rentals in France
Ada, tel 08 05 28 59 59, ada.fr
Avis, tel 08 21 23 0760, avis.fr
Europcar, tel 08 25 35 83 58, europcar.fr
Hertz, tel 01 73 13 78 00, hertz.fr
Driving in Paris is not advised—the traffic is heavy, street parking scarce, and you can get wherever you want to go using the good urban-transport system or plentiful taxis.

Driving Regulations

An international driver's license is not required for short-term visitors, but the U.S. Embassy recommends it. When driving, keep all relevant documents in the car. Remember that at unmarked intersections, the car coming from the right has priority and will not stop; slow down and look to the right when crossing an intersection. Seat belts are required for all passengers, even in the back seat. Children under ten are not allowed to ride in the front seat unless a special seat is provided for them. It is illegal to use a cell phone while driving.

In the absence of speed-limit signs, the limit is 30 mph/50 kph in villages, towns, and cities; 55 mph/90 kph (50 mph/80 kph in wet weather) on country roads;

70 mph/110 kph (60 mph/100 kph in wet weather) on divided roads and highways in urban areas; and 80 mph/130 kph (70 mph/110 kph in wet weather; 30 mph/50 kph in foggy conditions) on highways. If you have had more than two servings of any type of alcohol, you are over the legal limit and should not drive. If your car is towed or clamped in Paris, go to the nearest police station to find out how to retrieve it.

Car Breakdown

Europ Assistance, tel 01 41 85 85 85

For rental cars, check the package of information in the glove compartment for the emergency number. Europ Assistance offers a towing service that costs at least €200. Otherwise, look for a *garagiste* (garage) along the road. An "N" symbol means that it is open at night. There is one repair service open in every town on Sunday. Call the police (17) or the local *gendarmerie* (police station) if you can't find a garage. On *autoroutes* (highways), emergency phones are located alongside the road at regular intervals.

Public Transportation

Métro

tel 3424, ratp.fr
Operates: 5:30 a.m.–1:15 a.m. (2:15 a.m. on Fri.–Sat.)

Noctilien (Night Bus)

Operates: 12:30 a.m.–5:30 a.m.

Balabus

Operates: 12:30 p.m.–8 p.m., Sun. & public holidays, Apr.–Sept. A double decker tourist bus operated by the RATP.

RER

Operates: 5:30 a.m.–12:30 p.m.
Métro The Parisian subway,

known as the Métro, is operated by the Regie Autonome des Transports Parisiens (RATP). A map is posted in every station, or ask for a free *Plan du Métro* at the information window. Each line has a number, and is identified by the names of the stations at either end: The east–west line 1, for example, is Grande Arche de La Défense–Château de Vincennes.

Tickets are available from vending machines in stations; an agent is always available for assistance. Individual tickets are available, but a *carnet* (book) of ten tickets is better value if you plan to use the Métro frequently. The Navigo Découverte card is good for unlimited trips on the Métro, RER, and buses for one month or one week *(Mon.– Sun.)*. You will need a passport-size photo. These tickets should not be validated on buses, just shown to the driver. A Paris Visite card, available from ticket machines in the Métro, good for one, two, three, or five days, entitles you to unlimited use of public transportation in Paris and the Île de France and discounts at some sightseeing attractions. The Mobilis card, also available from ticket machines in the Métro, is good for one day only, exclusively for transportation.

Do not throw away a one-use ticket until you have left the station; a *contrôleur* (conductor) may ask to see your ticket, and will fine you if you do not have one.
RER The suburban train network, the RER, has stops in Paris, and you can use a Métro ticket to travel on it within Paris. Prices are higher for destinations outside the city.
Buses Métro tickets can also be used on city buses (validate one-use tickets in the machine behind the driver) or tickets can be purchased from the driver (exact change not required). A map of bus lines is posted at bus shelters. Some bus lines do

not operate after 8:30 p.m., or on Sundays and holidays. This information is posted at bus stops. Forty-seven late-night bus lines, called **Noctilien**, leave from Châtelet, Montparnasse, Gare de l'Est, Gare St.-Lazare, and Gare de Lyon. The **Batobus** *(batobus.com)* river buses run between the Eiffel Tower and the Jardin des Plantes. **L'Open Tour** *(tel 01 42 66 56 56, opentourparis.com),* a sightseeing bus line, has four routes. One-, two-, or three-day passes are sold. Commentaries are in ten languages (on headphones). The tours operate seven days a week, year-round.

Taxis

Taxis can be hailed on the street or found at a *station de taxi* (taxi stand) at major intersections. When the entire light on top is glowing, the taxi is available, but if only the small bulb is lit, it is not. Many cabs have green/red lights to indicate availability. Extra charges are added to the fare for pickups at train stations, luggage weighing over 12 lbs (5 kg), a fourth passenger (drivers can refuse to take more than three people), and an animal (except a seeing-eye dog). Tipping is at your discretion, but about 10 percent of the fare is customary.

If you call for a taxi, the meter starts running when the driver gets the call, and the fare can be expensive. It is a good idea to ask for a receipt in case you leave something behind, or have a problem with the driver. Fares go up at night and when the cab passes the city limits.

Any complaints about Paris taxis should be addressed to Service des Taxis, Préfecture de Police, 36 rue des Morillons, Paris 75015, tel 01 55 76 20 05.

Radio-Dispatched Taxis

Alpha-Taxis, tel 01 45 85 85 85,

reservation.alphataxis.fr
Taxis G7, tel 3607, g7.fr

Motorcycle taxis

With driver, helmet supplied:
City Bird, tel 08 26 10 01 00,
city-bird.com

Limousine services

City Bird (see above)
Corporate Paris, tel 01 47 30 54
54, corporateparis.com

Trains

SNCF The national French railroad, the SNCF (Société Nationale des Chemin de Fer) links
Paris and all major cities.
Information and reservations,
tel 3635 (7 a.m–10 p.m.); for
suburban lines, tel 3658, sncf.
com.

   The Paris mainline SNCF train
stations (each with a Métro station of the same name) are the
Gare de Lyon (for traveling to/
from the southeast of France and
Italy); the Gare du Nord (Brussels, London, and other northern
destinations); the Gare de l'Est
(the east); the Gare St.-Lazare (the
northwest, including Normandy);
the Gare d'Austerlitz (Spain and
the southwest); the Gare Montparnasse (the west, including
Brittany); and the Gare de Bercy
(auto-trains and overflow from
the Gare de Lyon). Phone for
times and reservations, reserve
online at voyages-sncf.com, or buy
your ticket at the station (phone
service is expensive).

   TGV The high-speed Train à
Grande Vitesse (TGV) will get you
to Marseilles in just over three
hours, Brussels in one and a half
hours, or London in two and a
quarter (by Eurostar via the Channel Tunnel). Reserve in advance for
all TGV and Eurostar trips.

   Before boarding any train, it
is essential to *composter* (validate)
your ticket in one of the yellow
machines at the start of each

journey, unless you have an e-ticket.
You may be fined by the conductor
if you don't.

Tours & Organized Sightseeing

Bus Tours

Tours of the city and its
monuments:
Balabus, ratp.fr
Paris City Vision, tel 01 44 55 60
00, pariscityvision.com
Paris L'Open Tour, tel 01 42 66
56 56, opentourparis.com (also
see p. 235)

Walking Tours

A variety of tours, from museums and monuments to historic
districts:
Paris Walks, tel 01 48 09 21 40,
paris-walks.com
Localers, tel 01 83 64 92 01,
localers.com

Bicycle & Segway Tours

Tours of different neighborhoods
and parks; some night tours
available:
Paris à Vélo, 22 rue Alphonse
Baudin, 75011, tel 01 48 87 60 01,
parisavelo.fr
City Segway Tours, 24 rue Edgar
Faure, 75015, tel 01 82 88 80 96,
citysegwaytours.com/paris

Boat Tours

The following companies offer
regular hour-long Seine tours all
day, starting at around 10 a.m.
and ending between 10 p.m. and
11 p.m. (later in summer). Some
also offer dinner cruises.

The Seine

Bateaux-Mouches, Pont de
l'Alma, 75008, tel 01 42 25 96
10, bateaux-mouches.fr, Métro:
Alma-Marceau.
Bateaux Parisiens Tour Eiffel,
Port de la Bourdonnais, 75007, tel
01 76 64 14 45, bateauxparisiens.
com, Métro: Bir-Hakeim.
Vedettes de Paris, Port de

Suffren, 75007, tel 01 44 18 19
50, vedettesdeparis.com, Métro:
Bir-Hakeim.
Bateaux Vedettes du Pont Neuf,
Square du Vert-Galant, Île de la
Cité, 75001, tel 01 46 33 98 38,
vedettesdupontneuf.com, Métro:
Pont Neuf.

The Canals

Canauxrama, 13 quai de la Loire,
tel 01 42 39 15 00 (reservations
required), canauxrama.com.
Two-and-a-half-hour canal
cruise. Departs: Bassin de la
Villette (Métro: Jaurès) or Port
de l'Arsenal (Métro: Bastille).
Paris Canal, 19 quai de la Loire,
tel 01 42 40 29 00 (reservations
required), pariscanal.com: the
Canal St.-Martin and the Seine in
three hours. Departs: Quai Ana-
tole France, near Musée d'Orsay
(Métro: Solférino) or Parc de la
Villette (Métro: Port de la Villette).

PRACTICAL ADVICE

Communications

Post Offices

Main Branch: 16 rue Etienne
Marcel, 75002, tel 3631, laposte.
fr, Métro: Louvre-Rivoli or Les
Halles. Open: Mon.–Sat. nonstop,
except between 6 a.m. and 8 a.m.;
Sun. 10 a.m.–midnight. Local
branches open: Mon.–Fri.,
8 a.m.–7 or 8 p.m.; Sat., 8 or
9 a.m.–noon or 1 p.m.

   Known as "La Poste," the
French postal service has branches
in every neighborhood. To
receive mail there, letters should
be addressed with your name
clearly printed, followed by "Poste
Restante" and the post office's
address. All Paris postal codes
begin with 75, and end with the
number of the arrondissement, or
quarter. For example, 75010 is in
the 10th arrondissement, 75002
in the 2nd arrondissement, and
so on.

   Mailboxes: Yellow *boîtes postales*
(mailboxes) are located outside

every post office. They may have separate compartments for local mail, *départemental* (mail within the *département*, and *autres départements/étranger* (elsewhere in France and foreign).

Telephones

To call France from the United States, dial 011-33 (international and French country code) and the nine-digit number (leaving out the initial zero).

The last telephone booth in Paris was dismantled in 2017. Before leaving home, check with your mobile operator to see what plans it offers customers traveling abroad and how to turn off "data roaming" on your cell phone to avoid prohibitive roaming charges. It's a good idea to use free Wi-Fi in hotels and cafés (look for the sign in the window) and at hotspots in public spaces for surfing the Web and buy a pay-as-you-go cell phone if you need to make calls.

All French phone numbers have ten digits, with Paris-region numbers beginning with 01. The four other national prefixes are: 02 for the northwest; 03 for the northeast; 04 for the southeast; and 05 for the southwest. Numbers beginning with 08 00 are toll free. There is an extra charge for other numbers beginning with 08.

To make an international call, dial 00, followed by the country code (1 for the United States and Canada), the area code, and the number.

Since deregulation, there are numerous directory-assistance numbers run by various operators. It is best to search the Web first (try infobel.com/France). If that doesn't work, call 118 000, but you will be charged for the call. The historic operator, Orange (formerly France Télécom), lists only its own customers on pagesjaunes.fr (businesses) and pagesjaunes .fr/pagesblanches (individuals) .

Newspapers

Most kiosks (newsstands) sell some English-language newspapers, including the *International New York Times, USA Today, The Wall Street Journal, The Financial Times,* and sometimes other British or Irish dailies. The major French daily papers are the left-wing *Libération,* the left-leaning *Le Monde,* and the conservative *Le Figaro.* The only paper published on Sunday is the *Journal du Dimanche.*

Television

France has 27 free digital television channels, some of which (notably Arte) show movies and TV series in English. Cable stations include Canal+ Cinéma, a movie channel with some films in the original language, CNN, France 24 (news), MTV, MCM (music videos), Eurosport, Planète (nature and science), RAI Uno (Italian), TVE 1 (Spanish), and Euronews. Many programs can be viewed in either the original language or in French. Look for the "VM" option in the TV guide.

Radio

For a mix of pop, rock, jazz, and classical with no commercials, try FIP (105.1 FM). Radio Nova (101.5 FM) offers mainly chill-out, ambient, and drum-and-bass music; Radio Latina (99 FM) Latin music; France-Info (105.5 FM) 24-hour news in French; Skyrock (96 FM) hip-hop, R&B, and French rap; RFM (103.9 FM) pop and rock; Radio Classique (101.1 FM) classical music; and TSF Jazz (89.9).

Movies & Books Set in Paris

The romantic setting of Paris has provided the background for innumerable works of film and literature. The list is endless.

Movies

An abbreviated list of some well-known American and international movies set here includes: *An American in Paris, Love in the Afternoon, Funny Face, Desire, Paris When It Sizzles, Paris by Night, Paris Calling, National Lampoon's European Vacation, The 400 Blows, Small Change, Breathless, The Last Métro, Last Tango in Paris, Frantic, French Kiss, Amélie, Midnight in Paris.* If you want to see any or all of these films, visit the Forum des Images *(2 & 4 rue du Cinéma, Forum des Halles, forumdesimages. fr),* which has an archive of just about every film having anything to do with Paris. For a small fee, you can watch any of them on your own video screen, or see scheduled films on a big screen.

Books

The following novels and memoirs are steeped in Parisian ambience: *Tropic of Cancer* and *Quiet Days in Clichy* by Henry Miller; *Quartet* by Jean Rhys; *A Moveable Feast* by Ernest Hemingway; *The Autobiography of Alice B. Toklas* and *Paris France* by Gertrude Stein; *Being Geniuses Together* by Robert McAlmon and Kay Boyle; *Shakespeare and Company* by Sylvia Beach; *The Paris Edition* by Waverly Root; *Down and Out in Paris and London* by George Orwell; *The Secret Paris of the '30s* by Brassaï; *The Diary of Anaïs Nin* by Anaïs Nin; *Force of Circumstance* by Simone de Beauvoir; *Paris Notebooks* by Mavis Gallant; *Paris Journal* and *Paris Was Yesterday* by Janet Flanner; *Paris Journal* by M. F. K. Fisher; *Paris* by Julian Green; *Paris in the '50s* by Stanley Karnow. The ultimate work set in Paris is Marcel Proust's *Remembrance of Things Past.*

Electricity

French circuits use 220 volts; a transformer and adapter plug are needed for American appliances that operate on 110 volts. Most computers and cell phones come with transformers that adapt automatically, but an adapter plug is still needed. Check with the manufacturer or ask at a *droguerie* (hardware store) or in the basement of the BHV store at 52 rue de Rivoli.

Local Customs

Say *"bonjour"* and *"au revoir"* to the staff when entering and leaving a shop, restaurant, or café. The French tend to keep to themselves more than Americans do, but as elsewhere a friendly approach usually gets a friendly response, and certainly the natives are always more than willing to give directions. If you are invited to dinner at a French person's home, bring flowers rather than wine.

Money Matters

Banque de France, 31 rue Croix-des-Petits-Champs, 75001, tel 01 42 92 42 92, Métro: Palais-Royal **American Express,** 4 rue Louis Blériot, 92500 Rueil-Malmaison, tel 01 47 77 30 00, RER (A): Rueil-Malmaison

In early 2020, one U.S. dollar equaled 0.90 euro. One euro equals 100 centimes, which come in coins of 1, 2, 5, 10, 20, and 50. The euro comes in coins of 1 and 2, and bills of 5, 10, 20, 50, 100, and 500, although many shops may not accept bills over 50.

Commercial currency exchanges are located in train stations, airports, and numerous locations around the city. Bank branches that exchange currency display a sign saying *"Change."* A commission is usually charged. The Banque de France often has the best exchange rate. Cash withdrawals against a credit card are possible at banks and currency exchanges. The American Express office exchanges currency, offering special services to Amex cardholders.

ATMs are the easiest way to get money, but an international PIN number is required. Check with your bank before leaving. In France, credit and debit cards now often have a chip containing the ID. Foreign cards usually have this information on a magnetic strip, which may occasionally cause problems. A fee is usually charged for credit card advances, but the exchange rate may be more advantageous than those offered by banks.

National Holidays

January 1, Easter Monday, May 1, May 8, Ascension (40 days after Easter), Pentecost Monday (10 days after Ascension), July 14, August 15, November 1, November 11, December 25.

Opening Times

Most banks are open Monday through Friday, from 9 a.m. to 5 p.m. Some close at lunchtime or open on Saturday morning. Major department stores are open from about 9:30 a.m. to 7 p.m., and some stay open till 10 p.m. one night of the week. Boutiques open around 10 a.m. and close at 7 p.m. or 8 p.m.; they may be closed on Monday and at lunchtime, usually between 1 p.m. and 2:30 p.m. More and more shops are staying open on Sunday, but check first. Cafés are open from early morning until 8 p.m., 10 p.m., or 2 a.m. Most restaurants are open from noon to 3 p.m. and 7:30 p.m. to 11 p.m. Many stores and restaurants close in August.

Time Differences

Paris is one hour ahead of Greenwich mean time. If it is midnight in Paris, it is 6 p.m. in New York, 3 p.m. in California.

Tipping

All restaurant bills include a 15 percent service charge. It is usual to leave a small additional tip for the waiter if the service has been good. It is customary to tip taxi drivers 10 percent, though this is not obligatory. It is usual to give porters, doormen, tour guides, and hairdressers a tip of €1–2, ushers and cloakroom attendants €1. There is no need to leave a tip for hotel maids unless you have required out of the ordinary service.

Toilets

The self-cleaning toilets on the street (now wheelchair-accessible) are free, and should not be used by children under ten unless accompanied by an adult. Some Métro stations have public toilets. Large department stores have public restrooms. If you are desperate, go into a café and head for the *"toilette"* sign. They are usually free, although a few may charge 50 centimes, but don't be surprised if you are asked to buy a coffee. Your chances of not being noticed are better in a large, busy café.

While all restaurants are required to have restrooms, they are not always up to the highest standards of cleanliness, and a few still have squat toilets.

Tourist Offices

In the U.S.
New York, tel 212 838 7800
Office de Tourisme de Paris (Paris Tourist Office)
Main office: Hôtel de Ville, 29 rue de Rivoli, 75004, parisinfo. com, Métro: Hôtel de Ville & Châtelet, RER (A & B): Châtelet Les Halles.
Open: daily 9 a.m.–7 p.m, Nov.–Apr. from 10 a.m.; closed Dec. 25.

Staff will answer questions and help with hotel reservations. There are branches at airports and train stations (see p. 9).

Travelers With Disabilities

Information: Office de Tourisme de Paris (Paris Tourist Office), Hôtel de Ville, 29 rue de Rivoli, 75004, parisinfo.com. Open: daily, 9 a.m.–7 p.m, Nov.–Apr. from 10 a.m.; closed Dec. 25.

The new Méteor Métro line is wheelchair accessible, otherwise access to the Métro is nearly impossible for wheelchair passengers. However, more and more RER stations are becoming accessible. Cité Universitaire, Auber, and Charles de Gaulle Étoile have public elevators, but in most cases you must ask a station employee to accompany you as the elevators require a key. In some stations employees are available to accompany you to the train only Mon.– Fri. from 6:30 a.m. to 8 p.m., for other times you can reserve the Accès Plus Transilien service before 12 p.m. on the day (tel 09 70 82 41 42; email: accesplus@ transilien-sncf.fr). RER lines A and B are "90 percent" accessible (see ratp.fr for a list of stations). The entire bus and trolley networks are wheelchair-accessible. Spaces are reserved for wheelchairs in the high-speed TGV trains, and there are accessible toilets. For a comprehensive plan of Paris transport accessibility visit iledefrance-mobilites.fr (in French).

Taxis are obliged to accept passengers with disabilities even if they require assistance, and to accept seeing-eye dogs. Persons with disabilities do not have to wait in line for a taxi at an airport or train station. When calling for a taxi, ask for a Renault-Espace van (see Taxis, pp. 235–236). Hertz and Avis (see Car Rentals, p. 234) have adapted cars; reserve 48 hours in advance. Taxis G7 Horizon (tel 01 47 39 00 91, g7.fr) has wheelchair-equipped cabs. Book in advance and specify that you need a "Horizon" car.

Most hotel elevators are usually too small for a wheelchair, and bathrooms can be tiny. Large, modern hotels are the most likely to be accessible. There is a ramp at the curb on every street corner. Street toilets are accessible and free.

For the visually impaired, there is a strip of bumps on the edge of Métro quais (platforms) and tactile numbers on elevator buttons.

U.K. publisher RADAR puts out Access in Paris, an English-language guide for disabled travelers (accessinparis.org). J'accede also publishes an annual guide listing accessible places. Its website (jac-cede.com) also provides useful information. The Paris Tourist Office has information on the accessibility of transportation, museums, and monuments. Pamphlets on train and Métro accessibility are available at all stations. Always clearly describe your needs when booking any travel service.

Escort Services for Travelers With Disabilities

Auxiliaires des Aveugles, 71 avenue de Breteuil, 75015, tel 01 88 32 31 40, lesauxiliaires desaveugles.asso.fr. Free escorts for the visually impaired.

Les Compagnons du Voyage, 34 rue Championnet, 75018, tel 01 58 76 08 33, compagnons .com.

EMERGENCIES

Embassies & Consulates

United States Embassy, 2 avenue Gabriel, 75008, tel 01 43 12 22 22; Consular Services (Visas and American Citizen Services) 4 avenue Gabriel, Métro: Concorde. **Canadian Embassy & Consulate,** 130 rue du Faubourg Saint-Honoré, 75008, tel 01 44 43 29 00. Métro: Saint-Philippe-du-Roule or Miromesnil.

For legal assistance in an emergency, contact your embassy or consulate for a list of English-speaking lawyers.

Emergency Phone Numbers/Addresses

Any emergency, tel 112
Police, tel 17
Fire or **emergency medical assistance,** tel 18
Ambulance, tel 15 or 01 44 49 23 23
Poisoning, tel 01 40 05 48 48. For the hearing disabled, send SMS to 114.
SOS Médecin, tel 01 47 07 77 77 or 08 20 33 24 24. Medical emergency house calls.
SOS Dentaire, tel 01 43 37 51 00 or 01 43 36 36 00; online booking at sos-dentaire.com. Emergency dental service available 24/7.
American Hospital, 63 boulevard de Victor-Hugo, Neuilly, tel 01 46 41 25 25. Métro: Pont de Levallois or Pont de Neuilly. Bus: 82. For 24-hour bilingual emergency medical and dental services.
24-hour pharmacy, Pharmacie Internationale, 5 place Pigalle, 75009, tel 01 78 38 12. Métro: Pigalle. (Closed pharmacies post a sign in the window with the address of the nearest one open.)
SOS Help, tel 01 46 21 46 46. English-language crisis hotline, 3 p.m.–11 p.m.

Lost Property

Bureau des Objets Trouvés (Lost & Found Bureau), 36 rue des Morillons, 75015, tel 3430. Métro: Convention. Open: Mon.– Wed. 8:30 a.m.–5 p.m., Thurs. 8:30 a.m.–12 p.m., Fri. 8:30 a.m.–4:30 p.m.
RATP lost and found: tel 3246

Lost Credit Cards

American Express, tel 1 336 393 1111 (call collect)
Diners Club, tel 1 800 234 6377 (call collect)
MasterCard, tel 08 00 90 13 87
Visa, tel 1 303 967 1096 (call collect) or 08 00 90 11 79

HOTELS & RESTAURANTS

Parisian hotels are officially rated from one star to four stars. Only the larger hotels have in-house restaurants, noted in the listings. Unless otherwise mentioned, all these hotels have private bathrooms with shower and/or bathtub. Value-added tax and service are included in the prices, but a hotel tax per person per night will be added to the bill.

Most hotels now charge extra for breakfast, usually continental style (bread, croissant, jam, and tea or coffee), but sometimes buffet style. Where two prices are given, the first is for continental breakfast, the second is for a more substantial buffet breakfast.

Street parking is extremely difficult to find in Paris, and most hotels do not have parking lots or garages. Reservations are recommended for all restaurants: The greats are often booked well in advance, and the small ones fill up quickly. All the following restaurants serve French cuisine unless otherwise noted.

Little has been done to make the city's hotels and restaurants accessible to the disabled. "Accessible room" means that a wheelchair would be able to get into a room and move around, and "adapted" means that the bathroom is up to standards. However, there are no specific facilities for the disabled, and buildings may have steps to navigate before entering. Travelers with disabilities should check when booking to make sure the hotel or restaurant meets their needs.

If your hotel is on a main street, ask for a room at the back where you will not be disturbed by traffic. Hotels in this directory are listed by location, price, then in alphabetical order.

Grading System

French hotels are graded according to a star system, from one to five stars, as well as the special designation of "palace" for five-stars with extras like Michelin-starred restaurants or spas. The system is based on room size and lobby size, with other amenities counted on a weighted scale. The requirements of the lesser grades are assumed in the higher ones. Minimum room size and the number of hours the reception desk is staffed increase with the number of stars.

Palace Five-star hotels with exceptional amenities that go above and beyond.

★★★★★ Bathrobes, elevators, room service, safe, mini-bar, restaurant open at least five days a week, valet parking, elevator. Staff speaks at least two European languages, including English.

★★★★ Air-conditioning, Wi-Fi, international TV channels, hair dryer, in-room breakfast, elevator if more than two stories.

★★★ En-suite bathrooms, color TV with remote, telephone, elevator if more than three stories.

★★ En-suite or shared bathrooms. Staff speaks at least one European language besides French. Elevator if more than four stories. Credit cards accepted.

★ Small reception area, breakfast area, en-suite or shared bathrooms, in-room sink, bathroom toiletries.

Always try to make reservations in advance, if possible confirming by e-mail. You may be asked for a deposit or credit card number.

Restaurants

One of the great pleasures of visiting Paris is its glorious food. Many hotels have their own restaurants, and some restaurants also have rooms to rent. Restaurants in this directory are listed by location, price, then in alphabetical order.

PRICES

HOTELS
An indication of the cost of a double room in the high season is given by € signs.

€€€€€	Over €300
€€€€	€220–€300
€€€	€150–€220
€€	€100–€150
€	Under €100

RESTAURANTS
An indication of the cost of a three-course meal without drinks is given by € signs.

€€€€€	Over €90
€€€€	€60–€90
€€€	€40–€60
€€	€25–€40
€	Under €25

L = lunch
D = dinner
See also the menu reader on pp. 263–264.

Credit & Debit Cards

Many hotels and restaurants accept all major cards. Smaller ones may accept only some, as shown in their entry. Abbreviations used are: AE American Express, DC Diners Club, MC MasterCard, V Visa.

Dining

Lunch usually starts around midday and goes on until 2 or 3 p.m. Dinner is usually eaten around 8 p.m., but may start about 7 p.m.

Menus must by law be displayed outside any establishment serving food, and studying and comparing these before making your choice is part of the pleasure. Most restaurants offer one or more *prix-fixe* menus, set menus at a fixed price, sometimes including wine. Otherwise (and usually more expensively), you order individual items *à la carte*—from the menu. The French usually eat salad (but rarely in restaurants) after the main course and sometimes with the cheese course, which always comes before dessert. Bread and water are supplied free. (French tap water is safe to drink.)

Smoking is forbidden in all public places in France. The smokers now congregate on the sidewalk.

Cafés

Cafés remain a French institution, good for morning coffee, leisurely drinks, modest meals, or just people-watching. They are usually busy all day, opening early to serve the traditional *grand crème* (large cup of white coffee) with croissants to people on their way to work.

Tipping

A 15 percent service charge is always included in the bill. Only add more if the service has been particularly good.

▶ THE ISLANDS

The Île de la Cité and the Île St.-Louis, while major sightseeing attractions, are home to mostly minor restaurants. There are, however, a few charming hotels on the Île St.-Louis.

HOTELS

🏨 DU JEU DE PAUME
€€€€€ ★★★★
54 RUE ST.-LOUIS EN L'ÎLE, 75004

TEL 01 43 26 14 18
jeudepaumehotel.com
A 17th-century tennis court creatively converted into a hotel with striking mezzanines. Rooms are comfortable and attractive, but small. Garden. Breakfast: €18.

🍴 30 🚇 Pont Marie 🔲 🔲
🟡 🔳 All major cards

🏨 DES DEUX ÎLES
€€€€ ★★★
59 RUE ST.-LOUIS EN L'ÎLE, 75004

TEL 01 43 26 13 35
deuxiles-paris-hotel.com
Located on the chic Île St.-Louis. Small, attractive rooms with exposed wooden beams. Breakfast: €15.

🍴 17 🚇 Pont Marie 🔲 🔳
🔳 MC, V

🏨 SAINT LOUIS EN L'ISLE
€€€€ ★★★
75 RUE ST.-LOUIS EN L'ÎLE, 75004

TEL 01 46 34 04 80
saintlouisenlisle.com
Small, quiet, and soberly elegant, it has exposed wooden beams, and terracotta flooring. Breakfast: €13.

🍴 20 🚇 Pont Marie
🔳 🔲 🔳 🔳 AE, MC, V

🏨 DE LUTÈCE
€€€ ★★★
65 RUE ST.-LOUIS EN L'ÎLE, 75004

TEL 01 43 26 23 52
paris-hotel-lutece.com
The wood-paneled lobby is cozy, and each modest room has an interesting detail, like exposed beams or a pretty mirror. Breakfast: €15.

🍴 23 🚇 Pont Marie
🔲 🔳 MC, V

▶ QUARTIER LATIN

Small hotels are the rule in the famous student quarter, which has hundreds of cheap restaurants (often of dubious quality), as well as one of the most expensive, La Tour d'Argent.

HOTELS

🏨 HOTEL DES GRANDS HOMMES
€€€€ ★★★
17 PLACE DU PANTHÉON, 75005

TEL 01 46 34 19 60
hoteldesgrandshommes.com
Ask for a room with a view of the Panthéon across the street in this pretty, comfortable hotel. Some rooms have canopy beds and exposed beams. Breakfast: €12.

🍴 31 🚇 Maubert-Mutualité, RER: Luxembourg 🔲 🔳
🔳 All major cards

🏨 PARC SAINT-SÉVERIN
€€€€ ★★★★
22 RUE DE LA PARCHEMINERIE, 75005

TEL 01 43 54 32 17
paris-hotel-parcsaintseverin.com
An attractively decorated hotel with a mix of modern and antique furnishings on a quiet street. Bright, spacious rooms, some with rooftop terraces. Breakfast: €16.

🍴 27 🚇 St.-Michel, Cluny La Sorbonne
🔲 🔳 🔳 All major cards

🏨 LE CLOS MÉDICIS
€€€ ★★★
56 RUE MONSIEUR-LE-PRINCE, 75006

TEL 01 43 29 10 80
closmedicis.com
Designer furnishings amid stone walls and exposed beams in this mid-19th-century hotel. Small, comfortable rooms, charming staff, fireplace, and garden. Breakfast: €13.

🍴 38 🚇 Odéon, RER: Luxembourg 🔲 🔳 🔳 All major cards

🏨 MAXIM QUARTIER LATIN
€€ ★★
28 RUE CENSIER, 75005

TEL 01 43 31 16 15
hotelmaximlatin.com
Decorated in a simple modern

style. Near the Jardin des Plantes. Breakfast: €10.

🛈 33 🚇 Censier-Daubenton
🛗 ⬛ ⬛ ⬛ AE, MC, V

🏨 GAY-LUSSAC

€ ★★

29 RUE GAY-LUSSAC, 75005

TEL 01 43 54 23 96

hotelgaylussac.com

Cheap, clean, comfortable, and located near the Luxembourg Garden. Breakfast: €9.

🛈 29 (some without private bathrooms) 🚇 RER: Luxembourg 🛗 ⬛ DC, MC, V

RESTAURANTS

🍽 LA TOUR D'ARGENT

€€€€€

15 QUAI TOURNELLE, 75005

TEL 01 43 54 23 31

tourdargent.com

Its reputation may have slipped a little, and it now has only one Michelin star instead of three, but it's still a great favorite with visitors for its duckling and its spectacular views of the Seine and Notre-Dame. Fixed-price L menu.

🚇 Pont Marie 🕔 Closed Sun.–Mon., Aug. 🛗 ⬛ All major cards

🍽 BAIETA

€€€€

5 RUE DE PONTOISE, 75005

TEL 01 42 02 59 19

restaurant-baieta-paris.fr

The young Nice chef Julia Sedefdjian offers a modern French cuisine with distinguished Mediterranean flavors. One Michelin star.

🚇 Maubert-Mutualité
🕔 Closed Sun.–Mon. ⬛ ⬛ AE, MC, V

🍽 L'AVANT-GOUT

€€

26 RUE BOBILLOT, 75013

TEL 01 53 80 24 00

lavantgout.com

This bistro is farther afield, near

the Place d'Italie, but it's small, cozy, and one of the city's greatest. Fixed-price menus.

🚇 Place d'Italie 🕔 Closed Sun.–Mon. ⬛ MC, V

🍽 L'INVITÉE

€€

8 RUE THÉNARD, 75005

TEL 01 43 54 59 47

linvitee.fr

Refined and yet with a convivial atmosphere, it offers a traditional cuisine with an international twist.

🚇 Maubert-Mutualité
🕔 Closed Mon. ⬛ ⬛ MC, V

▶ ## ST.-GERMAIN & MONTPARNASSE

The chic and beautiful neighborhood of St.-Germain-des-Prés has many charming hotels, some of them quite reasonably priced, as well as many interesting little restaurants. Lively Montparnasse is more down-market, but it has plenty of points of interest.

HOTELS

🏨 LUTÉTIA
🍽 €€€€€ ★★★★★

45 BOULEVARD RASPAIL, 75006

TEL 01 49 54 46 00

hotellutetia.com

Recently reopened after a major overhaul, this art nouveau grande dame, the leading hotel on the Left Bank, gained a five-star rating with its refreshed decor, new spa and swimming pool, fine restaurants and bars, and winter garden.

🛈 184 inc. suites 🚇 Sèvres-Babylone 🌊 🍴 🛗 ⬛ ⬛ All major cards

🏨 RELAIS CHRISTINE

€€€€€ ★★★★★

3 RUE CHRISTINE, 75006

TEL 01 40 51 60 80

relais-christine.com

Discreet, Left Bank luxury in a former convent, in whose

vaulted, 13th-century kitchens breakfast is served. Garden and courtyard. Breakfast: €30.

🛈 48 🚇 Odéon 🅿 🛗 ⬛
🌊 ⬛ All major cards

🏨 D'ANGLETERRE SAINT-GERMAIN-DES-PRÉS

€€€€ ★★★

44 RUE JACOB, 75006

TEL 01 42 60 34 72

hotel-dangleterre.com

A friendly staff, historical associations (Washington Irving and Ernest Hemingway stayed here), and loads of charm in individually decorated rooms keep regulars coming back. Breakfast included if booked directly.

🛈 26 🚇 St.-Germain-des-Prés
🛗 ⬛ All major cards

🏨 DE L'ABBAYE

€€€€ ★★★★

10 RUE CASSETTE, 75006

TEL 01 45 44 38 11

hotelabbayeparis.com

Charming 18th-century building with a courtyard garden on a quiet street. Four duplex suites with terraces. Some rooms are small. Breakfast: €18.

🛈 44 inc. suites 🚇 St.-Sulpice
🛗 ⬛ ⬛ AE, MC, V

🏨 HÔTEL DE L'ODÉON

€€€€ ★★★★

13 RUE ST.-SULPICE, 75006

TEL 01 43 25 70 11

hotelparisodeonsaintgermain.com

Antiques and tapestries in this 16th-century manor house create a romantic setting. Most rooms overlook the garden. Breakfast included.

🛈 27 🚇 Odéon 🛗 ⬛
⬛ AE, MC, V

🏨 HÔTEL DES SAINTS-PÈRES

€€€€ ★★★

65 RUE DES STS.-PÈRES, 75006

TEL 01 45 44 50 00

paris-hotel-saints-peres.com

Beloved of the fashion crowd, most of its antique-furnished

rooms have views of the garden. Breakfast: €17.

1 39 **⊠** St.-Germain-des-Prés
⊟ **⊗** **⊛** **⊛** AE, MC, V

🏨 L'HÔTEL
€€€€ ★★★★★

13 RUE DES BEAUX-ARTS, 75006

TEL 01 44 41 99 00

l-hotel.com

Has a marvelous, round stairway, cozy bar, and extravagantly decorated rooms. Oscar Wilde died in room 16. Breakfast included.

1 20 inc. suites
⊠ St.-Germain-des-Prés
⊟ **⊗** **⊛** **⊛** All major cards

🏨 ODÉON-HÔTEL
€€€€ ★★★

3 RUE DE L'ODÉON, 75006

TEL 01 43 25 90 67

odeonhotel.fr

A quiet location between the Boulevard St.-Germain and the Luxembourg Garden, with individually decorated rooms. Breakfast included.

1 32 **⊠** Odéon **⊟** **⊗**
⊛ All major cards

🏨 PULLMAN PARIS
🍴 MONTPARNASSE
€€€€ ★★★★

19 RUE COMMANDANT RENÉ MOUCHOTTE, 75014

TEL 01 44 36 44 36

all.accor.com

Reopened in spring 2020 after thorough renovation, this modern, high-rise hotel offers business facilities and good views from the upper floors. Choice of five restaurants and bars.

1 957 inc. suites
⊠ Montparnasse-Bienvenüe
⊟ **⊗** **P** **⊛** All major cards

🏨 RELAIS ST.-GERMAIN
€€€€ ★★★★

9 CARREFOUR DE L'ODÉON, 75006

TEL 01 44 27 07 97

hotel-paris-relais-saint-germain.com

Run by the wife of beloved chef Yves Camdeborde (see

Le Comptoir du Relais on this page), the hotel offers lavishly decorated rooms with a touch of humor and a gourmet breakfast (included).

1 22 **⊠** Odéon **⊟** **⊗**
⊛ All major cards

🏨 LEFT BANK
ST.-GERMAIN
BEST WESTERN
€€€ ★★★

9 RUE DE L'ANCIENNE COMÉDIE, 75006

TEL 01 43 54 01 70

hotelleftbank.com

In the heart of the Left Bank, this small hotel has an antique-filled lobby, wooden beams, and marble bathrooms. Breakfast: €12.

1 31 **⊠** Odéon **⊟** **⊗**
⊛ AE, MC, V

🏨 VILLA DES PRINCES
€€€ ★★

19 RUE MONSIEUR LE PRINCE, 75006

TEL 01 46 33 31 69

Great location for this renovated little hotel with small, simple rooms. No wheelchair access. Breakfast included.

1 11 **⊠** Odéon **⊟** **⊗**
⊛ All major cards

🏨 ISTRIA–MONTPARNASSE
€€ ★★★

29 RUE CAMPAGNE PREMIÈRE, 75014

TEL 01 43 20 91 82

hotel-istria-paris.com

A well-kept, comfortable hotel on a quiet street near Montparnasse; its past guests have included such greats as Rainer Maria Rilke, Marcel Duchamp, and Man Ray. Breakfast: €12.

1 26 **⊠** Raspail **⊟** **⊗**
⊛ AE, MC, V

RESTAURANTS

🍴 CLOSERIE DES LILAS
€€€€€

171 BOULEVARD MONTPARNASSE, 75006

TEL 01 40 51 34 50

closeriedeslilas.fr

Pricey but worth it for the so-Parisian ambience at this famous Montparnasse bar/brasserie/restaurant, a former hangout of Hemingway, Picasso, and more. A good place to drink amid the literary crowd. Fixed-price menus available.

⊠ Vavin **⊛** All major cards

🍴 GUY SAVOY
€€€€€

11 QUAI DE CONTI, 75006

TEL 01 43 80 40 61

guysavoy.com

In its new location comprising six elegant dining rooms in the Monnaie de Paris, this fine eatery offers creative specialties such as artichoke soup with black truffles or oyster concassé with seaweed and lemon.

⊠ Pont Neuf **⊗** **⊕** Closed
Sat. L, Sun.–Mon., & Christmas
⊛ All major cards

🍴 BRASSERIE LIPP
€€€€

151 BOULEVARD ST.-GERMAIN, 75006

TEL 01 45 48 53 91

brasserielipp.fr

A place to go for its literary connections (patrons have included Ernest Hemingway and F. Scott Fitzgerald), and its wonderful, intact, turn-of-the-20th-century decor, but not for the indifferent food and service.

⊠ St.-Germain-des-Prés **⊗**
⊛ All major cards

🍴 LE COMPTOIR DU
RELAIS
€€€€

9 CARREFOUR DE L'ODÉON, 75006

TEL 01 44 27 07 97

hotel-paris-relais-saint-germain.com

The immensely—and deservedly so—popular restaurant of bistronomy pioneer Yves Camdeborde, where diners are assured of a delicious meal in convivial surroundings. No reservations for lunch or dinner

---

on weekends; reserve for dinner Mon.–Fri.

🚇 Odéon 💳 All major cards

🍴 LE DÔME
€€€€

108 BOULEVARD MONTPAR-
NASSE, 75014

TEL 01 43 35 25 81

restaurant-ledome.com

Fine fish in the lively ambience of this famous Montparnasse brasserie. À la carte menu.

🚇 Montparnasse, Vavin 💳
💳 All major cards

🍴 LE DUC
€€€€

243 BOULEVARD RASPAIL, 75014

TEL 01 43 20 96 30

restaurantleduc.com

Fresh fish, prepared simply and served in a yacht-like setting. Fixed-price menus available.

🚇 Raspail 🕐 Closed Sun.–
Mon., & public holidays 💳
💳 All major cards

🍴 ZE KITCHEN GALERIE
€€€€

4 RUE DES GRANDS AUGUSTINS, 75006

TEL 01 44 32 00 32

zekitchengalerie.fr

Colorful contemporary art decorates the walls of this bright, cheery (but noisy) restaurant. Kitchen workers toil away in full view of diners as they whip up chef William Ledeuil's equally colorful, artistically presented and Asian-influenced dishes.

🚇 St.-Michel 🕐 Closed Sat. L, Sun. 💳 All major cards

🍴 CAFÉ DE FLORE
€€€

172 BOULEVARD ST.-GERMAIN, 75006

TEL 01 45 48 55 26

cafedeflore.fr

The prices are astronomical for café fare, but it's worth a visit for the art deco interior, classy service, and celebrity-spotting opportunities.

🚇 St.-Germain-des-Prés 💳
💳 All major cards

🍴 LA CAGOUILLE
€€€

10 PLACE CONSTANTIN
BRANCUSI, 75014

TEL 01 43 22 09 01

la-cagouille.fr

Exquisite seafood, yummy desserts, and friendly service in a stark setting. Terrace in summer. Fixed-price menus available.

🚇 Gaîté 💳 MC, V

🍴 LA COUPOLE
€€€

102 BOULEVARD MONT-
PARNASSE, 75014

TEL 01 43 20 14 20

lacoupole-paris.com

A lively, art deco brasserie with great service, good food, and impeccable historical credentials—everyone who was anyone came here in the 1920s. Fixed-price menu available.

🚇 Montparnasse, Vavin
💳 💳 AE, MC, V

🍴 LE CHRISTINE
€€€

1 RUE CHRISTINE, 75006

TEL 01 40 51 71 64

restaurantlechristine.com

French cuisine, with dishes inspired by seasonal ingredients and delicious dessert. The ambience is contemporary and cozy, with exposed stone walls and warm lighting.

🚇 Odéon 🕐 Closed Sat. L, Sun. L 💳 💳 All major cards

🍴 POLIDOR
€€

41 RUE MONSIEUR-LE-PRINCE, 75006

TEL 01 43 26 95 34

polidor.com

A 19th-century bistro that serves classics like boeuf bourguignon at basic prices. Fixed-price menus available.

🚇 Odéon 💳 No credit cards

PRICES

HOTELS

An indication of the cost of a double room in the high season is given by € signs.

€€€€€	Over €300
€€€€	€220–€300
€€€	€150–€220
€€	€100–€150
€	Under €100

RESTAURANTS

An indication of the cost of a three-course meal without drinks is given by € signs.

€€€€€	Over €90
€€€€	€60–€90
€€€	€40–€60
€€	€25–€40
€	Under €25

🍴 LE PETIT SAINT BENOÎT
€

4 RUE ST.-BENOÎT, 75006

TEL 01 42 60 27 92

petit-st-benoit.com

Cheap, funky, old-time bistro with decent food.

🚇 St.-Germain-des-Prés
🕐 Closed Sun.
💳 No credit cards

🍴 SUPU RAMEN
€

53 QUAI DES GRANDS-
AUGUSTINS, 75006

TEL 01 43 25 45 94

supuramenguysavoy.com

Three-star chef Guy Savoy marries unusual ingredients and flavor combinations to create innovative ramen dishes. The place is bright and lively furnished, with walls completely covered with writings.

🚇 St.-Michel 💳 💳 All major cards

🏨 Hotel 🍴 Restaurant 🛈 No. of Guest Rooms 🚇 Métro 🅿 Parking 🕐 Closed 🛗 Elevator

▶ **CHÂTELET &
LES HALLES**

The heart of the city is noisy and congested, but the hotels listed below are on relatively quiet streets. Many of the area's restaurants are throwbacks to the days when Les Halles was the major food market; they serve hearty, copious meals that are heavy on meat.

HOTELS

🏨 **BRITANNIQUE**
€€€€ ★★★

20 AVENUE VICTORIA, 75001
TEL 01 42 33 74 59
hotel-britannique.fr
Cozy, British-style comfort on a quiet street in the busy city center. Breakfast: €14.

🛏 39 🚇 Châtelet 🔲 🅂
🅂 AE, MC, V

SOMETHING SPECIAL

🏨 **HÔTEL LE PRESBYTERE**
€€€ ★★★

78 RUE DE LA VERRERIE, 75004
TEL 01 42 78 14 15
hotel-le-presbytere.com
This used to be a presbytery of the St.-Merri Church, whose flying buttresses form part of the decor of room 9. Expensive rooms have authentic, 18th-century carved-wood Gothic furnishings; cheaper ones are charmingly decorated with matching wallpaper, bedspreads, and curtains. Breakfast: €15.

🛏 12 inc. 1 suite 🚇 Hôtel de Ville 🅂 All major cards

RESTAURANTS

🍽 **LA POULE AU POT**
€€€

9 RUE VAUVILLIERS, 75001
TEL 01 42 36 32 96
lapouleaupot.com
A popular, all-night restaurant serving traditional food that attracts a variety of night owls

and theater people. Fixed-price menu available.

🚇 Les Halles 🅂 🅂 MC, V

🍽 **LES CHOUETTES**
€€€

32 RUE DE PICARDIE, 75003
TEL 01 44 61 73 21
restaurant-les-chouettes-paris.fr
This unusual restaurant on three levels in a former industrial space offers not only a handsome designer decor with a variety of atmospheres but also high-quality, seasonal food.

🚇 Temple 🅂 All major cards

🍽 **AU PIED DE COCHON**
€€

6 RUE COQUILLIÈRE, 75001
TEL 01 40 13 77 00
pieddecochon.com
Lively, all-night restaurant specializing in such brasserie fare as pig's feet and shellfish. Fixed-price menus available.

🚇 Louvre-Rivoli, Châtelet Les Halles 🕐 Open 24 hours a day, 🅂 All major cards

🍽 **FRENCHIE**
€€

5 RUE DU NIL, 75002
TEL 01 40 39 96 19
frenchie-ruedunil.com
A French chef trained by Jamie Oliver has created a small empire on this off-the-beaten-path street. Reserve in advance for the main restaurant or go early (around 7 p.m.) to the wine bar (no. 6; no reservations) or have a delicious sandwich at Frenchie To Go (no. 9; open daily for lunch).

🚇 Sentier 🅂 All major cards

🍽 **L'AMBASSADE
D'AUVERGNE**
€€

22 RUE DU GRENIER ST.-LAZARE, 75003
TEL 01 42 72 31 22
ambassade-auvergne.fr
Hearty country food from the Auvergne in a rustic setting,

with specialties like *aligot* (creamy cheese and potato), lentils, duck, and cured ham.

🚇 Rambuteau 🕐 Closed part of Aug. 🅂 AE, V

🍽 **LE HANGAR**
€€

12 IMPASSE BERTHAUD, 75003
TEL 01 42 74 55 44
Welcoming popular local bistro close to Beaubourg serves traditional fare from steaks to rabbit, salads, and chocolate soufflé.

🚇 Rambuteau 🕐 Closed Sun., Mon., & Aug.
🅂 All major cards

▶ **LE MARAIS &
BASTILLE**

The historic Marais does not have many hotels, but there are a few interesting options, as well as lots of good, small restaurants. The bustling Bastille area is slowly moving upscale, thanks to the opera house, but is still not the most desirable area to stay.

HOTELS

🏨 **PAVILLON
DE LA REINE**
€€€€€ ★★★★★

28 PLACE DES VOSGES, 75003
TEL 01 40 29 19 19
pavillon-de-la-reine.com
Antique-furnished rooms, some with four-poster beds. Garden. Breakfast: €17/35.

🛏 54 🚇 St.-Paul, Bastille
🅿 🔲 🅂 🎽 🅂 All major cards

🏨 **CARON DE
BEAUMARCHAIS**
€€€ ★★★

12 RUE VIEILLE-DU-TEMPLE, 75004
TEL 01 42 72 34 12
carondebeaumarchais.com
The 18th century brought back to life in this pretty hotel. Breakfast: €13.

🛏 19 🚇 St.-Paul, Hôtel de Ville
🔲 🅂 🅂 AE, MC, V

🅂 Nonsmoking 🅂 Air-conditioning 🅂 Indoor Pool 🅂 Outdoor Pool 🎽 Health Club 🅂 Credit Cards

🏨 CROWNE PLAZA PARIS RÉPUBLIQUE
€€€ ★★★★

10 PLACE DE LA RÉPUBLIQUE, 75011

TEL 01 43 14 43 50

ihg.com

International-style rooms in a turn-of-the-20th-century building. Garden, bar. Breakfast: €25.

ⓘ 328 🚇 République

🔁 🅿 🛗 🃏 All major cards

🏨 HÔTEL DE NICE
€€€ ★★★

42 BIS RUE DE RIVOLI, 75004

TEL 01 42 78 55 29

hoteldenice.com

Antique furnishings and a central location at reasonable prices. Breakfast: €10.

ⓘ 23 🚇 Hôtel de Ville 🔁 🅿

🃏 MC, V

🏨 GRAND HÔTEL DU LOIRET
€€ ★★★

8 RUE DES MAUVAIS-GARÇONS, 75004

TEL 01 48 87 77 00

hotel-du-loiret.fr

Clean, cheap, modest hotel on the evocatively named street of "bad boys." Breakfast: €10.

ⓘ 25 🚇 Hôtel de Ville 🔁

🃏 All major cards

🏨 HÔTEL JEANNE D'ARC LE MARAIS
€€ ★★★

3 RUE DE JARENTE, 75004

TEL 01 48 87 62 11

hoteljeannedarc.com

A fine little hotel, much in demand because of its location and low prices. Breakfast: €12.

ⓘ 35 🚇 St.-Paul 🔁

🃏 AE, MC, V

RESTAURANTS

🍴 L'AMBROISIE
€€€€€

9 PLACE DES VOSGES, 75004

TEL 01 42 78 51 45

ambroisie-paris.com

Classic three-Michelin-star French food by chef Bernard Pacaud.

🚇 St.-Paul 🕐 Closed Mon.

🅿 🃏 AE, MC, V

🍴 LE TRAIN BLEU
€€€€

GARE DE LYON, 20 BOULEVARD DIDEROT, 75012

TEL 01 43 43 09 06

le-train-bleu.com

Go for a drink to see the belle époque decoration in this train-station restaurant rather than for its pricey food. Fixed-price menu available.

🚇 Gare de Lyon 🅿

🃏 All major cards

🍴 LE 404
€€€

69 RUE DES GRAVILLIERS, 75003

TEL 01 42 74 57 81

Moroccan restaurant with fine couscous and tagines. Fixed-price L menu available.

🚇 Arts et Métiers 🅿

🃏 All major cards

🍴 LES ENFANTS ROUGES
€€€

9 RUE DE BEAUCE, 75003

TEL 01 48 87 80 61

les-enfants-rouges.fr

This charming little place with a Japanese chef (trained by Yves Camdeborde) who cooks up original versions of French dishes is a new favorite with the bistronomy crowd.

🚇 Temple 🕐 Closed Tues.–Wed. 🃏 MC, V

🍴 AU BASCOU
€€

38 RUE RÉAUMUR, 75003

TEL 01 42 72 69 25

au-bascou.fr

Basque and French specialties prepared in a lively restaurant. Fixed-price L menu available.

🚇 Arts et Métiers 🕐 Closed Sat., Sun., Aug. & Christmas week 🃏 AE, MC, V

🍴 CHEZ JANOU
€€

2 RUE ROGER VERLOMME, 75003

TEL 01 42 72 28 41

chezjanou.com

Lively, crowded, friendly, and trendy, this bistro serving solid, well-prepared Provençal specialties has a great outdoor terrace in summer and a fixed-price menu at lunch.

🚇 Chemin Vert 🃏 All major cards

🍴 CHEZ OMAR
€€

47 RUE DE BRETAGNE, 75003

TEL 04 90 04 63 88

Excellent couscous, old-fashioned bistro decor, and extra-friendly service.

🚇 Temple 🕐 Closed Christmas Day, New Year's Day

🃏 No credit cards

SOMETHING SPECIAL

🍴 CLOWN BAR
€€

114 RUE AMELOT, 75011

TEL 01 43 55 87 35

clown-bar-paris.com

The Clown Bar's new owners have not touched the listed art nouveau facade and the colorful 1920s clown tiles behind the zinc bar, but they have changed the menu, serving creative small plates, most of them positively stunning. If available, try the deep-fried *bulots* (sea snails), the *pithiviers de canard de Challans* (duck in pastry crust with yuzu-flavored date purée). The cheese and desserts are as dazzling as the other courses. Reserve in advance.

🚇 Filles du Calvaire 🕐 Closed Mon.–Tues. 🃏 MC, V

SOMETHING SPECIAL

🍴 LA BELLE HORTENSE
€€

31 RUE VIEILLE-DU-TEMPLE, 75004

TEL 01 48 04 71 60

cafeine.com

This wine bar/café/bookshop/wine shop (you can buy a bottle to go) offers two distinct ambiences. The small bar in the front is crowded and friendly, while the back room is a quiet oasis where you can read a book. Exhibitions, literary readings, and a good sound system are added attractions. If you're hungry, they will send out for a meal from their sister restaurant on the same block.

🚇 Hôtel de Ville, St.-Paul
💳 MC, V

🍴 LE PETIT FER À CHEVAL
€€
30 RUE VIEILLE-DU-TEMPLE, 75004
TEL 01 42 72 47 47
cafeine.com
Fashionable little bar/restaurant; one of the few places in the Marais where you can eat at any time until 1 a.m.

🚇 St.-Paul, Hôtel de Ville
💳 MC, V

🍴 LE TRUMILOU
€€
84 QUAI DE L'HÔTEL DE VILLE, 75004
TEL 01 42 77 63 98
letrumilou.fr
An old-time bistro on the Seine. Fixed-price menus available.

🚇 Hôtel de Ville, Pont Marie
💳 MC, V

🍴 TAXI JAUNE
€€
13 RUE CHAPON, 75003
TEL 01 42 76 00 40
restaurantletaxijaune.fr
This venerable bistro's chef/owner is an accomplished cook who relies on his inspirations and what's in the market to come up with meals of excellent quality, sometimes with unusual ingredients you won't taste elsewhere, e.g., horsemeat.

🚇 Rambuteau, Arts et Métiers
🕐 Closed Sat.–Sun. 💳 MC, V

▶ THE LOUVRE & PALAIS-ROYAL

A few grand hotels and some chic restaurants can be found in this palatial neighborhood.

HOTELS

🏨 DU LOUVRE
🍴 €€€€€ ★★★★★
1 PLACE ANDRÉ MALRAUX, 75001
TEL 01 73 11 12 34
hyatt.com
Pissarro painted the view from his window in this luxury hotel. Café. Breakfast: €30.

🛈 164 🚇 Palais-Royal
🔄 ❄ 💪 💳 All major cards

🏨 LE MEURICE
€€€€€ ★★★★★
228 RUE DE RIVOLI, 75001
TEL 01 44 58 10 10
dorchestercollection.com
This lavish hotel was once Salvador Dalí's favorite in Paris. Business facilities. Breakfast: €58.

🛈 160 🚇 Concorde, Tuileries
🔄 ⬛ ❄ 💪 💳 All major cards

🏨 THE WESTIN PARIS
🍴 €€€€€ ★★★★
3 RUE CASTIGLIONE, 75001
TEL 01 44 77 11 11
marriot.com
The century-old splendor of this hotel has been refurbished. Two restaurants, spa. Breakfast: €14/29/39.

🛈 425 🚇 Tuileries 🔄 ❄
💪 💳 All major cards

🏨 HÔTEL DE LA PLACE DU LOUVRE
€€€€ ★★★
21 RUE DES PRÊTRES-ST.-GERMAIN-L'AUXERROIS, 75001
TEL 01 42 33 78 68
paris-hotel-place-du-louvre.com
Facing the Louvre. Breakfast (€16) served in an ancient, vaulted basement.

🛈 20 🚇 Louvre-Rivoli, Pont Neuf 🔄 ❄ 💳 All major cards

🏨 AU RELAIS DU LOUVRE
€€€ ★★★★
19 RUE DES PRÊTRES-ST.-GERMAIN-L'AUXERROIS, 75001
TEL 01 40 41 96 42
relaisdulouvre.com
A cozy little hotel between the Louvre and St.-Germain-l'Auxerrois. Breakfast: €15.

🛈 21 + suites 🚇 Louvre-Rivoli, Pont Neuf 🅿 🔄 ❄
💳 All major cards

RESTAURANTS

🍴 CARRÉ DES FEUILLANTS
€€€€€
14 RUE CASTIGLIONE, 75001
TEL 01 42 86 82 82
carredesfeuillants.fr
Excellent traditional, southwestern French cuisine: variations on foie gras and truffles. Fixed-price menus available.

🚇 Concorde, Tuileries
🕐 Closed Sat., Sun., & Aug.
❄ 💳 All major cards

SOMETHING SPECIAL

🍴 LE GRAND VÉFOUR
€€€€€
17 RUE DE BEAUJOLAIS, 75001
TEL 01 42 96 56 27
grand-vefour.com
The most romantic restaurant in Paris has a decor unchanged since the 19th century, a fine Savoyard chef, charming staff, and an amazing list of historical customers (Napoleon, Cocteau, Garbo). This two-Michelin-star restaurant is the place to splurge. Recommended dish: lièvre à la royale (hare cooked in red wine and stuffed with foie gras and truffles). Fixed-price L menus available.

🚇 Palais-Royal, Bourse
🕐 Closed Sat.–Sun., Aug.
❄ 💳 All major cards

🍴 CLOVER GRILL
€€€€
6 RUE BAILLEUL, 75001
TEL 01 40 41 59 59

clover-grill.com
High-quality meats dominate the menu, but fish, vegetables and fruit are also covered. Almost all of them grilled or roasted.

🚇 Louvre-Rivoli 🔇 🅿 MC, V

🍴 CAFÉ MARLY
€€€
COUR NAPOLÉON
93 RUE DE RIVOLI, 75001
TEL 01 44 54 37 04
cafe-marly.com
Incredible setting in the Louvre for a chic café-restaurant with fine international food.

🚇 Palais-Royal 🔇
🅿 AE, MC, V

🍴 LE GRAND COLBERT
€€€
2 RUE VIVIENNE, 75002
TEL 01 42 86 87 88
legrandcolbert.fr
Attractively restored brasserie decor, friendly service, and respectable food. Fixed-price menu available.

🚇 Bourse 🅿 AE, DC, V

🍴 MACÉO
€€€
15 RUE DES PETITS-CHAMPS, 75001
TEL 01 85 15 22 56
maceorestaurant.com
A trendy restaurant. Second Empire decor and creative cuisine with an international flavor. Fixed-price menus available.

🚇 Pyramides ⊕ Closed Sat. L & Sun. 🅿 DC, MC, V

🍴 ASTARA
€€
7 RUE DES PETITS-CHAMPS, 75001
TEL 09 74 19 76 70
astara1981.com
Delicatessen and restaurant specialized in fish and seafood for forty years; it offers affordable prices and ingredients of Controlled Origin.

🚇 Bourse, Pyramides 🔇
🅿 AE, MC, V

🍴 JUVENILES
€€
47 RUE DE RICHELIEU, 75001
TEL 01 42 97 46 49
www.juvenileswinebar.com
Small, laid-back wine bar with tasty food and excellent international wines. Fixed-price menus available.

🚇 Pyramides ⊕ Closed Sun.–Mon. 🅿 AE, MC, V

🍴 WILLI'S WINE BAR
€€
13 RUE DES PETITS-CHAMPS, 75001
TEL 01 42 96 37 47
williswinebar.com
Even the French like it, although it's owned by an Englishman. Top-notch wines, fine cooking, debatable service. Fixed-price menu available.

🚇 Bourse ⊕ Closed Sun. 🅿 MC, V

▶ CHAMPS-ÉLYSÉES & 16TH ARRONDISSEMENT

The Champs-Élysées isn't what it used to be, but most of the palace hotels are located in its environs, along with some top restaurants. The 16th and 17th arrondissements are a stylish residential area with some equally stylish hotels and restaurants.

HOTELS

🏨 ASTOR ST.-HONORÉ
🍴 €€€€€ ★★★★
11 RUE D'ASTORG, 75008
TEL 01 53 05 05 05
maisonastorparis.com
Elegant Regency-revival decor on a quiet street in a tiny neighborhood. Some rooms have balconies or terraces. Gourmet restaurant, **L'Astor.** Breakfast: €25.

🛈 131 inc. suites 🚇 Saint Augustin 🔼 🔇 🅿 📺
🅿 All major cards

PRICES

HOTELS
An indication of the cost of a double room in the high season is given by € signs.

€€€€€	Over €300
€€€€	€220–€300
€€€	€150–€220
€€	€100–€150
€	Under €100

RESTAURANTS
An indication of the cost of a three-course meal without drinks is given by € signs.

€€€€€	Over €90
€€€€	€60–€90
€€€	€40–€60
€€	€25–€40
€	Under €25

🏨 BALZAC
🍴 €€€€€ ★★★★★
6 RUE BALZAC, 75008
TEL 01 44 35 18 00
hotelbalzac.com
Luxurious, elegant, belle époque building with huge rooms. The restaurant is the home of the great chef Pierre Gagnaire (see Pierre Gagnaire, p. 250). Breakfast: €28/38.

🛈 69 🚇 George V 🔼 🔇
🅿 All major cards

🏨 BRISTOL
🍴 €€€€€ ★★★★★
112 RUE DU FAUBOURG ST.-HONORÉ, 75008
TEL 01 53 43 43 00
oetkercollection.com
Top luxury and discretion for the rich and/or famous, with fine works of art and antiques, Gobelin tapestries, Persian carpets. Garden, bar, tearoom, and an excellent restaurant, **Epicure.** Breakfast: €45/60.

🛈 190 🚇 Miromesnil
🔼 🔇 🏊 📺 🅿 All major cards

🏨 Hotel 🍴 Restaurant 🛈 No. of Guest Rooms 🚇 Métro 🅿 Parking ⊕ Closed 🔼 Elevator

CAMBON
€€€€€ ★★★★
3 RUE CAMBON, 75001
TEL 01 44 58 93 93
hotelcambon.com
Stylish, modern comfort near the Place de la Concorde. Breakfast: €21.
① 40 Concorde
🚫 🅲 📵 All major cards

COSTES
€€€€€ ★★★★★
239 RUE ST.-HONORÉ, 75001
TEL 01 42 44 50 00
hotelcostes.com
In Paris, the name Costes guarantees good design and fashionableness. Lavish, neoclassical decor. Bar, business facilities, and fine restaurant with terrace. Breakfast: €35.
① 83 🚇 Tuileries 🚫 🅲 📶
📵 All major cards

CRILLON
€€€€€ ★★★★★
10 PLACE DE LA CONCORDE, 75008
TEL 01 44 71 15 00
rosewoodhotels.com
This beloved 18th-century palace overlooking the Place de la Concorde has been a luxury hotel since 1909, hosting celebrities such as Charlie Chaplin and Marilyn Monroe. It reopened in 2017 after a major overhaul, which did not diminished its opulence, also adding a lavish new subterranean spa to the offer.
① 78 + 46 suites 🚇 Concorde
🚫 🅲 📶 📵 All major cards

FOUR SEASONS
HOTEL GEORGE V
€€€€€ ★★★★★
31 AVENUE GEORGE V, 75008
TEL 01 80 08 19 50 53
fourseasons.com/paris
This venerable palace hotel with its fine antiques and tapestries is an art deco landmark. Courtyard garden and in-house Michelin-starred restaurants,

including **Le Cinq** (see p. 250). Breakfast: €38/44/49.
① 244 🚇 George V 🚫 🅲
📶 📵 All major cards

GALILÉO
€€€€€ ★★★
54 RUE GALILÉE, 75008
TEL 01 47 20 66 06
galileo-paris-hotel.com
This refined, comfortable, and calm small hotel near the Champs-Élysées boasts art deco–inspired interiors. Breakfast: €14.
① 27 🚇 George V 🚫 🅲
📵 AE, MC, V

HOTEL MARIGNAN
CHAMPS-ÉLYSÉES
€€€€€ ★★★★★
12 RUE MARIGNAN, 75008
TEL 01 40 76 34 56
hotelmarignanelyseesparis.com
The hotel has moved into the 21st century with a chic modern decor and rooms with a Scandinavian design touch. Bar and restaurant, **Canopée.** Breakfast: €29.
① 55 + 6 suites
🚇 Franklin D. Roosevelt
🚫 🅲 📵 All major cards

HOTEL RENAISSANCE
PARIS LE PARC
TROCADERO
€€€€€ ★★★★★
55 AVENUE RAYMOND-POINCARÉ, 75116
TEL 01 44 05 66 66
marriot.com
Elegant decor in this luxury hotel in five buildings, with a garden. Breakfast: €30.
① 100 + 27 suites
🚇 Trocadéro 🅲 🚫 🅲
📶 📵 All major cards

LE PAVILLON DES
LETTRES
€€€€€ ★★★★
12 RUE DES SAUSSAIES, 75008
TEL 01 49 24 26 26
pavillondeslettres.com
A "literary" hotel run by Le Pavillon de la Reine, with

each room devoted to a different writer or poet (from Shakespeare to Proust) and decorated in the appropriate period style, with excerpts of the author's writing on the wall. Breakfast: €26 (adults)/€14 (children).
① 26 🚇 Miromesnil 🚫 🅲
📵 All major cards

LE PLAZA ATHÉNÉE
€€€€€ ★★★★★
25 AVENUE MONTAIGNE, 75008
TEL 01 53 67 66 65
dorchestercollection.com
Rooms in Louis XV, Louis XVI, and Regency styles, chandeliers, and potted palms in the lobby. Five restaurants (see **Restaurant Alain Ducasse,** pp. 250–251), bar, business facilities. Breakfast: €44/60.
① 208 🚇 Franklin D. Roosevelt 🚫 🅲 🅲 📶
📵 All major cards

MAJESTIC
€€€€€ ★★★★★
30 RUE LA PEROUSE, 75116
TEL 01 45 00 83 70
majestic-hotel.com
Bourgeois comfort, with period furnishings and spacious rooms, near the Arc de Triomphe. Breakfast: €30/€40.
① 48 🚇 Kléber 🚫 🅲 📶
📶 📵 All major cards

PENINSULA PARIS
€€€€€ ★★★★★
19 AVENUE KLÉBER, 75116
TEL 01 58 12 28 88
peninsula.com
This elegant new grand hotel in a historic belle époque building boasts carefully restored period details, the latest high-tech gadgets, a contemporary art collection, and six restaurants, including the rooftop **L'Oiseau Blanc.** Breakfast: €45.
① 200 inc. suites
🚇 Kléber 🅿 🚫 🅲 📶 📶
📵 All major cards

🏨 PRINCE DE GALLES
🍴 €€€€€ ★★★★★
33 AVENUE GEORGE V, 75008
TEL 01 53 23 77 77
marriot.com
This palace named for the Prince of Wales underwent a total makeover and was restored to its original art deco splendor, complete with mosaic-covered columns in the courtyard. Breakfast: €40.
🛏 159 🚇 George V
🛗 🎫 📺 🅿 ⚡ All major cards

🏨 RAPHAËL
🍴 €€€€€ ★★★★★
17 AVENUE KLÉBER, 75116
TEL 01 53 64 32 10
raphael-hotel.com
Truly classy, luxury hotel with a painting by Turner in the lobby. Spacious rooms amid elegant furnishings. Wonderful, wood-paneled bar. Business facilities. Breakfast: €40.
🛏 82 🚇 Kléber 🛗 🎫 📺 ⚡
⚡ All major cards

🏨 ROYAL MONCEAU
🍴 €€€€€ ★★★★★
37 AVENUE HOCHE, 75008
TEL 01 42 99 88 00
leroyalmonceau.com
Rooms and suites in neutral colors are designed by Philippe Starck to feel like a home, with artworks and a mixture of styles. Breakfast: €62.
🛏 149 🚇 Ternes 🅿 🛗 ⚡
🎫 📺 ⚡ All major cards

🏨 VERNET
🍴 €€€€€ ★★★★★
25 RUE VERNET, 75008
TEL 01 44 31 98 00
hotelvernet-paris.fr
This century-old gem of a hotel has a sleek new contemporary decor and a restaurant with a stained-glass dome designed by Gustave Eiffel. Breakfast: €35.
🛏 50 🚇 George V 🅿 🛗
⚡ ⚡ All major cards

🏨 HÔTEL CASTILLE
🍴 €€€€ ★★★★★
33–37 RUE CAMBON, 75001
TEL 01 44 58 44 58
starhotelscollezione.com
Venetian-style luxury near Place Vendôme in a former annex of the Ritz. Italian restaurant with terrace. Breakfast: €35.
🛏 108 🚇 Madeleine 🅿 🛗
⚡ ⚡ 🎫 📺 ⚡ All major cards

🏨 L'HÔTEL PERGOLÈSE PARIS
€€€€ ★★★★
3 RUE PERGOLÈSE, 75016
TEL 01 53 64 04 04
pergolese.com
Warm, modern decor with marble bathrooms. Near the Bois de Boulogne and Arc de Triomphe. Bar. Breakfast: €19.
🛏 40 🚇 Argentine 🛗 ⚡
⚡ ⚡ All major cards

🍴 MÉRIDIEN ÉTOILE
€€€€ ★★★★
81 BOULEVARD GOUVION ST-CYR, 75017
TEL 01 40 68 34 34
marriott.com
Modern high-rise with standard comforts and little charm. The Jazz Club Étoile in the lobby presents live concerts every night Tues.–Sat. Bar and two restaurants. Breakfast: €32.
🛏 1025 🚇 Porte Maillot
🛗 🎫 ⚡ 📺 ⚡ All major cards

RESTAURANTS

🍴 ASTRANCE
€€€€
4 RUE BEETHOVEN, 75016
TEL 01 40 50 84 40
astrancerestaurant.com
Elegant, exclusive restaurant with stylish original dishes and superb service. Book ahead.
🚇 Passy 🕐 Closed Sat.–Mon.
⚡ ⚡ All major cards

🍴 LE CINQ
€€€€€
31 AVENUE GEORGE V, 75008
TEL 01 49 52 71 54

restaurant-lecinq.com
The arrival of chef Christian Le Squer (once of Ledoyen) at the Four Seasons George V hotel's elegant restaurant bodes well. Dishes like roasted foie gras with Gewurztraminer granita are presented as colorful works of art but still thrill the taste buds. The exceptional staff, discreet but full of fun, makes dining here a joy.
🚇 George V ⚡
⚡ All major cards

🍴 PAVILLON LEDOYEN
€€€€€
8 AVENUE DUTUIT, 75008
TEL 01 53 05 10 00
yannick-alleno.com
One of the greats, three-star chef Yannick Alléno, has taken over the kitchen of this 18th-century pavilion. The elegant Napoleon III dining room looks out on the gardens of the Champs-Élysées. Fixed-price L menus available.
🚇 Champs-Élysées Clemenceau 🅿 🕐 Closed Sat. L, Sun. ⚡ ⚡ All major cards

🍴 PIERRE GAGNAIRE
€€€€€
HÔTEL BALZAC (see pp. 248)
6 RUE BALZAC, 75008
TEL 01 58 36 12 50
pierre-gagnaire.com
One of France's greatest chefs officiates at this three-Michelin-star restaurant and is wowing the city with his artistic haute cuisine. Specialties include *encornets* (small squid) with walnuts. Fixed-price menus.
🚇 George V 🕐 Closed Sat. & Sun., Christmas, & Aug.
⚡ ⚡ AE, MC, V

🍴 RESTAURANT ALAIN DUCASSE
€€€€€
HÔTEL PLAZA ATHÉNÉE
25 AVENUE MONTAIGNE, 75008
TEL 01 58 00 22 43
alainducasse-plazaathenee.com
The three-star restaurant in this classy hotel serves up

langoustines au caviar and the famous Bresse chicken.

🚇 Franklin D. Roosevelt
🕐 Closed Sat., Sun., Mon.–Wed. L, mid-Jul.–mid-Aug., & Christmas 🆂
🆂 All major cards

🍴 DOMINIQUE BOUCHET
€€€€

11 RUE TREILLARD, 75008
TEL 01 45 61 09 46
dominique-bouchet.com
In a chic, contemporary setting, Bouchet brings out the best in seasonal products with his fine soups (try the chestnut cream if it is on offer), slow-cooked lamb, fantastic mashed potatoes, and vanilla mille-feuille.

🚇 Miromesnil 🕐 Closed Sat.–Sun., public holidays, & Aug.
🆂 AE, MC, V

🍴 CHEZ SAVY
€€€

23 RUE BAYARD, 75008
TEL 01 47 23 46 98
chezsavy.com
Heaven for meat and offal lovers and for anyone looking for an authentic, old-style bistro with high-quality, no-nonsense food: huge steaks, tripe, pig's feet, perfect fries, chocolate mousse, and more. The white-aproned waiters continue the brasserie tradition of carrying on jovial repartee with customers while sprinting from table to kitchen to table.

🚇 Franklin D. Roosevelt
🕐 Closed Sat.–Sun.
🆂 AE, MC, V

🍴 MINI PALAIS
€€–€€€

GRAND PALAIS (PONT ALEXANDRE III SIDE), AVENUE WINSTON-CHURCHILL, 75008
TEL 01 42 56 42 42
minipalais.com
Three-star chef Eric Frechon of the Bristol created the menu for the restaurant in the Grand Palais, which is quiet and comfortable in spite of its high ceiling and cavernous size.

Exquisite ingredients, fine preparation, and top-level service, all for quite reasonable prices, make this a great place to eat or have a drink on the wonderful colonnaded terrace.

🚇 Champs-Élysées Clemenceau 🆂 AE, MC, V

🍴 ANGELINA
€€

226 RUE DE RIVOLI, 75001
TEL 01 42 60 82 00
angelina-paris.fr
Join the ladies-who-shop and the fashion crowd for a cup of sinfully rich, "African" hot chocolate in this elegant, turn-of-the-20th-century Viennese tearoom. Busy weekends.

🚇 Tuileries 🆂 AE, MC, V

🍴 LE RELAIS DE L'ENTRECÔTE
€€

15 RUE MARBEUF, 75008
TEL 01 49 52 07 17
relaisentrecote.fr
When you are not in the mood to decide what to eat, line up at the Relais de l'Entrecôte (the line moves quickly). Once you are seated, a waitress in a black uniform, frilly white apron and high heels will ask you how you want your steak cooked. It comes with a green sauce full of herbs and great shoestring fries, preceded by a simple green salad with walnuts. If you take dessert, you actually have a choice. Reliable quality, efficient service, great fun. See website for other locations.

🚇 Franklin D. Roosevelt 🆂
🆂 AE, MC, V

▶ ## LES GRANDS BOULEVARDS

Pockets of tranquility, like the ritzy Place Vendôme, along with an increasing number of fine restaurants and brasseries, can be found here.

HOTELS

🏨 LE GRAND HÔTEL
🍴 INTERCONTINENTAL
€€€€€ ★★★★★

2 RUE SCRIBE, 75009
TEL 01 40 07 32 32
ihg.com
The public rooms are truly grand, but some rooms are small. Home of the famous Café de la Paix; bar, lounge. Breakfast: €45.

🛏 470 🚇 Opéra 🅿 🔁 🆂
🆂 All major cards

🏨 RITZ
🍴 €€€€€ ★★★★★

15 PLACE VENDÔME, 75001
TEL 01 43 16 30 30
fr.ritzparis.com
After a top-to-bottom renovation, the Ritz reopened in 2016 with its gilt, chandeliers, and luxurious interiors all spruced up. Two restaurants and two bars, including the famous Hemingway Bar. Spa. Breakfast: €66.

🛏 142 (half of them suites)
🚇 Concorde 🔁 🆂 🆂 🆂
🆂 All major cards

🏨 MANSART
€€€€ ★★★★

5 RUE DES CAPUCINES, 75001
TEL 01 42 61 50 28
paris-hotel-mansart.com
Next door to the Ritz, with spacious, individually decorated rooms and striking decoration in the lobby—an homage to Mansart, Louis XIV's architect. Breakfast: €18.

🛏 57 🚇 Opéra 🔁 🆂
🆂 All major cards

🏨 STENDHAL PARIS PLACE VENDÔME
€€€€ ★★★★

22 RUE D. CASANOVA, 75002
TEL 01 44 58 52 52
all.accor.com
Stendhal once lived in this little hotel with a new contemporary decor. Breakfast: €22.

(i) 20 🚇 Opéra 🔌 🔲
🆎 AE, MC, V

🏨 BANKE HOTEL
€€€–€€€€ ★★★★★
20, RUE LAFAYETTE, 75009
TEL 01 55 33 22 22
hotelbanke.com
Set in a former belle époque
bank, this hotel has a splendid
two-story lobby in the round
with a glass cupola and a
mosaic floor. The rooms
are decorated with rich yet
sober furnishings. Near the
Opéra and major department
stores.
(i) 91 🚇 Chausée d'Antin,
Le Peletier 🔌 🔲
🆎 All major cards

🏨 BEST WESTERN
PREMIER OPÉRA
FAUBOURG
€€€ ★★★★
49 RUE LAFAYETTE, 75009
TEL 01 42 85 05 44
hotel-opera-faubourg-paris.
com
New owners have given this
hotel a simple contemporary
decor. Breakfast: €19.
(i) 101 + suites
🚇 Le Peletier 🔌 🔲 🆎 All
major cards

🏨 GAILLON OPÉRA BEST
WESTERN
€€€ ★★★
9 RUE GAILLON, 75002
TEL 01 47 42 47 74
bestwestern.com
A helpful staff runs this
tastefully decorated little hotel
near the Opéra Garnier. Breakfast: €13.
(i) 25 + 1 suite 🚇 Opéra
🔌 🔲 🆎 All major cards

🏨 LAUTREC OPÉRA
€€€ ★★★
8-10 RUE D'AMBOISE, 75002
TEL 01 42 96 67 90
paris-hotel-lautrec.com
"Toulouse Lautrec slept here"
could be the slogan of this
reasonably priced hotel that

the artist once made his home.
The rooms are simple with
contemporary decor. Breakfast: €15.
(i) 59 🚇 Richelieu-Drouot 🔌
🔲 🆎 All major cards

RESTAURANTS

🍴 LE VAUDEVILLE
€€€
29 RUE VIVIENNE, 75002
TEL 01 40 20 04 62
vaudevilleparis.com
Art deco decor, amiable,
efficient service, lively
ambience, and reasonable
brasserie fare. Fixed-price
menus available.
🚇 Bourse 🆎 All major cards

🍴 CANARD &
CHAMPAGNE
€€
57 PASSAGE DES PANORAMAS,
75002
TEL 09 83 30 06 86
frenchparadox.paris
A modern restaurant in a classic setting, it serves free range
duck and champagne from
small producers. Sunday brunch
for adults and children.
🚇 Richelieu-Drouot 🆎 MC, V

🍴 TERMINUS NORD
€€
23 RUE DE DUNKERQUE, 75010
TEL 01 42 85 05 15
terminusnord.com
Bustling brasserie with handsome decor, perfect for a late
dinner. Fixed-price menus
available.
🚇 Gare du Nord 🔲 🔲
🆎 All major cards

▶ TOUR EIFFEL &
LES INVALIDES
A quiet, upper-class, residential
area with some lovely hotels and
fine eateries.

HOTELS

🏨 MONTALEMBERT
🍴 €€€€€ ★★★★★
3 RUE MONTALEMBERT, 75007
TEL 01 45 49 68 68
hotelmontalembert.-paris.
com
Fashionable hotel with
designer lobby and attractive,
contemporary- or traditional-
style rooms. Business facilities,
Le Montalembert restaurant.
Breakfast: €30.
(i) 50 🚇 Rue du Bac
🅿 Nearby 🔌 🔲 🔲
🆎 All major cards

🏨 HOTEL ACADÉMIE
€€€€ ★★★★
32 RUE DES STS.-PÈRES, 75007
TEL 01 45 49 80 00
academiehotel.com
A 17th-century building with
exposed beams in rooms and
18th-century furnishings. Breakfast: €19.
(i) 34 🚇 St.-Germain-des-Prés
🅿 🔌 🔲 🆎 All major cards

🏨 HÔTEL DUC DE
SAINT-SIMON
€€€€ ★★★★
14 RUE ST.-SIMON, 75007
TEL 01 44 39 20 20
hotelducdesaintsimon.com
A luxurious haven on the Left
Bank, with fine antique furnishings. Courtyard garden, charming basement breakfast room.
Breakfast: €19.
(i) 34 🚇 Rue du Bac 🔌 🔲
🆎 All major cards

🏨 LE BELLECHASSE
€€€€ ★★★★
8 RUE BELLECHASSE, 75007
TEL 01 45 50 22 31
lebellechasse.com
A short walk from the Musée
d'Orsay, with colorful graphics
in the rooms. Breakfast: €21.
(i) 33 🚇 Solférino 🔌 🔲 🔲
🆎 All major cards

HÔTEL DE L'UNIVERSITÉ
€€€ ★★★

22 RUE DE L'UNIVERSITÉ, 75007

TEL 01 42 61 09 39

universitehotel.com

Antique-furnished hotel distinguished by attention to detail. Two rooms have private terraces. Breakfast: €15.

🛈 27 🚇 St.-Germain-des-Prés
⬇ 🅂 🄰 All major cards

HÔTEL DU PALAIS BOURBON
€€€ ★★★

49 RUE DE BOURGOGNE, 75007

TEL 01 44 11 30 70

bourbon-paris-hotel.com

A quiet hotel with classic decor and comfortable rooms, a short walk from the Musée Rodin and Les Invalides. Breakfast: €12.

🛈 24 🚇 Varenne
⬇ 🅂 🅂 🄰 AE, MC, V

RESTAURANTS

L'ARPÈGE
€€€€€

84 RUE DE VARENNE, 75007

TEL 01 47 05 09 06

alain-passard.com

Alain Passard, one of Paris's top chefs, runs this highly rated restaurant with a modern decor. If available, try the sole with ginger and lime, or the baby onion fondue with herbs and broad beans. Fixed-price menus available.

🚇 Varenne 🕐 Closed Sat.–Sun. 🅂 🄰 All major cards

LE JULES VERNE
€€€€€

EIFFEL TOWER, 2ND FLOOR, 75007

TEL 01 83 77 34 34

restaurants-toureiffel.com

A gourmet restaurant with sleek, modern decor in one of the world's most famous monuments. Dinner with a view and a menu created by the restaurant's new chefs Frédéric Anton and Thierry Marx. Fixed-price menus available.

🚇 Trocadéro 🅂
🄰 All major cards

LES FABLES DE LA FONTAINE
€€€€–€€€€€

131 RUE ST.- DOMINIQUE, 75007

TEL 01 44 18 37 55

lesfablesdelafontaine.net

Cramped but excellent fish restaurant with high-quality products, founded by two chefs trained by Christian Constant.

🚇 École Militaire 🅂
🄰 All major cards

VIOLON D'INGRES
€€€€

135 RUE ST.-DOMINIQUE, 75007

TEL 01 45 55 15 05

leviolondingres.paris

Owned by Christian Constant, a well-loved chef who successfully reinterprets tradition and has trained and supported dozens of Paris's most talented young chefs, its cuisine is now directed by Bertrand Bluy.

🚇 École Militaire 🅂
🄰 All major cards

L'AFFABLE
€€€

10 RUE ST.-SIMON, 75007

TEL 01 42 22 01 60

laffable-restaurant.fr

A cozy restaurant where you can count on creative cooking. Fixed-price L menu available.

🚇 Rue du Bac 🕐 Closed Sat.–Sun. 🅂 🄰 AE, MC, V

LE 122
€€€

122 RUE DE GRENELLE, 75007

TEL 01 45 56 07 42

restaurant-le122.fr

Modern decor, high-quality dishes with flair, and unexpectedly reasonable prices in this chic, pricey neighborhood near the National Assembly and many government ministries.

🚇 Solférino 🕐 Closed Sat.–Sun. 🅂 🄰 AE, MC, V

LES COCOTTES
€€

135 RUE ST.-DOMINIQUE, 75007

TEL 01 45 50 10 28

lescocottes.paris

Same owner as the **Violon d'Ingres,** same high-quality products, but lower prices and a livelier ambience. Diners sit on stools at high tables. No reservations.

🚇 École Militaire 🅂 🄰 AE, V

AU PIED DE FOUET
€

45 RUE DE BABYLONE, 75007

TEL 01 47 05 12 27

aupieddefouet.com

Small restaurant with 19th-century decor, homey atmosphere, and low-priced selection of French classics. No reservations.

🚇 Sèvres-Babylone 🕐 Closed Sun. 🄰 MC, V

▶ ## MONTMARTRE

Montmartre still has a bohemian feel, and Pigalle is becoming less sleazy as more fashionable nightspots open.

RESTAURANTS

L'ARCANE
€€€

52 RUE LAMARCK, 75018

TEL 01 46 06 86 00

restaurantlarcane.com

Chef Laurent Magnin offers a French cuisine that follows the seasonal rhythm, particularly oriented toward sea flavors. Fixed price menus.

🚇 Lamarck-Caulaincourt
🕐 Closed Sat.–Sun. & Tue. L
🅂 🄰 MC, V

LA MASCOTTE
€€€

52 RUE DES ABBESSES, 75018

TEL 01 46 06 28 15

la-mascotte-montmartre.com

Old-time Paris the way we like it in this lively brasserie, where the waiters still wear the traditional vest and long apron and like to joke with the customers while they sample their seafood and steaks.

🚇 Abbesses 🄰 MC, V

🍴 À LA CLOCHE D'OR

€€

3 RUE MANSART, 75009

TEL 01 48 74 48 88

alaclochedor.com

A lively actors' hangout that serves decent, basic meals.

🚇 Blanche 🕐 Closed L & Sun. ❄️ 🈂️ MC, V

🍴 LE CABANON DE LA BUTTE

€€

6 RUE LAMARCK, 75018

TEL 01 42 57 20 46

Traditional French cuisine in a small and cozy restaurant, with big windows overlooking the rooftops of Paris only steps away from the Sacré-Coeur Basilica.

🚇 Lamarck-Caulaincourt 🕐 Closed Mon.–Tues. 🈂️ V

▶ AROUND THE PÉRIPHÉRIQUE

These are areas not often visited by tourists, but the restaurants listed below provide good reasons to make an excursion.

RESTAURANTS

🍴 LA GRANDE CASCADE

€€€€€

BOIS DE BOULOGNE,

ALLÉE DE LONGCHAMP, 75016

TEL 01 45 27 33 51

restaurantsparisiens.com

Fine Second Empire restaurant in a beautiful setting in the Bois de Boulogne, once a hunting lodge for Napoleon III. Fixed-price menus available.

🚇 Porte Maillot, then Bus 244 (till 8 p.m.) 🅿️ 🕐 Closed Christmas 🈂️ AE, MC, V

🍴 LE PRÉ CATELAN

€€€€€

ROUTE DE SURESNES, 75016

TEL 01 44 14 41 14

restaurant.leprecatelan.com

Talented chef Frédéric Anton livens up the cuisine of this lovely restaurant with a garden terrace in the Bois and three Michelin stars. Fixed-price menus available.

🚇 Porte Maillot, then Bus 244 (till 8 p.m.) 🕐 Closed Sun.– Mon. & Aug. 🅿️ ❄️ 🈂️ All major cards

🍴 SONATINES

€€€–€€€€

42 RUE FRIANT, 75014

TEL 01 45 39 74 91

The Japanese-descent chef creates original dishes adding an Asian touch to the traditional French flavors, yet without altering their original characteristics. Only *carte blanche* menu.

🚇 Porte d'Orléans 🅿️ 🕐 Closed Sun.–Mon. ❄️ 🈂️ AE, MC, V

🍴 FLODERER

€€€

7 COUR DES PETITES-ÉCURIES, 75010

TEL 01 47 70 13 59

floderer-paris.com

A sparkling, 19th-century Alsatian brasserie near the Gare de l'Est with typical dishes and friendly service. Fixed-price menus available.

🚇 Château d'Eau ❄️ 🈂️ All major cards

SHOPPING

Spending money is easy in this shopper's paradise, where tempting window displays abound. Shop owners are required to price each item displayed, so you'll know what you're in for, but bring a little extra cash if you don't want to go home frustrated. Items purchased include a 20 percent sales tax that is refundable to visitors from outside the European Union on purchases over €175 made from the same shop on the same day (ask the assistant for a *détaxe* form).

Accessories

Frenchwomen seem to be born with a knack for accessorizing. Ask the salesperson for tips on tying that *foulard*.

Alexandra Sojfer 218 boulevard St.-Germain, 75007. tel 01 42 22 17 02. alexandrasojfer.com. Closed Sun. Métro: Rue du Bac. A truly Parisian shop more than 150 years old, stuffed with every type of umbrella and cane imaginable.

Anna Kaszer 24 rue Titon, 75011 (showroom). www.anna kaszer.com. By appointment only. Métro: Faidherbe Chaligny. This is the address for funky bags, scarves, and foulards. Kaszer uses classic materials and jazzes them up in an original way.

Causse 12 rue de Castiglione, 75001. tel 01 49 26 91 43. causse -gantier.fr. Closed Sun. Métro: Tuileries. The shop of a venerable luxury glove maker acquired by Chanel.

Christian Louboutin 68 rue du Faubourg St.-Honoré, 75008. tel 00 800 945 804 (option 1). christianlouboutin.com. Closed Sun. Métro: Madeleine. To fashionistas, thanks in great part to "Sex in the City," Louboutin is less a shoemaker than a god. His vertiginous heels do indeed bring wearers closer to heaven.

Droguerie 9–11 rue du Jour, 75001. tel 01 45 08 93 27. ladro guerie.com. Closed Sun. Métro: Les Halles. Colorful yarns, feathers, unusual buttons and beads, and other trimmings.

Groom Studios 13 rue du Cherche-Midi, 75006. tel 01 43 22 42 51. groom-studios. com. Closed Sun.–Mon. Métro:

St.-Sulpice. A handsome line of colorful handbags and small leather goods, scarves, and other tasteful accessories.

Pour vos Beaux Yeux 10 Passage du Grand Cerf, 75002. tel 01 42 36 06 79. pourvosbeauxyeux. com. Closed Sun.–Mon. Métro: Etienne Marcel. Choose the era you want to belong to by buying never-worn vintage eyeglasses at this shop owned by a collector of bygone eyewear styles.

Tam Tam dans la Ville 3 rue Pas de la Mule, 75004. tel 01 48 04 98 93. tamtamdanslaville.paris. Closed Sun. a.m. Métro: Bastille. Fun, reasonably priced costume jewelry, scarves, and small leather goods.

Antique Shops

Antique shops can be found on the Quai Voltaire, Rue de Beaune (*Métro: Rue du Bac*), and neighboring streets, where exclusive dealers sell museum-quality pieces; the Louvre des Antiquaires (*closed Mon., Métro: Palais-Royal*) has 250 boutiques. At the Village St.-Paul (*closed Tues., Métro: St.-Paul*), the '50s seem to be the most popular era.

Books & Music

Paris has many English-language bookshops, and even the French stores listed below carry some foreign-language books.

Abbey Bookshop 29 rue de la Parcheminerie, 75005. tel 01 46 33 16 24. abbeybookshop .wordpress.com. Closed Sun. Métro: St.-Michel. New and used English-language books.

Artazart 83 quai de Valmy, 75010. tel 01 40 40 24 03. artazart. com Métro: Jacques Bonsergent. Canal-side shop with a fine selection of the latest books on design, architecture, and photography, plus a small gallery.

FNAC 74 avenue des Champs-Élysées, 75008. tel 08 25 02 00 20. fnac.com. Open till 10:30 p.m. Métro: George V. Every record and (French) book imaginable is sold in the newest branch of this chain. All CDs can be tested on headphones.

Galignani 224 rue de Rivoli, 75001. tel 01 42 60 76 07. galignani .fr. Closed Sun. Métro: Tuileries. English and French books in an Old World–style shop with wooden shelves.

Melomania 38 boulevard St.-Germain, 75005. tel 01 43 54 07 25. Métro: Maubert-Mutualité A temple for classical and operatic music, mainly on CD. Finding rarities here is not unusual.

Shakespeare and Company 37 rue de la Bûcherie, 75005. tel 01 43 25 40 93. shakespeareand company.com. Open 10 a.m.–10 p.m. Métro: St.-Michel. Nothing to do with Sylvia Beach's original bookstore, though it co-opted its name. Holds readings by well-known authors. Its stacks are dusty, but it still attracts plenty of visitors.

Boutiques

The real joy of shopping in Paris, however, is boutiquing. Wander through the Marais, Montmartre, St.-Germain-des-Prés, or the Place des Victoires to discover your own favorite boutique.

Children

Even W. C. Fields went all gooey at the sight of the unbelievably cute children's clothing in Paris. Prices are just as unbelievably high.

Centre Commercial Kids 22 rue Yves Toudic, 75010. tel 01 42 06 23 81. centrecommercial. cc. Métro: Jacques Bonsergent. Closed Sun. a.m. and Mon. Even kids have their concept store now: trendy clothing, furniture, accessories, and toys. Activities and cooking classes, too.

Du Pareil au Même 128 boulevard de Courcelles, 75017. tel 01 47 66 03 31. dpam.com. Closed Sun. Métro: Ternes. The main store of a chain with great prices on colorful, quality children's clothes and the cutest baby shoes imaginable.

Jacadi 17 rue Tronchet, 75008. tel 01 42 65 84 98. jacadi.com. Closed Sun. Métro: Madeleine. Flagship of chain store selling traditional French children's clothing.

Clothing

The boutiques of the top designers are concentrated on Rue du Faubourg St.-Honoré, Avenue Montaigne, and in St.-Germaindes-Prés. Along with these, the other boutiques listed here have something a little different, with many offering bargain prices on designer labels.

Agnès B 6 rue du Jour, 75001. tel 01 45 08 56 56. agnesb.com. Closed Sun. Métro: Les Halles. Reliable quality and stylish cuts from this much loved designer, for men, women, and children.

Azzedine Alaïa 5 Rue Marignan, 75008, 01 76 72 91 11. maison-alaia.com. Métro: Franklin D. Roosevelt. By appointment only. The lovely newest boutique of a unique designer whose clothes make women look sexy.

Carmen Ragosta 8 rue de la Grange aux Belles, 75010. tel 01 42 49 00 71. carmenragosta.com.

Closed Mon.–Tues. Métro: Jacques Bonsergent. Italian designer Carmen Ragosta sells not only her own handmade women's clothing designs—simple styles with a twist— but also serves up "vegitalian" dishes at lunchtime.

Chanel 31 rue Cambon, 75001. tel 01 44 50 66 00. chanel.com. Métro: Concorde. The sacred, snooty precincts of Chanel fashion, designed by Karl Lagerfeld.

Christian Dior 30 avenue Montaigne, 75008. tel 01 40 73 73 73. dior.com. Métro: Franklin D. Roosevelt. Extravagant creations in the plush setting of Dior salons off the Champs-Élysées.

Come On Eileen 16–18 rue des Taillandiers, 75011. tel 01 43 38 12 11. Closed Sat., Sun. a.m., & every day 4 p.m.–6p.m. in winter. Métro: Bastille or Breguet Sabin. Huge shop packed with vintage clothing, good quality though not particularly cheap.

Emporio Armani 149 boulevard St.-Germain, 75006. tel 01 53 63 33 50. armani.com. Métro: St.-Germain-des-Prés. Closed Sun. a.m. The Italian designer's huge store in the heart of St.-Germain-des-Prés, all stark-white clean lines.

Fifi Chachnil 68 rue Jean-Jacques Rousseau, 75001. tel 01 42 21 19 93. fifichachnil.paris. Closed Sun. Métro: Les Halles or Étienne Marcel. Designer Fifi Chachnil sells real lingerie in the kitten miaow tradition in her lollipop pink atelier and boutique. Sexy color mixes and ensembles with bows and trim.

Hermès 24 rue du Faubourg St.-Honoré, 75008. tel 01 40 17 46 00. hermes.com. Closed Sun. Métro: Madeleine. Famous for its silk foulards (scarves), this venerable house is trying to liven up its classic image with Nadège Vanhee-Cybulski designing its women's collection.

Jean-Paul Gaultier boutique 44 avenue George V, 75008. tel 01 44 43 00 44. jeanpaulgaultier

.com. Closed Sun. Métro: George V. Jean-Paul Gaultier's men's and women's ready-to-wear, lower-priced Gaultier jeans, accessories, and perfumes.

L'Eclaireur A judicious selection of clothing and accessories by designers including Linda Farrow and Gareth Pugh. leclaireur.com. Boutiques at:
40 rue de Sévigné, 75004. tel 01 48 87 10 22. Closed Sun. a.m. Métro: St.-Paul. Women's fashions in shop with spectacular design.
10 rue Hérold, 75001. tel 01 40 41 09 89. Closed Sun. Métro: Palais-Royal.
10 rue Boissy d'Anglas, 75008. tel 01 53 43 03 70. Closed Sun. Métro: Concorde.

L'Habilleur 44 rue de Poitou. 75003. tel 01 48 87 77 12. habilleur. fr. Closed Sun. Métro: St.-Sébastien-Froissart. New, seriously discounted designer clothes from Plein Sud, Paul & Joe, and others.

La Marelle 25 galerie Vivienne, 75002. tel 01 42 60 08 19. la-marelle-paris.fr. Closed Sat. a.m. & Sun. Métro: Bourse. Upscale used clothing in perfect condition, by the likes of Dior and Chanel.

Marché Saint-Pierre 2 rue Charles-Nodier, 75018. tel 01 46 06 92 25. marchesaintpierre.com. Closed Sun. Métro: Anvers. This five-floor Montmartre store sells all kinds of fabric amid dozens of other nearby fabric shops.

Pigalle 7 Rue Henry Monnier, 75009. pigalle-paris.com. Closed every day a.m. Métro: Saint-Georges. High-end men's streetwear by Stéphane Ashpool, former basketball player and celebrated fashion designer who grew up in the once seedy neighborhood of Pigalle.

Roseanna 5 rue Froissart, 75003. tel 09 86 62 58 32. Closed Sun. & Mon. a.m. Métro: Saint-Sébastien Froissart. The first boutique of this Parisian brand of women's high-end prêt-à-porter. Clothing, shoes, and accessories for a casual and yet very stylish look.

Vanessa Bruno Designer Vanessa Bruno's sophisticated but easy to wear women's clothing with great cuts are prized by Parisiennes. vanessabruno.com.

Boutiques at:

51 avenue Victor Hugo, 75016. tel 01 82 28 07 98. Closed Sun. Métro: Victor Hugo.

25 rue St.-Sulpice, 75006. tel 01 43 54 41 04. Closed Sun. Métro: Odéon.

100 rue Vieille-du-Temple, 75003. tel 01 42 77 19 41. Closed Sun. a.m. & Mon. a.m. Métro: Filles du Calvaire or Saint-Sébastien Froissart.

Yves St. Laurent 38 rue du Faubourg St.-Honoré, 75008. tel 01 42 65 74 59. Closed Sun. Métro: Concorde. Current designer Anthony Vaccarello is shaking things up with a rock-and-roll chic approach to the late master's high style.

Department Stores

For those who prefer large department stores where they can find everything in one place, next-door neighbors Galeries Lafayette and Printemps (Métro: Havre-Caumartin or Chaussée-d'Antin) have it all. The smaller Bon Marché (Métro: Sèvres-Babylone) is less crowded and more exclusive. BHV (closed Sun., Métro: Hôtel de Ville) is a mid-market department store. The low-priced chain Monoprix (closed Sun.) has branches all over town, and is good for children's clothes, cosmetics, and accessories. Attractive, youthful women's fashion at reasonable prices can be found at specialist chain stores like Naf Naf, Promod, Zara, and H&M.

Flea Markets

There are several permanent flea markets on the edges of Paris: the enormous Puces de St.-Ouen (closed Tues.–Fri., Métro: Porte de Clignancourt), specializing in antiques; the more junk-oriented Puces de Montreuil (open Sat.–Mon., Métro: Porte-de-Montreuil); and the Puces de Vanves (open Sat. & Sun., Métro: Porte-de-Vanves), with some antiques and lots of miscellaneous stuff. As with most flea markets, go as early in the a.m. as possible, and don't hesitate to bargain. Prices are generally high, especially for antiques, but there are a lot of finds.

Housewares & Interior Design

The French claim to know the most about l'art de vivre (the art of living). The following stores sell some of the elements that go into this fine art.

E. Déhillerin 20 rue Coquillière, 75001. tel 01 42 36 53 13. edehillerin.fr. Closed Sun. Métro: Les Halles. A fantastic array of kitchen utensils and cookware at this emporium, open since 1820.

La Chaise Longue Cheap, chic accessories for the kitchen and the bathroom. lachaiselongue.fr. Boutiques at:

22 rue du Pont Neuf, 75001. tel 01 40 13 06 49. Closed Sun. Métro: Les Halles.

68 rue De Rivoli, 75004. tel 01 48 04 30 03. Métro: Hôtel de Ville.

2 rue De Sèze, 75009. tel 09 63 29 88 26. Closed Sun. Métro: Madeleine or Opéra.

Maison de Famille 29 rue St.-Sulpice, 75006. tel 01 40 46 97 47. maisondefamille.fr. Closed Sun. Métro: St.-Sulpice. Kitchen gadgets to bedding and decorative objects, plus selected men's and women's clothing.

Matins Bleus 85 avenue du Général Leclerc, 75014. tel 01 42 22 94 40. descamps.com. Closed Sun. Métro: Alesia. Fine bed linens, as only the French know how to make.

Merci 111 boulevard Beaumarchais, 75011. tel 01 42 77 00 33. merci-merci.com. Closed Sun. Métro: St.-Sébastien-Froissart. This trendy concept store in a huge multilevel space with a glass roof sells home furnishings and much, much more: kitchenware, fresh flowers, vintage and new clothing, books, etc. Café and restaurant. Part of the profits goes to sustainable development projects in Madagascar.

Muriel Grateau 37 rue de Beaune, 75007. tel 01 40 20 42 82. murielgrateau.com. Closed Sun. Métro: Rue du Bac. Luxurious, 100-percent linen bedsheets in a palette of colors, and tableware with pure, modern, elegant lines.

Storie 20 rue Delambre, 75014. tel 01 83 56 78 23. storieshop.com. Closed Sun. Métro: Vavin. Unusual design objects with a "story" to tell.

The Conran Shop 117 rue du Bac, 75007. tel 01 42 84 10 01. conranshop.fr. Métro: Sèvres-Babylone. Terence Conran's design domain, with attractive furniture and home accessories.

Miscellaneous

CSAO 9 rue Elzévir, 75003. tel 01 42 71 33 17. csao.fr. Closed Mon. Métro: St.-Paul. Stepping into CSAO, on a street in the Marais called "la petite Afrique," is like entering an African bazaar. There's an amazing variety of handcrafted fabrics, naïve paintings on glass, gas-can lamps, pottery, baskets, and household furnishings—many made from recycled and salvaged goods. CSAO works with local African craftsmen and has helped certain villages survive. It also has a gallery featuring African art next door at 9 bis.

Perfume

This is a city where any man can name the scent being worn by a woman. Your preferred Poison (Christian Dior) may not be Opium (Yves St. Laurent), but you will surely find a fragrance to your liking.

Palais Royal–Serge Lutens
142 galerie de Valois, 75001. tel
01 49 27 09 09. sergelutens.com.
Closed Sun. Métro: Palais-Royal.
Luxurious boutique where you
can pamper yourself with a
perfume by fragrance designer
Serge Lutens.

**Parfumeries Bernard Marion-
naud** 104 avenue des Champs-
Élysées, 75008. tel 01 53 96 50 00.
marionnaud.fr. Closed Sun. Métro:
George V. A wide selection of
brand-name perfumes and cosmetics offered by this chain. Visit the
website for other locations.

Sephora 70 avenue Champs-
Élysées, 75008. tel 01 53 93 22 50.
sephora.com. Métro: Franklin D.
Roosevelt. The ultimate perfume
and cosmetics store, with testers of
nearly every brand in existence.

Shopping Centers

Paris has few American-style
shopping centers. The notable
exceptions are the recently
upgraded Forum des Halles
(*Métro: Les Halles*) and the shops
under the Carrousel du Louvre.
The beautiful, 19th-century Galerie Vivienne (*Métro: Bourse*) and
the 18th-century arcades of the
Palais-Royal (*Métro: Palais-Royal*)
might be called forerunners of
the mall, but they are worlds

apart from the modern U.S. version, the closest being the Beau-
grenelle (*Métro: Bir-Hakeim*).

Taste Treats

Barthélémy 51 rue de Grenelle,
75007. tel 02 22 82 24. Métro:
Rue du Bac. Closed Sun.–Mon.
Some of the best cheeses in Paris,
in a charming, old-fashioned shop.

Berthillon 31 rue St.-Louis
en Île, 75004. tel 01 43 54 31 61.
Métro: Pont Marie. berthillon.fr
Closed Mon.–Tues., Aug., & during
school vacations, except Christmas.
Makers of the famous Parisian ice
cream, also sold in other outlets
throughout Paris.

Demoulin Patisserie 6 boulevard Voltaire, 75011. tel 01 47
00 58 20. Closed Mon. Métro:
République. This pastry shop makes
mouthwatering almond croissants
and incredible chocolate tarts.

Du Pain et des Idées 34 rue
Yves Toudic, 75010. tel 01 42 40
44 52. dupainetdesidees.com.
Métro: Jacques Bonsergent. Closed
Sat.–Sun. Fantastic bread–try the
pain des amis–made by a former
businessman. Worth waiting in
line for.

Épices Roellinger 51 bis rue
Sainte-Anne, 75002. tel 01 42 60
46 88. epices-roellinger.com. Closed
Sun. Métro: Pyramides or Quatre

Séptembre. With a variety from all
over the world, but also a French
selection, it is a paradise for those
who love spices or want to discover
them. In addition to the wide variety of peppercorn and spice mixes,
the flagship of the shop is the "Cave
à vanilles," which preserves the finest qualities of vanilla.

Fauchon 24, 26, 30 place de
la Madeleine, 75008. tel 01 70 39
38 02. fauchon.com. Closed Sun.
Métro: Madeleine. The finest of
foodstuffs.

Izraël 30 rue François-Miron,
75004. tel 01 42 72 66 23. Closed
Sun.–Mon. & L on weekdays.
Métro: St.-Paul. Don't miss this
imported-food shop, redolent of
spices and filled with good food.

Legrand 1 rue de la Banque,
75002. tel 01 42 60 07 12. caves-
legrand.com. Closed Sun. Métro:
Bourse. One of the best wine
merchants in Paris; also sells carafes,
other wine accessories, and French
regional food specialties.

Nicolas Main store: 31 place
de la Madeleine, 75008. tel 01 44
51 90 22. nicolas.com. Closed Sun.
Métro: Madeleine. A chain of fran-
chised wine shops with a reliable
selection and knowledgeable (often
English-speaking) owners. Branches
in all Parisian neighborhoods.

ENTERTAINMENT

As a major world capital, Paris has more than its share of entertainment possibilities. Parisians love to go out, so many performances are sold out in advance—try to book tickets ahead of time for the theater, concerts, dance performances, and the opera. For details on concert times and movie listings, buy a copy of the weekly *Pariscope (pariscope.fr)* or *l'Officiel des Spectacles (offi.fr)* at any newsstand. Both come out on Wednesday.

Bars/Nightclubs

Paris nightlife offers something for everyone: bobos (bourgeois bohemians) who like to gossip and smoke (outdoors only!) in funky cafés with flea-market furniture (Café Charbon, Lou Pascalou); lounge lizards who enjoy relaxing in comfy armchairs to the mellow sounds of chill-out music (Buddha Bar); sophisticates who want to sip a cocktail (Prescription Cocktail Club, Harry's Bar); and clubbers who refuse to go to bed before dawn spreads its rosy fingers behind the Eiffel Tower (Le Bus Palladium, La Machine).

Bizz'art 167 quai de Valmy, 75010. tel 01 40 34 70 00. bizzartclub.com. Métro: Louis Blanc. Bar, club, and restaurant (French) with soul, Latin, funk, and R&B concerts. Package deals for meal with concert and/or club.

Buddha Bar 8 rue Boissy-d'Anglas, 75008. tel 01 53 05 90 00. buddhabar.com. Closed Sun.–Mon. Métro: Concorde. Huge basement restaurant/bar for beautiful people, with an enormous Buddha statue.

Cabaret Sauvage 211 avenue Jean Jaurè, 75019. tel 01 42 09 03 09. cabaretsauvage.com. Métro: Porte de la Villette. In a round building with a peaked roof like a circus tent; a bar in the center and a stage on one side. Hosts concerts (world, electro/techno, jazz/funk, hip-hop, reggae), cabaret shows, and dance parties. Restaurant.

Café Charbon 109 rue Oberkampf, 75011. tel 01 43 57 55 13. lecafecharbon.fr. Closed Sun. Métro: Parmentier. A former music hall, this was the first hip café to open on this street, now lined with funky, inexpensive bars. Its decor must be seen (high ceiling, turn-of-the-20th-century mural of cabaret dancers), but avoid the crowds on weekend nights. Also check out **Nouveau Casino** at the same address (tel 01 43 57 57 40). Now part of the Charbon, it has live techno, alternative rock, and pop music.

Candelaria 52 rue de Saintonge, 75003. tel 01 42 74 41 28. quixotic-projects.com/candelaria. Métro: Filles du Calvaire. Go through the door in the back of this tiny hole-in-the-wall taqueria and you'll find a cozy, friendly speakeasy with great cocktails.

Castor Club Club 14 rue Hautefeuille, 75006. tel 09 50 64 99 38. Closed Sun.–Mon. Métro: Odéon or Cluny la Sorbonne. It is a cozy and discreet place, whose entrance is an anonymous door, with only a slot through which to peek. This chic and slightly retro speakeasy with a British pub atmosphere is ideal for sipping excellent cocktails with a fifties-sixties-seventies soundtrack, especially blues.

Chez Georges 11 rue des Canettes, 75006. tel 01 43 26 79 15. Métro: St.-Germain-des-Prés. Friendly, unpretentious, cheap bar in a classy neighborhood.

Chez Jeannette 47 rue du Faubourg St.-Denis, 75010. tel 01 47 70 30 89. Métro: Château d'Eau. This old-fashioned neighborhood café taken over by a good-natured crew of young people is now a popular watering hole and meeting place for a hard-partying crowd. Decent food, too.

Chez Moune 54 rue Jean Baptiste Pigalle, 75009. tel 06 32 76 12 25. Closed Sun.–Tues. Métro: Pigalle. Long a lesbian cabaret (hence the sign depicting a tuxedoed lady with a cigarette), now one of the hottest clubs in town. Edith Piaf herself used to hang out here.

Harry's Bar 5 rue Daunou, 75002. tel 01 42 61 71 14. harrys bar.fr. Métro: Opéra. The venerable American bar in Paris where the Bloody Mary was first concocted. Best martini in Paris.

L'International 5 rue Moret, 75011. tel 09 50 57 60 50. linter national.fr. Closed Sun.–Mon. Métro: Ménilmontant. Exactly what Parisian nightlife was lacking: a place with free admission and reasonably priced drinks where you can listen to live music: folk, rock, electro, world, and more.

La Casbah 18–20 rue de la Forge-Royale, 75011. tel 01 88 33 41 78. lacasbah.paris. Métro: Ledru Rollin. The lavish Moroccan decor is the main interest of this restaurant/club. House, R&B, pop, and dance music.

La Chapelle des Lombards 19 rue de Lappe, 75011. tel 01 43 57 24 24. lachapelle.paris. Closed Mon. Métro: Bastille. Latin rhythms, R&B, funk, and live concerts in a warm and friendly atmosphere. Free admission Thurs.

La Machine du Moulin Rouge 90 boulevard de Clichy, 75018. tel 01 53 41 88 89. lamachinedu moulinrouge.com. Closed Sun.–Thurs. Métro: Blanche. Enormous three-level club with concerts and DJ nights, featuring rock, electro, and world music.

La Perle 78 rue Vieille-du-Temple, 75003. tel 01 42 72 69 93.

cafelaperle.com. Métro: Rambu-teau. There is nothing special about this café except that its cheap drinks attract hordes of glamorous young people in the evening and that it was the site of the anti-Semitic rant that caused fashion designer John Galliano's downfall.

Le Bus Palladium 6 rue Fontaine, 75009. tel 01 45 26 80 35. buspalladium.com. Métro: Blanche. Live music and DJs Thurs.–Sat. Restaurant.

Le China 50 rue de Charenton, 75012. tel 01 43 46 08 09. lechina .eu. Métro: Ledru Rollin. The atmosphere and decor of old Shanghai in Paris. Bar, Asian restaurant, and concerts of blues, jazz, jam, electro, and world music.

Le Fumoir 6 rue de l'Amiral Coligny, 75001. tel 01 42 92 00 24. lefumoir.com. Métro: Louvre-Rivoli. A lively but refined setting for a cocktail or meal, right across from the Louvre. Decorated to look like a library in a stately home.

Le Sans Souci 65 rue Jean-Baptiste Pigalle, 75009. tel 01 53 16 17 04. Closed Sun. Métro: Pigalle. A neighborhood bar and restaurant that has profited from the popularity of Chez Moune, across the street, and has become a hangout for young people, enlivened by a DJ Thurs.–Sat.

Lou Pascalou 14 rue des Panoyaux, 75020. tel 01 46 36 78 10. cafe-loupascalou.com. Métro: Ménilmontant. One of the original trendy/funky bars in the Ménilmontant area, just to the north of Rue Oberkampf. Free concerts on Sunday and Tuesday evenings.

Pachamama 46–48 rue du Faubourg St.-Antoine, 75012. tel 01 55 78 84 75. pachamama-paris.com. Closed Sun.–Mon. Métro: Bastille. A four-floor bar/club and restaurant with a structure by Gustave Eiffel is living its second life. While maintaining the South American inspiration of the place it previously hosted, the new decor, with vintage pieces (including cult objects) and

recycled items from Brazil, Mexico, and even China and South Africa, has given the ambience a very bohemian charm. It's worth a trip just for an eyeful.

Prescription Cocktail Club 23 rue Mazarine, 75006. tel 09 50 35 72 87. Métro: Odéon. A stylish cocktail bar with an excellent cocktail list, comprising both the classics and creative house drinks; to be sipped under Magritte-style hat lampshades.

Raidd Bar 23 rue du Temple, 75004. tel 01 53 01 00 00. Métro: Hôtel de Ville. *The* trendy gay bar of the moment, with butch bartenders who often leave their post to take a public shower in a glass booth. Women sometimes admitted. Open until 4–5 a.m.

Wanderlust 32 quai d'Austerlitz, 75013. tel 06 27 79 30 65. wanderlustparis.com. Métro: Gare d'Austerlitz. A restaurant, bar, and club at Les Docks-Cité de la Mode et Design, a nightlife center for mostly young people with its large terraces overlooking the Seine.

Cabaret

These famous, Vegas-type shows with topless dancing girls are expensive, and attended mostly by busloads of tourists. If going, skip the overpriced, mediocre meals and just have a pricey drink at the bar.

Crazy Horse Saloon 12 avenue George V, 75008. tel 01 47 23 32 32. lecrazyhorseparis.com. Métro: Alma-Marceau. Considered the most erotic of the cabarets. The dancers have names like "Kismy Patchwork," with shows like "Teasing."

Le Paradis Latin 28 rue du Cardinal Lemoine, 75005. tel 01 43 25 28 28. paradislatin.com. Métro: Cardinal Lemoine. In a building designed by Gustave Eiffel, Paris's oldest major cabaret presents the French Cancan and acrobats in

a review entitled "Paradis à la Folie."

Lido 116 bis avenue des Champs-Élysées, 75008. tel 01 40 76 56 10. lido.fr. Métro: George V. The Bluebell Girls sing, dance, and ice-skate in fabulous costumes.

Moulin Rouge 82 boulevard de Clichy, 75009. tel 01 53 09 82 82. moulinrouge.fr. Métro: Blanche. The Doriss Girls still do the can-can in thousands of varied costumes. Dance numbers are interspersed with circus acts.

Cinema

Parisians are movie-mad; they love everything from the latest American blockbuster to the most intellectual East European offering. Many cinemas regularly show the classics as well, from the Marx Brothers to Frank Capra. Cinema snobs go only to films in "VO" *(version originale)*, so you will find many screenings in English. "VF" means *version française,* and the film will be dubbed into French. Make sure you check before you buy your ticket. On Friday and Saturday nights there are long lines outside cinemas on the Champs-Élysées and les Grands Boulevards. Don't be surprised if you have to sit through 20 minutes of advertising before the film starts; this is standard practice. The following are a few of the more interesting cinemas.

Grand Action 5 rue des Écoles, 75005. tel 01 43 54 47 62. legrand action.com. Métro: Cardinal Lemoine, Jussieu. Art-house movies, with festivals of everything from Tennessee Williams to the Marx Brothers.

La Cinémathèque Française 51 rue de Bercy. 75012. tel 01 71 19 33 33; cinematheque.fr. Métro: Bercy. A stunning Frank Gehry building houses the Cinémathèque, with four screens, a bookshop, and a restaurant.

Le Champo-Espace Jacques Tati 51 rue des Écoles, 75005. tel

01 43 54 51 60. cinema-lechampo .com. Métro: St.-Michel or Odéon. Woody Allen, Monty Python, and French classics, recent films you may have missed, and new releases.

Le Louxor 170 boulevard Magenta, 75010. tel 01 44 63 96 98. cinemalouxor.fr. Métro: Barbès-Rochechouart. Refurbished and reopened by the City of Paris, this handsome Egyptian-themed art deco cinema dating from 1921 shows first-run movies and has the advantage of not screening advertising before the film. Don't miss the café with a balcony on the top floor.

Max Linder Panorama 24 boulevard Poissonnière, 75009. tel 01 48 00 90 24. maxlinder.com. Métro: Grands Boulevards. New releases in a serious cinema with good seating, digital THX sound, and a balcony.

MK2 Bibliothèque 128/162 avenue de France, 75013. mk2.com. Métro: Bibliothèque F. Mitterrand or Quai de la Gare. Artsy films for the masses: 14 screens, three restaurants, a bar, a big shop, and "love seats" for couples in the theaters.

Studio Galande 42 rue Galande, 75005. tel 01 43 54 72 71. studio galande.fr. Métro: St.-Michel. The *Rocky Horror Picture Show* is shown every Fri. and Sat. at 10 p.m. plus other recent and not-so-recent films.

Opera/Dance/Classical Music

All the greats in the worlds of classical music, opera, modern dance, and ballet come to perform in Paris. Many churches regularly hold concerts of classical music. Check *Pariscope* or the *Officiel des Spectacles* for details, or call La Toison d'Art (tel 01 44 62 00 55), or Musique Sacré à Notre-Dame de Paris (tel 01 44 41 49 99). You can book online for major shows at fnacspectacles.com or billet reduc.com. Also for concerts: concertclassic.com.

Opéra-Comique 1 place Boieldieu, 75002. tel 01 70 23 01 31. opera-comique.com. Métro: Richelieu-Drouot. Operas, operettas, and classical concerts are staged in this beautiful, sumptuously decorated 100-year-old theater, built by Louis Bernier.

Opéra National de Paris-Bastille Place de la Bastille, 75012. tel 08 92 89 90 90. operaparis.fr. Métro: Bastille. Major opera and dance productions in the opera house that Parisians love to hate, but flock to anyway.

Opéra National de Paris Palais Garnier Place de l'Opéra, 75009. tel 08 92 89 90 90. operaparis. fr. Métro: Opéra. Opera and dance performances (by the Ballet de l'Opéra National de Paris and visiting companies) in this wonderfully overdecorated, 19th-century opera house with frescoes by Chagall.

Philharmonie de Paris 221 avenue Jean-Jaurès, 75019. tel 01 44 84 44 84. philharmonie deparis.fr. Métro: Porte de Pantin. The new Philharmonie de Paris (2,400 seats) stands next to the former Cité de la Musique, with its smaller Philharmonie 2 concert hall, a museum of music, research center, and conservatory. Concerts of all musical genres.

Salle Gaveau 45 rue de la Boétie, 75008. tel 01 49 53 05 07. sallegaveau.com. Métro: Miromesnil. The belle époque Salle Gaveau, which seats 1,020, is known for its fine acoustics and has been restored to a faithful version of its early 20th-century appearance. It features primarily piano and chamber music, along with occasional orchestral concerts.

Salle Pleyel 252 rue du Faubourg St.-Honoré, 75008. tel 08 92 97 60 63. sallepleyel.fr. Métro: Ternes. The Orchestre Philharmonique moved to its new home in Parc de la Villette in January 2015, leaving the beautiful art deco Salle Pleyel to a new life of contemporary music.

Théâtre des Champs-Élysées 15 avenue Montaigne, 75008. tel 01 49 52 50 50. theatrechamps elysees.fr. Métro: Alma-Marceau. Hosts the Orchestre National de France, plus visiting orchestras and opera companies.

Théâtre de la Ville 2 place du Châtelet, 75004. tel 01 42 74 22 77. theatredelaville-paris.com. Métro: Châtelet. The major venue for an adventurous program of dance performances by all the best international companies.

Théâtre du Châtelet Place du Châtelet. tel 01 40 28 28 40. chatelet.com. Métro: Châtelet. Musicals, classical concerts, and dance productions are held in this attractive theater.

Pop/Rock/Jazz

The French have adopted American jazz and made it their own, with many Parisian basement jazz clubs. They can get very crowded; arrive early.

Caveau de la Huchette 5 rue de la Huchette, 75005. tel 01 43 26 65 05. caveaudelahuchette.fr. Métro: St.-Michel. A Latin Quarter basement club with '50s-style rock, boogie, and swing. Still going strong.

Duc des Lombards 42 rue de Lombards, 75001. tel 01 42 33 22 88. ducdeslombards.com. Métro: Châtelet. The club heats up with lively jazz concerts beginning at 8 or 10 p.m.

Élysée-Montmartre 72 boulevard Rochechouart, 75018. tel 01 44 92 78 00. elysee-montmartre .com. Métro: Anvers. A historic Pigalle music hall, devastated by fire in 2011 reopened for concerts in 2016.

Instants Chavirés 7 rue Richard Lenoir, 93100 Montreuil. tel 01 42 87 25 91. instantschavires.com. Métro: Charonne. Just outside of Paris, this friendly club is the best for avant-garde jazz.

Jazz Café Montparnasse 13

rue du Commandant-Mouchotte, 75014. tel 01 43 21 58 89. jazzcafe-montparnasse.com. Métro: Montparnasse or Gaîté. Taking the place of the historic Petit Journal Montparnasse, this completely renovated venue offers a great live jazz program, with dinner & concert or drink & concert formula.

Jazz Club Étoile Hôtel Meridien, 81 boulevard Gouvion St.-Cyr, 75017. tel 01 40 68 30 42. jazzclub-paris.com. Métro: Porte Maillot. Good, live jazz and blues in the lobby of the otherwise unexciting Méridien hotel.

La Cigale 124 boulevard Rochechouart, 75018. tel 01 49 25 89 99. lacigale.fr. Métro: Pigalle. Rock concerts by international and local groups in a former theater.

Le Divan du Monde 75 rue des Martyrs, 75018. tel 07 68 78 68 01. divandumonde.com. Métro: Pigalle. All types of music—rock, *chansons française* (French songs), gospel, and Central European.

New Morning 7–9 rue des Petites-Écuries, 75010. tel 01 45 23 51 41. newmorning.com. Métro: Château d'Eau. Top jazz, blues, African, and South American musicians perform in this club.

Olympia 28 boulevard des Capucines, 75009. tel 08 92 68 33 68. olympiahall.com. Métro: Opéra. Iconic concert hall with a variety of music acts, including many French *chanteurs* and *chanteuses* (singers).

Petit Journal Saint-Michel 71 boulevard St.-Michel, 75005. tel 01 43 26 28 59. petitjournalsaint michel.com. RER (B): Luxembourg. Closed Sun.–Mon. Basement club featuring New Orleans–style jazz.

Point Ephémère 200 quai de Valmy, 75010. tel 01 40 34 02 48; restaurant: 01 40 34 04 06. point ephemere.org. Métro: Louis Blanc. Lively cultural center with art exhibitions, events, and a wide variety of pop, rock, and dance concerts for a young crowd. Restaurant with terrace overlooking the Canal St.-Martin.

Sunset Sunside 60 rue des Lombards, 75001. tel 01 40 26 21 25. sunset-sunside.com. Métro: Châtelet. Central jazz club with two spaces featuring good French and international groups.

Zénith 211 avenue Jean-Jaurès, 75019. tel 01 44 52 54 56. le-zenith. com. Métro: Porte de Pantin. Cavernous rock venue where international superstars perform.

Theater

Going to the theater in Paris provides an opportunity to soak up the ambience, but otherwise there is not much point unless your command of French is excellent—most of the plays are in French. However, a few theaters occasionally stage plays in English (listed below; otherwise, in French). Booking usually starts two weeks in advance.

Café-théâtres are small theaters (without cafés), with the equivalent of off-off-Broadway plays and stand-up comedy of varying quality.

Bouffes du Nord 37 bis boulevard de la Chapelle, 75010. tel 01 46 07 34 50. bouffesdunord .com. Closed Sun. Métro: La Chapelle. Directors Olivier Mantei and Olivier Poubelle stage plays of excellent quality—many in English—in a handsome old theater.

Café de la Gare 41 rue du Temple, 75004. tel 01 42 78 52 51. cdlg.org. Métro: Hôtel de Ville. A *café-théâtre* presenting plays and comedy sketches.

Cartoucherie-Théâtre du Soleil Route du Champ-de-Manœuvre, 75012. tel 01 43 74 24 08. theatre-du-soleil.fr. Métro: Château-de-Vincennes, then shuttle service or bus 112. Acclaimed director Ariane Mnouchkine's troupe performs plays in an old warehouse near the Bois de Vincennes.

Comédie Française 1 place Colette. tel 01 44 58 15 15. come die-francaise.fr. Closed Sun. Métro: Palais-Royal. Molière's company was the founding troupe of this

venerable theater next to the Palais-Royal; his works are performed, along with pieces by Chekhov, Corneille, Racine, Shakespeare, Anouilh, and others. The acting is usually superb. French language only.

Odéon-Théâtre de l'Europe Place de l'Odéon, 75006. tel 01 44 85 40 40, theatre-odeon.eu. Métro: Odéon or Luxembourg. A terrific and eclectic repertoire, with theater companies from all over Europe and performances in many languages.

Point Virgule 7 rue Ste.-Croix-de-la-Bretonnerie, 75004. tel 01 42 78 67 03. lepointvirgule .com. Métro: Hôtel de Ville. A small, popular *café-théâtre* with mostly comic sketches.

Théâtre de Nesle 8 rue de Nesle, 75006. tel 01 46 34 61 04. theatredenesle.com. Métro: Odéon. Tiny Left Bank theater with occasional English-language plays by Pinter and others.

Théâtre du Rond-Point 2 bis avenue Franklin D. Roosevelt, 75008. tel 01 44 95 98 00. theatre durondpoint.fr. Métro: Franklin D. Roosevelt. Some of Paris's most exciting theatrical productions are presented in this former ice-skating rink. French language only.

Théâtre du Vieux-Colombier 21 rue du Vieux-Colombier, 75006. tel 01 44 39 87 00. vieux.colombier. free.fr. Métro: St.-Sulpice. A smaller, Left Bank outpost of the Comédie Française, with a selection of both classic and modern pieces.

Théâtre MC93 Bobigny La Maison de la Culture, 1 boulevard Lénine, Bobigny. tel 01 41 60 72 72. mc93.com. Métro: Bobigny–Pablo Picasso. Avant-garde pieces (Robert Wilson, Peter Sellars) are the mainstay of this modern theater in one of Paris's "red" suburbs.

Théâtre National de Chaillot 1 place du Trocadéro, 75016. tel 01 53 65 31 00. theatre-chaillot.fr. Métro: Trocadéro. Enormous theater presenting dance, theater, and circus productions.

LANGUAGE GUIDE

General

Yes *Oui*
No *Non*
Excuse me *Excusez-moi*
Hello *Bonjour*
Hi *Salut*
Please *S'il vous plaît*
Thank you (very much) *Merci (beaucoup)*
You're welcome *De rien*
Have a good day! *Bonne journée!*
OK *D'accord*
Goodbye *Au revoir*
Good night *Bonsoir*
Sorry *Pardon*
here *ici*
there *là*
today *aujourd'hui*
yesterday *hier*
tomorrow *demain*
now *maintenant*
later *plus tard*
right away *tout de suite*
this morning *ce matin*
this afternoon *cet après-midi*
this evening *ce soir*
Do you have . . . ? *Avez-vous . . . ?*
Do you speak English? *Parlez-vous anglais?*
I am American *Je suis Américain* (**man**); *je suis Américaine* (**woman**)
I don't understand *Je ne comprends pas*
Please speak more slowly *Parlez plus lentement, s'il vous plaît*
Where is . . . ? *Où est. . . ?*
I don't know *Je ne sais pas*
No problem *Ce n'est pas grave*
That's it *C'est ça*
Here it is *Voici*
There it is *Voilà*
What is your name? *Comment vous appelez-vous?*
My name is . . . *Je m'appelle . . .*
Let's go *On y va*
At what time? *À quelle heure?*
When? *Quand?*
What time is it? *Quelle heure est-il?*

In the hotel

Do you have . . . ? *Avez-vous . . . ?*
a single room *une chambre simple*
a double room *une chambre double*
with/without bathroom/ shower *avec/sans salle de bain/ douche*

Help

I need a doctor/dentist *J'ai besoin d'un médecin/dentiste*
Can you help me? *Pouvez-vous m'aider?*
Where is the hospital? *Où est l'hôpital?*
Where is the police station? *Où est le commissariat?*

Shopping

I'd like . . . *Je voudrais . . .*
How much is it? *C'est combien?*
Do you take credit cards? *Est-ce que vous acceptez les cartes de crédit?*
size (clothes) *la taille*
size (shoes) *la pointure*
cheap *bon marché*
expensive *cher*
Have you got . . . ? *Avez-vous. . . ?*
I'll take it *Je le prends*
Anything else? *Avec ça?*
enough *assez*
too much *trop*
bill *la note*

Shops

bakery *la boulangerie*
bookshop *la librairie*
drugstore *la pharmacie*
delicatessen *la charcuterie/le traiteur*
department store *le grand magasin*
fishmonger *la poissonnerie*
grocery *l'alimentation/l'épicerie*
junk shop *la brocante*
library *la bibliothèque*
supermarket *le supermarché*

Sightseeing

visitor information office *l'office de tourisme/le syndicat d'initiative*
open *ouvert*
closed *fermé*
every day *tous les jours*
all year round *toute l'année*
all day long *toute la journée*
free *gratuit/libre*

abbey *l'abbaye* (**f**)
castle, country house *le château*
church *l'église* (**f**)
museum *le musée*
staircase *l'escalier* (**m**)
tower *la tour* (**La Tour Eiffel**)
tour (walk or drive) *le tour*
town *la ville*
old town *la vieille ville*
Town Hall *Hôtel de Ville/la mairie*

MENU READER

breakfast *le petit déjeuner*
lunch *le déjeuner*
dinner *le dîner*
I am on a diet *Je suis au régime*
I'd like to order *Je voudrais commander*
Is service included? *Est-ce que le service est compris?*

Le Menu

menu à prix fixe **meal at set price**
à la carte **dishes from the menu, charged separately**
entrée/hors d'oeuvre **first course**
le plat principal **main course**
le plat du jour **dish of the day**
le dessert **dessert**
boisson compris **drink included**
carte des vins **wine list**
l'addition **the bill**

Les Boissons Drinks

café **coffee**
au lait ou crème **with milk or cream**
déca/décaféiné **decaffeinated coffee**
express/noir **espresso/black**
allongé **American-style coffee**
le thé **tea**
le lait **milk**
eau minérale **mineral water**
gazeux **fizzy**
non-gazeux **non-fizzy**
citron pressé **fresh lemon juice served with sugar and water**
orange pressée **fresh squeezed orange juice**
frais, fraîche **fresh or cold**
bière **beer**
en bouteille **bottled**

à la pression **on tap**
panaché **mixed**
le panaché **shandy**
la carafe/le pichet **pitcher of tap water or wine**
la demi-carafe **half liter**
un quart **quarter of a liter**
vin de maison **house wine**
vin de pays **local wine**
digestif **after-dinner drink**

Le Repas The Meal

le pain **bread**
le poivre **pepper**
le potage **soup**
le sel **salt**
le sucre **sugar**

Meat Dishes

l'agneau **lamb**
l'andouille **tripe sausage**
le bifteck **steak**
à point **medium rare**
bien cuit **well done**
bleu **very rare**
contre-filet **cut of sirloin steak**
entrecôte **rib steak**
faux-filet **sirloin steak**
grillé **grilled**
hachis **chopped**
saignant **rare**
bordelaise **with red wine and shallots**
bourguignonne **cooked in red wine, onions, and mushrooms**
le canard **duck**
la carbonnade **stew of beef in beer**
le carré d'agneau **rack of lamb**
le cassoulet **stew of beans, sausages, pork, and duck**
la choucroute **sauerkraut**
le confit **duck or goose preserved in its own fat**
le coq au vin **chicken in red wine**
le côte d'agneau **lamb chop**
les cuisses de grenouille **frog's legs**
la daube **stew with red wine, tomatoes, and onions**
le dinde **turkey**
l'escargot **snail**
farci **stuffed**
le jambon **ham**
le lapin **rabbit**
le magret de canard **breast of duck**
le médaillon **round piece of meat**
l'oie **goose**

le porc **pork**
le pot-au-feu **casserole of beef and vegetables**
le poulet **chicken**
le poussin **young chicken**
les rognons **kidneys**
rôti **roast**
la saucisse **fresh sausage**
le saucisson **salami**
le veau **veal**

Fish Dishes

l'anchois **anchovy**
l'anguille **eel**
le belon **Brittany oyster**
la bouillabaisse **fish soup**
le cabillaud **cod**
le colin **hake**
le coquillage **shellfish**
la coquille Saint-Jacques **scallop**
la crevette **shrimp**
la daurade **sea bream**
l'encornet **squid**
le flétan **halibut**
les fruits de mer **seafood**
l'homard **lobster**
l'huître **oyster**
la langoustine **jumbo shrimp**
la limande **flounder**
la lotte **monkfish**
la moule **mussel**
moules marinières **mussels in white wine and onions**
la poulpe **octopus**
le saumon **salmon**
le thon **tuna**
la truite **trout**

Some Sauces

aïoli **garlic mayonnaise**
américaine **sauce of white wine, tomatoes, butter, and Cognac**
béarnaise **egg, butter, wine, and herbs**
forestière **mushrooms and bacon**
hollandaise **egg, butter, and lemon**
meunière **butter, lemon, and parsley**
meurette **red wine sauce**
Mornay **cream, egg, and cheese**
Provençale **usually tomatoes, garlic, and olive oil**

Vegetables

l'ail **garlic**
l'artichaut **artichoke**

les asperges **asparagus**
l'aubergine **eggplant**
l'avocat **avocado**
le champignon **mushroom**
les chips **potato chips**
le chou **cabbage**
le chou-fleur **cauliflower**
le concombre **cucumber**
le cornichon **pickle**
la courgette **zucchini**
cru **raw**
les crudités **raw vegetables**
les épinards **spinach**
le haricot **dried bean**
les haricots rouges **kidney beans**
les haricots verts **green beans**
les lentilles **lentils**
le maïs **corn**
le mange-tout **snow pea**
le mesclun **mixed leaf salad**
la noisette **hazelnut**
la noix **nut, walnut**
l'oignon **onion**
le poireau **leek**
le pois **pea**
le poivron **bell pepper**
les pommes de terre **potatoes**
les pommes frites **french fries**
le riz **rice**
la salade verte **green salad**
la truffe **truffle**

Fruits

l'ananas **pineapple**
la cerise **cherry**
le citron **lemon**
le citron vert **lime**
la figue **fig**
la fraise **strawberry**
la framboise **raspberry**
le pamplemousse **grapefruit**
la pêche **peach**
la poire **pear**
la pomme **apple**
la prune **plum**
le pruneau **prune**
le raisin **grape**

Snacks

le croque-monsieur **toasted ham and cheese sandwich**
l'oeuf à la coque **boiled egg**
oeufs au jambon **ham and eggs**
oeufs brouillés **scrambled eggs**
oeufs sur le plat **fried eggs**
le yaourt **yogurt**

INDEX

ILLUSTRATIONS CREDITS

National Geographic
TRAVELER
Paris
FIFTH EDITION

Since 1888, the National Geographic Society has funded more than 14,000 research, exploration, and preservation projects around the world. National Geographic Partners distributes a portion of the funds it receives from your purchase to National Geographic Society to support programs including the conservation of animals and their habitats.

National Geographic Partners, LLC
1145 17th Street NW
Washington, DC 20036-4688 USA

Get closer to National Geographic explorers and photographers, and connect with our global community. Join us today at nationalgeographic. com/join

For rights or permissions inquiries, please contact National Geographic Books
Subsidiary Rights: bookrights@natgeo.com

Fifth edition edited by White Star s.r.l.
Licensee of National Geographic Partners, LLC.
Update by Iceigeo (text updates: Maria Chiara Piccolo; editorial staff: Francesco Filippini, Maria-Angela Silleni, Renata Grilli)

Drive maps drawn by Chris Orr Associates, Southampton, England
Illustrations drawn by Maltings Partnership, Derby, England

The information in this book has been carefully checked and to the best of our knowledge is accurate. However, details are subject to change, and the publisher cannot be responsible for such changes, or for errors or omissions. Assessments of sites, hotels, and restaurants are based on the author's subjective opinions, which do not necessarily reflect the publisher's opinion.

ISBN: 978-88-544-1678-9

Printed by
Rotolito S.p.A. - Seggiano di Pioltello (MI) - Italy

NATIONAL GEOGRAPHIC TRAVELER
THE BEST GUIDES BY YOUR SIDE

More than 80 destinations around the globe

 ARIZONA
 AUSTRALIA
 COSTA RICA
 CUBA
 IRELAND

 ITALY
 JAPAN
 LONDON
 NEW YORK
 PERU

 PORTUGAL
 PUGLIA
 ROME
 SCOTLAND
 VIETNAM